THE WOUNDED BODY

SUNY series in Psychoanalysis and Culture
Henry Sussman, editor

The Wounded Body

Remembering the Markings of Flesh

Dennis Patrick Slattery

STATE UNIVERSITY OF NEW YORK PRESS

Published by
State University of New York Press, Albany

© 2000 State University of New York

For information, address State University of New York Press,
State University Plaza, Albany, N.Y., 12246

Production by Cathleen Collins
Marketing by Patrick Durocher

Library of Congress Cataloging in Publication Data

Slattery, Dennis Patrick, 1944–
    The wounded body : remembering the markings of flesh / Dennis
Patrick Slattery.
        p.   cm. — (SUNY series in psychoanalysis and culture)
    Includes bibliographical references and index.
    ISBN 0-7914-4381-7 (alk. paper). — ISBN 0-7914-4382-5 (pbk. :
alk. paper)
        1. Body, Human, in literature.   2. Psychoanalysis and literature.
3. Mimesis in literature.   I. Title.   II. Series.
PN56.B62S59   2000
809'.9335—dc21   98-55986
                                                                            CIP

10 9 8 7 6 5 4 3 2

To my three Muses, Mary, Sandy, and Louise
And to my sons, Matt and Steve

Contents

Foreword

This is a profound book which is both scholarly and elegant. The author writes with a sure command of his field of literature, and with a poet's ear sensitively attuned to the subtly nuanced voices of the soul. Spanning a range in Western literature which is remarkable for its depth as well as breadth, Slattery weaves a text that offers original insights into the poetics of the flesh. Each reader, I am certain, will find a favorite chapter within this weave, but every reader will be seduced by the power and beauty of the entire work. For myself, I was most touched by the chapter on Rousseau. The subtitle alone, "Autobiography, Body Cleansing, and the Invention of the Paris Sewer System," is enough to entice even the most tired reader.

As a student of the body for more than a quarter century, both as a writer and a psychotherapist, I am most impressed by Slattery's attempt to present a poetics of the flesh. In this respect his book is decidedly not a psychology of the body, and any attempt to read it in that way would fail to capture its unique vision. It is true, however, that he draws upon psychology in rich and rewarding ways, particularly the traditions of depth psychology and phenomenology.

But the author's poetics of the flesh takes a step beyond these traditions, and in doing so enriches them. For example, phenomenology has always understood that the human body is a cultural-historical matter, that the lived body, or the body-I-am, as distinct from the object body, or the body I have, is a fiction. As such, the human body is a site where, for example, the politics of gender inscribe or mark it in various ways. These fictions of the body have been explored by philosophers, feminists, psychologists, art historians, and cultural critics, the most important of whom make their appearance in Slattery's work.

But to these fictions of the body, Slattery adds the dimension of the bodies of fiction, and in this regard his work often reads as if it is the fleshing out of the bones of these other perspectives. In the bodies of literature which he explores, one experiences the fictions of the body in their figured and archetypal forms. One meets the fictions of the body as characters in a tale. In this regard, I would suggest that Slattery's work is a kind of cultural-historical manual of psychotherapy, a kind of descriptive diagnostic of the embodied soul in all its odd appearances and guises.

Slattery's poetics of the flesh rests upon a specific moment of the human body, a moment which is simultaneously personal and universal. I am referring here to the author's emphasis on the wounded body. But why is the wound so important? Slattery writes that "Wounding is one way the body shows its hyperbole . . ." (Chapter 1, p. 11). This is a profound insight, and one which every student and practitioner of depth psychology can appreciate. When Freud's hysterics crossed the threshold of his consulting rooms, they dissolved in their symptoms the four-hundred-year-old heritage of a Cartesian split between a mind divorced from the flesh and the body regarded as a soulless, inanimate machine. Their symptoms were a piece of dramatic hyperbole, an exaggeration of what I have described in my own work as the gestural body of everyday life.

In this caricatured exaggeration of the gestural body, the symptom or the wound is always a return of the animate body, the ensouled body, the passionate body. At the origins of Freud's and Jung's work is the recognition that in the wound is the soul. The chapters in Slattery's book are an extensive elaboration of the wounded gestural body. They persuasively demonstrate how our wounds are haunted gestures, and how our gestures carry and allude to the woundings of the soul. In this last regard, Slattery's book offers some original insights, for which I can express only deep gratitude.

This book deserves a wide and varied readership. Psychologists, psychotherapists, literary scholars, historians, and interested lay readers will find genuine nuggets of gold in the author's reflections. But most important, the reader will find in this work a compassionate understanding of our shared human condition as flawed human beings who hurt, age, grow ill, and die. There is in this work an implicit invitation for each of us to accept with more tolerance, forgiveness, and even grace, the shock of incarnation. The literary characters who are present in Slattery's work begin to accompany the reader, like friendly ghosts, making the journey along the path of life a little less lonely, a little more bearable. Limp with the injured and blind Oedipus, feel again the scar of Odysseus, suffer the disease of Ivan Ilych, and bear with the abusive markings on the back of the slavewoman Sethe. It is a journey well worth taking.

Robert D. Romanyshyn

Acknowledgments

Finishing a book provokes a series of memories. Any journey one takes and remembers should begin with gratitude to those who supported its meandering ways. My parents, Roger and Mary Slattery always encouraged me, often under strained circumstances, to persevere. My sister Mary Beth and brothers Martin, Bob, and Bill I thank for always welcoming me home. To the rigorous Marianist brothers and priests and lay faculty of St. Joseph High School in Cleveland, Ohio, for singling me out as someone with potential, I extend my gratitude. They launched me into the world of ideas, loaned me their own books, and showed me that reading was the key to it all. In them I discovered the desire to learn.

I thank the faculty at Cuyahoga Community College, especially Harold Gaines, John Faust, and Margaret Schroeder for showing me how exciting teaching and learning can be. I acknowledge the fine teaching I received at Cleveland State University, including Julius Drossin, cellist in The Cleveland Orchestra, Mr. Small who taught Spanish, and Mr. Cabrini in English. At Kent State University I found exceptional teachers in Glenn Frank of the Geology Department, Bernard Benstock, Barbara Child, Howard Vincent, John Keating, Glen Burn, Bill Hildebrand, and Doris Franklin in English. They were exceptional and contagious in their love of literature and language. From them I learned of the poetic instinct and the power of myth.

The Institute of Philosophic Studies' interdisciplinary program at The University of Dallas, founded by Donald and Louise Cowan, allowed me and my colleagues an authentic sense of what being part of a shared myth can mean when applied to the Academy. Their leadership and vision opened our eyes to the sacred invisibility in all things that could be discerned by the imagination. To them and to Robert Romanyshyn, Robert Sardello, James Hillman, and Patricia Berry in Phenomenology, Fritz Wilhelmson in Philosophy, Father Benedict in Physics, Peter Phan in Theology I owe gratitude for showing us that a passion for learning is a worthy vocation that is available to everyone. All illustrated by example the sacred trust that teachers have and how the classroom should always remain an inviolable space of generosity. I acknowledge them and my student colleagues in that program for the hours of rich conversation they afforded.

At Southern Methodist University in Dallas, I thank the bright and enthusiastic teacher-colleagues in rhetoric who helped me get across the more obstinate speed bumps that such teaching demanded. Among them I acknowledge Marilyn Stewart, Mitchell Smith, Tony Howard, Peter Feldman, Virginia Oram, Michael Sims, Marshall Terry, and Theresa Enos.

I also acknowledge and thank my colleagues at the University of Incarnate Word in San Antonio who made teaching there a joy and a privilege, including Basil Aivaloitis, Roger Barnes, Laurie Taylor-Mitchell, Nancy Pawell, Eloise Stoker, Mary Beth Swofford, Sister Martha Ann Kirk, Sister Margaret Patrice Slattery, Sister Germaine Corbin, Larry Hufford, Peggy Bowie, Doug Gilmour, Jo LeCoeur, Bob Lamb, Jim Donovan, Pat Burr, Pat Fite, Gil Hinajosa, Eduardo Paderon, my colleagues in the English Department, as well as the vision and energy of President Louis Agnese. My good friend and artist-humanitarian, Amy Freeman Lee, has also been a constant inspiration and support in all of my work. I thank as well all the undergraduate and graduate students willing and excited about exploring various topics with me in courses on culture, literature, and the body; their fine penetrating insights helped to give form to this study. I learned from them that the best in a teacher is largely determined by the willingness and energy of one's students to learn collaboratively.

I must also acknowledge the joy I experienced teaching literary classics at two Teachers Institutes: The Dallas Institute of Humanities and Culture under the leadership of Gail Thomas and Louise Cowan, and the Fairhope Institute of Humanities and Culture in Alabama under the direction of Larry Allums. In these two summer havens I discovered the powerful presence of adult learners. I am fortunate to have been invited to study and learn in these rich graduate programs of alternative learning.

Finally, at Pacifica Graduate Institute, a sacred space of soulmaking envisioned by its founder, Stephen Aizenstat, I have been encouraged by Charles Asher, Provost, Dianne Skafte, academic vice president, Patrick Mahaffey, Director of the Mythological Studies program, and Mary Watkins, Director of the Counseling Program supported extensively by my colleagues and administrative staff, and challenged by very special adult learners to explore and write about dimensions of culture and imagination that attract me. Through contact with them, literary insights have been broadened and deepened. No greater good fortune can befall a person than to be gifted with colleagues and students who support one another in allowing the imagination to find its own voice in the world.

Two National Endowment for the Humanities Summer Seminars for Teachers, one on the Origins of the Modern Imagination at Harvard under the direction of Leo Damrosch, the other in The Homer Institute at The

University of Arizona under the direction of Norman Austin, provided great stimulation for my work. In addition, an Andrew Mellon Grant to Study Modern Critical Theory at Rice University under the direction of Frank Lentricchia and Wesley Morris also aided the development of ideas within these pages.

I thank all of the creative writers of both fiction and theory in this volume who have shared their insights on a dimension of human being that is as profound as it is fathomless: the phenomenon of being embodied. I therefore acknowledge their perceptions, their insights, and their powerful voices from the past. The depth of their thoughts and images stimulated my own thinking into these deep waters.

I thank as well Ms. Nina Falls at Pacifica Graduate Institute for so diligently working with me to prepare this manuscript by finding time outside her regular and very full duties to assist me in closing the wounds of a very marked volume. I thank Mary Lou Kravetz, director of our library, and her kind staff for their generous help in procuring permissions for works cited in the study. I am grateful to Mr. James Peltz of SUNY Press for believing in and staying with this project and helping me shepherd it to completion. I wish to thank Cathleen Collins of SUNY Press for giving finer shape to this work as it moved into production. And to Maria denBoer, my copy editor and indexer for her careful and caring eye. I thank you for making it a better work.

To my sons, Matt and Steve, fierce defenders of their father's work, I can do no more than give you this book in love. And to my ever-faithful, patient, and circumspect wife, Sandy, who is as close to Homer's Penelope I ever hope to get outside of his magnificent epic, I can only promise: I owe you one.

I am grateful to the following publishers for their willingness to allow me to cite from all or part of these works:

"Corrupting Corpse vs. Reasoned Abstraction: The Play of Evil in *The Brothers Karamazov*, by Dennis Patrick Slattery. *Dostoevsky Studies: The Journal of the International Dostoevsky Society*. Vol. 1, New Series (1993). pp. 3–24. © 1993 Charles Schlacks, Jr.

"Puer Wounds and Ulysses's Scar" by James Hillman. In *Puer Papers*, *Spring*, 1979. pp. 3–53. © 1979 James Hillman.

"I am Going to Speak of Hope." Cesar Vallejo, *Complete Posthumous Poetry*. Edited/translated by Barcia Eshlame. © 1979 by the Regents of the University of California.

"Evil and the Negation of the Body: Flannery O'Connor's 'Parker's Back,'" by Dennis Patrick Slattery. *The Flannery O'Connor Bulletin*, Vol. 17, 1988. pp. 69–79. © 1988 Sarah Gordon, editor of *The Flannery O'Connor Bulletin*.

"Whiteness" by Dennis Patrick Slattery. Edited by Carolyn Cuellar. Del Rio, Texas: The Maverick Press. Reprinted by permission of the editor.

"Telling the Story: from *Words Under the Words: Selected Poems by Naomi Shihab Nye,* © by Naomi Shihab Nye. Used by permission of Far Corner Books.

Chi poria mai pur con parole sciolte
dicer del sangue e de le piaghe a pieno
ch'i' ora vidi, per narrar piu volte?

(Who, even with untrammeled words and many
attempts at telling, ever could recount
in full the blood and wounds that I now saw?)
                              —*Inferno*, Canto 28, ll. 1–3.

Earth felt the wound, and nature from her seat
Sighing through all her works gave signs of woe,
That all was lost. Back to the thicket slunk
The guilty serpent, . . .
                              —*Paradise Lost*, Book IX, ll. 782–84

1

Introduction

The Wounded Body:
Remembering the Markings of Flesh

The wounds work as thresholds between inner and outer
realities. Seeing into the wounds and scars reveals that
everyone is wounded and teaches one how to see the person coming out of the wound.

—Michael Meade, 4

TWO MEMORIES AND AN OVERVIEW

When I have spoken to various authors about what prompted their research into a particular area of interest, even passion, most will answer by recounting an academic preoccupation, a scholarly concern that
bears on their teaching, or some other equally well-meaning but usually
very neutral response. But occasionally, if pressed a bit, and if I offer to buy
the first round, some writers will open up and relate something in their
lived life that prompted them to pursue an area in their professional field.
Suddenly they open to a desire to know what was only vaguely comprehended and in the process they give greater credence to novelist Marcie
Hershman's very provocative observation: "It's a myth that writers write
what they know. We write what it is that we need to know. What keeps me
sitting at my desk, hour after hour, year after year, is that I *do not know*
something, and I must write in order to find my way to an understanding.
. . . The questions that drive me as a writer . . . are not born of some good
idea, but of a deep inner need" ("The World and the Library," 20). While
forgiving her the popular use of the word "myth" to mean something false,
nonetheless her insight into a desire based on need is perhaps more often
behind the writing of a book than is generally admitted in introductions.
Two personal memories have fueled the writing of this book, with its major
theme of the wounded body in literature.

1

I remember coming from a partially completed Ph.D. program in Comparative Literature at Kent State University after finishing a master's degree in the same area. I was drawn, even magnetized, to a new interdisciplinary series of courses in the recently created Institute of Philosophic Studies at The University of Dallas in 1972. Combining the collective thought of five disciplines, including a very strange breed of psychology called phenomenology, which at the time had only a few supporters in the country's academic programs, the Institute wanted to shatter some of the stubborn walls of academic departments and allow the imagination to roam a bit more freely between disciplines in turf that we could all, by digging in, call our own. The idea was ingenious; the success beyond measurement. For all of us who piloted this new way of envisioning graduate studies under the leadership of Donald and Louise Cowan, these were four glorious years of study, of argument, of cross-fertilizing one another's disciplines. So happy were we that we tended to sneeze offhandedly at our detractors.

I remember feeling both sophisticated in what I knew and anxious about the future as I read and reveled in all of these French, German, and Dutch names in phenomenology that were alternately intimidating and challenging, for unbeknownst to each of us, we were being formed into a worldview. One of the first of several complete shifts in my thinking occured when I was introduced to the works of Maurice Merleau-Ponty by Robert Romanyshyn. All of us surely can recount with ease, if not a little quickening of the blood, where we were when first we met a titanic thinker and writer or painter or musician who changed our lives forever by altering the way our vision took in the world in a radically new way. *The Phenomenology of Perception* opened up for me the body as a lived experience in a way that I had never comprehended, except in the vaguest way. Working as a security guard at night at a steel factory in Dallas to help my family pay the bills, I read this mysterious, dark, and poetic figure from midnight until 6 A.M. for many nights; then I reread him. Not only did he give a different attitude toward the body, something that had little occupied my thoughts until then; he also gave a different language in which to speak about the body, about its gestural movements, its appetites, and its intimate relation to language. His prose was by turns philosophic, poetic, and prosaic. I felt that here was a linguistic feast incorporating all the major food groups the soul needed to survive and flourish. Merleau-Ponty's insights and observations stopped me in my conventional tracks on almost every page:

> The identity of the thing through perceptual experience is only another aspect of the identity of one's own body throughout exploratory movements; thus they are the same in kind as each other. Like the body image, the fireplace is a system of equiva-

lents not founded on the recognition of some law, but on the experience of a bodily presence. I become involved in things with my body. . . . (185).

It sounded like common sense in its simple language, but it was surrounded by a mystery of being incarnated. Incarnation took on the aura of a miracle in the language's plainness and in its commonality, much as the rudimentary but striking images of poetry will occasionally arrest us with a shock of recognition. I began to sense that the body's movements are poetic gestures toward the world. Simple bodily movements had a meaning that needed to be spoken; they were in fact a speech themselves and the body was a rich and deep rhetorical and poetic field of study that was only slightly grasped by the objective measurements of science, much less by the academic discourses of the time. They would need another ten years to discover the body's intrinsic design.

Perhaps 1962, the date of publication in England of this major epic in the study of human embodiment and language, may mark the beginning of the study of the body that today has become almost epidemic in its popularity. My study of literature and the body, or the literary body and finally the wounded terrains offered in poetic works that explored embodiment, began with this reading.

TITANIUM LIMBS AND THE MECHANICAL BODY

My second memory is more recent and perhaps more enfleshed. It is early morning at Northeast Baptist Hospital in San Antonio. At 5 A.M. all lights are on in the halls, as they have been all night. The corridors are full of talk and activity, and the energy level is high as the night crew is replaced by the day interns, orderlies, nurses, and surgeons. Beds are rolling past my door like the cars beginning their buildup on Loop 410 just down the street from the hospital. Some of the beds have already found their passengers; others are roaming the halls looking for particular rooms to gather their charges to take them to early surgery. My anxiety increases as I hurriedly get up and brush my teeth and wash up at the sink before I am beckoned. I am alone at this hour and feel the growing anxiety attendant upon falling into a medical sinkhole.

An empty bed slows outside my door, stops, and the orderly checks his slip with the name and number on the door and enters, clanging his bed against walls and the bed across from mine (which has blessedly remained empty all night). Cheerful and terrifying at the same time, this young man, a corridor warrior, dressed in his light green fatigues, has come for me.

As a runner, I was used to the aches in the joints that often followed a jog around Bachman Lake in Dallas or the track at Fort Sam Houston in San Antonio. But as a persistent and increasingly angry left hip called for more sustained attention, I visited a sports medicine doctor and was told my problem was tendinitis. Nothing serious and easily corrected, I was assured.

Fitted with an expensive pair of orthotics, I continued my runs four times a week, until the pain grew. What had been diagnosed as tendinitis, under x-ray examinations in San Antonio, became in an instant osteoarthritis. The cartilage was almost completely gone and bone was grinding on bone. I could feel the crunch when I walked and to alleviate it I began to limp excessively.

My disease was given back to me through a growing number of voices at work, who began to ask with more frequency if I had hurt myself over the weekend or the previous night. Soon, everyone was asking what was wrong as my limp, my own body's way of conveying my malady through an unambiguous gesture, a gesture of favoritism, grew steadily worse until only a complete hip replacement would ease the pain and stop the damage to my spinal column that was the consequence of such a weathered gait.

And so the orderly came for me, the next installment to alleviating disease through a procedure that had become commonplace in the medical lexicon. My two bodies became very apparent to me during this time, for the night before the surgery, a close friend came to see me and to pray with me for a successful surgery. When we had finished, Sister Martha Ann turned to me, and asked me *the question* that brought to the fore the body as lived. She asked if I wanted to say anything to the bones in my hip that were to be removed, bones that had served me for five decades but now, worn out, must be removed and consigned to the oblivion of the furnace in the basement of the hospital where certain body parts are disposed of; they were to be replaced by prosthetic devices made of stainless steel, titanium, and cupped with a polyurethane container.

With some coaxing by her, I began to speak to my hip, to thank it for the years of faithful service and to tell it that I would miss our intimate association. And then something happened that is rare for me. I began to weep over the loss of the hip, this part of me that had suffered the arthritis in so much silence, but which now wanted to speak. It was a moment in which I am not sure if I have ever been closer to the sense of my own enfleshed being in the world (unless it was being present and assisting at the birth of my second son). And to pray over bones, I was to learn, is a custom in earlier people's religions, as well as in the Catholic Church through the relics embedded in altars, that brings the body into a living, emotional presence. Perhaps something of our own souls is permanently in our body, in each of its parts. To lose something of ourselves is to lose something of psyche, even of a memory that is embedded deep in every organ. I felt that the body had taken on a poetic and sacred sense that is usually hidden from us in our everyday lives. That was the body that I felt deeply was my identity. Thanking the old bones and the crushed joint, raspy and irritable though they had been of late, seemed to calm the hip down and I was able to sleep well the night before the surgery.

But this morning, as I climbed into the hospital bed and began the trip down the brightly lit linoleum hall, shiny with wax and full of other beds heading generally in the same direction as morning traffic began to snarl, I felt a growing alienation from myself, and specifically from my own flesh. Lying on my back, I watched the ceiling full of small holes in the soft tile and began to count the bright lights that passed in pairs above my head. They looked brightly down on me, efficient and indifferent, just doing their job. As I entered the prepping room, I could see on the large board with the schedules of surgery for that day some two dozen or more names, each one to have a major procedure before 4 P.M. It was a traffic jam of beds, orderlies, surgeons, and anesthesiologists, all jockeying for their respective patients and all very careful to ask each one being prepped for repair to state the nature of their procedure. One orderly took a black magic marker and gingerly drew a black "L" on my left leg so there would be no confusion once I was transported into another galaxy via the anesthetic.

During this entire experience, I felt myself moving away from my body, thinking of it as something like my automobile, whose front end had gone out of alignment and now needed its castors and cambers realigned or replaced. This body was a mechanical apparatus, its hips mere struts. Toe in, toe out. The operating theater became a very clean and cool body shop to which, like a car dealership's morning traffic of vehicles being dropped off in various stages of infirmity or woundedness, bodies were brought for professional readjustments; "do it now, while the warranty is still valid," I kept repeating to myself.

This is the body of medicine, I reflected later. Here I am a commodity, one that needs to be made unconscious so the work can take place without my presence. Consciousness needed to be severed from the body, to turn it into a corpse for a short time—the psychic trade-off for replacing the parts. I thought as well of how place defines not only *how* we are but *who* we are. In this context, my body was something separate from me. Joking, the anesthesiologist remarked that I would now get my morning Marguerita mix, so called because of its lime green color and its cool feeling as it enters the circulatory system, and that I would begin to feel pretty good.

Talking to myself loudly about nothing in particular, I saw a nurse at the end of my bed and told her I was freezing; could she give me more blankets. She came to me and I asked her when I would have surgery so that the ache in my left side would stop; my legs were jerking in discomfort from the cold. She responded with a smile that I had just come out of a surgery that had lasted three hours. I had tubes in me, a bleeding catheter between my legs, and an ache in my side that was unbearable. I also had a new prosthetic hip, made of stainless steel, titanium, and polyurethane to replace the decomposed socket and the worn-out femur's ball. Part of my body was now artificial, technological and better than what had been removed. But part of me was also gone forever, a hip that I had been born with and which had been a lifetime companion. Disease had dictated its removal. I felt the wound both along the left side of my outer hip and deep within me, a place that had opened up where stitches could not reach.

As the days of healing began in the hospital, and then at home, I could slowly deal with the pain through the pain killers, but I could not bear to look at the scar 12 inches long on the outside of my left thigh and extending to the point where the hip bone joins the socket, even when my loving wife faithfully changed the dressing and cleaned it twice a day. The sutures, when I did look once as she cleaned the wound, were like small black insects hovering around the gape; it was red and swollen and raw where the knife had run its course, hands had gone in with tools, pushing aside the muscles to get at the bones making up the joint, sawing, cutting, drilling, screwing, hammering, fitting, and sewing back up. A gaggle of green-suited technicians, busy measuring, calculating, severing, replacing, needn't pay any attention to my conscious needs. The wound told the entire story in all of the violent invasions that I was not part of because of not being present during the surgery.

But the wound, now only a thin red line down the side of my leg, still contains the tale, as the lines of a pen on white paper mark out the line of words that come together to form a narrative, or like the white hash marks on the blue background of this computer screen that scratch out the narrative I am relating. My body now had a wound which was, for a short time, the handy orifice into the inside of my body, into its structural skeleton. My left leg a ziplocked bag, the wound its freshly made aperture. How powerful it is in the way that this slice of red line contains or carries such indelible memories. The wound is the trace of the memory, what I have left of the experience; it also marks the place of what I would call deep memory, an indelible recollection that one feels always at the edge of the field of consciousness. The other part is the absence of pain, which is the memory of the worn-out bone.

And so the body wounded is a very mortal flesh remembered in a particularly unique way. What is this phenomenal body, this poetic body of markings? What is the wound in its relation to language, to identity, and to being named? Does being wounded, marked, scarred, tattooed, violated in some bodily way change our relation to the way we express ourselves incarnationally through body gesture or in language? Does it change the way we are placed, or in place in the world? Yes, the body is the site of cultural, political, and gender battles, explorations, and assertions. But it is not just that, or not first that. There is an imaginal tissue that exists between psyche and soma that antedates these more overt concerns. There is, in fact, a subtle or imaginal body and it is this one that the poets offer us for contemplation, to offer by analogy our own wounds to us. For example, Richard Jones reminds us in "Scars" of "This ragged scar" that is "earned" (6) by rubbing against the world. Our ragged wounds allow the body to speak its language.

To the poetic sense of the body we must yield in order to find in the interstices of the flesh the more profound mysteries of our incarnation. Such a belief lies at the heart of this exploration. I will explore the body as it is changed, deformed, incarcerated, fatigued, bludgeoned, decomposed, made into something else by the world—where the world marks it. And I would ask: Is being wounded a gift? Is there a gift embedded in the wound? For me, the gift is the prosthetic that it took wounding me to install; now I walk freely without a limp and without the chronic pain that had begun to consume my life. Is being wounded, then, a way of inhabiting the world in a new way, such that what was conventional is no longer sufficient? Do they become inoperative as we move to another plane of consciousness through our wounds? The wound is a special place, a magical place, even a numinous site, an opening where the self and the world may meet on new terms, perhaps violently, so that we are marked out and off, a territory assigned to us that is new, and which forever shifts our tracing in the world. Mark Seltzer's study, *Serial Killers*, reveals that "in wound culture, the very notion of sociality is bound to the excitations of the torn and opened body; the torn and exposed individual, as public spectacle" (254). The wounded body certainly reflects the wound culture that gives it life and a place. Serial killers are part of its lexicon that needs closer examination to show body and world as a piece, or as mirrors of one another.

The wounded body is sacred in some deep level of its existence; it is a body specialized and formed by experience; in its new way of being present to the world, the wounded body gains something not possessed before. The wound is a gift; it may be a witness to a god or goddess working in the wound. The wound may be the violent presence of the numinous, or the sacred that enters us through the actions of others. Body woundedness forces us to imagine it in relation to violence, to the sacred, to language, and to the city, for the body as a rich metaphor encompasses all of these areas and gives them all an incarnational meaning. Approaching this same issue, but from the other side, Lionel Corbett observes that in a postmodern world where organized worship does not work for many, "for an approach to divinity that has personal relevance, it is necessary to focus on its manifestations within the psyche, in the body, in relationships" (2). The sacred dimensions of the body have close affinities with divine woundedness for it offers another site of openness to the interior psyche and the transcendent.

I believe it is the poet who dreams the body back to its deepest layers of meaning most forcefully and convincingly, in order to show us the finitude of being enfleshed but also the way the world as we create it is a mirror, a rich and textured metaphor for the way we understand and interpret the body in any given cultural-historical period.

THE CULTURAL-HISTORICAL BODY

Given the almost obsessive interest in the human body in literary and psychological theory during the past twenty years, one might think that the body had been invisible until just recently. In some sense it has, for until a few years ago it had not quickened interest in academic circles, nor was it viewed until recently as the shifting image in various political, social, psychological, and mythical fields. With the rediscovery of Freud and the discovery of Michel Foucault, the body has walked onto center stage with the same forceful fascination as had the corpse for medicine in the first dissecting and operating theater at the University of Padua in the thirteenth century.

What has been recovered is not just the physical body—although culturally its literalness has been promoted through the rather superficial call to health, wellness, and body management—but the body as metaphor, as political emblem, as social construction, as symbol, and as symptom, as Robert Romanyshyn has described it in his original and insightful extensions of Merleau-Ponty's work,[1] and is only now being felt full flush in the academic and social disciplines. The body today is a deeply complex cultural image that carries within it our history and our meanings. Writing eloquently of the body and language, Merleau-Ponty believes that "For us the body is much more than an instrument or a means; it is our expression in the world, the visible form of our intentions" (*Primacy of Perception*, 5). His observation captures in a short but critical and imaginative way the connection between expression and styles of intention that is uniquely ours as individuals. Our style of inhabiting the world in an embodied way is already an expression of the meaning that the body carries. In this way, the body can be imagined as the locus of both our individual and cultural mythologies. I understand the body to be both a location and a field for experience as well as for interpretation.

This is a book about embodiment from the point of view of the poetic or literary imagination. I wish to uncover in these chapters a poetic sense of flesh, of how the flesh remembers and how it finds its language through the body and subsequently into the world, although these may not be two moments, but rather one action in a single instant. And by "world" here I hope to include not just the world's matter as well as the body's substance, but also a vital sense of the sacred, the holy—what might be called the numinous, that haunts our flesh and can give voice to the transcendent. The literary works included in the Contents all also reflect in some measure the observation made by Carl Jung: "The body is merely the visibility of the soul, the psyche, and the soul is the psychological experience of the body, so it is really one and the same thing" (*Vision Seminars*, 475).

Presently there exists a deep desire in literature and psychology, especially psychoanalysis, to uncover the flesh in new and innovative ways, perhaps in a renewed and renewing partnership. For as a cultural invention, according to Robert Romanyshyn (*Technology as Symptom and Dream*, 23), the body is always metaphorical in its relation to the world and symbolic in its inherent power to unite self and world in a richly textured field of meaning. This "intertwining," in the language of Merleau-Ponty, the literary artist accomplishes most fully and complexly, as the book's chapters will illustrate. What underlies my own way of viewing the body through a range of literary images in a variety of poetic works are the ideas first introduced and articulated by Aristotle in the *Poetics*: poiesis and mimesis. For just as studies on the body have of late coagulated around issues of gender and politics primarily, I have found a deeper interest in the poetics of the body, even preferring to call it the mimetic body, the body of possibilities in its wounded or marked nature. Perhaps there is a poetic physiology hidden in this approach that would take us deeper than a political or gender reading allows.[2] I take seriously the penetrating explorer of the imagination, Gaston Bachelard, who in one of his last works, *Fragments of a Poetics of Fire*, suggests that the poetic image has a "power of enhancement, unhappily lacking in ourselves, which we find gripping when we read the work of poets" (11). The poetic wound, the mimetic disease or mutilation or decay, as poetic images, "have immediate powers of their own. . . . There is a poetic ontology in every literary image" (11) that must be approached with a certain naivete so that they can emerge in their full splendor to reveal what we have not yet discerned about the body's mortal gestural nature. Wounds offer us gestures that need to be dwelled with over time. Aristotle intuited this reality in the *Poetics*.

We recall that he distinguishes between the poet and the historian in the following way: The historian's task is to write of events that have actually occurred, whereas the poet's task is to narrate events "such as *might occur* and have the capability of occurring in accordance with the laws of probability or necessity" (*Poetics*, 16, my emphasis). The historian's world is one of fact, the poet's more intimate with *ananke*, the necessity of actions or perhaps the necessity *in* actions. As such, Aristotle continues, poetry is "more philosophical" than history and "more concerned with the universal" (17). The poet, moreover, is concerned with a poiesis, a making, an action artificially constructed. The poet has the task of both forming and deforming images and stories to arrive at something of their essence, some inherent pattern or design that resonates a universal or archetypal significance. The poet is engaged in a mimesis, an imitation, a making or forming by means of the poetic imagination, and one of the instruments at his or her hand is the body in its distorted, wounded, corrupted, marked, or scarred condition.

Making the deep connection between the case histories of therapy in analysis and the genre of stories in fiction, James Hillman brings together this act of poiesis, an "imagining in words" (*Healing Fiction*, 4), with the plot of an action that is as much a part of psyche as it is of the body, and perhaps participates in the same quality of *ananke* suggested by Aristotle. Hillman reminds us that in the *Poetics*, wherever the word "plot" is used, in the original Greek, Aristotle used *mythos*: "Plots are myths. . . . To be in a *mythos* is to be inescapably linked with divine powers and to be in mimesis with them" (*Healing Fiction*, 11). The implicit suggestion in this connection is that not only does there exist a body of myths but also a *mythos* of the body, of which the marked or wounded or scarred body offers us one emblem of poetic meaning. I wish, therefore, not to politicize the body, but to poeticize it, to allow its mimetic sense to surface in the figures and to understand the action through the wounds of both body and language.[3]

Part of my belief is that within the poetics of the body, mimesis finds its origin as well as its destiny. It finds its origin through memory and its destiny through desire. The poetic image of the body offers us more than politics or gender; it offers "a template," an image I take from George Elder's Preface to *The Body*, for images, as he suggests. From them "we may perceive larger meanings, reflections of those psychological and sacred depths from which the energy comes that powers fascination with our incarnate form" (vii). The body is an image of both depth and surface, of deep mysterious interiors and often codified exteriors; what affects it in either region becomes the ground for constructing those meanings that haunt the body visible and invisible.

What is powerfully inherent in the poet's vision of embodiment as a rich and inexhaustible metaphor is that it escapes the literalism attendant upon three popularly shared images of incarnation: (1) the body is a series of systems to be analyzed and finally managed; (2) the body is something that we have, like another possession; (3) the body is something that is objective and adheres to the laws of mechanism. What travels in our cultural ruts today and seems to be accepted with little question is that the body is often little more than a technical function but is understood only vaguely or not at all as a cultural symptom (Romanyshyn, *Technology*, 28).

The literary imagination, by contrast, retrieves the body from cliché and the scourge of literalism to reveal its more subtle and nuanced contours as a phenomenon. The wound becomes the distortion through which we revision its phenomenology as a lived experience. Wounding is one way the body shows its hyperbole, drawing our attention to it in unexpected ways. The chapters on various literary works make explicit what Merleau-Ponty has claimed of the body and the world, and which helps us to see that the genesis of the Ecology movement is coincidental with a renewed interest in the body as an organic unity. Gaia and the body are born within the same cultural clock time. They also share a birth in psychological time, a time of soul's multiple speech. Merleau-Ponty underscores this relationship: "The world is made of the same stuff as the body . . . and vision happens among or is caught in, things" (*Primacy of Perception*, 163). The body becomes most authentic and textual when "between the seeing and the seen, a blending of some sort takes place, when the spark is lit between the sensing and the sensible" (163).

Each of the poetic works discussed in this volume may perhaps contribute to this blending of the world and the self through the body wounded, diseased, putrefied, pierced, marked, tattooed, bloated, or murdered, for in the body distended and distorted there is revealed something true about the interaction of individuals and the world concerning their own fatedness, their individual destiny, and their evolving character.[4]

Richard Zaner reminds us, given the latter observation, that "embodiment is not a fact, but a complex event and a task" (*Context of Self*, 57). Physiologically it is a given; psychologically and poetically it is a becoming. How the artists of the works explored in this volume reveal the complexity of embodiment, how the task of living an embodied world of meaning, and how one's own destiny as well as one's history are predicated on bodily being are its central concerns. In addition, several chapters will make more explicit the body's relation to language, to a world wherein flesh and word find a common landscape if not a shared heritage given the incarnational quality of speech and the enfleshed nature of words. What becomes immediately apparent to anyone who reads widely on the body is the clearly outlined vocabulary that is adopted and thus shapes the body according to its own preconceived contours through that language. The body becomes a being languaged into existence and formed by the vocabulary that gives it expression; its style and gestures and functions are assertively sketched out by the discipline that studies it. The body is made in the image of the myth that powers its envisioning.

THE WOUNDED BODY: CULTURE, GENDER, POLITICS

Elaine Scarry's *The Body in Pain* (1985) was one of the first studies to inaugurate an exploration of the body in literature. Anthropologist Mary Douglas' *Purity and Danger* (1966) was also a key work that opened up ways of perceiving the body ritualized in literature.[5] Since then there has been a spree of works on embodiment in its wounded, marked and inscripted condition. Early on was Peter L. Hays' *The Limping Hero: Grotesques in Literature,* (1971) which seemed to get stuck in impotency and did not extend the phenomenon of the wound beyond it. Yet his catalogue of works that contain wounded figures shows how prevalent they have been.

More recent studies I have consulted that work the particulars of the body as social, gendered, and political site, and which take body criticism in another direction from mine, include Rosemarie Garland Thomson's *Extraordinary Bodies: Figuring Physical Disability in American Culture and Literature* (1997); Laura Mulvey's *Fetishism and Curiosity* (1996); Judith Butler's *Bodies That Matter: On the Discursive Limits of "Sex"* (1993); Paul A. Komesaroff's (ed.) *Troubled Bodies: Critical Perspectives on Postmodernism, Medical Ethics, and the Body* (1995); Andrew J. Strathern's *Body Thoughts* (1996); David Hillman and Carla Mazzio's (eds.) *The Body in Parts: Fantasies of Corporeality in Early Modern Europe* (1997); William Doty's (ed.) *Picturing Cultural Values in Postmodern America* (1995); Donald M. Lowe's *The Body in Late-Capitalist USA* (1995); Caroline Walker Bynum's *The Resurrection of the Body in Western Christianity, 200–1336* (1995); Shannon Bell's *Reading, Writing and Rewriting the Prostitute Body* (1994); Thomas Laquer's *Making Sex: Body and Gender from the Greeks to Freud* (1990); Margaret Lock's "Cultivating the Body: Anthropology and Epistemologies of Bodily Practice and Knowledge" (1993). Lock's essay makes it clear how much the body is invented as an epistemology of knowledge itself. Her studies are helpful in allowing one to survey the terrain of body criticism today, and of how body exploration is semiotic, "in other words, how the body functions as both a 'transmitter' and 'receiver' of information" (136). She goes on to highlight how in studies today the body "is no longer portrayed simply as a template for social organization, nor as a biological black box cut off from 'mind,' and nature/culture and mind/body dualities are self-consciously interrogated" (136). What becomes clear in reading her survey of critical approaches to the body is how deeply metaphorical it is as a mirror of values carried by the culture that invents it anew.

BODY, NAMING, AND PLACE

I want to extend explorations of somatic similes to go beneath cultural concerns to poetic experiences of the body contained in the works of this study and to envision the meanings incarnated in the particularities of woundedness by paying attention to the body as the analogue of psyche, and by seeing how bodily pain and suffering lead to a greater awareness of our human limits and vulnerabilities. If Aristotle is correct in suggesting that "The first principle, then, and to speak figuratively, the soul of tragedy, is the plot" (*Poetics*, 13), the *mythos* of the work, may there not be a corresponding relation in the body of one engaged in the imaginative reading of that action? There exists, I believe, an element in the soul of a work that resonates deeply within our own bodies by means of imagining *with*. The essence of *mimesis* is somatic, visceral, a shared psychic element wherein we feel the action, the wounding, the marking of the body, in our own being. I believe that this mimetic quality of poetry is where the body of the reader and the embodied figures, the characters, which Aristotle lists as second in importance (13), thicken. Within the imaginative experience there arises a sympathy of place, of being part of the same terrain, of feeling the generic quality of a literary work echo in one's own being not in an exclusively intellectual, but in a visceral way.

In part this study is informed by David Michael Levin's observation that each person begins life "with a body genetically precoded for movement. This infantile body is also an ancient body which belongs as much to the culture of our ancestors as it does to nature. It is the body of the collective unconscious; its actions call for interpretation through archetypal symbols" (100), which is a further elaboration of Merleau-Ponty's "intertwining," for the body reveals, as a large, overarching metaphor of our humanness, that a richer experience of being open to the world occurs through wounding.

To be wounded is to be opened to the world; it is to be pushed off the straight, fixed, and predictable path of certainty and thrown into ambiguity, or onto the circuitous path, and into the unseen and unforeseen. One begins to wobble, to wander, and perhaps even to wonder not only about one's present condition but also about one's origins. Circling the edges of the wound, so to speak, one's vision may clear, one's perception sharpens, and one may grasp for the first time what James Hillman describes in *The Soul's Code* as that "innate image" that lies at the heart of the acorn that is me (4), that defines my heritage and my destiny. How one lives one's own embodiment out, especially in its hyperbole—its woundedness—reveals the acorn's possibilities as well as its origins. It is to see the form of one's life at once, without development, without linearity, and without theory. It is to grasp the form of one's being in an instant.

Wounds, misshapen bodies, scarred or marked flesh always tell a story through their opening onto the world. For the Homeric Greeks, claims Hillman, the word *kairos* referred "to a penetrable opening" ("Notes on Opportunism," 153). It was the goal of archers practicing their accuracy to aim their arrows at openings, the Achilles' heel that wounds. *Kairos* is also the right moment, the appropriate time. The world is let in through the opening, the place where the flesh has been wounded, where there exists a gap, a fissure. It is the place of dialogue and of narrative. "What comes through the hole has its source beyond the wall and cannot easily be detached from the gap (chaos) of its entry" ("Notes on Opportunism," 154).

To be wounded is to be in a drama, in a narrative, often one of initiation, of a passing from one domain to another, that can provoke both interest and perhaps sympathy. One thinks, for example, of the crooked paw of the large bear, Old Ben, in Faulkner's *Go Down, Moses* or of the crooked, deformed lower jaw of Moby-Dick. The god Haephaistos is exiled from Olympus for having crippled feet (Elder, *The Body*, 375); Achilles is left exposed on the ankle of his left foot where his mother Thetis held him as she dipped his infant body into the River Styx; the sight of his maternal support is precisely where he is most vulnerable and eventually injured mortally. His heel grounds him in the human world within an otherwise divine body. God wounds Adam in order to draw from his side the rib from which He creates Eve; Christ is circumcised at eight days of age, the wound a sign that links God with mortals; the ritual of circumcision is a cutting away of the animal that "is most associated with personal desire" (Elder, *The Body*, 339). At the end of his life he suffers five wounds during his crucifixion. From birth to death his body suffers the markings of sacrificial and initiatory rituals that are both personal and cosmic. Philoctetes suffers a snake bite on the island of Tenedos as the Greeks sail for Troy; he is left behind because the stench from his oozing wound overpowers the sensibilities of the Greek sailors; Jacob dares to wrestle with one of God's angels and receives a maiming wound in his left thigh (Elder, *The Body*, 379–81); Parzival's Fisher King receives a wound in his thigh; it then becomes the young knight's task to ask the King the right question about his injury; Roy Hobbs in Bernard Malamud's *The Natural* plays his last baseball game with a bleeding open wound he received from a silver bullet sixteen years earlier. Part of heroic action is therefore defined by the suffering attendant upon the open wound, which has lain dormant for almost two decades, but which then opens up and out at the moment of one's greatest moment of action.

The Gospel of Luke tells us that Christ was circumcised on the eighth day after his birth and that on that same day he was given the name already designated by an angel before he was conceived. Naming and being wounded take place in the same ritual. Our wounds name or identify us; do our names in some way wound us as well? Odysseus is named by his uncle Autolycos before he is wounded by the boar; Oedipus' name, meaning "swollen foot," is intimately associated with his wound. Mythically then, personal identity is bound up tightly with our wounds. Our wounds name us and give the trajectory of our destiny. They identify and mark us. Our name, along with our wound, records us in the world. And in our identity rests our vulnerable mortal limits. If we can be recognized, then we can be wounded. Where we have been marked is where the soft spot of our being is, where we are most finite; but it is also where the hinge is located that marks the pivot of our history and our destiny. Our name is perhaps our Achilles' heel, the spot in which we are most mortal, most identifiable. A soiled reputation is the consequence of a name publicly wounded.

The archetypal questions we might therefore pose at this juncture are: What god or gods reside in the wound? What does the wound want? What is the disease asking? What is the story that it poses or proposes? What plot wishes to be born through the wound? Behind these questions is the implication that the body carries, in all of its lineages and lineaments, an archetypal correlate that corresponds to some deep psychic and even numinous reality. The body is a visual aid, a vision that aids our imagination in order to deepen the texture of our lives through the wounded bodies explored here.

The body already has within its nature as a text "a divine code" (Levin, 205) which has a beginning and an end. It has a personal myth, an engraving, a marking, a wounding that gives it its particular character and its own unique way of being in the world. At heart it is, as Anthony Synnott believes, the core of "social life and social interaction, and also at the heart of personal identity" (262). Within this particularity is an archetypal wholeness that allows each of us reading that body in a world of meaning to sense by analogy our own wounded condition as well as something more: in many of the works, a gashed openness to the divine, to transcendence that the show of vulnerability reinforces, if not encourages. The "measure of our mortality" (Levin, 218), and perhaps our immortality, is to be found in the body, as well as our sense of place, of being placed and belonging to place and to a narrative, most especially through our wounding.

Placement, being placed or finding a place in the world through our wounds, is also an important consideration in this study.[6] Echoing some of the original insights of Merleau-Ponty, Edward Casey links body to place: "We might say, in sum, that body and place *are congruent counterparts.* Each needs the other. Each suits the other. Put otherwise, *place is where the body is"* (103).[7] Place, and with it a story, might be given through a wound, a tattoo, a scar, a corpse, a body in decay or diseased.

The wound is where something buried or hidden splits open, breaches, and reveals a memory, a site of pain, of suffering and death, but it can also include a joyful sense of new freedom as well. Hephaistos, with his wounded foot, is our best and fullest archetype for how, out of our "terrible deformity" (Elder, *The Body,* 377) we create imaginatively something that is deeply our own, a creativity that "develops out of defect or out of need," as Edward Edinger believes (qtd. in Elder, *The Body,* 377). Our wounds have the capacity to advance our consciousness to new levels of awareness. Our wounds, our defects that are embodied emblems of our imperfections, have the capacity to "'bring us down to earth' . . . or drop us deeper into depths of ourselves to ponder the strange relationship of strength and weakness, success and failure, good and evil" (Elder, *The Body,* 377). Our wounds, scars, and markings may be the loci of place that put us in the most venerable and vulnerable contact with the world, with divinity, with one another, and with ourselves. As such, the body may invoke an entire cosmology; it is cosmic in its symbolic nature.[8]

This series of ruminations explores those dimensions of the flesh that signal fundamentally shared experiences of embodiment as metaphors, through the following images: the appetites, the corpse, disease, the body inscribed, scarred, mutilated, wounded, murdered, fragmented, textualized, decaying, corrupting, lost, remembered, imagined, and languaged into being. The questions that arise might then be framed this way: What is unique about the poetic body in literature that sets it apart from our unconsciously lived everyday body, such that it offers a way of seeing in and through it to other dimensions of human experience? The poetic body offers to the imagination a particular way of experiencing the world, of being in the world, that is fundamentally different from other ways of knowing. Is this poetic body closer to the subtle body of dream? Does the poet dream the body forward and upward into our imaginative consciousness? Is there a reverie of the body that the literary work wants us to participate in, to feel the sense of the flesh in a visceral way? What the philosopher Gaston Bachelard believes about poetry—that "all poetry is androgynous"(*Right to Dream,* 174)—may also apply to human embodiment as well.

THE IMAGINAL/POETIC BODY

Each literary work I discuss develops the body as a central metaphor of signification in all of its senses. Each of the works reveals fictional characters who imagine themselves in the world from a particular body perception and from an imaginal perspective that is unique to their world. Implicit in their way of perceiving is an imagination that David Abram describes as "a way the senses themselves have of throwing themselves beyond what is immediately given, in order to make tentative contact with the other sides of things that we do not sense directly, with the hidden or invisible aspects of the sensible" (*Spell of the Sensuous*, 58). In other words, the body is the aperture or the corridor into invisible presences that can be imagined only through the flesh. Various forms of wounding or body attacks and distortions, body markings, and even body murder suddenly open avenues of significance that would not be available through any another means. The body is therefore the controlling metaphor for the work's essential meaning, even perhaps its most profound opportunity, for the body promises, even within its limits, possibilities when imagined creatively.

The following list sketches briefly the central concern of each chapter:

In Chapter 2, Homer's *Odyssey* offers the monstrous body of appetite and of excess as well as the body wounded and scarred in an initiatory rite of passage between the human and animal realms. Both of these images are tightly intertwined with the images of right order of speaking, of soundness of mind and the establishment of home. Central to the body's modulated appetites is the narration of one's history, such that one begins to find the place of home first and primarily in one's own bodily existence. Homer's poem might be called the epic of the curbed appetite and the remembered wound.

In Chapter 3, Sophocles' *Oedipus Rex* expresses the forgotten, wounded body, the body of pollution, which is remembered, and another wound which is self-inflicted as the individual gains insight into his destiny through a remembrance of origins and a recognition of his first wounding as an infant by his father, Laius.

The polluted body, the wounded ear, and the tainted state of Denmark is Chapter 4's central action in Shakespeare's *Hamlet*. Blood sacrifice, a descent into the underworld of violence and murder, and the action of purifying the polis at the expense of the feminine comprise the resolution of a heroic mind whose first impulse is to escape the body's limits entirely. The tragedy of *Hamlet*, as one of our first modern interrogations of the flesh, could also be called the Tragedy of the Abandoned Body.

With Rousseau's *Confessions* in Chapter 5, the modern body is invented and the self as a cultural concept takes full form. Here the relationship between body and city is more sharply delineated: disease and body management, especially in Rousseau's failing health, his desire to empty himself of all his personal pollutions, the obstructions in his own body ailments, especially in his retaining urine because of a blocked urethra, and his use of catheters to relieve and drain himself of body poisons, reveal the body as a place of catharsis. These body and autobiographical cleansings I explore and correlate with the invention of the Paris sewer system, wherein the city is flushed of its impurities. Like *The Confessions* themselves, the sewer sluices below the surface of polite society bear witness to the new technology of autobiography as waste management, of which *The Confessions* is a linguistic analogue. Rousseau's reflections on his own flesh, his origins, and the desire for pure and unsullied feelings of a virgin heart are linked with Paris' own urban desire for waste elimination and a corresponding obsession with cleanliness and personal hygiene as the invention of the individual gains fuller prominence in society. Autobiography becomes a rhetorical and poetic form of body and city purification.

In Chapter 6, *The Brothers Karamazov* attempts to reconcile intellect with flesh through the two central images of the novel: the corrupting corpse of Father Zosima, whose offensive stench scandalizes the acceptable conventions of miracle, and the intellectual prose poem of Ivan Karamazov, in which evil is given its fullest expression. In this context, evil *is* abstraction.

Chapter 7 deals with Herman Melville's *Moby-Dick* and continues the interrogation of the body given form by Dostoevsky through Melville's exploration of three patterns of incarnation: Ahab's dismembered leg and his scarred flesh; the inscribed body of the white whale; and the tattooed bodies of Queequeg and Ishmael. Each of these images of being enfleshed compete for the soul of the sailor-scribe Ishmael, whose narrative incarnates the force of and gives voice to all four figures as Captain Ahab leads the *Pequod* to the waters that contain the site of his original affliction. The body and the text continue an epic exploration begun by Homer's *Odyssey*.

In Chapter 8, Leo Tolstoy's *The Death of Ivan Ilych* poetically expresses the body's journey from health to disease, from caring for the body of anatomy and for an anatomical, compartmentalized, and efficient life devoid of unpleasantness, to exploring the phenomenal body as lived. Disease is the occasion and opportunity for a fullness of life through the gesture of generosity toward one of his own family. Ivan Ilych experiences a shift in focus that leads to spiritual insight only through the invasion of illness. The heroic life of success is exposed through disease and exchanged at the last moment for a more deepened life that redeems his lifelong pursuit of secular achievement.

The two short stories of Flannery O'Connor, "Revelation" and "Parker's Back" which comprise Chapter 9, create two distinct but related bodies: the animal body of Ruby Turpin and the tattooed body of images. Salvation is glimpsed by both figures as inclusive, comic, and the consequence of violent suffering. Grace is present in the form of a violent action followed by the tattooing on O. E. Parker's back of an image of the Byzantine Christ.

Toni Morrison's *Beloved* illustrates in Chapter 10 the phantom body of slavery explored through the action of a mother's slaying her own child to protect it from a life of servitude. Memory, flesh, and the Word are the modes of redefining poetically the experience of slavery and freedom on many levels. Through the Word, and then through its extension into story, the scarred and beaten body of community is freed from the slavery of the past.

The poetic body, or the wounded body created by the imagination and given flesh in these works that span approximately 2,800 years, offers insights into the visceral, lived experience of being enfleshed in the world. All of them disclose language's power, through stories and remembrances, of how the body offers inexhaustible possibilities of envisioning the horizon of meaning attendant upon our own incarnation. The body exists in the world in limited space and time such that much of its meaning is gained by means of remembrances and desires, expressed through language and the body's woundedness. Gesture, in fact, is at the core of these poetic creations. Said another way, the body is a language, a gesture, a sign, and a form of speaking in and to the world. David Abram observes that "to touch the coarse skin of a tree is thus, at the same time, to experience one's own tactility, to feel oneself touched *by* the tree. And to see the world is also, at the same time, to experience oneself as visible, to feel oneself *seen*" (68). This same act of touching and being touched is found in the poetic expressions of various forms of woundedness in the literary works under study.

Flesh, as Merleau-Ponty develops it in his later writing, "is the mysterious tissue that underlies perceiver and perceived" (qtd. in Abram, 66). Each of the fictional bodies of the characters I focus on in the various literary works all engage this mystery of the subtle tissue that intertwines the individual to a larger world of meaning. The wounded or marked body exaggerates and makes more poignant this connectedness that all of us incorporate. It insists that the process of growing down deep into who we are to become requires a continual bruising, scarring, and marking, even dismembering of who we are presently, so that the fullness of our embodied being may find itself fully revealed in the world in its relation with others.

While waiting for a flight home some time ago, I saw a woman with a deeply cut arm freshly sutured, raw and red, where the skin pulled angrily from the stitches. Arrested by this sight, and wondering about the nature of the narrative that would expose such a deep gash in her life, I could only find expression for it in the following:

Wounded

Wound stretching the length of her
Lower arm,
She cradles the sliced flesh in her left hand.
Black stitches, spaced in perfect symmetry along
The whiteness of skin—a vertical single file
Of large insects immobile, arrested in suture and sew.
Sitting beside her in the airport
Terminal
Matriarchal, unmoving, resting
Both wrinkled hands on her cane propped primly
Before her,
An old woman gazes straight ahead, listening,
Thinking.
The wounded woman recounts the attack; three men in a kitchen
Broken glass, a cleaver spinning into
A life of its own.
She looks puzzled, as if the wound
Is a sudden surprise, a stitched chasm that
Abrupted itself, unawares, on to her flesh.
She questions it, speaks softly to the smooth
Curve of its progress from wrist to forearm.
She runs her finger tips along the braided slice.
Reading a Braille line of prose, raised
Bumps of plot.
Her mouth remains open after she ceases
To speak.

2

Nature and Narratives

Feeding the Fictions of the Body in Homer's Odyssey

The mind's patterns of thinking are clothed by the Body
—*The Temple in the House,* 97

Perhaps as Eric Voegelin affirms, both the *Iliad* and the *Odyssey* are markers within ancient Greece for the emergence of a new kind of consciousness, one that deals in a rudimentary but sophisticated way with "symbolization of a new experience of human existence under the gods, of nature, of order, of the causes of disorder" (*World of the Polis,* 48). But more important, Voegelin continues, Homer was the first "to give us a theogony, to image the gods, to give them form, and to put them into dramatic conflict with man" (51) so that in the epics he crafted, at no time do human beings act without the presence, and often the intervention, of divinity in either a celestial or human form.

In fact, as Bruno Snell observes of this connection between divinity and mortality, "every new turn of events is engineered by the gods" (*Discovery of the Mind,* 35). Clearly human beings have, in the poetry of Homer, entered more fully into direct and deeply entangled relations with the citizens of Olympus. On to this relationship the epic stories of the heroic men and women are fastened with great subtlety and charm, often anticipating in their concerns so many of the cultural concerns of our own postmodern world. And yet with this overt and tangibly embodied connective tissue between mortals and divinities, Odysseus is perhaps rightly called, according to Norman Austin, "the first modern European hero, . . . whose aspirations belong to us, and whose voyage has dominated European consciousness from Homer's time to our own" ("Odysseus/Ulysses," 201). Odysseus seems almost omniscient in his multivalenced role as the man of many turns and one deeply memorable scar.

Homer's great achievement includes as well his offering very powerful images of the heroic, the body, home, war, the persuasive and psychological force of stories themselves, which, in the polyphonic world of Odysseus' polytropic persona, is directly related to what I perceive as a retrieval not just of the household—or its magnificent analogue in the figure of the polis—but of a more fundamental salvaging of human embodiment itself. And part of this retrieval revolves around Odysseus' scar, which marks him unequivocally even through his many disguises, his many woven fictions. Odysseus' journeys and subsequent telling of those voyages is an imaginal attempt to retrieve and reunite biology and biography—to get the story right—and to return home in a way that does not end in his or his family's destruction. The Phaecians, marvelous and mysterious people who inhabit a world Edenic in its charm and fruitfulness, will offer him an opportunity, Christopher Vogler notes, to "find a frame to fit it all together" (*Writer's Journey,* 223), to allow him to inhabit fully his own narrative and to live once again fully in his own body. Odysseus, to be sure, has his stories; what he is searching for is the right genre in which to situate these narratives, the right *mythos* or plot in which to place them. What he chooses is a genre that begins in tragedy but has its *telos* in comedy. For comedy is the genre that celebrates the body and has as its strongest impulse the sanctity and preservation of life, of existence, and of love that binds communities in a largesse that transcends any one individual and approaches a more sacred imagination as it approaches the gods.

Moreover, even as Cedric Whitman believes that the struggle of Achilles is not just with Briseis or with honor in the *Iliad*, but is rather "a struggle for identity, of locating one's place in the world, and of deciding which values may aid one in finding his place in things" (197), so are Odysseus' journeys home and, most crucially, his relating these narratives to the Phaecians in Books 9–12 also his own unique way of finding and constructing both place and self after ten years of heroic efforts in the service of destroying a city. But while Achilles' concerns in the *Iliad* were with grief and heroic striving toward the gods, Odysseus' struggle implicates his bodily appetites and desires and the curbing of excess. Moderation in life replaces a metaphysics of an honorable death.

Held hostage by appetite, Odysseus' journey is psychic as well as physical; he must not just literally recapture and rule his city once again. He must first journey in his own imaginal language, as he has traveled for two decades in his own body from Troy to Ithaca, to give his life a fictional, or poetic quality, through the utterance of story. He must imagine his life as a fiction, enter its psychic reality and its monstrous images, as preparation to deal quite literally with the monstrous appetites in the form of the suitors devouring his own household. The stories he offers to the Phaecians illustrate in their complexity what W. B. Stanford claims is a seminal quality of this roguish hero. He writes that "Homer was large-minded enough to comprehend a unity in apparent diversity, a structural consistency within an external changefulness, in the character of Ulysses" (*Ulysses Theme*, 80).

Within his diversity, and on a more imaginal and mythic level, his task is to journey in memory through his past and to give those events poetic form in story. In the process, he regains some wholeness to being embodied that goes beyond stomach in a dimly conscious instinct for satisfying desire. A full homecoming includes a retrieval of embodiment itself so that "Noman" or "Nobody," which he calls himself when he battles Polyphemos, whose titanic stature mirrors appetites in their most distorted and distended form, becomes "Somebody," with a full past and a desirable future. Present in Homer's images is a connection between retrieving the fullness of the body through reintegrating the feminine, matter, the earth, which are integral to Odysseus' shattered psyche after ten years of warring. Embodiment is as central to homecoming as is storytelling.[1] Not only must he journey home in story; he must also travel home integrally embodied. His scar carries within it his unique narrative.

The epithet "Nobody" is just one of the tropes that the polytropic figure of Odysseus has in his fictional sack of disguises. As a man of many turns, his options, alone or in conjunction with divinity, are multiple and varied. He knows, for example, how to turn stories, to turn things around when he is in trouble; he can turn a harmful situation into one less life-threatening, or he can turn the tables on a predator, remain constantly in motion, turning things over in his mind as he voyages from Troy to Ithaca, or he can turn himself around, turn, or be turned into something else through camouflage or disguise so that, within the comic impulse of this epic, things turn out right, with a new order and design to them. Fabrication finesses a new order.

By looking at the belly, at animals, at Odysseus' own stories, and at his scarred or inscripted body, we see through a series of poetic turns how this comic hero reclaims his own mythologem, how he begins to see and speak mythically through the pathologized images of his narratives, the great stories of distortion and twistedness that reflect deeply and mimetically the twists and turns of his own soul, often through the excesses of appetites, both psychic and somatic. Hunger drives the memory's desire forward. As J. Nigro Sansonese writes of the epic poet, " a "human being in Homer is a human body: the locus of experience" (*Body of Myth*, 34).[2] What Odysseus has lost in ten years of battle is not only his own mythology, rooted deeply in his own embodiment, but the myth of his city, kept alive and intact, however minimally, by his circumspect and faithful Penelope. The twists and turns of his own journeys and their subsequent imaginative forms in his storytelling inspire a successful re-turn of the cunning leader to his homeland. These coils are reflected in the loom of Penelope as she fabricates deceit by twisting the threads into a funeral shroud for her father-in-law, Laertes. They are a mutually weaving and plotting couple, intent on preserving both household and city. Said another way, the anticipated death of the father is what gives continued life and coherence to the household. Is Homer wishing us to see the inextricable threads weaving life and death together as well here, and that one does not exist without the other in a continuous fabric of meaning?

Penelope's weaving is as important as Odysseus' meandering voyage home. Her weave may even be more ontological, since the act of weaving is associated with *kairos*, a term, Hillman reminds us, comes "from the art of weaving" ("Notes on Opportunism," 153). "Weaving, time and fate are often connected ideas. An opening in the web of fate can mean an opening in time, an eternal moment when the pattern is drawn tighter or broken through" (153). Penelope threads her husband home by offering *kairos* to his chronological time. Time and eternity are the warp and woof of this threading him home. And I believe the same may be said of the scar he carries on his thigh, a threading marker that he received from a boar hunt early in life that marks his identity to Eurycleia when he returns home.

Odysseus' narratives may be understood as the vessel in which he sails home, propelled as it were by an imaginative remembrance of fantasies past and desires sustained. It is as if Odysseus is a marvelously complex metaphor for poetry itself, with all of its ambiguities, uncertainties, intertwined plots, paradoxes and possible meanings. Polytropic and polyphonic are characteristics of both the man and poetic verse. Homer offers on one level not just the making of a poet out of the lustrous metalworks of a warrior, but the craft of poetry itself, with its right angles of meaning and quirky turns of significance. Like the rest of the world, however, poetry needs to be enfleshed. And its most forceful reservoir, the imagination, is what seeks within him a fullness of freedom.[3]

Furthermore, even while the *Iliad* emphasizes a psychology and metaphysics of individual heroism, according to Whitman, the *Odyssey* concerns itself, as a much more self-reflexive and self-conscious story, with "the typology of humanity and experiences" (233). As Achilles seems to transcend the ordinary mortal limits of mere warriors in battle, spurred on by the grief attendant on his loss of Patroklos, Odysseus, once free of Troy's blood, descends further into appetite and engages haphazardly in what appears to be a reflex slaughter of anything and anybody with whom he drifts into contact. He is perhaps the shadow of the warrior code of Achilles, his brother in battle, whose code he still embodies, but without its attendant *kleos*. His journeys will take him through the dual existence of wounder and healer. As an archetypal image of what Edward Whitmont describes as a representative of "the healing dynamic," Odysseus is "a healer that both is wounded and inflicts wounds. . . . He is a wound-carrying and wound-conveying healer" (*The Alchemy of Healing*, 193). To wound, to be wounded, and to heal are all essential parts of Odysseus' story that must be confronted and lived through as he weaves his way to Penelope. Where healing is promised, there shall wounds also appear.

War, in Homer's poetic worldview, seems as much to offer an attitude toward the world as it is an appetite for gain, not just of *kleos* but of goods. And what takes place as normative human behavior to define honor on the fighting field of Troy will fail within the more constricted and ordered boundaries of Ithaca. So the question may be posed: What does Odysseus learn and leave from a decade of battle? And what does it cost him? For the epic is engaged in illustrating through a comic, if not finally a joyful complexity, a recovery of the poetic sense of the world, one based on craft and inspired by memory.

Perhaps what Odysseus loses, in addition to home, is the full sense of embodiment itself, especially as it is joined mythically to the sacred feminine. The goddess is the image that anchors Odysseus in the world through the flesh. Through the figure of Calypso, with whom he spends seven of the ten years in his journey home, he is able to contemplate his mortal home and Penelope. In this goddess of "the sacred feminine," as Tom Absher refers to her (*Men and the Goddess*, 36), Odysseus begins to retrieve a wholeness of self that modulates appetite and curbs excess after living in the belly and through the desires of the body for so long. It is as if in war he had lost himself physically or, more accurately, had been reduced physically to one organ of the body: the stomach. He and his castoffs from Troy seem reduced to roving bellies, nomadic wandering editions of the more stationary suitors.

Appropriately, then, one of their first confrontations is with Polyphemos, for they discover through his image their own likeness: a singled-eyed and monstrously bellied figure without piety, law, *oikos*, or human community. The belly's preoccupation with satisfying desire endstops the movement of soul toward community and civilization in its most complete participation while it gives form to their wild bellies by forcing them to confront it directly. Polyphemous' island places them in the wild, where, as they discover that the old laws of the *oikos* regarding guest and host do not apply, they find themselves completely bewildered, "a kind of place or region (land or sea) in which one readily loses one's way, goes astray," according to Edward Casey (229).

It is also another place of wounding for Odysseus. The more difficult journey that will carry Odysseus alone, stripped of all remnants of the Trojan landscape, is that from warrior to bard or poet, fighter to storyteller, solely reflexive to a more embodied and integrated figure, patient and ruled by constraint, having found a necessary soulful balance with the feminine, the earth, and the household. Through the stories of his experiences, he is better able to return home to reclaim what has fallen into complete disorder through the appetites of the suitors, themselves mortal miniatures of Polyphemos—but not without deeply wounding others and being wounded by having himself stripped of all that he left Troy with: men, gifts, and plunder. His wounds will leave him naked and alone, washed onto the shores of Scheria where, next to the help from the goddess Athena, only his scar and his narrative will accompany him as he transits from warrior to poet.

If one of the powers of poetry is to impose an order, an intricate design or pattern on experience, then Odysseus must first learn to give both order and aesthetic form to his past in order successfully to imagine himself toward the future, finally to the hut of Eumaeos, the swineherd in his homeland, and then to the space of the devouring suitors in his own home, where he is wounded by them. In imagination, the distance between the cave of Polyphemos and the dining hall of Odysseus is only a stutter-step, since both reflect the same hungry spaces of appetite. Odysseus' deeper journey is one in which he will be translated from the imaginative domain of Scheria to the more literal world of Ithaca—a city which, like Troy, holds the feminine hostage—in his passage through and his reciting passages of, his wild and wandering past. In the fantastic and imaginative space of Scheria he will offer his story to the Phaecians and satisfy their own appetite for narratives. They, too, have a hunger; they are starved for the food of the world in story form, and so they offer Odysseus a safe harbor in which to anchor his narrative and regain his past.

Having been fully and abundantly, but not excessively fed, the Phaecians are happy to show abundant hospitality in escorting him home, but not without full knowledge of the violence that will befall them at the hands of Poseidon, to whom they are distantly related, for their generosity. Homer then links belly to place in several spaces of the epic and reveals how stories themselves can modulate, even appease appetite, by conferring on one's history a degree of moderation that the leader needs in order to rule well.[4] Desire is replaced by a higher consciousness, "a poetic ontology," according to Gaston Bachelard (*Poetics of Fire,* 12), that gives soul a new, more divine sense of being, with a loss of appetite.

Furthermore, by linking Poseidon to both Polyphemous and to the Phaecians, we intuit the intimate affinity between appetites and story and discern the fact that stories themselves satisfy a deep appetite in the psyche; without stories the appetites have no governance. May Homer's suggestion be that stories modulate appetite and in a way civilize them? Built into these relations of Poseidon is an aesthetic exploration of the imagination's power to re-create the world and modulate desires. Remembering Odysseus' creation of the Trojan horse helps us here.

We recall that it is to Odysseus' handiwork in the shaping of the Trojan horse that all the Acheans pay great homage, for only by hiding in the belly of the beast are they able to open up the walls of Troy by craft (*metis*) and then conquer it by force (*bie*). By contrast, if the fundamental action in the *Iliad* is mortally wounding the Trojans with weapons of destruction, slicing, fragmenting, and emptying them of the winged spirit of life (*thymos* or breath); and the fundamental cohesive image that pulls all the action toward its center is the hard, bronzed shield of Achilles fashioned by Haephestus at the request of Thetis, Achilles' immortal mother, then the fundamental action in the *Odyssey* is weaving things, people, and plots together in a con-spiracy (a breathing-with). In the latter, the central image is the soft, shape-revealing clothing for the body which bends, folds, and yields to the contours of what it is to both reveal and conceal, much like language itself in its persuasive, poetic possibilities.

As the shield of Achilles protects him in battle by hiding his body from Trojan assaults, so does clothing act as a great counterfeit to conceal the essence of who or what one is. Just as the heel of Achilles marks the body's most vulnerable locus and is the target of Paris' arrow that mortally wounds the hero, the boar scar of Odysseus analogously marks the indelible inscription of his history and his true identity. As the *Iliad* is revelatory, reveling in *kleos* by the hero, the *Odyssey* is by contrast conciliatory, circuitous, and concealing. Metals give way to cloths and rigid structures surrender to the softer contours of disguise. Disguise wins over exposure, polysemousness over what is more univocal.

What, then, does Homer wish us to imagine about the body and identity, the wounds of the flesh and our own narrative design in the world? It is partly, as James Hillman outlines the imaginal realm of archetypal psychology, observes: "the body has its home in the soul" (*Revisioning Psychology*, 80). The body is less a thing than it is "a situation," as Robert Romanyshyn defines it (*Technology*, 24), an event where meaning finds its expression in language. Here we see that within the ancient epics, the scars or vulnerable points of both heroes' bodies implicate the flesh directly in their respective destinies and score the flesh with one's history. The body itself is indeed a narrative to be marked by the world so that it carries the chapters of one's own experiences. If the body is always an emblem of our history, then its wounded markings are the permanent witnesses to that same body's identity. In the markings of the body are the tracings of that person's mythology. Achilles had to be held by his mother by his right heel as his infant body was dipped into the River Styx. Where he was supported is the site of Paris' arrow that wounds him in the one vulnerable place on his body. The boar scar Odysseus receives happens after he is named by his grandfather. The heel and the thigh are the wounding sites of both heroes, one in war, the other in a boar hunt. They mark the heroic with wounds that occur at peak moments of breakthrough—through the walls of Troy and the hiding place of the boar. The wounds are received at points or intersections of transitions; the wound marks one mythically with his destiny.

While I will explore the boar scar on the young Odysseus' body later in the chapter, I mention here that this scarring is an inauguration, an initiation not just into the codified life of the hunter-warrior, but into something more; it installs Odysseus within the tradition of language itself and plants the seeds for the poet to grow. This poetic quality of Odysseus is most evident in Books 9–12 when he recounts his history, not without a few embellishments to thicken the fiction. Finally, the initiation he undergoes is as much a confirmation of his own name, "Man of Wrath: Odysseus" (19.409), named by his grandfather. With the hunt and the scar by the boar who charges at him in the wild when he is the first hunter present to ferret it out of the thickly entangled olive bushes, Odysseus is inaugurated by the world, by the animal powers, into his destiny. The world would seem to speak to him and to leave its mark, a remembrance of its dialogue with him in the hunt. It seems poetically appropriate, then, that when he reenters his own household after twenty years' absence and is washed by the faithful maidservant, Eurycleia, that his identity is uncovered by means of the scar, as the boar's identity is uncovered when he charges from the bush, and Odysseus' own identity is recovered when he uncovers himself from the leaves on Scheria and finds a place to reveal his wrapped story to the Phaecians. Such a recognition completes the circle of the small hunt of the boar and the larger battle of Troy where another animal aids in ending that conflict.[5]

Joseph Campbell's identification of the hero's journey that includes three moments—departure, initiation, and return (*Hero with a Thousand Faces,* 30)—is repeated often in this richly fabricated epic of storying and journeying in what might be called a *poetics of retrieval,* a fiction of covering and recovering. Such a retrieval also includes a rediscovery of the feminine archetype, both goddess and mortal, and of the flesh itself. Hidden for seven years with Calypso, a time perhaps when his own psyche incubates, Odysseus weeps for home.[6] These seven years are an imaginal period of both gestation and digestion. They also suggest that the psyche of Odysseus needs to experience again being in place, belonging somewhere in space and time and having that feeling of belonging to a particular habitation, before he can successfully return to his own place.

Calypso gives him his first sustained sense of being embodied and in place, even as her habitation is far from the center of civilization, but rests on the margins. This marginal quality seems to be a universal mythical setting for anyone seeking a shift in their conventional way of being. In her home exists a profound poetic paradox about our finding place in the world, for the epic suggests that one must at some point inhabit the margins, be willing to be decentered, to live on the edge, to wander in the wild, before becoming wholly centered where one belongs. Edward Casey writes, in fact, that "knowledge of place begins with bodily experience" (*Getting Back into Place*, 47).[7] This observation makes sense when we recall that Odysseus, glutted with three years of appetite experiences, including gorging, sleeping, vomiting forth, devouring, perhaps now with Calypso needs to digest, to make part of himself, his own psyche, the import of these experiences. Then, he must tell them to a public audience.

Staying in place, learning to dwell, therefore, prepares him for a different work, that of creating an artifice in speech through storytelling. For after being placed and dwelling with Calypso, he is freed by those two divinities connected most closely with speech—Athena and Hermes—and journeys to the Phaecians where, in a kind of double duty, he both remains in place and imaginatively journeys through telling his biography of all the places he has confronted. And in this imaginative-remembered journey, he weaves his life, through these stories, into a unity so that their rich tapestry is powerfully delightful and seductive. Richard Sennett observes about the Greek *polis* that "The Greek word for city, *polis*, meant far more to an Athenian like Pericles than a place on the map; it meant the place where people achieved unity" (*Flesh and Stone*, 38–39). If Ithaca is an inchoate city, then Odysseus must return as a unity, integrated with the elements of the psyche that will guarantee some measure of healing, so that he may preserve it from the ravishes of the appetites that have filled his household.

Persuaded initially by Athena, Zeus believes that the time is right (*kairos*) for Odysseus to be released and once again to journey home. This timing is a sacred and divine decision, one that can be known only to the gods. Crafty as well as full of craft, Odysseus asks Calypso to swear an oath that she will not harm him as he builds his own raft to sail home on. They become, perhaps for the first time, bound and united not just by their bodies, but by language itself. Oath-taking begins to emerge as another form of being in unison with others and will serve the preservation of Ithaca when Athena in Book 24 demands that Odysseus and the families of the slain suitors swear oaths that will protect the life of Ithaca.

After Calypso agrees to his request, he leaves her island intent on a quick and direct *nostos* to Ithaca. But Poseidon intends differently. He continues to suffer deeply from the wound his offspring, Polyphemos, received at Odysseus' hands, through his craft. The wound passes from offspring to parent, and seems to gain a greater intensity. Through wounding the animal side of humanity, Odysseus may have at the same time wounded something divine in that same figure. It is not too different from how the boar that he mortally wounds, but not before it gashes his leg, is also connected to divinity, most particularly to the goddess tradition that antedated Homer.

Odysseus' raft is splintered and, aided by Ino, he is hurled onto the land of the Phaecians, where, naked and alone, he finds shelter in the natural world, much like an animal would who is in danger of exposure to the elements or to enemies. It is the condition of the animal, the domain of instinct that Odysseus must recover before he can begin the journey into civilization. In perhaps the most poignant simile in the epic, one that requires a close and comparative reading with a later one that contains a similar description, Homer describes Odysseus' design to seek shelter:

> He went on into the wood; he found it near the water
> In the clearing around, and came upon two bushes growing
> From the same place, one of wild olive, one of tame.
> Nor did the moist force of the blowing winds breathe through them,
> And the shining sun never struck them with its beams,
> Nor did rain ever reach through to them, so thick
> Did they grow over and under each other. Odysseus
> Went in beneath them. . . .
> He lay down in the middle, heaping the fallen leaves over him
> As a man may cover a torch with black embers
> At the edge of a field, where no neighbors may be by,
> And save the fire's seed, . . .
> So Odysseus covered himself with leaves. (5.475–92)

Athene then covers his eyelids over with sleep so he can be relieved from "toilsome fatigue" (5.493).[8]

Compare this scene to the one in Book 19 describing the boar's lair as the young hunter, Odysseus, stalks it:

> And there in the thick-copse was lying a great boar.
> The blowing winds' watery force did not blow through to it,
> Nor did the Sun strike it with the beams of his rays,
> Nor did the rain get all the way through, so thick
> It was, and a plentiful deposit of leaves was there. (439–43)

Out of this thicket the boar charges at the same time that Odysseus rushes him, holding the long spear: This scene repeats his earlier instruction by Hermes to charge Circe in order to strike terror into her after she has changed his men into swine. The myth of this hero becomes more intensely intertwined through the poetics of space of these two shelters, both natural images of a dwelling, or a home for an animal, hosted by the earth. Now in the hunt by the young man, "the boar got the start and struck him/Above the knee, and gashed his flesh deep with a tusk,/Charging at him slantwise, but did not get to the man's bone" (19.449–51). Odysseus' spear goes deep into the body of the boar, which squeals under its intrusion "and his spirit flew off" (453). Furthermore, after this wounding, Autolycos binds up the wound "and with an incantation they held back/The black blood" (456–57). The old man works on his grandson's wound and heals him; they send Odysseus "in joy speedily to his fatherland,/To Ithaca" (461–62) in just the same patterned manner of action that the good hosts, King Alkinoos and Queen Arete, Phaecian parents of Nausicaa, redeem Odysseus and send him home after he has emptied himself of his stories and in a sense, wounding himself again in the telling of their pain and his losses. Here too he is bound up, or at least laid in cloth "Inside the hollow ship, [beside] all of the food and drink./They spread out a blanket and linen cloth for Odysseus/On the deck of the hollow ship, so he might sleep without/waking,/Upon the stern" (13. 72–75).

What is the poetic intertwining offered by the poet in these two scenes, which, in their own woven pattern, implicate other crucial events in the narrative and may contain the large mythic pattern governing the entire epic? We discern a pattern of fabrication, of story itself, embedded in the design that leads us poetically to an insight on naming, words' signification, the body marked through a painful initiation, and the advent of one's personal narrative. As Laura Slatkin writes, "the narrative of the *Odyssey* asserts its own supremacy and justifies the assertion by inviting its audience to reflect on the process of storytelling" (237).

The first incident in Book 5 reveals Odysseus almost home, with one more port to call on: Scheria. He has spent seven years with one goddess, another with Circe, and the other two, presumably, filled by the stories of Books 9–12, when his narrative voice begins to order and give shape to his past experiences in a complex weaving of memory and imagination.

He first finds a place in the woods of Scheria that might offer shelter "in the clearing around" (5.476) from wild beasts. He decides to burrow between the two bushes "growing from the same place, one of wild olive, one of tame" (479). Naked and hungry, covered with brine from battling the chaos of Poseidon's sea, Odysseus feels joy when he discovers a place big enough for three men, in the middle of which he covers himself with leaves that have fallen from the surrounding trees. It is in large measure the dead leaves in nature that allow the spark of his own life to survive the cold night air. Homer reveals to us here that deep mythic pattern of life-death-regeneration.

The natures within, animal and human, warring and domestic, are knottily spliced through the images of the two olive bushes. This idea of things being twisted or elements folding over and under one another to create an intricate metaphor of branching and intertwining, seem to surround him, rather than images of the straight and narrow. He enters a great weave of nature—the natural order that reflects his own duality, and is nowhere closer to Penelope in her intricate design to trick the suitors. Her name, as Nancy Felson-Rubin observes, means "thinking all around," as well as etymologically carries "the pun on her name as 'weaver'" (168). She is as deceptive as her husband, "aware of the plots she creates, and, like Odysseus, cunning in securing her own best interests in terms of survival, duty and pleasure" (168).

Richard Onians' classic work, *The Origins of European Thought*, is also provocative at this point. He observes that Homer uses *thymos* (breath, blood, consciousness), the breath that is consciousness (49), as what "determines or are the quality and condition of [the Greek] mind" (25). Mind and breath, associated with the lungs, reveal an intimate relationship; as he writes earlier, for Homer "thinking is described as 'speaking' and is located sometimes in the heart but usually in the 'midriff' or 'diaphragm'" (13). What one thinks, therefore, is exhaled in the breath from the *thymos*; one might say it is inspired or inspirited into the world. The point is that this word *thymos* is also associated with a word used to describe "things close together, or of close texture, e.g. a thicket, the twigs and branches of a tree . . . which fit admirably the multitude of branching passages and veins within each lung and the intricate tracery, the polygonal lobules of the outside" (28).

Onians further affirms that in the Homeric world, "mind, thoughts, knowledge are breath which can also be breathed out" (56). So Homer's richly and thickly textured dwelling for Odysseus explores several themes at once: it associates Odysseus with the animal world, specifically with the boar that wounds him as a youth; it shows him once again as builder, artificer, in making his own bed and lying in it; it weaves him even more closely to Penelope; it gives the body's inside through the natural setting outside, with its winding intricate patterns woven into a tight natural fabric and therefore links world and body in an intimately webbed relationship; it comments once again on his circuitous, wily, and polysemous nature; and, perhaps most important, it prepares for his debut as poet when he breathes his story onto his eager Phaecian audience after he arrives at the palace and is treated to grand hospitality. The body's insides find their objective correlate in the world and marry thought and feeling and the body together. These intricately webbed images are poetic keys to show us the deeply interrelated imagination of the Greeks where abided no fundamental separations between the large patterns of existence.

These intermingled images appeared earlier under the aspect of the goddess with the four springs on Calypso's island: "one after another flowed with white water/All close together, one turned one way, one an-other" (5.70–71). Later, as Poseidon engages his raft "So the winds carried it here and there over the sea./Sometimes the South Wind threw it to the North Wind to carry/And sometimes the East Wind yielded it to the South Wind for/pursuit" (5.330–34). All of this danger prompts Odysseus to re-alize: "Alas for me, I fear one of the immortals is weaving/A snare for me, to have bade me get off the raft;/I shall not yet obey her" (5.336–38). Later, as he tells his stories in a great woven pattern to the Phaecians, he under-scores his contest with Polyphemos and how he cleverly escaped from the cave by tying each of his men "under the breasts of the thick-fleeced/sheep" (9.443), while he himself hung upside down like a bat pressed against the belly of the ram, after filling the great belly of the Cyclops who, drunk with wine, lies "on his back . . . with his massive neck twisted" (9.373). He de-scribes how he fastens himself to the ram, the animal most associated with Helios, god of the sun.

According to Marija Gimbutas, the ram was "sacred to the Bird God-dess, followed by the fleece symbol and the association of the Goddess with weaving and spinning" (*Language of the Goddess,* xxii). So Odysseus is lit-erally and figuratively weaving not only his escape but his passage home: "There was a lead ram, by far the finest of all the sheep,/Whose back I grasped and lay under his shaggy belly/Curled up. And with my hand twisted in his marvelous/wool/I held on relentlessly with an enduring heart" (9.431–34). His escape is ingeniously polytropic, a contorted, twisted, circuitous, meandering, and fabricated journey out of the cave, with his own belly pressed against the ram's. Belly to belly, human and an-imal, mind and body *plait* mortal to the immortal realms of being.

There is in addition certainly a poetic resonance here of the Trojan horse's hollow belly out of which the Achaeans emerged, a kind of stom-ach/cave into the hollow of the city to mortally wound it as well as the hol-low ship of the Phaecians that transports Odysseus as cargo to Ithaca. Onians offers a discovery here that we might apply to the place of the body in this fleshy epic. As *thymos,* mentioned above, the "the vital principle" as Onians refers to it, "moves about in the passages of the lungs and promotes thinking, feeling and action. Associated to it is the epithet 'bushy, shaggy,' which could be applied to a sheep, a tree or a thicket and which Homer ap-plies to the heart, between which and the lungs the consciousness seems to be shared" (28).

He goes on to describe the heart's appearance, which, like the lungs, re-veals "the tracery of branching veins and arteries running over its surface and with the multitudinous branching veins and arteries growing immedi-ately out of it, like bushes, many of them through the lungs" (29). All of these coagulating images of complex and interwoven designs point not only to a complexity of mind and thought, but of speech as well, as we witness in Books 9–12, in which Odysseus weaves the ornate design of his past through the stories that catch in their webbing the hearts of the Phaecians and guarantee his own passage home. This same intricate webbing will appear in the story of Aphrodite's failed tryst with Mars and their both being captured in the invisible filaments of Haephestos' grand and clever webbing, a fabrication of his own cleverness. Complexity, subtlety, and indirection are the virtues in the *Odyssey*, not force, might, and unyielding courage typical of the *Iliad*.

In addition, in Odysseus' hands twisting the marvelous wool, is an embedded analogy to Penelope. Is it wool that she uses on her loom as she twists the threads into whole cloth for her father-in-law and in the process dupes the suitors through the complexity of her own mind that their appetites blind them to? And are Odysseus' escape tactics also his own motion of twisting the wool in fabric as he first fabricates himself to Polyphemous as "Noman," the identity of the great wounder of the god's offspring?

I believe this subtle weave is part of Homer's poetic genius, even while Penelope's loom shuttles the thread for Laertes' funeral robe through her weaving instrument. What she does with cloth her husband does with words through his crafted story. Certainly in her weaving/unraveling actions, a form of traveling over the same ground repeatedly, she too is devious-devising against the suitors who have turned the Odyssean household into a cave of Polyphemos, a hollow place of insatiable appetite and a single-leveled consciousness. There is an abundance of goods to devour in his palace as there are in the unlawful monster's hollow home. And within each dwelling lives the simple-mindedness of those single-eyed in satisfying only the body.

As Penelope and Odysseus are linked by a thread in this adventure, actually stitched or woven together, so too are the worlds of Polyphemos and Odysseus' *oikos*. Both Odysseus and Penelope are intimately related in their craft and accuracy, for as the weaver must shoot her spool or shuttle "through the warp-threads at a critical time, the right moment (kairos), for the opening in the warp lasts only a limited time" (Hillman, "Notes in Opportunism," 153), so must Odysseus string the bow and shoot the arrow through the twelve ax handles with uncanny accuracy, just as he had to run his spear through the boar at the right instant and in the right spot even as he was wounded in so doing. Both feats of accuracy and *metis* define his identity and both implicate wounding. In addition, he had to tell his story to the Phaecians with deadly poetic accuracy to win their graces and a ride home. So the weave in the wound, in the words, and in the narrative all conspire to weave Odysseus into the fabric of Penelope's design.

When Odysseus uses animals to aid his homeward journey from Troy, he weaves his story into his son and to Menelaos,[9] who narrates to Telemachos the story of plotting to capture the god of the depths, Proteus, by hiding beneath the offensive-smelling seal skins amid a pack of these same wild animals, Proteus' companions. His daughter Eido instructs him and his men, as Menelaos recounts the action: "She bedded us down in a row and threw a skin over each;/There the ambush would have been most dreadful. The dire/smell/Of the sea-nourished seals oppressed us dreadfully,/For who would lie down to sleep with a monster of the sea?" (4.440–46).

The smell of sweet ambrosia saves the men from betraying their cover as they watch for the mercurial and shape-shifting form of Proteus, who appears "Under the blowing West Wind, hidden in a black ripple" (4.402). She tells them, in effect, to look into where the shadow grows from the water, where the wave is wounded in that it is the place where the water darkens in the subtle shadow. What Homer weaves so tightly is the intimate relation between monster and mind, nature and craft, as well as the subtle and transitory nature of knowing; knowledge would appear to grow from both.

These seals, as Carl Jung has written, are "warm blooded—that is to say, they can be thought of as contents of the unconscious that are capable of becoming conscious' (*CW*, 9, 2 par. 338). Proteus himself, as a shape shifter, is for Jung "like a revolving image that cannot be grasped. What he says is 'in sooth," infallible; he is a 'soothsayer'" (339). James Hillman extends this image by showing that Proteus represents "the multiple and ambiguous form of soul" (*Revisioning Psychology*, 203). It is in his "polyvalent nature, which includes the grotesque, vicious, and the pathological" (203), as here in the stench of the seals that nauseates Menelaos and his men. Nonetheless, they wait patiently for an opportunity to apprehend and question this watery figure who will instruct them on how to reach home, as Tiresias in the underworld will instruct Odysseus and his men on how to travel home.

This brief vignette by Menelaos to Telemachos is a foreshortened narrative of what happens to his father when Circe, not Eido, instructs them in how to make contact with Tiresias, the blind prophet, in Hades. Both Menelaos and Odysseus must confront these soul figures who are apertures into truth, into revelation, like Hermes himself (*CW*, 13, par. 218), before they can arrive home. So they too, like Odysseus, hold on relentlessly "with an enduring heart" as Proteus shifts his appearance, not forgetting "his wily skill" (4.455). He changes "from a lion, to a serpent, a panther, a boar, watery water, a tree" (4.457–59).

This tenacity of animal strength and endurance in the above scenes relates the animal/human/divine each time over some form of trickery, disguise, protection, or cover—some subtle economy of mind—that leads to a retrieval of what is desired. Without this tight interweaving of the natural/human/immortal impulses of soul, home and homecoming remain hopelessly out of reach, and even if achieved, would be incomplete. The stories of each man—here Menelaos and later the full-blown chapters of Odysseus' own narrative journeys with the Phaecians—give final shape and meaning to the events, making out of them deeply patterned psychological experiences. Hermes, not Ares, is the guide here, for the words of stories are his domain; there is colossal power inhabiting the language of stories, and Hermes "knows the workings of deceptive fictions" (Hillman, *Revisioning Psychology,* 163).[10]

William Randall refers to one's "inside story," the one we create from within, rather than the ones created about us from without; such stories are full of speculations and projections into the future (53). The boar scar that initiates the young Odysseus through his fresh wound is about Odysseus the wanderer trying to return home decades later. When he therefore crawls from the tightly intertwined olive bushes to confront Nausicaa, daughter of Alkinoos and Arete, he *is* the boar that earlier marked his young body. Proteus is the shifting image between the two worlds.

Homer appears to link Proteus with his home in the sea, the perennially mythic symbol, Jung writes," of the collective unconscious" (*Nietzsche's Zarathustra,* 71) itself. Odysseus, certainly a psychological son of Proteus, emerges naked out of the sea, a Protean figure in his rhetoric, his disguise, his fictions, and his polysemousness. It is within his nature to proffer the Phaecians something they hunger for—imaginal narratives of the world from which they seem blissfully separated. Odysseus himself comes out of the unconscious, out of a time of incubation with Calypso, divinity's great goddess. She has been described as a divine mediatrix among heaven, earth, and the underworld. She is able to embody all of these worlds (Absher, *Men and the Goddess,* 39), as the Great Goddess did in an earlier tradition, one that Homer is poetically retrieving and giving voice to once again.

Odysseus' stories are themselves protean in their shifting imagery, full of monsters, the grotesque, the abhorrent and fascinating, as well as intricate in their design. In their fantastic imagery they imaginally mirror the fantastic architecture and geography of Scheria. This enchanted isle possesses "bronze walls," "Golden portals," "Silver doorposts," "gold and silver dogs/ That Hephaistos with his skillful faculties had formed," "cloths/ . . . fine and well-woven, the work of women" while outside there are "tall blossoming trees . . . growing/Pears and pomegranates, apple trees with shining fruit," "Pear matures upon pear, apple upon apple, Grape cluster on grape cluster, and fig on fig" (7.85–120). Their lavish world of things finds its analogue in Odysseus' lavish world of tales, protean stories that reflect the deepening shapes of the poet's own soul. Only in such a soulfully abundant place could Odysseus give them all the monstrous, grotesque, and violently embodied figures in action that speak together of violations of the home because of excessive appetite. One might then compare here the less complex anatomy of the stomach with the more intricate branches of a tree that comprise the lungs and heart, veins and arteries. From this tangled interior Odysseus' stories emerge, as from twisted olive bushes.

Scheria is mythically linked to Polyphemous' world by the actions of Poseidon. Both are foods whose intention is to assuage appetites. Ginette Paris' observation is appropriate here: Greek mythology, she believes, "is an exploration of an imaginal world which in many ways resembles our own" (*Pagan Meditations*, 6). Is it too much to suppose that the stories told by Odysseus find their resonance in the soul of the Phaecians themselves, deep in their own bodies? They are a people who have felt no wounding, not until they aid Odysseus in getting back to Ithaca, which action draws to them the wounding by Poseidon, who in his anger fulfills the oracles by transforming their returning ship to stone. Petrified at sea, the ship rests within sight of Scheria, a visual reminder to the people of the trouble Odysseus invites when one encounters him in the world. To confront Odysseus in the world, it seems inevitable that one will be wounded in some fashion by him. He is the archetype of the wily wounder, dangerous to behold and always risky to befriend; he is the figure of our wounds whose words can bring disaster.

By the same token, the world of Polyphemous—indeed, all the psychic, imaginal places Odysseus visits—are mirrors of his own nature, his appetites, and his level of instruction. The habitations he and his men visit are like architectural structures of the psyche, if not of different organs of the body itself, primarily of the stomach. Anthony Lawlor suggests that architectural structures "become repositories for our thoughts and feelings. They hold and nurture the psychological energy that animates our ways of living" (*Temple in the House*, 9).[11]

Certainly Odysseus' tales are not just about him; he has entered a much deeper structure in his travels, with the most important journey being to Hades, a deep psychological place where he confronts not only the imaginal bodies of his own history but also all the suffering wives and mothers of the heroes who have died in battle. The experience is both personal and collective.[12] So too with Odysseus' stories. What is true of these stories he tells, these myths of his own psyche that have validity on a more universal scale, is equally valid of all stories of the ancient myths, as Paris writes. Within the realm, of myth, she asserts, "there is no copyright" (*Pagan Meditations*, 5).

The *Odyssey* explores, then, how the act of knowing can also be an act of wounding. I sense a deep connection between wandering and wounding, as the Oedipus myth will make more poetically explicit in the following chapter. One therefore ought not miss the protean nature of this water deity who earlier appeared to Menelaos and whose body can metamorphose into other figures, into basic elements, in order to evade captivity. He is like the imagination itself, or the soul imaging itself through different images and actions. Freedom and knowledge are the offshoots of this god's nature in that if contained, he will offer to Menelaos the knowledge he needs to return home. In a sense, he is the divine mirror of Odysseus' mind in its subtle, intertwined complexity.

In a less radical way, Athena projects different shapes on Odysseus to enhance or underscore his own protean, polytropic nature. She makes him *appear* by turns a god or a beggar or an old man with wrinkled skin and stooped posture; even his nakedness beneath the wild and tame olive trees makes us pause over the body's place in the action. Who is it that continues to change the shape and figure of Odysseus, casting him into various roles, turning him into various fictions as he weaves his way toward Ithaca? For one thing, apparently it is something that exists in the myth of the body that has an imaginal correspondence in the body of myth. Sansonese has suggested that "something is being described in myth, something about the human body, something essential to its workings but also truly technical and beyond mere fetish: 'the wisdom in the inward parts'"(38). Both soul and story are revealed incarnately, in and through the body. It is as if the parts of the body have corresponding poetic appendages in one's life story; our stories are located in our bodies, and perhaps the genesis of this story rests deeply nestled in our wounds.[13]

In his body transformations, Odysseus is a mortal analogue of Proteus, of divinity itself. Vernant tells us that the "vocabulary of the body or aspects of the corporeal, makes up the code that allowed a Greek to express and think about his relation to himself, his presence to himself; it also encompasses the relation to the divine or supernatural, whose presence within oneself, in and through one's own body, expresses itself in the same symbolic register" (*Mortals and Immortals,* 31).[14]

At the same time, the body's vulnerability and changeability, its mortalness and susceptibility to wounding, "reminded the audience of the ephemeral nature of the body, human life, and thus more so, the importance of home" (32).

In some ways, the telling of stories from the mouth of a mortal accomplishes several things: not only does the audience delight by gratifying an appetite of the soul for fictions themselves, for a mimetic experience that includes rich subtlety and intricate design, but it also helps to shape and order the "wild" experiences of one's past by giving them a "tameness," a shape and structure that can be apprehended by others.

The difference between wild and tame, therefore, suggests the difference between experience and expression, or between event and experience, the latter becoming true only in the *poiesis* of utterance, seeing the story as fiction and the fiction embodying the meaning of the event remembered, not literally but imaginally. Mimetic action, then, consists in taming through story the wildness of one's nature.

Odysseus' autobiography is therefore a grand weaving of not what literally happened to him but, on a much deeper and mythical level, what he imagines what happened to him *means*. He realizes his stories' significances within the magically enchanted and nonthreatening space of imagination itself—Scheria. Here he can imaginatively remember his past as preparation for his literal journey home. Now he is better prepared to face the ambiguity of twenty years' absence by inscribing on his future some images by which to guide him into what should be most familiar and familial—his own household.

However, his various voyages imaginatively remembered, as well as his trip to the underworld with Circe as his instructor and Tiresias as his mentor, have all prepared him to accept the fact that his home's condition may not match his remembered image of it. What we are allowed to witness in this journey is the embodied soul itself struggling toward meaning, changing shapes, attacking seducers, entering the earth, the underworld, lands of enchantment, seduction, animal life, vegetative surroundings, imagining death, marriage, love, sexuality, leadership, sleep, survival alone, being lashed to his own mast and listening to the Sirens' call, being sucked into whirlpools and riding a ship's spar to safety and to seven years of incubation. The soul's propensity seems to be to remain in motion, to be embodied, to be involved with the stuff of the world and to find artistic or poetic expressions of itself in making, crafting, telling, talking, in the great web formed by *poiesis*.

If Proteus is the patron saint of soul, of polytropism itself, then Hermes is its guide and Athena its ruling architect.

So this idea of intertwining includes events being transformed into experiences through stories as well as the past being woven tightly into the future through the narratives voiced in the present, as our two passages from Books 5 and 19 reveal. In their descriptive similarity and in the events surrounding them, they give several of perhaps hundreds of skeins of the larger yarn that the epic laces together.

WORDS AND WOUNDS

We return, then, to our two passages in which Odysseus seeks shelter in his nakedness between the wild and tame olive bushes growing from the same place, and his confronting the boar who scars him as a youth.[15] What else would bring Homer to compare these two passages and situate Odysseus in the middle of the comparisons?

When Nausicaa rescues him and instructs him to supplicate her
mother, Arete, in order to guarantee a passage home, Odysseus finds himself on the threshold of identifying himself most completely, not only in
name but also in narrative. Demodocus warms the audience by singing of
Troy and the Trojan horse, thus setting the stage for the poet, Odysseus, to
reclaim himself through his history imaginatively recalled. Initially Demodocus sings of the first ten years of Odysseus' separation and the various battles at Troy, all of which make Odysseus cover his head and weep silently.
It is as if he is wounded once again by the grief attending his losses there as
well as his absence from home. Then Odysseus recites the rest of the
story—the *nostos*. He finds his place, again in the middle, but a narrative
middle this time. He is between the Trojan War and his own homeland. To
move from the middle home, he must pay his passage by recalling and reciting the passages of his adventures, thus placing himself in a story within a
larger legend. We might say that he places himself or finds a place within
his personal myth. Books 9–12 contain the voice of the warrior turned wanderer turned poet.

At this juncture Odysseus opens a wound in the corpus of the larger
epic tale, a tear in the fabric of the story, for here is the incision of his own
story within the larger body of epic narrative, just as any human life, perhaps, is after "making a mark," opening a space and a place, or inscribing
one's self into the larger story of his or her time.

On a smaller scale, the story of the scar is offered by the bardic voice
of the epic as a wound quickly spliced between the time Eurycleia touches
the scar holding his foot and then letting it drop into the bowl of water,
sending it spilling and clanging over the stone floor as she gasps in a moment of recognition. When she traces her fingers over the scar she immediately retraces, or retrieves the life of the man she is cleansing. Touching and
tracing the scar returns the story to her and to us of the original wounding.

Let us look closely for a moment at the details on both sides of the
memory that practically gush through the healed gash to tear open the scar
tissue, revealing its originary injury and the story of its genesis.

Odysseus is worried as the old house maid who raised and nursed him
begins to wash his camouflaged body, wrapped in a disguise, in a fiction, of
identity. With just the two of them present—for Athena has averted the
gaze of Penelope who sits nearby—Odysseus has returned to just more than
home; he has returned to the original source of his feeding by the old servant, who embodies fidelity and trust. Eurycleia is the original source of his
nourishment; his feeding begins at her breast. In preparing for this ritual of
hospitality, she takes a "glittering basin" and mixes (intertwines or has flow
together?) hot and cold water (19.385) and at this moment of possibly pre-
mature identity, Odysseus becomes alarmed; sitting by the hearth, he "sud-

denly turned toward the/darkness/For at once he was apprehensive in heart lest when she touched/him/she notice his scar *and the facts become apparent*" (19.386–90, italics added). As he earlier mixed the wild and tame in nature, now he mixes the fire and darkness in the household even as Eurycleia mixes the hot and cold water. What the scar tissue reveals is who he is, and the *fact* that he is, even as most of the Ithacans have lost hope of his ever returning.

The moment is revelatory for Eurycleia when she draws near, for she knows "right away . . . /The scar which once a boar dealt him with its shining tusk/When he had come to Parnassus to see Autolycos and his sons" (392–94) who is himself one that excels "In trickery and oath making" (396) and who was endowed by none other than Hermes, the wily god of deception, storytelling, telling lies, fabricating, disguising, thieving, and interpreting. He is a transmitter and translator of words from divinity to mortals. But more than that, as Ginette Paris points out, he is "the God of mythic thought, more interested in the truth of symbols than the truth of facts" (*Pagan Grace*, 84).[16]

The wound, which opens a deep and painful connection between present and past, is surgically administered by the poet in the verse, which moves from time present to the past, to the origin of the scar, in the same sentence. There is a seamlessness about this incident that resonates the seamlessness among the events of Odysseus' life and his later imaginative construction of them, as well as a tightness of fit among animal, vegetative, human, and divine worlds; each is part of the same grand mythic plaiting of Being elaborated here.

Odysseus receives the boar wound after Autolycos names him in Ithaca, a name that comes out of the man's own *rage* at men and women "throughout the much-nourishing earth,/And let him be named Man of Wrath: Odysseus" (19.407–8). Again, there is a seamlessness between Odysseus' birth and his visit to Parnassus to claim gifts Autolycos promised him when he came to hunt, an action Odysseus repeats years later when he departs Scheria and arrives on Ithaca with many gifts. Coupled in these two passages are the two actions of telling stories and being wounded. Both end the same way: with his being bound up and sent back to Ithaca with many gifts for his troubles and his tales. In one way, Odysseus' telling his tales to the Phaecians does wound them, or sets a prophesied wounding by Poseidon in motion. Harboring Odysseus fulfills the words of the oracle that initiates their wounding. When they transport him home they fulfill the prophecy set by Zeus wherein the traveler they help will cause the ship, on its return, to be transformed into stone within sight of the island, a perpetual wound of grief (3.160–85). They pay dearly for his stories.

In the narrative of Odysseus' wound, tucked inside the narrative of his homecoming, the hunters trace the boar with their dogs, "tracking the footprints, and behind them/came the sons of Autolycos" (19.437–39). The footprints themselves are important, for poetically they are scars, imprints on the earth, reminders of what has passed by and a guide to what is ahead. Footprints act as memories of a body's presence, and depending on how well one can hermeneutically read and interpret, the text of the prints will determine the range of success in finding their source. The footprints of the boar are analogous to the scar of Odysseus, for they track to where what is hidden may finally be revealed, in an instant. They lead to where the fact is revealed.

The boar prints are a text revealing what is concealed, as is Odysseus' scar. The prints are like an embodied story that links body with story or embodies story itself, as something to be read as the visible markings of what is absent, as the scar of Odysseus is the visible marking of what is no longer visible, but which can be retrieved through the scar itself. As we read this part of the history of Odysseus, we remember that in a sense we are reading it from within the space of the scar, reading it from the inside out, for the scar is the visible residue of what is no longer visible, but which exists memorially. Further, as Hillman notes, "the wound that is necessary to initiation ceremonies ends the state of innocence as it opens in a new way at another place. . . . It is as if the soul can find no path out of innocence other than physical hurt" ("Puer Wounds," 113).

As the young hunter Odysseus approaches the boar with his spear in Book 19, as he will in the analogous scene approach the Phaecians with the power of his narratives, and as he will approach the suitors by stringing the bow and then killing first their leaders with his arrows, the entire larger action of the story is woven into this scar story. Said another way, his history and his future congeal around the thigh's scar: "And there in the thick-copse was lying a great boar," protected in almost an exact way as is the naked and estranged Odysseus on Scheria whose greatest worry is being hunted by animals, as here in this narrative he hunts an animal. Animal and human natures converge in the story along the path of hunter and hunted; Homer insists that we understand the young Odysseus as a hunter and the older Odysseus as an animal; the former inflicts a wound and is wounded while the latter inflicts his story on to the Phaecians, whose appetite is only too happy to devour all the morsels of the episodes.

The young, wounded, animal-marked Odysseus then returns to Ithaca bandaged and surrounded by gifts, a condition repeated in the generosity of the Phaecians. Both trips are described as happening "speedily" (19.462), which suggests an urgency toward *nostos* at both times of his life. Both of his parents want to know quickly of the story of the scar, and Odysseus "told them about it fully" (463). And then, almost without a pause, we return from the wounded thigh to the present: "The old woman took the scar in the palms of her hands and / knew it /As she touched it; she let the foot drop that she held, /And his shin fell into the basin and the bronze clattered. It tipped back to one side and the water spilled out onto the ground" (19.467–70). He quickly warns her to "keep your story in silence and turn it over to the gods" (503). The appearance of the scar hides the story; the hidden scar reveals Odysseus' story. The wound and its memory, the scar can, like words, conjure something that has been absent into the present. Here is what words and wounds share—their relation to the past and to the memory of the past being brought forward into the present. The tangible body is a second order of narrative presence; first words, then presences. Words, like the scar, can conjure absence into presence. When the body becomes inscribed, according to Peter Brooks, then the flesh becomes a text," (*Body Work*, 75), or in the case of Odysseus, it grows into an embodied narrative.

What is there, then, about the animal in the story with its remembrance in the scar? How are we to think of the body of Odysseus when it seems poetically to metamorphose into animal and then back to naked babe, alone and womb-covered in the earth? Is there an animal kind of consciousness that is crucial to the hero in epic?

Laurens Van der Post suggests that for the growth of psyche "we need the animals; we can't know ourselves unless we see ourselves reflected. Animals reflect us; they make possible our reflective consciousness" (qtd. in Hillman, "The Animal Kingdom in the Human Dream," 311). And Jung's observations are even more salient: "The animal is a well-behaved citizen in nature. It is pious, it follows the path with great regularity. . . . If you assimilate the nature of the animal, you become a peculiarly law-abiding citizen. You go slowly and become reasonable in your ways" (qtd. in "The Animal Kingdom in the Human Dream," 313). Yes, Jung was speaking metaphorically in using the word "citizen," but there is his sense that one belongs more appropriately to place, finds a home there, by means of the animal. And this idea of citizenship is crucial to the restitution of the *oikos*.

The boar tusk driving itself into the body of Odysseus and the spear of Odysseus slicing deeply into the flesh of the boar suggest an exchange of natures: the animal gets into him, into his body and soul; he adopts an animal soul here, which, if Jung is correct, is not different from embodiment. He writes in the *Zarathustra Seminars* that "the difference we make between the psyche and the body is artificial. . . . In reality there is nothing but a living body and psyche is as much a living body as body is living psyche. It is just the same" (396). And later, to this same point, Jung asserts that "only through extreme pain do you experience yourself. . . . before that you can't imagine that you are anybody" (449). Identity involves suffering, a suffering into the self through soul.

The pain the young Odysseus feels when the animal enters him and he it is a physical/soulful analogy to what happens when he is forced out of his anonymity by the Phaecians, who demand that he tell them his story. Moreover, that we are to link closely the actions within the tales he tells with *the act of telling* becomes evident when Odysseus, fatigued from commanding the helm of his own narrating, asks to be able to stop and sleep, as he fell asleep more than once during his physical journeys. But Alkinoos is not to be dissuaded: "The night is prodigiously long. It is not yet time/To sleep in the hall. Do tell me your wondrous deeds" (11.3373–75). To which Odysseus, bleary-eyed, responds: "But if you are still longing to listen, I would not myself/Refuse you in this, to tell other more piteous things" (378–81). His tenacity, witnessed often on his journeys, serves him well here as assenting guest.

Lest we be too quick about skipping over the effect the tales of Odysseus have on the Phaecians, we should look once more at the power of *thymos* as outlined by Onians. He believes that as *thymos* is a vapor from liquid, and liquid drunk goes to the lungs, "then prophetic inspiration was sought by inhaling vapors, or by drinking blood or water, wine, or honey" (66). Now if the mind or thought, and speech, are synonymous, then when a person speaks, his intelligence, or we can say, his stories, the embodiment of his intelligence, is transferred to the lungs of his audience: "the listener takes them into *thymos*, thus adding to his store, his knowledge. They pass from lung to lung, mind to mind. Thoughts are words and words are breath" (66–67). Stories are a kind of nourishment to the mind and to psyche. In an oral culture, what is taken in can be dramatically in-spiring, for the breath of another can become part of one's own knowledge. In the act of telling his stories, Odysseus disperses his mind among the Phaecians and forever changes them. Perhaps telling stories is a kind of con-spiracy, for the breath of one is taken in by the breathing of others. The stories are not just figurative, but physiologically embodied. Odysseus' stories become part of the Phaecians' communal life. No wonder they are stricken to silence when he ceases speaking.

Perhaps he trades off in the telling the heroic world of the boar hunt, and its painful initiation, with the darker, more rounded, and less sharp world of Hermes, who "is not heroic. Its phallic power is in the word, not the sword" (Hillman, *Revisioning Psychology,* 163). Hermes is the shadow god in the *Odyssey,* now here, now there, helping to free Odysseus from Calypso, aiding Odysseus in deflecting the enchanting powers of Circe, guiding the souls of the suitors into the underworld, giving his blessings to the trickster nature of Autolycos, delighting over the prospect of being in bed with Aphrodite, even if the snares of her husband would hold the two of them together in a fine web of entrapment; passing the words of divinities to the mortal realm, "weaving deceptive fictions" (163) and embodying in Odysseus the power of narratives that reveal what is perhaps most fundamentally true as Odysseus completes the circular journey: Ithaca-Troy-Ithaca.

His stories encircle the Phaecians and trap them like the filaments of Haephestus' webbing, illustrating again that the craft of artifice and *poiesis* is central to the comic epic. An artifice of words is in sharp contrast to the force of hard steel and might of the *Iliad*. In the Odyssean epic, which is circular, folding back on itself like cloth, less stiff and resilient, the qualities of cloth, camouflage, disguise, story, narrative, deception, cleverness, animal consciousness, words, persuasion are far more potent than warring, slaying, cutting, slicing, dismembering, and leveling that is typical of the more masculine linear trajectory of heroic aggression. As the later epic, *Moby-Dick*, will reveal how Ahab and Ishmael both have "dark doubles" in the figures of Fedallah and Queequeg as two of the most apparent but not inclusive "images of the self everywhere," as John T. Irwin suggests (*American Hieroglyphics*, 289), Odysseus' dark doubles are the stories themselves, images and actions of his own soul as it moves inexorably, though always circuitously, toward home. The folds and wrinkles in the fabric of his narratives are most analogous to the physical journeys home. His stories double his travels in design and intention. He actively imagines the plots of his past life, not as literal events but as imaginal simulacra, so that he may *imagine his way* into the household, appearing first as a fiction in his disguise, at the same time as he embodies invisibly the markings of his truest self.

His scar, images of the belly, and appearances of the swine or wild pig condense in the narrative with conscious repetition as Odysseus first establishes himself "at home" with Eumaeos, the keeper of his pigs, while continuing his fictitious identity until just before he reveals himself to Telemachos and with his son plots to slay the suitors. But first Athena tells the wanderer, "I will make you unrecognizable to all mortals, / I shall shrivel the lovely flesh on your supple limbs, / Destroy the blond hair from your head, and cloak you about / In rags" (13.397–400). She wraps him in the skin of a deer and sends him to the swineherd's hut. The faithful servant and his master then unite in hospitality: "And so they told such stories to one another. / And the two of them did not sleep much time, but a little" (15.492–93), which prepares the way for Odysseus and Penelope in their first night together in bed. After satisfying one another in old patterns of lovemaking, they share stories of the past twenty years as Athena accommodates them by holding back the dawn. But first within the household of

Eumaeos, Odysseus prepares the meal and extends his own hospitality to the faithful servant by serving him.

Eumaeos' hut is a necessary liminal space for the hero in several ways: it is between the ocean and his home; it marks the space of hospitality for him within his own domain; and it serves as the setting in which father and son meet for the first time and share their loss in grief. Here father and son create another plot as they begin to plait their lives together. Books 15 and 16 might be called the great weaving and reconciliation books of the epic because in them Odysseus' life threads begin to be woven back into the fabric of his fatherland and his family as he imagines entering his own home. Odysseus reconciles belly and mind; he gains thereby a sense of place and of belonging to what he has longed for.

Approaching in disguise the threshold of his own home, he is alternately served by his son and reprimanded by the suitors: Melanthios questions Eumaeos suspiciously: "Miserable swineherd, where are you leading this wild pig,/This tiresome beggar, desecrator of feasts/Who stands by many door posts and rubs his shoulders on them, . . . And to ask food for his insatiable belly?" (17.215–27). Even Odysseus is willing to play the role of scapegoat as he pleads for food to appease "an eager stomach" (17.286). Appetite and mind, excess of the body and the moderation or restraint of thought are tested here; within the person of Odysseus each finds its proper place in relation to one another. Odysseus occupies a liminal psychic space between the sound-mindedness of Athena and the appetites of the suitors. Speech then, carried on the breath (*thymos*) is the element that reflects this intertwining of body and mind (*nous*). The scar on Odysseus' thigh is the image that unites the two elements of the hero.

This scene is crucial because it prepares for Eurcyleia's washing him as part of the proper role of hospitality initiated by Penelope, who suspects in her own mind that her husband may be beneath the disguise. If she knows or intuits that perhaps this is the man she has been waiting for, she then knows of the scar as his identifying marking. Her cleverness, her own *metis*, both reveals and conceals her intention; she is his formidable mirror. The scene therefore repeats in a reversed way the crisis with Polyphemos; Odysseus remembers the strategy used there, knows that he is in the company of smaller but no less impious Cyclopes in his home, so he understands he must outflank them through what the earlier experience has taught him.

His stories have aided him in imagining his home in any of several forms, all of which contain some distorted imagery. For example, he says to Eumaeos in admiring the great hall where Phemios sings, that there is such beauty, surely "No man could look down upon them" (17.268), referring to his fictional identity when confronting Polyphemos. Again, almost comically, Homer has Antinoos berate Odysseus standing so close to the table and in so doing, refers to him through one of his name's meanings: "What God has brought this trouble, this annoyance at the/banquet?"(17.446–47), after which he is struck by Antinoos "on account of my woeful belly,/A cursed thing that gives many evils to men" (472–74).[17]

In one way, Odysseus speaks the absolute truth to the suitors, but it is couched in the appearance of a beggar so no sense of analogy is discerned by them, no mimesis surfaces in their mind. They take his words at face value and read nothing beyond or between them. Like poetry or story itself, he speaks what is true through the distortion of disguise. In short, he delivers the truth through a fiction, but if the audience has no mimetic powers of discernment, they will hear and understand only the literal. In some important psychological way Odysseus repeats his great stunt at Troy, namely, presenting one image that is seemingly harmless, and using it to disarm his adversaries so that the Trojans can climb out of the belly of the horse to conquer Troy. Here again he uses his belly to render himself a harmless beggar so he can once again repeat the trick of Troy. His dissembling is masterful in making his audience believe that the outside is a fair and accurate replica of the inside. And the suitors, ironically, led by their bellies in all things, see no signals of their impending destruction.

Odysseus nowhere else has the delight of speaking so forthrightly of exactly what is on his mind to the suitors, protected by the appearance of a beggar or "wild pig," and in so doing, asks us to remember the connective tissue between the two passages discussed at length earlier. Here they begin to coalesce in these scenes prior to Odysseus throwing off his disguise in order to retrieve his home.

And as if to have fun in language with what *he* knows and *they* don't, Odysseus taunts Antinoos further: "But if perchance gods and Furies exist for beggars,/May the end of death find Antinoos sooner than marriage" (475–76). Indeed it will.

Odysseus' belly remains the focus of this section of the story, as a kind of body diversion so that his words are not seen through, even as Eumaeos promises him that Penelope will give him all that he wishes. He suggests to the beggar: "begging bread through the district,/You will feed your belly; whoever wishes will give to you" (558–59), which would be a clever way of testing the entire Ithacan community's hospitable impulses as well as the extent of their fidelity.

We then are asked to shift our own field of vision in order better to see Odysseus in the role of Polyphemos. I believe it works this way: Odysseus physically enters the belly of the house and imaginally the belly of the suitors; he is thickly embroiled in their appetite, in their mean-spiritedness and lack of hospitality; he studies it, seeking a possible strategy to overthrow them. Once more, he has entered the cave of Polyphemos as one who is both victimized by appetite and yet having an appetite, like Poseidon's son, for avenging their excess. And he is, after all, "Man of Wrath." This time, however, he enters knowing the terms of that appetite's code of behavior to guests. Appetite is moderated by mind. He and his son will block all exits from the great hall, as Polyphemos blocked the cave with the large stone, but this time there is no escape route; Odysseus' polytropic plan admits of no compromises or prisoners. Here exists the remnants of the warrior of Troy modulated to fit the occasion of his home's condition.

Homer continues to focus our imagination on the unwieldy appetites at large here as well as the limits of patience Odysseus has mastered in himself. The seven years with Calypso are put to good use at this juncture. Iros, the beggar of the district, "outstanding for his greedy/belly" (18.2–3), also insults Odysseus as he remarks on his speech: "How fluently does the wild pig talk,/Like an oven woman; I should devise evils for him" (18.26–27). When they prepare to fight, the suitors hold up a prize of a "goat stomach," which Odysseus, continuing the deception, confesses: "my criminal belly/Urges me on" (54–55). Completely taken in by his self-chastising, the suitors relax their suspicions and award the new beggar the goat stomach full of blood as the prize. Such a prize must have been pleasing to Hermes. It shows the interior of the body brought forth as an emblem of victory, not unlike Odysseus' own actions, which will shortly shed the disguise to reveal his identity as he reclaims his household.

The epithet "wild pig" that the suitors hurl at Odysseus more than once in their attempts to wound him with words calls to mind the wild boar's attack on him as a youth as well as outlines the animal he serves here. The scar, revealed shortly after the above scene, marks the boundary between the animal and the human order; here the gods intervene even when they hide. The scar is an etching, a line of demarcation between two worlds. It is a threshold marker as Odysseus spends much time patiently at the threshold, assessing the contents of the belly of his house. The white scar of the animal, wounding the human order, is a place between two destinies: the animal nature is human as the human nature is animal: wild, instinctive, and unwilling to be tamed.

It might be more precise poetically to say that in Odysseus resides an animal imagination, much like the animal imagination he has retrieved through his episodes; he takes on the animal habits, finds himself in an animal place between the two olive trees growing intimately together. This site becomes a sacred place, almost a birthing grove sacred to the goddess, for it unites the animal and the human orders, with the implicit sanction of Athena's divine assistance.

The worlds or the realities of animal, vegetable, human, and divine are all tightly woven here to construct a poetic field in which Odysseus as central player marshals all those who will be spared to carry on the household and all those who will perish. He can imagine himself through them and is thus able to penetrate the belly of his home and slay those whose appetites have violated the codes of hospitality. He is able to liberate Penelope in her own home as the Achaeans liberated Helen in Troy. But her own instincts prompt her to establish the stringing of Odysseus' old bow and the accuracy of the contestants as they attempt to shoot the arrow through the twelve ax handles. Already, before the beggar's identity is known, Telemachos, Penelope, and Odysseus are engaged as accomplices in retrieving their rightful place in the home. In silence, and under the noses of the suitors, they have united to become one mind.

In the eyes of the hungry suitors, Odysseus is certainly a wild pig. But their imagery is far more accurate than they would ever suspect. He is the wild boar, Hermetic in temperament, furious like Athena, ferocious as the wild boar, as he sheds his cover to wound the suitors, in effect charging out of the copse to wound every one one of them mortally. He thus replays his earlier destiny and links it to the stories that uncovered for the Phaecians his true identity fully imagined.

Moreover, just before he slays the suitors and hangs the maidens who were unfaithful to the household with the same cold abandon in which Achilles drags the body of Hector three times around the Trojan walls, but after his scar convinces Eurycleia of his true identity, he refers to his wound as an emblem of proof of who he is. First he offers it to Eumaeos and to the oxherd: "Come now, I shall show you another manifest sign/So you may know me well and trust me in your hearts: A scar a boar once inflicted on me with his shining tusk/ . . . . He drew his rags away from the great scar" (21.218–21). They weep over his return and promise to help him reclaim his home. Later he uses the scar to prove to his own father, Laertes, who is inconsolable over the loss of his son: "First of all, take notice with your eyes of this scar/That a boar inflicted on me with shining tusk on Parnassos/When I had gone there" (24.330–33), after which Laertes' "knees and his own heart went slack/When he recognized the sure tokens Odysseus had shown him. He threw his arms round his dear son and went faint for breath" (24.345–47).

The wound and the narratives of his past serve Odysseus in his ultimate homecoming. Like the scar, his stories reveal his identity; they create a boundary between past and future and anchor Odysseus in the present, surrounded by all those who were faithful to the home. Body and narrative share a common heritage in the self-creation or construction of the domestic hero; one cannot have a full identity, Homer implies, without an intertwining of both human embodiment and a history fully remembered. The stories we tell and the wounds we carry together constitute a major measure of who we are. Odysseus successfully marries belly to mind, appetite to story, and divinity to mortality in order to retrieve the earlier love that he sacrificed to fight for another woman.

This mythic action of an early wounding, which can be seen psychologically as a form of polluting the body, or reminding us of our mortal and frail limits, Sophocles uses as a centerpoint around which once again to highlight the complex relation of wounding to memory and to authentic identity in *Oedipus Rex*. Old afflictions and present pollutions will define the proud king in his grandeur and in his feeble old age at Colonus.

3

Wandering Wounds and Meandering Words

The Tragic Body of Memory in Oedipus Rex

I have longed to know what flesh is made of.
—Tiresias, in Wole Soyinka's
Bacchae of Euripedes, 243)

Over time, our bodies are continually marked with experience, from an original birthmark to a scar, surgical wound, or physical deformity that reveals something crucially significant about our identity, the nature of our actions, and the texture of our biography, as Odysseus' boar scar from hunting has just shown us. The genre of tragedy, or a tragic event that may lead to some redemptive conclusion, is the most fertile terrain in which the body has received some wound from the world; it may also be the cause of the world's wounds, even if that world implicates one's self as the wounder.

The psychological or spiritual suffering in tragedy, for instance, often has its analogy in some form of body wounding. The cause may be found in Pascal's observation that "we never remain in the present. The truth is that the present commonly wounds us" (qtd. in Brandon, 144). This intimacy between temporality itself and being wounded is expressed more recently by Jacob Needleman: "the kind of changes we seek to make in our lives are usually no more than superficial wounds in the body of time" (6). He goes on to suggest that if we are not able to discern the real turning points or crossroads in our lives, then poke or probe our lives how we will, it "will have no more effect than a temporary disturbance that soon closes over again, as tissue closes over a minor wound" (5). Through this image of wounding he presents, we can see ourselves clearly in the dark mirror of Oedipus. We recall the vulnerable heel of Achilles that Paris' arrow eventually finds, or perhaps the most famous scar in literature which we discussed in the previous chapter, the scar of Odysseus that Eurycleia discovers as she washes her disguised master's leg and touches the healed wound he received from a boar while hunting as a young boy.

51

In more current literature, one that will be explored in a later chapter, is the wound that Ivan Ilych receives in Tolstoy's novella, *The Death of Ivan Ilych,* incurred when he slips from a ladder while rearranging the drapery in his new home and hits his left side against a window knob; or the set of scars on the back of Sethe, the slave woman who has been severely beaten by two men before they rape her of her milk in Toni Morrison's novel, *Beloved.* Her healed wounds assume the shape of a chokecherry tree, the branches like raised Braille etchings on her back. Through these markings she remembers their cruelty. Each of these marked figures carry on their bodies some trace of their history, some indictments of memory, of incidents in the past that have become permanently part of the body's landscape and the psyche's mythic terrain. Each marking keeps a story alive on the flesh to be retrieved and told. These markings not only configure the past but also play a critical role in the character's future. They are sites of one's developed sense of identity. It is as if the wounded action lives with haunting permanence through the markings, indelible etchings which have associated with them intimate psychological suffering as well as acute physical pain. Tragedy may be traced through their lineage.

The action of body woundedness in Sophocles' *Oedipus Rex* reveals the body as a metaphor, a way of seeing through and questioning what kind of knowing grows from the violence inflicted on the body, especially the knowledge that grows out of the scar or the festering wound of injury to it. The body offers itself as an image of the poetic imagination that, if imagined within the context of the action of the work, reveals dimensions of identity that are not so readily apparent when the body is taken for granted or even ignored in its frailty. While the body reflects "a cultural invention" and more important, "a situation," as Robert Romanyshyn describes it (*Technology,* 73), it is also a rich poetic metaphor that offers its own ontology to us; a kind of knowledge is offered through the wounded or violated body that helps us to understand the poetic work's entire meaning.

Body wounds are the loci of the action's meaning; they are as well the origin of personal myths and the place in which one enters a communal mythos. Rose Emily Rothenberg suggests that "scars are imprints of traumas once present and now left behind, vestiges that serve as distinct reminders of the injuries that body and psyche have encountered" (142). It is where critical mass congeals, constellates, and develops its own persuasive language. There exists a rhetoric, a powerful speaking, deeply embedded in body woundedness that needs to be heard fully, so that we can understand more profoundly what it means, for example, that the city of Thebes and the natural order have been blighted, or wounded, along with the wounded body of Oedipus, for the psyche of the individual and the city are not to be separated. I would include here in this sense of wounding the condition of pollution as well, as when we pollute the earth today with toxins or waste, we wound the Earth Mother and bring her closer to death. On this area of study, Richard Sennett writes that "Our civilization, from its origins, has been challenged by the body in pain. . . . The puzzles of bodily pain marked Greek tragedies and early Christian efforts to comprehend the Son of God" (*Flesh and Stone*, 25).[1]

James Hillman guides part of this discussion on body woundedness when he writes of the puer figure in psychology, especially when this youthful, somewhat innocent, and untried character suffers wounds that mark his destiny. In fact, "the wound itself seems to identify the puer spirit with heroic destiny." Parents, he goes on to suggest, "can be the wounders. Everyone carries a parental wound and has a wounded parent" ("Puer Wounds," 101). In a poetic reading of the wound initiated by a parent, as is Oedipus' wound inflicted on him by his father, Laius, Hillman insists that "the parent is the wound. . . . Our wounds are the fathers and mothers of our destinies" (103).

Such wounding would be the cause of one's weakening rather than strengthening of self in the world; however, as part of the search for identity, the wound can be a way of wakening and actually allowing one an opening into a fuller state of being; the wound may be both or alternately a learner and a teacher (109). As such, it may initially appear as a curse but in time be perceived as a gift (107), one given to each person. For none of us, from birth to death, escape some form of body or psychic woundedness. Far from making us more vulnerable, Hillman observes, the wound can open one to dimensions of self that are closed to those who will not pursue their afflictions. Through wounding one may enter a crossroads, some mediating ground between innocence and maturity, from a superficial life of distance to a more intimate and penetrating awareness of being in a far richer place. Wounds suggest to us that where we are most vulnerable is the place/time which must be most venerated, for they mark a sacred space in us that we would have ignored had not the wound brought it forcefully into consciousness.

Such an action Sophocles poetically inaugurates in the drama of *Oedipus Rex* and fulfills or completes in Oedipus' wandering, meandering journey to the sacred grove of Colonus in the later play which space does not allow me to discuss in this book. There in this suburb of Athens the suffering old man finds peace and cleansing as well as an embracing by the gods. His close relationship with divinity begins, however, in his initial wounding. His originary wound through the ankles to tether him to the side of Mount Cithaeron, and inflicted on him soon after his birth, opens him to the wonder of divinity immediately prior to his death. Those same wounded feet lead him with his daughter to the moist grove of Colonus. Our wounds are connected, therefore, to time, to memory, and to the divinity within the soul; vulnerability and divinity exist close to the affliction, marking us as both.

The paradoxical language of the wound suggests that in tragic action it is the gash that heals; but it also leaves its trace, its mark of memory on the body, a physical and psychological emblem of one's mortality, one's limits, and one's ability to endure. *Oedipus Rex* is a dramatic rendering of the wounded memory, a remembering that recovers through the wound the true origin of one's identity. Not only does the parent wound him, but the wound eventually parents him. Oedipus becomes most completely himself through the knowledge gained through his old wound.

When the wound becomes a scar, there is always present the "after-thought" of the original violation. The scar, we might say, is the wound that has matured and taken on its own shape on the body; from there it signals a greater level of psychic wholeness because wounds, Hillman has discovered, always lead to depth and to soul, to insight and to a greater weathering of life's events. Wounds also instruct the wounded on a sense of place, time, and belonging, for wounds speak of some form of violation of both self and place. We will see, for example, that through the wound that he is forced to remember, the shackles put through his ankles shortly after his birth, Oedipus comes to know that he is out of place, and that this is the genesis of his polluting effect on the city and the land.[2] Pollution would seem to have close ties to displacement and to disorder.

Since my focus will be on several acts of wounding in *Oedipus Rex*, with particular attention paid to the original wound inflicted on Oedipus almost immediately after his birth, then remembered when he is king, there is a way of speaking about the scar that covers wounds as a trace or marking that hides the shadow of the original affliction. What I wish to develop here is an imagination of wounding. The shadow of original affliction may be the knowledge or the insight that has to be brought to light in tragedy. Tragic action is a rite of passage and this passage "involving the birth of the new and death of the old," writes Rothenberg, "inevitably creates a wound" (145). The shadow is the knowledge that is buried in the original wound. The scar, we might understand, opens up to the shadowy wound that it now covers; it may remind one who incurs the original wound of its place. Furthermore, Rollo May suggests from his practice as an analyst that memory depends mainly on myth and that memory has the capacity to form the past into a myth (*Cry for Myth*, 66, 70); the wounds one receives in life, whose origins are remembered, may be the genesis of one's personal myth. Our myth may reside most thickly in those places, tissues and times of our deepest wounds, the place of crossroads, intersections, and newly discovered boundaries. Wounds mark these places in space and time. Our wounds, then, map out our history *and* our destiny.

When Charles Boer explores the shadow in Greek tragedy, he makes a provocative insight that opens the wound to further exploration: Nowhere is the Shadow more valuable, he suggests, than in Greek tragedy. The very complexity of characters like Oedipus "are related to the God-shadows they carry in these plays (in Oedipus' case, the Shadow side of Apollonian purity). Even though Shadow invariably means trouble—indeed, it means tragedy—it is only in the fact that a God visibly carries their Shadows that one finds largeness or depth in these characters. . . . Without Shadow, tragedy is nothing" (135). We can phrase the search of Oedipus for his origins as a journey back and through to remembered body woundedness, back to the shadow of his past, his murder of his father, and finally to the wound that gives him, face to face, his origins and his destiny. In the same manner that a scar may be the shadow of a wound, so in the life of the psyche the symptoms of one's past may be shadowed in the gap in self-knowledge one carries in the present.

Of course it is not new that Oedipus' name, "swollen foot," already implicates his identity through his body malady. Bernard Knox has gone a step further in illustrating how the Greek *oidi*, "to swell," is very close to *oida*, "to know" (9). It is the movement or action from not knowing to knowing that comprises the drama's central mimetic action. What Oedipus succeeds eventually in knowing is that most of his life has been spent meticulously avoiding Apollo's oracular knowledge that he is fated to slay his father and marry his mother. Here oracular knowing is a form of wounded knowing. By means of his swollen feet Oedipus walks the land believing that he is successfully avoiding his destiny; he discovers later in life that his swollen feet, following their own wounded fate, took him precisely to where he needed to fulfill it. Not "flaw" but "wound" is perhaps the better word to use to describe the condition of a tragic character. Oedipus' knowledge comes through the orifice of a "tragic wound." E. R. Dodds is correct when he writes: "the theory that the tragic hero must have a grave moral flaw, and to say Aristotle said so, is false" ("Misunderstanding," 38).

To suggest that the tragic figure of Oedipus is wounded and then to attend to this wound reveals more of how he comes to understand his own biography—especially in how it is deeply embedded in biology. To attend to the notion of flaw, which is much more abstract than wound, is perhaps a signal that criticism itself has fallen prey to the cleverness of the Sphinx, who in her facile riddle, which appears to be deceptively easy for the astute Oedipus to solve, actually sets him up to complete his fated journey. The riddle creates a blind spot in its vision, so that what is not at least as apparent has been overlooked: the prize of the city of Thebes and the queen is in fact the situation he was most intent on avoiding. Does tragic action therefore reveal to us that we are most blind where we are most acutely wounded? Are our wounds initially our blind spots, the loci of our most wounded way of seeing? And is where we are most unconsciously wounded the place where we believe our greatest power lies? Perhaps, then, it is in the changing nature of the wound's presence that tragic action gathers momentum.

Solving the riddle of generic man, mankind in the abstract, exposes both the clever mind of Oedipus *and* the astute reverse psychology of the Sphinx. Oedipus is fated to show his cleverness in locating the riddle's solution and is therefore snagged by what he believed he was, by his own efforts, able and freely to avoid. His own blind spot is his inability to see that the riddle is all about feet and man's upright posture. Would he have avoided his fate had he felt the pain in his own feet through the Sphinx's riddle? His original vulnerable spot is that he does not understand that built into the riddle, the gods are underfoot, making sure that Oedipus wends his way into Thebes. Jonathan Lear believes that "for Oedipus to have recognized his abandonment, all he had to do was look down. The wounds through his ankles emblazon abandonment in every step. But his wounds are too painful . . . to think about them" (48). The deeper wound is loss of the father and loss of belonging to place. The poetic appropriateness of being wounded where one contacts the earth and is grounded becomes more apparent. The pain from his wound is the parent that guides him.

Oedipus, therefore, hits the mark of the city he believes he has no relation to because, in part, his relation to his past and to his present is based, along with his mother's, point for point, on a series of wrong assumptions. Again, a wrong assumption may be understood as a pollution or a corruption of logic itself, which Oedipus prides himself in exercising. We might say that the assumption grows from avoiding the wound at his feet, what is transparently hidden.

First, Oedipus wrongly assumes that Polybus and Merope are his biological parents; he wrongly assumes that if he is to avoid the oracle's sentence, he must avoid Corinth; and he wrongly assumes that the man he murders, along with his guards on the narrow path leading out of Mount Cithareon, is not his father, for he wrongly assumes, he later discovers, that the narrative of the man who escapes, a narrative which insists that not *one* but *several* men attacked the king and his men, is true. Oedipus has all along been on the wrong trajectory of logic in his attempt to avoid his destiny. But as long as his life is governed by information, by the words of the oracle, and so long as his identity is constellated in his cleverness, and the wounds at his feet are disremembered, his mathematical precision about things, and a sense that this knowledge is not connected in any important way to his body and to the act of slaying another, he is safe from himself and his destiny because he is insulated from his history. He cannot look down. Not until his wounded feet bring to consciousness their own memory will Oedipus begin his wandering toward the true origins of his identity. Failing this, he is certain to avoid what he calls "that old affliction."

What Oedipus does bodily is not correctly or even directly connected to what he thinks and assumes. It appears less important that Oedipus physically weds and sires children with his mother in the polluted and drought-ridden city of Thebes than that he is disconnected, like Hamlet after him, to matter itself and to accurate or authentic knowing. The barrenness of the city finds its correlate in his own lack of his personal myth. This divorce from matter and from knowing fully is intimately tied to the fact that he is unknowingly wedded to his mother, that he has entered her (yet another way of understanding woundedness) and has had four children by her. The wound at his feet may be defined further through Jonathan Lear's remark that "what Oedipus doesn't know is that he doesn't know" (46). His original affliction is a wound in the body of knowledge itself, the gap in knowing, itself.

It therefore becomes clearer that there is something more profound in Sophocles' plot than that Oedipus murders his father and marries his mother; there is an action in his drama that is much more primordial. The drama is more intimately tied to matter and to the archetype of the wound Oedipus receives as an infant before being exposed, shackled, his ankles pierced, and abandoned on the side of Mount Cithaeron by his parents that bears witness to Oedipus' divorce from matter and knowing. It implicates by extension the wound he is fated to inflict on his father as well as the self-inflicted wound he suffers at his own hands with the brooches from his mother's dress after she has hanged herself. That he uses two objects from his mother's clothing in the wounding keeps the relation of mother and son, even matter and son, imaginally present. Oedipus develops profoundly through this dramatic action from being his mother's son, an impetuous youth quick to anger, swift to act, impatient with others, who lives on the surface of experience, guided by intellect through logic and divorced from any profound depth in the meaning of life, to a man who has visited the underworld and touched the realm of soul, of depth, of reflection, and of a profound understanding of his life; his wounded ankles are the genesis of this voyage.

He makes the underworld journey through two apertures: words and wounds. We see the nature of this intricate relation of words and wounds, first through the oracle that threatens the father and the wound that the father inflicts to anchor the son on the mountain, to guarantee the three-day-old infant's vulnerability and certain death and Laius' own deflection of the oracle. Exposing his son is the father's method of disowning the truth of his own knowing from the oracle. Jung believes that, in the modern world, the gods have gone into the body to become diseases: "Zeus no longer rules Olympus but the solar plexus, and produces curious specimens for the doctor's consulting room" (*Alchemical Studies,* 37). Paraphrasing this idea, I suggest that the gods have gone into the body in the form of body-woundedness, there to become part of the destiny of the individual as well as the memory of that same person's history. Divine knowing will emerge from the bottom up, not the top down, in Oedipus' embodiment. Memory will begin in the wounded feet and move slowly through the body to the intellect, where logic and lineage will congeal. His gouging out his own eyes in guilt and shame shows us how this knowledge of his condition is the deepest self-wounding.

TIME, PLACE, AND THE POWER OF WOUNDING WORDS

Words as well as body wounds comprise the riddle of identity for Oedipus, especially as they have the capacity to lead one to his or her origins through the narrative of both biology and biography. His wound from infancy is as much a part of that same riddle as are words themselves. Jocasta relates the literal history of the early event with noble motives: to free him from any concern that he is the abandoned son returned. His father Laius, fearing the oracle's prophecy that he would be murdered by his son, shackled his feet and exposed him on Mount Cithaeron. But we need to look closely at the juxtaposition of this tale to her son's infancy, which is separated only by an ellipsis in the drama. The ellipsis is a kind of linguistic wound in the text in an otherwise free flow of words, as she continues the story: "But Laius,/so the report goes at least, was killed by strangers,' thieves, at a place where three roads meet . . . my son—/he wasn't three days old and the boy's father fastened his ankles, had a henchman fling him away/on a barren, trackless mountain" (ll. 788–93). The ellipsis is also a bridge between father and son. The absent words are what we and Oedipus seek. In addition, Jocasta's literal and exact chronicle of the events also rests uneasily on a false assumption: that exposing the infant on the side of Mount Cithaeron inevitably led to his death. So she can speak through her assumption with a clarity that undoes what she had hoped for.

These lines comprise the most important narrative in the play, especially since immediately after them, Jocasta offers, with perfect logic, a kind of narrative syllogism that rests comfortably but precariously on yet another false assumption: "There, you see? Apollo brought neither things to pass. My baby no more murdered his father than Laius suffered—his *wildest* fear—death at his own son's hands. That's how the seers and all their revelations *mapped out the future*. Brush them from your mind" (ll. 793–98, emphasis added). The central issues of the play all constrict and compress into these words uttered proudly and a bit mockingly by the unknowing mother who assumes she knows. Could she be seen as matter in ellipsis, elliptical matter as mother?

THE WOUNDED EARTH

First, her words splice the murderous act performed spatially where three roads meet to the temporality of the infant Oedipus wounded by the parent. The wound links Oedipus' heritage to his destiny; the wound is the bridge, or the shackle that painfully binds past to future. I want to take some liberty with this notion of woundedness to allow wounding to be entangled with words themselves. It seems a little fact, to be sure, but then this drama hinges on the incidental, on the trivial, the tri-via of journeying, acting, and finally speaking.

We remember for a moment the words that set Oedipus in motion from Corinth. He tells us himself that "Some man at a banquet who had drunk too much/shouted out—he was far gone, mind you—/that I am not my father's son. Fighting words!/I barely restrained myself that day . . . I had to make my move" (ll. 858–63). Clearly these words wound Oedipus deeply; it is this wounding by words that incites him to action and propels him out of Corinth in search of a cure for his wound. These words are not neutral; on the contrary, they are fighting words! Second, this voice spewing *excessive* words that wound him are actually part of the destiny that Oedipus will wander into as he creates a wide arch on his journey to avoid Corinth and slaying his father. The words of the oracle wound him further, for they suggest to him that he will murder whom he most loves.

He has the right idea, along with the correct words that point him to the truth of his destiny; he simply applies them to the wrong place. His words have not found the right home; they are misplaced words, even wandering words, that tend to meander around the truth but do not strike it until later; however, they do wound him into action, not unlike the wounded feet of the infant Oedipus that prompt the shepherd ("I pitied the little baby, master," 1302) to act against the words of Laius and Jocasta. Indeed, he violates their words and instead gives the infant over to the herdsman who takes him to the king and queen of Corinth, themselves a barren couple without children of their own. He is given to them to assuage their barrenness as he is later delivered to Thebes to fertilize that earth's barrenness and so save the city.

The focus here, nonetheless, is on the Oedipus wounded at birth, who is now wounded by language, by knowledge that he seeks to corroborate through divinity's voice. His words are telling in this context: "I heard all that and ran. I abandoned Corinth, from that day on I gauged its landfall only/by the stars, running, always running/toward some place where I would never see the shame of all those oracles come true. And as I fled I reached that very spot/where the great King, you say, met his death" (ll. 876–82). His feet and his eyes are in complicity with his words as he runs following the stars to avoid what is not a threat; but his false knowledge is in fact corrected and guided by his fated feet, which know the truth. His fated destiny he reasons to avoid not just what is under his feet, but the feet themselves. Body knowing through their wounds is more powerful than reasoned calculation. As we will see with Ahab in *Moby-Dick*, there is a compelling psychological need to return to the origin of the original affliction; that affliction's knowledge is known deep in the body.

When he confronts Laius where three roads meet, he leaves the trackless destiny of his running and comes to the constricted, tight, and very clearly tracked terrain in the earth—a wound perhaps, on the earth's surface. The roads here conspire in the form of a triple wound, a place where the earth remembers the passage of countless feet and carts. Oedipus describes this constricted space to the chorus of Theban elders after he has inflicted new wounds on himself: "O triple roads—it all comes back, the secret,/dark ravine, and the oaks closing in/where the three roads join" (ll. 1531–34). Now he is not in "a barren trackless" place but its opposite, a confluence of tracks, a confusion of paths; yet he is at the center of them at the same time, the place of destiny's partial fulfillment.

Here Oedipus resides almost in the shadow of his destiny. He describes the terrain, after his self-mutilation at the play's end, as "the secret,/dark ravine, and the oaks closing in/where the three roads join" (ll. 1530–33). This is the geography of soul, of depth, of darkness, of destiny, where his actions of wounding and killing and the words of the gods find common ground, if not downright complicity. At the crossroads he and his father inhabit the realm of soul, where wounded becomes wounder and the wounder is wounded. Soul and world are one here at the crossroads; father and son meet and fulfill their respective destinies and the world, as witness, presents herself as multipathed, dark, close, tight, restrictive, shaded, and secretive, offering a poetics of soul and world in their unity.

The fatedness of father and son has its reflection in the landscape of the world; there exists, as Hillman suggests, "psychic depths to the world" ("Anima Mundi," 72) as much as there is to persons. Here in this deeply psychological place the father is slain by whom he sought to destroy and the son slays the very figure he sought to avoid. And, in the genius of the play, each acts in secret from the other, for the son and the father do not know one another in their anger. Their wounds, however, are familial in this richly metaphoric and soul-ful world place; they are both where the gods have spoken they need to be. Crossroads is the home of their respective destinies, fulfilled unknowingly by each toward the other. Their unknowing peoples the feet of their coming and going. They meet because of the oracular speaking that both tended to avoid. And now, where the three roads meet, their destines are outlined. Dianne Skafte, writing perceptively on oracular consciousness, reminds us that "divination is concerned with the past, present and the future, in addition to providing spiritual and psychological guidance" (32). Her words are another way of describing the confluence of the three roads. Time and space in their synthesis congeal here in a wound that cuts through the fabric or veil separating mortals and divinities; the words of the oracles are fulfilled in the wound to the father who wounded the son.

We need, however, to let Oedipus himself tell the story to his mother, for the narrative recapitulates the action of Oedipus' destiny. Following the mythopoetic logic of the play, the narrative remembers his destiny. He therefore recollects to Jocasta that the king's men are about to thrust him off the road; in his anger he begins to wound each of them in turn: "And the one shouldering me aside, the driver, / I strike him in anger!—and the old man, watching me / coming up along his wheels—he brings down / his prod, two prongs straight at my head! / I pay him back with interest. . . . I killed them all—every mother's son!" (ll. 890–98). The one who was wounded first in birth, then by the drunken fellow at a tavern in Corinth, then by the oracle at Delphi, and now again at the crossroads, becomes the wounder, in a sense replacing his father's originary act toward his son.

According to the oracle's prediction, Oedipus is partway home, for the crossroads is the dwelling of his destiny; it is where the traces in the earth in the form of the three roads offer a constellation of worlds; there he confronts, unknowingly, his origin and his destiny simultaneously, lived out through his ferocious and unchecked anger, a wound in character his father shares. The crossroad itself is analogous to the wound, for at crossroads possibilities open, choice is optioned, there is a gap in the original path where others are introduced. The crossroad, George Elder writes, is where things split open, promising other directions to take, in the same way that wounding opens up to deeper possibilities of knowing and of remembering. Like the crossroad, the wound opens the present to the past and to the future. Divinity enters at the crossroad and through the wound. The crossroad, George Elder writes, opens up the space of Hekate and of Hermes, of the place where souls were buried ("Crossroads," 166), where directions were given, where a new orientation becomes possible. All of these potentialities are inherent in Oedipus and Laius' meeting. Crossroads and wounds share all the potential for a new quality and form of knowing. Knowledge coagulates in both locations.

Perhaps Sophocles saw what psychoanalysis later rediscovered: that remembering can be an act of self-wounding, an opening up of the past that allows what has festered to burst open, brought forth, drained, so that a deep healing can begin. His character is indeed his destiny, and we see how like father is the son. Father and son together reveal how accurate is the Greek idea that *ethos* equals *telos*, which may be a mantra for analysis itself. It understands that our destiny is somehow buried in the wounds of our history. Uncovering this interconnection or this crossroads is at the heart of what Edward Whitmont has called a "mythological perspective," for what is included in this perspective is "a living emotional reality" ("The Destiny Concept in Psychotherapy," 191) that takes one's history out of an abstract series of events to discover in them the meaning as experience.

The crossroads "is the place," according to Dennis Tedlock, "where time and space intersect and one's fate is fulfilled" (43).[3] In the wounded terrain of the crossroads Oedipus may be said to wound his origins, and through the action, brings that much closer to full embodiment in the world the words of the oracle. In his wounding, the words he has been told gain further validity.

The imagery of Jocasta's narrative, unbeknownst to her, also puts forth another psychological reality that must be tracked in reading into the complexity of this entangled dramatic action, or the tracking of the *meaning of an action* that has already occurred but must be retrieved by a combination of words and wounds that move emphatically and linearly forward and those words that grow from a more wandering or meandering way of thinking. It is the second order of words that more intensely snags the bits and pieces of truth that are revealed through the unknowing speech by Oedipus and Jocasta. Perhaps the second way of remembering, when the course is less steady, more wavering and wandering in its direction, is closer to a kind of imaginative remembering, one in which the parts begin to cohere slowly to form a full dramatic action. Remembering that original wound, he begins, like Ivan Ilych almost two thousand years later, to imagine his life rather than simply to recall it. Imagining it brings forth its meaning, its relevance, and its interconnectedness in the myth that it shapes.

At the juncture of knowing and not knowing in the drama, the messenger from Corinth, with word of Polybus' death, arrives to clarify and unburden Oedipus of his history; but in the now-familiar backward swing of irony that seems to characterize tragic action, the effect is the reverse of its intention. The one who has lived a life of surefootedness is shortly called back to those same feet's afflictions. The messenger, with a tone of bravado coating his words, and a cloud of unknowing encasing his thought, believes his role to be Oedipus' savior, to free him from his history and unburden him of his suspicions.

Oedipus' penetrating question to the messenger is revealing: "Oh—/ when you picked me up, was I in pain? What exactly?" and the messenger:

"Your ankles . . . they tell the story. Look at them," to which the king responds: "Why remind me of that, that old affliction? The messenger enlightens him: "Your ankles were pinned together. I set you free." And Oedipus: "That dreadful mark—I've had it from the cradle" (ll. 1131–35). Immediately, impatiently perhaps, he wishes to discover the origin of his wounding, for in that revelation he believes he will know who he is, especially, the messenger reminds him, "you got your name from that misfortune too,/the name's still with you" (ll. 1135–36).

Both his name and his pain are at the heart of his identity; the meaning of both, moreover, still eludes him. This recognition of that old affliction is the key crossroad for Oedipus; in remembering the wound he seeks out the wounder, which shortly takes him to hearing another name identified, that of his father: "Who? Do you know? Describe him." And the messenger: "He called himself a servant of . . . /if I remember rightly—Laius" (ll. 1141–44) to which his mother, overhearing all that transpires, responds in the stage directions, "Jocasta turns sharply." The wound opens up to the origin. Now the name of the origin has been uttered—the wounded feet have led to the revealed word and the hero begins to see disclosed for him both his heritage and his destiny through the wounds and the word naming his father. The name of the father is the deepest wound for Oedipus in this pause in the narrative journey.

Oedipus' impatience gains momentum, just as his anger gained momentum at the crossroads where he slayed his father and his attendants: "Out with it," he demands of the messenger. "The time has come to reveal this once for all" (ll. 1150–51). And as if through the wounded feet all begins to pour forth, the entire story, much as in Homer's *Odyssey* some eighty-five lines spew forth from the scar in his thigh to reveal the history of the youth wounded by the boar tusk (*Odyssey*, 19.390–475). Here Oedipus breaks open: "Let it burst! Whatever will, whatever must! I must know my birth, . . . I must see my origins face-to-face" (ll. 1183–85). His name has given him both his history and his future; the closer he journeys back in naming and in the wounds of his feet to his beginnings, the closer Oedipus gains a knowledge of his deepest sense of self in the world and that knowing ensnares what he thought himself distant from: the wounding father. In the archetypal action of father and son, before the father dies, the son must wound him in return; one's individual destiny and freedom depends on this primordial action, begun with the original wounding. John Horder's image comes from the wounding father who asks his son, "Shall I break your legs . . . before throwing you to the ground? ("The Sick Image of My Father Fades," 130).

The chorus' language is critical at the moment when Oedipus has invited all of the polluted past, which he thought was safely contained, to burst forth. The analogue of this moment at the crossroads, the other half of this linguistic metaphor, is the slaying of the father; here it is the naming of the father, followed quickly and forcefully by the true naming of the son. In the space generated by Oedipus' absence, and before the messenger enters to tell the horror of what has occurred offstage, the chorus observes: "Time has dragged you to the light,/judged your marriage monstrous from the start—/the *son and the father tangling, both one*" (ll. 1341–43, emphasis added). Enmeshed one into another, father and son are related intimately in their mutual wounds mutually inflicted. Not the linear logic but the entangled experience connects father to son as they met in the chthonic region of the dark ravine, where the constricted space did not allow them to pass one another without one or the other giving way. As neither was willing to yield, they became entangled; plural becomes singular, many and one are synonymous, which violates all law of arithmetical logic as the truth of the man bursts forth. In their confrontation at the crossroads and in their relation to Jocasta, father and son are a psychological unity. They live together as one mythic presence, and perhaps as one festering wound.

Oedipus Rex is most poignantly a drama about words, which, when used to retrace the steps back to the slain king, who the Theban people say vanished without a trace and whose body was never recovered, will finally lead to the wounded one, Oedipus. The knowledge gained wounds both himself and his wife/mother. These acts of wounding both punctuate his life as well as describe the answer to the Sphinx's riddle. The one who is wounded becomes the wounder, the one who is meant to heal the land becomes its greatest violator, and the one who, after wounding his origins in slaying Laius, wounds himself and thereby gains a level of consciousness not afforded him previously, a consciousness that sets him closer perhaps to the level of consciousness that only Tiresias possesses. In another of the great ironies of this action, Tireseias is the figure whom Oedipus rails most against and whom he most becomes in his blindness, his insight, and, eventually, his holiness.

Two movements exist in the dramatic speaking and the thought that it promotes: one is very linear, logical, mathematical, almost syllogistic, and it is the side of Oedipus that is able to solve riddles as long as they are at a distance from him. The other is the imaginal movement of recollection, which moves circuitously and wanders to the truth. Donald Cowan has referred to this magnificent king as one possessing an "overestimated intellect" and an ego's drive toward conquest ("The Self-made Leader," 162). His mother exhibits the same pattern of thought, evidenced in her clear and precisely detailed recollection of Laius' murder. We see it in other places, for example, when Creon and Oedipus are interrupted in their initial argument by the mother: "Tell me clearly, how did the quarrel start?" (773). And referring to the words of the one man who escaped Oedipus' slaughter on the road, she affirms: "I told you *precisely* what he said" (938); Oedipus, desperately attempting to wriggle out of being implicated in the murder, falls on the arithmetic of the escapee's words: "So if he still holds to the same number, I cannot be the killer. One can't equal many" (932–34). His fate and his history become an arithmetical proposition. Yet this logic will not be enough, for its language is far too limited and disincarnated from his wounded body.

THE WANDERING WOUND

The other set of images that further directs the action has to do with chance asides, pieces of information that seem insignificant, incidental, and tri-vial, but which suddenly take on great power and import as they fit into the larger form of the plot. It is the incidental things that one catches out of hand, so to speak, impurities rather than the pure logic of the intellect, that bring Oedipus home to himself. Jocasta, for instance, describes the space of the mountain where her son was exposed, shackled, and left to die by the father as "barren and trackless" (792), qualities that might describe Merope, Polybus, and Corinth. No map, no footpath to follow, a geography, so to speak, where one may wander directionless and with no goal or destination, and finally, with no support in order to survive. She also rebuffs the oracles and seers who have ineffectually, to her mind, "mapped out the future" (798). The map we might understand here as a kind of distorted spatial image so that one can stay on track, go the shortest route from point to point with a clarity of vision denied those who are ignorant of the way.

But just as she speaks of this false mapping, which is of course not the case, and meaning to deflect Oedipus from his pursuit, he stops and begins to reflect in a way we have not seen him engage before: "Strange,/hearing you just now . . . my mind wandered,/my thoughts racing back and forth" (810–11). Here the linear pursuit is broken by the less intellectual, less logical, but more accurate search. He reaches a crossroads in his thinking about his history, one which abandons linear certainty and begins to roam, reflect, and take other avenues to knowing. Images loop back on themselves in Oedipus' mind. Identification of place stops Oedipus, so to speak, in his tracks; it then sends him tracking on a different heading in a more meandering and therefore more accurate form of inquiry.

Jocasta's question to her son as she begins to feel less comfortable at this juncture is revealing: "What haunts you so?" (813). Wandering, roaming, reflecting, following a trackless terrain rather than one clearly marked, indicates a more genuine journey toward his origins, for Oedipus is always moving in two directions with his questions and assertions: back and down, both toward his origins and down into depth, into the soul of who he is, the most originary form of being at home. He will reach his origins when he re-contacts the "old affliction" of his wounded feet. And Oedipus' haunting realization of place soon afflicts as well as probes his mother's memory, for when she thinks of the body of her husband and the man in front of her, she has an insight that seems to escape her in words before she can think it through: " and his build . . . wasn't far from yours" (818).

To speak of his psychological journey from the point of view of em-bodiment, Oedipus' thinking moves out of his head, that is, out of intellec-tual and logical explanation, and into the level of images, which are given him through his body generally and the wounds in his feet specifically, to his own origins; they serve a greater purpose in regrounding him to the earth, which carries the wounds of Oedipus into herself. Being itself is cor-rupted and wounded deep into its roots through his presence in Thebes. There is no gap here between physics and metaphysics. Stepping into king-ship and into his mother's bed wounds all of nature; the entire order of Being suffers a profound gash, which sprouts from and then grows out of the wounded ankles of the hero. But he is not at a point in his own devel-opment to understand such a truth of his existence. When Oedipus wounds himself toward the end of the play, the action of self-blinding through self-mutilation is a willful, freely chosen act that sends him not only out of Thebes so that the pollution and corruption can be removed from the earth, but also to wandering for years until he "stumbles" onto the sacred grove of Colonus. Wandering and stumbling across the earth also has its lineage in how the infant Oedipus was discovered by the shepherd, who found him exposed and shackled in infancy on the mountain's side: "I stumbled on you,/down the woody flanks of Mount Cithaeron" (1123).

Spatially, Oedipus begins his life in the mountains, wanders the earth's surface for many years between the action of the two plays, and ends his days in *Colonus* underground, in the sacred grove, a protecting fury and a sacred figure for the land in his bodily infirmity. He now has the capacity, earned in suffering and acceptance, to promote the health of the city of Athens ruled by his "adopted" son, King Theseus. The wounded hero becomes for a time the wounded healer. His wound has carried him to his destiny, one that is not steeped in remorse but one which now allows him " a creative response" (Whitmont, "The Destiny Concept in Psychotherapy," 197) of what he has become. The wounded figure who pleads in *Oedipus Rex*, "Let me slip/from the world of men, vanish without a trace/before I see myself stained with such corruption" (ll. 920–23), becomes a figure whom all will remember at Colonus. In the sacred grove Oedipus will be honored as a chthonic force of healing and an emblem of the painful search for self-knowing.

It seems truer to say that Oedipus *is complex* than to gloss him over as *a complex*; his life has been comprised of crossroads, penetration, wounding, and finally healing. He is wounded in body and then through language; biologically, he penetrates his mother and has four children by her; temporally, he penetrates the present in the past with the swords of language to reveal his true identity; he penetrates his own seeing; and finally he penetrates the earth herself in burial, having been cleansed of pollution, cleansed by his daughter in a ritual baptism and ritually called to the earth by the gods and placed within her by Theseus at the end of *Oedipus at Colonus*. His language now reflects a deeply self-aware and soulful perspective, what Hillman describes as an underworld perspective or way of seeing (*Dream*, 46); it is to see with the eyes of soul rather than with the vision of intellect; Oedipus' shift in vision radically alters his life's trajectory and points him inwardly to the sacred and to home—the sanctified place of the grove at Colonus.

4

Speak Daggers But Use None

Denmark's Wounded Body

From the city the dying groan, and the throat of the
wounded cries for help.

—Job, 24:12

In few of Shakespeare's plays does the body's relationship to the city or
the kingdom receive such close poetic scrutiny as it does in *Hamlet*. The
large concern in the tragedy's action is the displacement, or debasement of
matter itself, and its relation to *mater*, to Hamlet's mother Gertrude, and to
the pollution that attends the murder of a king by his brother, with the
queen as the prize of his violation. Such usurpation is a witness to the disintegration of an established order, and, if we understand it more univer-
sally, to the collapse of a worldview.

In *Hamlet*, pollution, poison, corruption, dirt, defects of nature, appetite, uncertainty, a mote or speck of dust, all emerge to trouble the
mind's eye and the flesh's ear. The usurping King Claudius warns his
nephew not to look for his father in the dust; Hamlet's soliloquies focus
on the flesh melting, the garden of state and nature remains unweeded,
neglected; the sheets of his mother's bed are soiled and incestuous, the ear
is poisoned, nature is defected and corrupted, crimes are most foul, the
world has become a giant riddle, and indeed, something, we do not yet
know the full implications of what, is decomposing in the state of Denmark. The matter of the play is the state or condition of matter itself; it is
without doubt one of the most recurring terms in the entire tragic action,
underpinning it and giving many of the major speeches their clearest
focus. In a tribute entitled "Loving Shakespeare," the playwright, Harold
Pinter believes that Shakespeare's work is always exploring the cut, the affliction: "Shakespeare writes of the open wound and, through him, we
know it open and know it closed. We tell when it ceases to beat and tell it
at its highest peak of fever" (4). Tragedy's most noticeable hallmark may

then be the open wound, polluted and festering on a personal and political level.

The king has been murdered and matter itself is most fouled. Hamlet's initial response to such pollution is to begin to abandon his own flesh in an attempt to escape the soiling. It is to this relation to matter, to the body most foul, to sacrifice and to the feminine violated that I wish to focus in this chapter. In some ways Shakespeare's vision in *Hamlet* is double; one poetic eye is on the Middle Ages with its emblems of order and degree; the other is clearly concentrated in modernity, on a world fragmented, with no shared myth to contain its motion or its direction. Between such disparate ports must Hamlet attempt to cleanse a city which has been violated; the political body is now infected with the microbe of murder and usurpation.

Clearly aligned with a fantasy of idealism, Hamlet must face the polluted body of nature and city; as a figure presaging the rise of the Romantic individual, Hamlet has in his temperament what Alfred de Vigny sees as the main characteristic of the modern self: "It is the misfortune of the imagination of enthusiasm to be misplaced in a vulgar and materialistic society" (qtd. in Watt, 223), he wrote; Hamlet, ahead of the other fictional Romantic figures, must suffer the slings of imperfection and finally enter into the ritual act of murder in order to salvage Denmark. Said another way, Hamlet must repeat the trauma to the state, where the word "trauma" is the Greek word for "wound" (Seltzer, *Serial Killers*, 254).

Wound begets wound so that a healing cure can be formulated; again, it must swirl around the figure of the queen, the occasion of the first wound, the murder of Claudius. Hamlet must wound the wound first with words then with action, so to say, as the cathartic action to rid the state of its poison, much like snake venom may be the necessary curative. He must double the original trauma to break the community from its poisoned state. Eros in both woundings is not far from violence.

What, then, does Shakespeare want us to apprehend in this most soiled of plays, an action in which matter itself seems most insistently explored, which bespeaks a foul contagion in the order of things? Not only matter but even time itself is out of joint; Hamlet, in a strained, ambivalent attitude, curses the cosmos because he has somehow been chosen to set things right, to reestablish a beneficent order of Being to a contagion most foul. He must heal the wounds of Denmark while not tainting his own mind.

Like his prototype Orestes of Aeschylus' *Libation Bearers* before him, Hamlet has been chosen by forces beyond himself; but with the young prince the rub is that instead of enjoying the clarity of Apollo's oracle to direct him, he is instead mired in the ambiguity of a ghost's guiding words. The ghost of his father is a figure who is neither corpse nor living body but inhabits a liminal ground somewhere between life and death. The play's entire action, in fact, is one of trying to deal with being in-between, neither here nor there, at a crossroads, neither past nor future. The spectral body of his father haunts the son's vision of justice.

Who is he to trust when deceit abounds around him? Clearly Hamlet's task is more difficult than that of his Greek progenitor; to slay his mother is Orestes' charge. But the ghost tells Hamlet to provoke his mother's guilt, to speak daggers, to wound her ear with them, but use none, to be content with the metaphor, not the literal wounding. He may use his words to wound but refrain from engaging the sword. The tragic action stretches from Mycenae to Denmark through the same archetype of violence and pollution. The Dionysian god of tragedy, and of the body as locus of sacrifice, mutilation, dismemberment, and as the vehicle for pollution, sexuality, and hiddenness, is very much a part of both young men's roles in reestablishing and perhaps redefining justice.[1]

Hamlet knows that the body of his city is ill, that it has been polluted, and that it needs to be cleansed without destroying its very nature. What he does not yet realize, however, is that this same city disease is already infecting his own sense of the body in his desire to separate his own matter from spirit. The drama discloses Shakespeare's astute sense of the relation between the city and the flesh as metaphors of one another's condition, a theme that gains fuller status in *The Merchant of Venice*. That play deals not only with the pound of flesh that Shylock demands for justice, but also with the unclean body of the Jew in Venice in the seventeenth century.[2]

Such an attitude infecting Hamlet invades his own bearing toward the flesh that will eventually demand a violent purging. The tragedy is therefore as much about redefining the nature of matter and the matter in nature, as it is about moving from an attitude based on revenge to one that revives those medieval values of honor, courtesy, and a sense of grace. But all of the action will be filtered through the body and pollution as the young prince attempts to cleanse the soiled kingdom and his own mother's bed.

Wanting at first to remain unsullied, Hamlet intuits the intimate relationship between the private household and the larger political order. No wonder, then, that so much of the last act haunts the gravesite of Ophelia and the open pit in the earth that is her grave. At this site the images of *mater*, matter, and the earth herself conflate in Hamlet's declared love for his lost love.[3] The play begins, then, on the dark ramparts of the castle with a question, "Who's there?" (1.1.1) as the guards see the ghost; it migrates from there to a remembrance through the decayed body of Yorick, whose skull Hamlet lovingly holds as he reflects on the images of friendship that his former servant offered him.

Hamlet explores a contemporary epidemic: the retrieval of the lived body in a world that constantly threatens its pollution. It is a dirty business, but Hamlet begrudgingly acquiesces to it. The question is: How? Through violence? Through ritual? Blindly? Madly? There exists not only method in his madness but madness in matter itself. His task is to retrieve the matter of the world from madness and at the same time retrieve his own being in embodied remembrance. As he is homeless in Denmark, he is also disembodied, for in his imagination he has abandoned matter herself. Matter, the play suggests, has itself become mad; substance has become demented; the earth staggers with the pollution of the first fall and with the thick reverberations of Cain's envy and then murder of his brother Abel.

Primitive, primordial human violence has penetrated the world's matter; only through the body can it be cleansed. Hamlet is therefore given the task of ritual priest by his father's ghost to cleanse matter itself not by violence but through words. But are words sufficient to heal the wound, or is wounding itself needed as a stronger rhetorical form? It is a daunting task because he believes that such pollution has actually penetrated so deeply into the city's order that it has infected time itself. Disjonted time and polluted matter create a soiled space and time that pleads to be redeemed.

Ritual violence, a Dionysian action, appears to be the only way in to the pollution so that matter itself may be restored, cleansed, and given its place in the world. Can language itself penetrate, wound, and lance the moral ruptures of Claudius' actions, and then redeem the time? If this play exemplifies its generic action, then tragedy insists that we go more deeply into the wound, the infection, the pollution that tragedy forces us to face; to escape from it is to invite its doubling intensity.

Such a penetration, it seems, takes place in this play in two ways: first in dramatic action in the form of the drama Hamlet designs and has the players rehearse, which will bring the king to his feet in guilt and remorse; second, in the ritual slaying of Polonius, which Hamlet must perform. Word must move to deed, to a physical wounding of the body, but a body corrupted, like Polonius, in order to begin a process of healing the polluted corpus of the city. Hamlet must, in effect, repeat the murderous action of his uncle in order to bend Denmark and kingship itself toward cleansing. It is as if the original wound needs to be opened again, punctured, so that its suppuration can be reexperienced on another level.

Archetypal psychologist Mary Watkins suggests that repeating the original wound always contains the promise of breaking into something new, a new awareness instead of being fated to compulsively repeat the original affliction. The second wounding is a way of deeply remembering the original violation; now the affliction can be revisioned, opened up, even revitalized (interview, June 18, 1998). By so doing, the original wounding of King Hamlet by his brother Claudius for both private and public theft of wife and throne by pouring poison into his ear while he sleeps must be atoned for by a second ritual act of wounding that is not motivated by self-interest. The second wounding executed by Hamlet is a sacrifice to appease the gods and the original wound, in order to shift the archetype of king back to the father.

And yet, in the midst of his desire to avenge his father's murder and to reclaim the matter of the world, Hamlet knows deeply, that, as Rene Girard suggests, "If vengeance is an unending process, it can hardly be invoked to restrain the violent impulses of society. In fact, it is vengeance itself that must be restrained" (*Violence and the Sacred*, 17).

I also sense that the first soliloquy of Hamlet has as its central impulse a deep, almost desperate desire to jettison his own embodiment and with it all the diseased matter of his city. Robb Pocklington gets close to the heart of the matter when he writes that "the young prince returns to Denmark from Wittenberg to have his very being ripped from within him. . . . Hamlet ceases to exist at the moment he observes someone else, Claudius, acting in his place" ("The Devil Made Them Do It," 19).

In what way, then, does Hamlet abandon the flesh of the world? What is the nature of this abandonment and what does he see as pollution? More important, how does he then transfer this pollution to the body of Polonius, whom he wounds mortally? Certainly we include here the body of the father whose ear has been polluted with poison at Claudius' hand;[4] the ghost implicates the entire country when he tells his son: "A serpent stung me. So the whole ear of Denmark/Is by a forged process of my death/Rankly abused" (1.5. 36–38); the polluted body of Gertrude, the corrupt body of Claudius, the sacrificial body of Polonius, the discarded body of love in the figure of Ophelia. With all of these figures, language, too, is out of joint. There is false speaking, guileful expression, polluting words. The pollution has infiltrated language itself. Duplicity, false speaking, and guile are now enthroned. In his ritual cleansing, Hamlet must redeem words themselves from further pollution. Poetic, artful, and generous speech will be the antibodies against the diseased ear. Such medicinal speech gathers around the remembered body of the now-decayed Yorick, the heroic body of Laertes, the honorable actions of Fortinbras ready to attack the gates of Denmark to redeem his father's honor, as well as the body of remembrance in Ophelia, as she is brought to rest in the grave.

Not only does incarnation comprise the central lineaments of the drama, it must also become a flesh that remembers. The most potent line that Hamlet utters at the end of the play occurs when he is dying; there he pleads to his philosopher/companion Horatio: "If thou didst ever hold me in thy heart,/Absent thee from felicity awhile,/And in this harsh world draw thy breath in pain,/To tell my story" (5.2.325–28). Hamlet has learned that perhaps the fullest form of embodiment is to be remembered in story, for it is as close to immortality to which a mortal can aspire.

Hamlet wishes his flesh as well as his story to be given a unity, to be enfleshed in narrative, to be gathered up into a sensible form. Embodiment allows him to recover his story and to have it told after his death. His action from Acts 1 to 5 includes a major shift from wishing that his "too too sallied flesh would melt,/Thaw and resolve itself into a dew" (1.2.129–30), to a state of wishing to be remembered through story. His desire swings from being dispersed into space at the beginning, to insisting on being placed at the end of the action. His story, to be told by Horatio and heard by the citizens of Denmark, will act as a soothing salve to heal "the wounded ear" (Kittelson, 55) of the citizens and us as audience. Claudius' act of wounding the king's ear in murder infects all of our hearing. Hamlet's request to be remembered in story is medicinal to the poisoned ear. His request to Horatio not only retrieves the world and sets it right in Act 5; he also retrieves his own mortal flesh in the process. The greatest victory in this action is an integration of his own flesh with the world's body. And it happens through speech and hearing.

Hamlet begins his initiation into polluted Denmark by treating his own body as a corpse, as a way of abandoning it. He ends by treating it as a consciousness with a future and a history. Yorick's skull is the emblematic crossroads of his own narrative biography because it locates Hamlet in a memory and establishes him in a place, giving to his being a local habitation and a name, if not a full identity. On this desire of human beings to be articulated in the world and yet cleansed of its pollution, the French phenomenologist, Merleau-Ponty writes: "My body is made of the same flesh as the world . . . and moreover . . . this flesh of my body is shared by the world" (qtd. in Levin, 66). Flesh, therefore, as David Michael Levin reflects, "is a notion which finally makes it possible for us to articulate the human body with respect to its ontological dimensionality" (Levin, 67).

Pollution, putrefaction, and moral decay are the conditions Hamlet intuits early in the play when he voices his desire in the first soliloquy to escape the body. His is a diagnosis that has its analogue in the condition of the world; it is a decaying place that he compares to "an unweeded garden/That grows to seed. Things rank and gross in nature/Possess it merely" (1.2.135–37). What he senses in himself is the inner moral condition of the outer world, though he cannot prove it; it is an intuition that the ghost gives fuller expression to. But are the words of the ghost trustworthy? Hamlet's original dilemma is not action but belief. What he will come to believe in at the end of the play is matter itself and the importance of his own memory to be deeply embedded in it. Matter may be redeemed through medicinal speech, speech that heals the ear.

A few examples of the play's preoccupation with matter follow to reveal how Shakespeare builds up a totality of effect: Polonius asks his daughter early in the play when she comes to him, "How, now, Ophelia, what's the matter?" (2.1. 73); Polonius asks Hamlet, "What is the matter, my lord?" to which Hamlet answers with a question: "Between who?" and Polonius corrects himself: "I mean the matter that you read, my lord" (2.2.191–93); Hamlet responds to the request of Rosencrantz and Guildenstern to wait on him, "No such matter" (2.2.256); he responds later to the same two men: "Therefore no more, but to the matter. My mother,/you say—" (3.2.295–96); and shortly after he asks Gertrude: "Now, mother, what's the matter?" (3.4.7); when she becomes alarmed at her son's discourse with the ghost, he responds: "I the matter will re-word, which madness/Would gambol from" (3.4.147–48); as he soon instructs her on how to behave toward the king, he advises her: "Make you to ravel all this matter out,/That I essentially am not in madness" (3.4.190–92); when a messenger presents himself to the king, Claudius questions, "What is the matter?" (4.5.96); the clown at Ophelia's gravesite comments that Hamlet has gone to England to have his wits restored, but "if a do not, 'tis no great matter there" (5.1.130); and Hamlet to Claudius before the duel says "What is the reason that you use me thus?/I loved you ever. But it is no matter" (5.1.267–68). Clearly matter in either its absence or presence gives direction to the entire action.

What the world's body yearns for in order to redeem matter is a sacrifice to cleanse both self and world of the disease that infects all of its parts. But a sacrifice done in vengeance is a dangerous move, for, as Girard observes, "everytime it turns up in some part of the community, it threatens to involve the whole social body. There is the risk that [it] will initiate a chain reaction whose consequences will quickly prove fatal to any society of modest size" (*Violence and The Sacred*, 15). To decontaminate the body is, in Hamlet's imagination, to decontaminate Being itself. Pollution is a dicey element to deal with because, like any form of stain, it can render oblivious the object of its taintedness if the proper methods are not used to eradicate it.[5]

In his fascinating study, *Origins of the Sacred*, Dudley Young illustrates how complex is the nature of pollution in observing that its root meaning suggests "a coming into presence of the usually absent divinity"; it also carries an ambiguous shadow, "the possibility of a spasm that may kill or cure, or kill as it cures" (232). The original meaning of the term "pollution" derives from the Latin *pollure,* meaning "to defile." But it is also linked to *pollere,* to be powerful. Pollution is then an injection of strength which disorders. The word "pollution" in every culture means the bad breath of divinity, an infectious, contagious affliction that calls for quarantine and cleansing (catharsis) of all exposed to it (234). And may that bad breath enter the community through soiled words to the ear?

The question that *Hamlet* asks us to meditate on could perhaps be phrased this way: How is the human being fouled, made dirty, tainted? and its corollary: How does one find the appropriate and least destructive contrary act or element of purification? One possible suggestion is that the ultimate dirt, decay, and dust are the ultimate elements or conditions that we are finally to return to. Our origin is indeed our destiny.

Yet even more important for Hamlet's future, some form of dismemberment, sacrifice, or pulling apart is necessary "for awakening the consciousness of the body," as James Hillman has observed. His presence in Denmark may then be likened to the entrance of Dionysus, known as a god who loosens, sets free, delivers, dissolves, collapses, breaks bonds and laws, "the final unraveling as of a plot in tragedy" ("Notes on Opportunism," 162). What Hamlet as Dionysus who once again gains consciousness of himself as an incarnated being must do is disseminate this consciousness into all the corners of the deadened city, much like Polynices' body was carried by animals throughout Thebes, because the pollution itself is ubiquitous. Such action culminates in the slaying of Polonius as sacrificial object of Dionysus in order to free the city from the stranglehold of pollution. Cleansing a city is a dirty business as well as a thickly mythical action and inaugurates a counter-archetypal action of violence that restores.

Dirt, Mary Douglas writes in her excellent study of pollution, "is never a unique isolated event; where there is dirt, there is a system" (*Purity and Danger,* 35) either condemning or condoning it. To confront a culture's dirt is already to enter into how a people understands purity, cleanness, even a moral hygiene of the soul. Dirt, pollution, or an invasion of impurities are testimony to a symbolic system of values that guide a people and further what might be called their collective myth.

Hamlet is thus a paradigm for the tragedy of defilement; in one sense Hamlet is the poetic and dramatic stepson of *Oedipus Rex.* To be soiled is in some mysterious way to return to the soil, to the ground of earth herself; it is to be reanchored back into the world through the most originary form—the body itself. Soiling makes us aware once again of our ephemeral embodiment and our sentient being, of how fragile is our embeddedness in time. In our soiledness is a memory of our future. Perhaps tragedy even addresses, in this act of soiling, the possibility that earth herself has been displaced, made homeless, and is therefore seeking her right place. Tragedy may even bring the earth back home even, as in *Hamlet,* Ophelia's ritually being brought into the earth creates a sacred ground in which Laertes and Hamlet begin to coalesce in their authentic love for her. Her memory provokes a stronger declaration of love for her perhaps because it is addressed to her dead body. I would suggest that in her death language itself is redeemed through Hamlet's and Laertes' declarations of love for her, within the wound in the earth herself, a cavity made to receive Ophelia's dead body.

Make the city right again, the ghost of his father admonishes his son, but in the process, "Taint not thy mind, nor let thy soul contrive/Against thy mother aught. Leave her to heaven" (1.5.85–86). This admonition appears only after a thick accretion of images to underscore the depth of the pollution in a whole litany of words like "foul," "unnatural," "garbage," "incestuous," "adulterate beast," "curd." Many of these images of violation and pollution swirl around Hamlet's own decree about his own embodiment: "My fate cries out/And makes each petty artery in this body/As hardy as the Nemean lion's nerve" (1.5.82–84). To which the ghost of Hamlet pushes the body image into that of the state itself, as was cited earlier: "So the whole ear of Denmark/Is by a forged process of my death/Rankly abused" (1.5.36–38).

Now his father, in ghostly guise, is perhaps the most unnatural figure in the play. Patricia Berry refers to him as "an imaginal presence, like a hallucination or a vision or a dream image" ("Hamlet's Poisoned Ear," 145). As such, he is a vague, ambiguous figure from the terrain of the supernatural, an emissary perhaps from divinity itself. He is also a spiritualized or imaginal body, insubstantial but real. Furthermore, as he relates to his son, he is in transition himself as a kind of halfway figure occupying the liminal space of the earth, the ground of matter.

An anomaly, the ghost of Hamlet's father may be a creation of the pollution itself. Said another way, the ghost is an image of pollution and violation; he is the ambiguous image of death in life and life in death. What he says, therefore, must be equated with the voice of ambiguity itself. The ghost is an in-between figure, not a person but not a corpse or a dead body, either. He is, to broaden the argument to include the genre in its form, the image and voice of ambiguity itself, for the ghost embodies in spectral garb the transitional nature of values being realigned in a new world cleansed from the decay of being, itself. And the question around him remains: Are his words to be trusted, are they medicinal, or are they further pollution for the ear?

If Mary Douglas is correct in her observation that uncleanness is matter out of place, then pollution is the primordial presence of boundary fragmentation and breakdown. Matter flows into itself with no boundaries, no limits; all becomes ambiguous and nothing is certain. Words themselves enter the pollution and are consequently tainted and untrustworthy, loaded with ambivalence and perhaps concealing more than what they reveal. Authenticity in speech or action promises a quick and short avenue to extinction. Needed, therefore, is a ritual cleansing that will be powerful enough to permeate the entire anatomy of the corporeal body. And Hamlet, poet that he is, seizes on the first step, a public display in which the guilty will be forced to disclose themselves: a play will unveil by imitation the killing of Hamlet's father; the key action is performed by Lucianus, who Hamlet explains to Ophelia, is "nephew to the king" (3.2.223).

The ritual of cleansing begins with Hamlet himself in the role of the ritual poisoner of the king's ear. Therefore, in a fiction, in a feigned performance, a *mimesis* of the actual poisoning, to paraphrase Polonius, Hamlet skillfully uses drama as a tool of indirection by which Claudius' guilty action is uncovered. The source of the pollution is identified in a dramatic probing through both gesture and speech that seems to poison Claudius' ear with the truth of his actions. The source of the pollution is rather quickly diagnosed. The malady of matter is now prepared for surgery, so to speak, and Hamlet is to fill the role of surgeon to remove it, an appropriate dramatic sequence to the ritual of the drama that identified the ailment. If the king does not bolt at the player's speech Hamlet has written, "then my imaginations are as foul as Vulcan's stithy" (3.2.73–74). We remember in Hamlet's simile that it was Vulcan, the imperfect or wounded artisan, who was able to craft the shield of Achilles, who formed on its surface images of an entire world containing scenes of both strife and peace. In like manner is Hamlet the playwright re-creating the world in dramatic form.

If the ghost of Hamlet's father is the figure of displacement in pollution, so too is the play within a play. Luciano recites his lines and gives voice in the process to "Hecate's nature Thrice blasted/Thrice infected" (3.2.235–36).

The king will shortly pray in order to attempt self-expiation, but his words and thoughts remain split within the diseased kingly body; his pollution is too deep to eradicate and he despairs of succeeding. His inauthentic words wither immediately.

Nothing short of a ritual sacrifice will suffice because the infection has grown so intense that even the source of the illness is incapable of reversing its deadly progression. A kind of moral metastasis has crippled the body politic. It is therefore poetically appropriate that, sparing his uncle under the assumption that his prayers are sincere, Hamlet goes to his mother's chamber to work his words into her diseased ear and once again, by indirection, force the pollution into public hearing.

Just before entering Gertrude's closet, it might be well to survey the polluted spaces in *Hamlet*. The world of the dead's boundary and the world of the living is polluted by the ghost; he is the drawstring that pulls eternity and temporality together; the boundaries of Denmark are being polluted by the encroaching force of Fortinbras; the internal boundaries of family are polluted by Polonius' spying on his own son. He instructs Reynaldo: "Put on such forgeries you please; marry none so *rank as may dishonor him*"

(2.1.20–21), and shortly after: "Lay these sallies on my son/As twere a thing a little soiled in the working" (2.1. 39–40). Also soiled are the boundaries of love between Ophelia and Hamlet and their impending marriage; the boundaries between son and mother, between nephew and uncle, between friend and friend, between life and death, between spirit and flesh.

Boundary pollution seems often essential for tragedy; it reveals a breakdown of the entire social and spiritual worlds where new boundaries may grow from the chaotic shake-up of norms. But in the process, no system is safe and no relationship protected from the effects of such pollution, which for Hamlet is located in the body, in Being itself. Claudius, like all great polluters, is doubly dangerous, for he performs two distinct acts in polluting: He crosses a line that is ritually taboo; he endangers others in that action, which marginalizes his subjects and casts to the periphery those values a culture needs to survive and which are most effectively reinforced through ritual observance.

Hamlet's language, when he is beckoned by Rosencrantz, and then when he enters Gertrude's closet, is critical, for it underlines the central place of matter itself in the action. As he says to Rosencrantz when he receives Gertrude's summons: "you shall command, or rather, as you/say, my mother. Therefore no more, but to the matter. My mother,/you say—" (3.2.293–95). Language tumbles over and doubles on itself, phrases turn themselves inside out here and in other passages. Doubling, repeating, mirroring, inverting inform the action, as fiction and fact drift in and out of each other's landscape. Not only time but language is out of joint. Words seem double-jointed and invert one another in phrases that reverse one another's order. At this point in the drama all is unmoored, free-floating, and in danger of destruction even as they seek some redeeming certainty.

The king's offense is fully vented as Hamlet pauses to slay the king on his journey to Gertrude's space; the stench of crime now surfaces and takes on the force of language: "O, my offense is rank, it smells to heaven;/It hath the primal eldest curse upon't,/A brother's murder" (3.3.36–38). Ritual sacrifice is now the only antibody for this primal curse, and it falls to Hamlet to redeem matter itself. The "discursive space" (Stallybrass and White, 80) of Gertrude's closet and Ophelia's tomb are two pivotal psychological places wherein somatic symbols and memory are clearly intensified; they are also the places of violence and dead bodies as ritual killing and ritual burial are the predominant actions. Finally, they are places of acute cleansings even while both women will die as ransom for the city's expurgation of the political malady.

In addition, to speak of his mother's space, Gertrude's image coalesces the relation of matter and mother. As such, it seems most mythically powerful, even appropriate, that the ritual sacrifice of another to cleanse matter itself occur here. Patricia Berry has written on the paradox of matter/mother in the West, signifying both something and nothing, or a lacking. She writes that "Mother/matter is the ground of existence. . . . When we get close to our 'matter,' our lower substrates, our roots, our past, the ground from which we came, our lower physical nature . . . it is not surprising that we feel something unsettling, something inferior, chaotic, soiled perhaps" ("What's the Matter with Mother?" 3). The large hinge on which the action of the tragedy swings is located here in Gertrude's room. If a ritual cleansing of the kingdom is to ensue, let it be most fully complete where matter and mother congregate in an unsettling, even marginal, space.[6] But we should not lose sight of the fact that Gertrude is Hamlet's origin, so her closet has a very primordial quality to it, a deep return to beginnings for him.

His first words set the issue squarely before her and the audience: "Now, mother, what's the matter?" (3.4.8); and a few lines further: "What's the matter now?" (3.4.12). But matter also has an interior dimension that its exterior surface hides, and so Hamlet wishes all of matter to be revealed through his mother: "You go not till I set you up a glass/Where you may see the inmost part of you" (3.4.19–20).

The presence of someone invisibly present behind the curtain in her room immediately after Hamlet's arrival and accusation invites speculation that Polonius is the image of corruption here. He will now become the sacrificial victim in the violent process of cleansing. Hamlet is now to venture deeply into the land's violation by ritually murdering Polonius, even as he wonders if it is the king behind the curtain. What is in the "inmost part" of Gertrude finds its correlative in the scheming Polonius behind the curtain. He occupies that liminal space on stage but hidden, neither truly off nor on stage.

Hamlet then, slays the father of his love, Ophelia, in the presence of his mother; but for an instant, in the act of slaying, he wonders aloud: "Is it the king?" (3.4.27). Only by entering physically, bodily, into avenging the slaying of his father *by himself slaying a father*, do Hamlet, his mother, and matter itself have any real hope for complete regeneration through cleansing. The action and momentum of tragic action allows no detours. Hamlet must enter fully into the pollution through sacrifice and then voice it in language, an action that Claudius has struggled mightily against. It is appropriate, too, that Hamlet slays Polonius without ever *seeing* him; he only hears him and responds to his cries by thrusting through the curtain. Voice, cries, words, not vision is dominant here as Hamlet enters into the pollution of Denmark through sound rather than sight.

Hamlet then very shortly speaks the nature of his crime, almost relishing the blood of murder: " How stand I then,/That have a father killed, a mother stained,/Excitements of my reason and my blood" (4.4.56–58). "O from this time forth,/My thoughts be bloody, or be nothing worth!" (4.4.64–65). Mythically he has entered completely into the presence of Dionysus, into an underworld consciousness, and there assumed the dismembering god's mantle. In so doing, he brings Gertrude down with him, into facing her own guilt in the crime against the political order, as she is loathe to confess: "To my sick soul, as sin's true nature is" (4.5.17). Gertrude collapses under the assault of words and begs her son: "O Hamlet, speak no more!/Thou turn'st my eyes into my very soul" (3.4.89–90). Whipped into a frenzy at this point, her son gives her no quarter as he disgorges in language the corruption of eros through her acts with the king. Images of body fluids, animal grunts, mud mixed with garbage, waste, all constellate here in a conflagration of putrid bodily miasma: "Nay, but to live/In the rank sweat of an enseamed bed/Stewed in corruption, honeying and making love/Over the nasty sty—" (3.4.93–95). He also uses the language of his own madness, which will "but skin and film the ulcerous place/Whiles rank corruption, Mining all within,/Infects unseen" (3.4.149–53). The slaying and the language is full of dead, decaying matter, which in its presence Hamlet begins his journey back into the world through murder.

The ghost, an insubstantial voice that only Hamlet sees and hears, pleads for his son not to bring Gertrude to despair. As Hamlet acquiesces, he confesses that he is not mad. If she does not believe him, then "Bring me to the test,/And I the matter will re-word, which madness would gambol from. Mother, for love of grace/Lay not that flattering unction to your soul" (3.4.146–49).

What has the capacity to redeem matter is the presence of grace, the most effective antibody to place matter's decay into remission. But this action could not occur without Hamlet first entering fully and bodily into the very act he has dedicated himself to avenging. Like his prototype, Orestes in Aeschylus' *Libation Bearers*, and his future image in Raskolnikov in Dostoevsky's *Crime and Punishment*, Hamlet pushes justice to a higher level through the sacrifice of Polonius and to the wounding of his mother's ear with the truth of her complicity.

Said another way, only when her son enters into the pollution that slayed his own father does the act of purgation grow strong. The act of killing the king in his imagination and Polonius *in fact*, is part of the primitive ritual that cannot be eluded if a true and lasting healing or decontamination is to revive Denmark. But first through the ritual slaying the margins and boundaries of Denmark have to be further violated and dissolved for any sense of the sacred, for grace, to be reinstalled within effective leadership. Douglas refers to this movement as instilling a "creative formlessness" into the culture (161) wherein power itself is risked in this dangerous and tentative boundary-shifting phase of pollution and cleansing. She extends this idea to suggest that "purity is the enemy of change, of ambiguity, of compromise" (*Purity and Danger*, 162). Safety resides in a life of fixed forms: danger and impurity are always present in transition when values are shifting.

Killing Polonius is then a sacrifice that takes place in the margins; it is a murder in metaxis, an in-between killing that is shored up on one side by the murder of King Hamlet and on the other by the now-open poisoned rapiers of Laertes and Hamlet and in the cup of poison mistakenly drunk by Gertrude amidst the king's silence, as well as the poisoned stabbing of Claudius himself. Pollution breaks viciously open once Polonius is slain. He is the catalyst for expelling all boundaries and allowing Fortinbras finally to enter Denmark unchallenged. He will bring with him a code of honor and retribution through the memory of his slain father and bless the actions of Hamlet, his Danish prototype. Mortally wounding Polonius is analogous to lancing a boil, expelling the pent-up poisons. Hamlet's pen and rapier puncture the pollution.

The imaginative ritual action of Hamlet's is essential because it consolidates the boundaries of drama and the world of everyday life. It also sets the stage for a retrieval of the body and matter itself through a series of woundings and poisonings. The now-dead body of Polonius liberates Hamlet from the festering pollution of Denmark. The young prince's language grows more certain, more even and controlled even as it treats lightly and comically the corpse of his victim.

When the king interrogates Hamlet as to the location of Polonius, Hamlet responds: "At supper." To which the king asks: "At supper? Where?" and Hamlet: "Not where he eats, but where 'a is eaten. A certain convocation of politic worms are e'en at him" (4.3.17–20). The body rhetoric intensifies as Hamlet offers that he wanted to show "how a king may go a progress through the guts of a beggar" (4.3.29) and, that if they wished to find the body, time will make it possible to "nose him as you go/up the stairs into the lobby" (4.3.34). Smell of decay and pollution now literally begin to saturate the castle. The interior moral pollution has been made overt and exterior through Hamlet's action. Its container weakened, it spills into areas that the king and queen would have preferred remain virginal.

Social pollution will be cleansed by the growing presence of honor and the retrieval of grace as restorative alternatives to vengeance. Mary Douglas adds another element here from her study of pollution in suggesting that whenever a culture is in transit from a state of pollution to purification, the members of that community are often marginalized, decentered, and perhaps recomposed. Transition and displacement are certainly part of this drama and perhaps of the genre of tragedy generally.

Matter itself in the form of the innocent Ophelia and the shamed but repentant Gertrude must also be sacrificed. This shame, as Patricia Berry writes, "is a way into the experience of mother earth" ("What's the Matter with Mother," 6). The gravesite is the earth's wound, a hole dug into her, a container not only of Ophelia but the place for Hamlet and Laertes to exchange expressions of love and honor to redeem the city. As her shame is felt for the first time through her son's words at almost the moment that Polonius is slain, and that Hamlet's grief over the loss of Ophelia at her gravesite prompts him to ask Laertes for forgiveness and to struggle with him for the sake of honor, Denmark begins to be restored to what matters.

Matter itself is redeemed, in part because love is remembered and a sense of honorable behavior is restored. Act 5 is full of images of death, of the earth, of remembrance and of wounding. Remembrance redeems the violence through the empty grave of Ophelia. As her father served in his ritual slaying to loosen the hold of pollution on Denmark, so does Ophelia redeem this action, giving ritual and remembrance, as well as love, a place. Burying her is a profound ritual act of remembering; through Ophelia Hamlet asks to be remembered and to have this drama told. Love is restored in Act 5 because the source of pollution has been excised. Matter is made whole and sacred through the request of Hamlet to Horatio to tell his story. Narrative itself, Shakespeare reveals in this very self-conscious play, is the most secure antibiotic to further infections. Poetic narrative may be absolutely essential for a culture or a people so they are not victimized by appetites and self-seeking rulers.

Hamlet's last words, uttered from his mortally wounded self, solidify two central aspects of healing. In writing of how traditions are kept alive in cultures, David Levin observes how "the body is a primary ritual bearer, and original metaphorical text, of such transmission" (*Body's Recollection*, 170–71). Hamlet's great contribution to his community is that he embodies the values of their tradition that have been occluded by violence. He has, through his own sacrifice, redeemed both language and matter through the body. If we think of stories, especially those related orally, which is what Hamlet requests of Horatio, then stories themselves are ritualized ways of re-membering the past, putting the past back together in a new form. Hamlet's story will now be given a home through Horatio's remembrance. Could it have been born without his entering the wounds of Denmark and then inflicting his own deadly wounds on Polonius and Laertes? Does Shakespeare wish us to understand the inherent wounds in stories, wounds that precipitate narratives? Within such remembrance, the community will indeed once again matter; through the violence and wounding of many victims, Denmark has emerged with a different, more honorable story through which to survive and prosper. A new social and political order begins to seep through the wounds of Denmark.

The following chapter will explore both the psychic wounds of Rousseau as well as his own internal body obstructions and their relation to the city of Paris. Rousseau's cleansing of his own history through self-storying has its civic analogue in the invention of the Paris sewer system. As such, the analogy I explore is not far removed from the polluted city of Denmark. Both Denmark and Paris are concerned with expelling waste.

5

Rousseau's *Confessions*

Autobiography, Body Cleansing, and the Invention of the Paris Sewer System

An old doctor says, "Health is a precarious state for man
that bodes no good."
　　　　　—Guido Ceronetti, *The Silence of the Body,* 56

No matter what response is elicited from readers of *The Confessions*, it almost always takes some form of exasperation, confusion, impatience, even if the degree of intensity varies. "Get a life!" one student shouted out during class in her frustration because of Rousseau's seeming long-windedness and his hedging, patronizing voice. He seems to many ears to yammer incessantly about his pitiful beginnings, his unfortunate nomadic adolescence, and his persecuted personal life as he matures into middle age.

He feels as well the rhythms of revolt internally, when he informs us that a malformed bladder from birth begins to take on a life of its own and directs his feelings as well as his memories; like the disease that infects Ivan Ilych, Rousseau's agitated and stubborn bladder (he suffered from uremia) shifts his entire way of seeing himself, the rapidly changing world around him, and his relation to others. *The Confessions* might be viewed as much as a diagnosis of his physical maladies as it is a record of Rousseau's own achievements and failures. It is certainly an embodied narrative that seeks to define the figure of Rousseau, who in his physical and psychological ailments seeks some form of cleansing by writing his autobiography. Aristotle and others before him understood how confession and catharsis are so frequently two sides of the same act of self-exposure.

The Confessions is no less a profound psychological work. Rousseau's deep penetration of his own psyche anticipates not only the Romantic emphasis on feelings, on trusting sensibility over all forms of thought, but also the depth psychology of Carl Jung and the archetypal psychology of James

Hillman, Thomas Moore, and Robert Sardello.[1] *The Confessions* may be considered an originary text of psyche that explores the complex interiority of one soul to see its reflection and refraction in the culture of France that was about to explode out of its own rigid boundaries with the energy and fluids of liberty, equality, and a newfound interest in and respect for the common person. Rousseau certainly reflects the voice of the common man coming to know himself, the self-made individual who in his common roots feels a destiny to his life that gathers power and multiplicity as it grows from the acorn of its original beginnings.[2]

Irving Babbit's observation in *Rousseau and Romanticism* is as relevant now as it was when it was first published in 1955: "Now nothing is more private and distinctive in a man than his feelings, so that to be unique meant practically for Rousseau and his followers to be unique in feeling. Feeling alone they felt was vital and immediate" (80). Rousseau's desire to connect all men under a universal sympathy found its home in the connection of the senses, "something that is, in short, intuitive and immediate" (80). Deep and shared feelings are what bind the common person to others and to greatness. Sensibility is the code of democracy and it is always and primarily an embodied code, one that the flesh reveals. Feelings themselves might be understood as the middle term between thought and flesh, ideas and incarnation; feelings bridge flesh and thought so that the inside of an individual can find expression in the world at large. The body is then "the primary ritual bearer and original metaphorical text" and "exists at the very source of all of our knowledge," writes Levin (171). Sensibility is an incarnational response to the world. And we, as readers of Rousseau's confessions, must, as he instructs us, judge him, finally. His task is no less than to bring the textual body into the culture so to reflect and refract it through the soul of one individual.

The areas I wish to explore through Rousseau's self writing include his relation to language as it creates both himself and his audience through the technology of a book, his own embodiment, and the city; none of these three arenas is separated in the sensibility of Rousseau. They are his idea of language, especially its powerful ability to create worlds of meaning that retrieve, even reinvent, intense feelings that far transcend those accompanying the original event that is later recollected, recast, and re-membered in language. At times it must even be "embellished," as Rousseau himself admits.

Along with this project to retrieve the past in its feeling sensations, Rousseau is also interested in uniting both the audience and himself in a conspiracy of self-creation as well as a creation of the "Other"; his relation to his own sense of embodiment, which includes a growing desire to abandon it for a pure form of liberty; and the invention of the Paris sewer system, an enormous project of waste management whose desire is to purify the city, and whose outward creation reflects one of the essential purposes of autobiography: a form of autobiographical waste management. Jung's psychic admonition of "as above, so below," might be extended here to include "as within, so without."

This same desire for purification is a complex controlling cultural and personal metaphor that is built into the intentions of *The Confessions*. Its author appears determined to exonerate himself, to cleanse his history and prove once and for all time his purity of heart in the social eye, as well as to remove the obstructions from his own bladder. His disease, in other words, implicates his culture, his own psychology, and his autobiographical project. In the process he wishes to redeem the self that is Jean-Jacques Rousseau, and to make transparent his shame by holding it up for close inspection to the perceiving eye of the reading audience, flood it with minute details, retrieve the feeling that gives it its energy, and then ask the reader to judge the results. *The Confessions* I therefore want to envision as a linguistic construction, an elaborate and labyrinthine container, of waste management on several levels; language itself, in a cooperative project with memory and imagination, may be the linguistic catheter that unblocks obstruction to allow or encourage the flow of Rousseau's interiority to reach the sensibilities of his audience, whom he insists, must pass judgment on him after he has reported all the facts of his life, down to the most minute detail, however embellished they might become in the telling.

The sewer system's creation under the city of Paris and Rousseau's constricted body are two sides of a common concentration on waste, its blockage and its flow, and the problems dealing with its accumulation and expulsion. As John Sturrock has written, "the autobiographer is seeking to plot the course of his remembered life after the event(s); he is, by virtue of his calling, a conspiracy theorist" (27). Thinking of Rousseau in particular he writes that "his conviction of his own uniqueness is underwritten by his anxiety to rescue his self-image from the custody of others" (27).

Autobiography is not just a remembrance of who and what one was; it is an elaborately created fiction that implicates the entire context out from which it appears; not what was lived is the fundament of autobiography, but *the life created* out of that living, most emphatically in its embodied feeling aspects as the centerpiece of the self-narrative. Rousseau's autobiography is not just a personal expression, "expressing inner dynamics, but a cultural product as well" (Sturrock, 39). Rousseau illustrates emphatically the unique nature of the individual who is pulled from anonymity through the expression of remembered experiences, who cannot be separated from the large cultural metaphors surrounding one and conspiring, themselves, to create the individual.[3] As such, his *Confessions* is an elaborate expression of psychological and social hygiene. As a written text, a body of language, Rousseau's *Confessions* has its own subtle reality different from oral expression. As the musings of Gaston Bachelard reveal, "Written language must be considered as a particular psychic reality" (*Poetic Imagination,* 102). He further asks us to pay attention to our own relation to the written word, especially when it takes the form of a book: "The best proof of a book's specific existence is that it is at once a reality of the virtual and a virtuality of the real. . . . Books place us in another life that makes us suffer, hope, sympathize"(102). The shape of Rousseau's *Confessions* must therefore be seen as partly fiction, but also more centrally as an organic extension of his own embodiment. Through written language, he incarnates himself forth into the world; the text is the witness of, and as a metaphor for, his own incarnated presence long after he is dead. The body of Rousseau takes the form of language here and shapes his reality for us in what might be called a long and deep reverie of his imagined self.

At this juncture we should pause to recall another great autobiography written by a man at about the same point in his life as Rousseau was in his when he undertook the project of life writing. Carl Jung's *Memories, Dreams, Reflections* is as profound in its depths as Rousseau's inner exploration. In his own deeply elaborate self-reflection, Jung reminds us that "everything in the unconscious seeks outward manifestation" (47). How much of Rousseau's outpourings are conscious, how much unconscious, may be difficult to discern. But those contents in the deeper cavities of his being have their own desire to become transparent, to be flushed from the reservoir of his own psyche.

In a book that is one of hundreds to examine this rich period of the eighteenth century, a time when so many of the properties of the postmodern world were fertilized, brooded upon, and developed, Stephen Cox's *The Stranger Within Thee: Concepts of the Self in Late 18th. Century Literature* illustrates that the consciousness of this period stressed "sensibility" as a key attitude in the search for self. The true self develops through sensibility, that is, how the self apprehends the world. "Sensibility is like sympathy," he writes. "It is an impulse that connects the inner with the outer world" (9). For the Enlightenment, the individual self gathers great inherent worth. Lord Shaftesbury writes at this time: "I am more freed in the esteem of what depends on my self alone, and if I have once gained the *taste* of Liberty, I shall know . . . both my true Self and interest" (qtd. in *The Stranger Within Thee,* 17). Sensibility in Enlightenment life is both an ethical and a psychological concept, one that is embodied deeply in the flesh of understanding and perception at a time which gave "a mystique of the individual self," a "sacred significance to the Self" (Cox, 47). Rousseau played this side of the street of the culture in order to give to the commonness of his own humble and precarious beginnings the sacred dimension that valuing the individual self allowed.

Jean Starobinski writes one of the most trenchant books on the psychology of Rousseau in which he reveals that Rousseau desired not just communication but a *transparency of the heart* (*Jean-Jacques Rousseau*, 24). His desire is not to avoid subjectivity, but to pass beyond "self-forgetfulness that has made us other than ourselves" (Morrisey, xi) in order to find the true self. Rousseau is the first full expression, Morrisey writes in the Preface, of the "modern consciousness as it manifests itself in literature" (xxiv). Rousseau pushes language beyond simply an instrument for conveying information. According to Starobinski, in *The Confessions*, "the writer singles himself out through his work and calls forth assent to the truth of his personal experience. . . . He was the first to experience the dangerous compact between ego and language, the 'new alliance' in which man makes himself the word" (Morrisey, xxiv). The flesh becomes word and the individual becomes the object of his own creation, an act of self-refracting that is as dramatic as it is effective in creating the self as an imperfect, albeit very complex and paradoxical fiction.

Look, for example, at what Rousseau writes in his *Discourse on the Origin of Inequality* which antedates by two hundred years the media marketing of the self and the full-blown invention of the celebrity: "It was necessarily to one's advantage to seem to be other than what one was *in fact*. To be and to appear became two completely different things" (42). Or again, in a letter to his friend D'Alembert, in 1758:

> What is the talent of the actor? the art of counterfeiting himself, of putting on another character than his own, of appearing different than he is, of becoming passionate in cold blood, of saying something other than what he thinks as naturally as if he really thought it. . . . What is the profession of the actor? It is a trade by which he performs ('gives himself in representation') for money, submits himself to the ignominy and affronts that others buy the right to give him, and publicly puts his person on sale. (74)

Such a statement opens up his autobiography to much speculation as to who the real Jean-Jacques is and how he elaborately creates in his audience the feelings that he has contrived through his narrative. It is a continuous dance between transparency and obstruction, for what looks clear and lucid may be the places of greatest occlusion in Rousseau's conscious manipulation of feeling management.

The Confessions may be envisioned as an elaborate and rich fiction; tied to the first-person narrative, it becomes most incredible as we read more deeply into the narrator's nature, including the passages that reveal through the body the psychological markings of his flesh. Rousseau reveals the embodied quality of the individual as few others have, especially as it is revealed through the remembered events of the past. Reflection offers deeper and sweeter, and at times more powerful feelings of shame, remorse, gratitude, regret, injury, alienation, joy, and fulfillment because of how they find their way into the language of memory.

THE TRANSPARENT BODY

In his remarkable book, *Coming to Our Senses*, Morris Berman observes that body image and interiority or "self-awareness" are two sides of the same coin (33). He goes on to highlight what I believe underwrites Rousseau's motives in creating his autobiography: that the self is created not exclusively by the Other but by one's self in a conspiracy. Our own body image is prominent and central in our visual image of our selves. As a metaphor, it gives us back to ourselves as Other. And it is not accidental, he points out, that in the sixteenth century, mirrors began to proliferate at approximately the same time that the individual as a concept comes into its own, with its attendant idea of self-consciousness (48). Reflection, then, takes on literal as well as psychological meaning for Rousseau. The invention of the mirror and a little later, the plate glass window, give rise to two ideas: self-reflection and transparency—with Rousseau's life writing becoming culturally the great exposé of the Self. Language, then, becomes a mirror in such a way that we see through the words darkly of *The Confessions* the image of Rousseau as he has crafted it, and then mirrored it for public consumption. Through the image we find revealed the authentic contours of his own interiority. His is not just a life story but, more important, a poetic expression of soul. Several specific illustrations from his autobiography will make this observation more emphatic.

Moreover, it is not just Rousseau who is created in *The Confessions*. We as audience, as readers or listeners, are as well. I would say it this way: Rousseau creates us as a mirror in which the self that he creates is reflected. He then creates the response to him that he desires, telling us, for example, after he has related an unseemly or horrid event from his past, that we must now be disgusted, confused, sympathetic, or to feel some other emotion that he assigns to us. He creates our feelings as he gazes on us through his narrative. Only by creating in us a response to his narrated events can he then exonerate himself in our eyes. For the image in the mirror of his creation is not the *person* Jean-Jacques Rousseau; rather, it is a *character*. And this character he planned to submit to the most minute and microscopic examination of its inward parts, as indeed the microscope as an instrument of visual eavesdropping on the smallest particle of the body came into its own, as Barbara Stafford reveals: "by the late eighteenth century. . . . Like these inward-bound faculties, the microscope exposed the thickness of experience, the depth of the level" (341). Rousseau's own interior interrogation as well as his preoccupation with his blocked bladder creates the image of a self that is both open and impeded by the world. I understand his interior blockage to be a wound that gave him great pain through most of his life, and that his autobiography is filtered through this defective physiology. His interior physiology became his external autobiography, refracted in the sewer system's creation.

Consider the early embedded instructions for reading *The Confessions* which he delivers periodically throughout the work, here in his own reading of fictions. When he explores the characters in Plutarch, for example, he writes: "I took fire by his example, and pictured myself as a Greek or a Roman. I became indeed that character whose life I was reading" (20–21) wherein the passion of entering into another's world and self was so strong "that my eyes sparkled and my voice rang" (21). This ability of the imagination to take on or to assume, in Keats' terms, a "negative capability" so to become the other, is a blueprint of how we are to read Jean-Jacques. We read *The Confessions* always with an analogical eye. But what is the effect of this reading?

Robert Romanyshyn offers us a way into this double vision, or perceiving as reflection. In describing the commonplace image of one's self in the mirror, he observes that when we see ourselves reflected in a mirror, it is not simply our selves that we see. Rather, if we stay with the experience of the image in the mirror, "the self in reflection is a figure in a narrative; the one being reflected is the one who tells the tale. If one sees only a duplicate of oneself, that is the self created by science" (*Psychological Life*, 10), namely, objective, distant, and simply a copy of the original. But to stay with the image given back to one—and here I would say whether it is the figure of oneself in a mirror or the figure of another in the mirror of narrative—"the reflection as a figure transforms the reflected. . . . The reflection as a figure in a story *infects the reflected* and the one who sees the reflection is caught up in a story" (10). This one who can get caught up in the story is both reader and the one creating the image. The power of the image that carries the emotion has the power to transform both audience and creator of the image. It transforms both *in their feelings*. Romanyshyn pushes this idea further, which ties us back to *The Confessions*: "Psychological life makes its appearance as a reality of reflection" (11). Only by writing of himself, and perhaps more generally speaking, only in autobiography, does the psychological life of the writer gain an opportunity for full disclosure. The self exists most acutely in its psychological life when one grants it a memory in writing.

Autobiographical life, by extension, is psychological life in its depths and in its feelings, both of the narrator's and of his audience. Rousseau then offers us what might be called a double sleight of hand, such that when we look or gaze back at him, he has already been created in a particular way in our own judgmental eyes. Indeed, his own reflection in *The Confessions* is a deepening and refiguring of the reflected. And that he never planned his personal story to appear while he was alive is in a sense his own insurance policy against confusing or disorienting the reader through having the Rousseau of *The Confessions* obstructed by the living person of Jean-Jacques: "My *Confessions* are not intended to appear in my lifetime, or in the lifetime of the persons concerned. . . . But since my name is fated to live, I must endeavor to transmit with it the memory of that unfortunate man who bore it, *as he actually was* and not as his unjust enemies unremittingly endeavor to paint him" (373, my emphasis). His opening volley is and has been very disarming for readers since its original publication because it conveys a daring experiment undertaken by an individual that proves to be very seductive in its sincerity:

> My purpose is to display to my kind a portrait in every way true to nature, and the man I shall portray will be myself. Simply myself. I know my own heart and understand my fellow man. But I am made unlike any one I have ever met; I will even venture to say that I am like no one in the whole world . . . and if by chance I have used some immaterial embellishment it has been only to fill a void due to a defect of memory. . . . I have bared my secret soul as Thou thyself hast seen it, Eternal Being! (18)

He is very instructive here about what we should look for. In addition, he suggests that language will be used as a glass in a double sense: it will allow him to be "displayed," as behind a plate glass window, and it will allow through reflection or mirroring those emotions and feelings, that cannot lie, to be retrieved and to infect, even to shape, the reader. He is also, as the earlier quote by Rousseau makes clear, the actor who presents himself on display for our judgment and sympathy. The line between autobiography and fiction would appear to dissolve quickly in these first pages. I say this because of the term "immaterial embellishment" which Rousseau says he will use in order to fill in the details of unremembered events. As we follow the progression of his autobiography more frequently, we notice that in the latter books he embellishes more regularly because his memory is not able to grasp as many facts of his experience as his life becomes more entangled and labyrinthine. The image he uses is revealing, as he instructs readers to retrace their steps through his work: "I am absolutely certain what the result of their researches will be, but I lose myself in the obscure and tortuous windings of the tunnels which lead to it" (544). This image will take on greater weight when we discuss the sluices and dark tunnels of the Paris sewer system being developed then, and of how it is, like *The Con-*

fessions, a place of intimate discharge. But for the present, perhaps exploring another passage, this one directly in the text in which a mirror figures prominently, will help to ground these observations on his method.

In Book 2 Rousseau recalls his passionate, erotic relationship with Mme. Basile, in whose house he is living for a time. We discern, too, how he is a master of the subtle gestures of the body. Because without speaking, the body has the capacity for deep communication. He spends time with this beautiful woman, alone, without any words passing between them. What is shared is their bodies as they appear to one another. Merleau-Ponty's observation on the public nature of flesh is instructive here when he writes that "my body sees and is seen. That which looks at all things can also look at itself and recognize in what it sees the 'other side' of its power of looking. It sees itself seeing; it touches itself touching" (*Primacy of Perception*, 162). It seems that we, as embodied beings, are always in a condition of reflection of both self and other. This phenomenological truth Rousseau offers us hundreds of times in his confessions as he engages in the deepest and most protracted self-reflection of his time.

THE GESTURAL BODY

In this little vignette with Mme. Basile is contained a clear sense of the entire work's design; Rousseau exposes to us what we need to know of the creation of the self. Consider the scene. Mme. Basile has gone to her room to be alone, and Rousseau, a young teenager at this time (1728–31), having finished his duties, follows her to the second-floor bedroom. He finds when he climbs the stairs that her door is ajar and so slips in unperceived. Why, we wonder as we read, is he playing cat and mouse with her? What is he creating in this scene as we the readers follow him up the stairs and wait with him on the threshold of her room? And, most important, what does he wish us to perceive? He would appear to want to be "alone" with her, but in a peculiar way. He wishes to be present to her without her awareness of his presence. He reveals himself to us in his writing while he conceals himself from her in his actions. He finds her beside the window (78) working on her embroidery, facing that part of the room opposite the door. To heighten the experience for us, and to capture the feeling for himself now, he chooses to tell us that "she always dressed well, but that day her attire was almost coquettish. She was in a charming attitude with her head slightly lowered to reveal the whiteness of her neck and she had flowers in her beautifully brushed hair" (78). All of this creates such an erotic effect on him that he feels deprived of his senses. In response, he throws himself on his knees in a posture of servile worship, feeling this desire course through him as he extends his arms to her in his fantasy. He acts out his desire for her as she faces away from him in front of the window, the place of transparency. She is completely transparent to him even as he is convinced that her vision of him is obstructed, which he believes makes him invisible to her. He tells us that he is "quite certain that she could not hear me, and imagining that she could not see me" (78). He imagines, then, that he is inaccessible to her vision. Yet what he imagines and what becomes painfully apparent to him is their disparity: "But over the chimney-piece was a mirror, which *betrayed me.* I do not know what effect this scene had upon her" (78).

This mirror of reflection shows her everything of his secret desire made manifest but, he thought, invisibly to her. He was completely transparent even when he believed her vision of him was completely occluded. How she interprets his silent gestures is given through her own silent gesturing to him. She invites him, by a slight turning of her head and by subtly pointing to the carpet at her feet, to join her there. In one sense, her silent embodied gesture mirrors and completes his desire. He bounds silently across the room and pounces on the carpet in one vigorous movement and is content to lie there without speaking. Now that the interior self has been made public and transparent, he can do or say nothing. He is paralyzed and cannot utter a single word. The self, caught, or made transparent, is frozen into inaction. Mme. Basile's response is a perfect mirroring of the young Rousseau's gesture of desire, which she became an accomplice to immediately; she reflects his own desires in her response to him, which is couched in silence. She reflects his self in her gesture, but now thinking about it, on reflection, the voice of the autobiography observes: "she neither drew me to her nor repulsed me. Indeed, she did not take her eyes from her work, and tried to behave *as if she could not see* me at her feet" (79, my emphasis).

It is worth citing Merleau-Ponty's observation on the mirror here. He writes that "the mirror itself is the instrument of a universal magic that changes things into a spectacle, spectacles into things, myself into another and another into myself" (*Primacy of Perception,* 168). The language of this almost charming exchange between her and Rousseau shows how much the two become mirror reflections of one another, exposing themselves in their interiorities by their outward embodied gestures. In effect, we might say they gesture one another into being, giving the other definition through their own movements—exterior forms of interior motives. The inside, the realm of feelings, which Rousseau firmly believed never lied, is offered through the body in its gesturing.

Now it is Rousseau's turn to reflect the other self, for he says that he realized that "she shared my embarrassment and perhaps [note the big perhaps!] my desires, and was restrained by a bashfulness equal to my own." So he now sees his own self reflected in the response of Mme. Basile; she has indeed become transparent to him as he had to her earlier. What emerges in this encounter is the inner dynamics by which each creates the self of the other through gesture, itself a manifesto of interior desires made bodily apparent and insisting on interpretation. He uses language to re-create and reflect on the meaning of the silent encounter, shrouded only in gesture. His words mirror his interiority as it is felt.

But we are not done yet in this mirroring and making transparent activity between the two desiring lovers. His reading of her response after making the initial gesture inviting him to her foot mat is still not enough for him to override his own fears. So he continues in his mind: since she was five or six years older, he believes all the initiative should come from her, but since she does nothing, he reads that lack of further motion as her wish for him not to engage any subsequent gestures in return.

In other words, Rousseau creates himself through the other by reading her behavior as nothing less than a mirroring of his own behavior and desires motivating him. And even to this day, in writing his autobiography so many years later, he continues to create her as he ends this richly mirrored and transparent moment: "I know that I was right, *for surely* she had too much sense not to see that such a novice as I not only required encouragement but actual instruction" (79). And yet, is this all to the event that is important? No, because here is the point of the entire autobiography that Rousseau will rehearse innumerable times in his writing. The event has a richer place in his heart now that he remembers it from a point of remembrance far removed from its actual occurrence: "The image of the charming woman has remained printed in such charming outline on my secret heart. It has gained added beauty, indeed, as I have become acquainted with the world and womankind" (79). The remembered figure is one of beauty when filtered through all he has learned of women since then. She has been re-created through the imagination and is now a deeper and more intense bodily experience in the language of recollection than she was in the immediacy of the original event. And in the recollection Rousseau has created in us our own feelings toward the event that he has himself felt, even as he has simultaneously created in us an image of himself. In fact, we have embodied the Rousseau that he has created in us. He implicates our own embodied feelings and actually creates them in a way that Merleau-Ponty suggests when he writes: "there is a human body when, between the seeing and the seen . . . a blending of some sort takes place, when the spark is lit between sensing and sensible" (163). Rousseau's autobiography is not then simply a reminiscence of one man toward his past; it brings in the cultural subtleties of the reader as well. We sense Rousseau through the remembered event even as we feel the sensibilities that he has evoked in us through the narrated experience. He has printed her charming image on our own hearts, there to become part of the palimpsest of the self that is Jean-Jacques.

Sturrock helps to clarify this action in writing that "For Rousseau, an autobiography can be read not only as a personal expression . . . expressing inner dynamics, but as a cultural product as well" (39). And further: "we often rewrite culture as much as we rewrite our lives" (40). The culture that he creates includes those of us reading and experiencing his past in the present. His *Confessions* is an elaborate and complex creation of a social body, with an exchange value consisting not of money but of the far more valuable capital of human feelings.[4]

Such a blending will display its greater complexity through two other incidents in *The Confessions* in this section of the chapter. They are exempla of what I believe takes place throughout the hundreds of pages of Rousseau's psychologically complex creation of modern consciousness in all of its private and subtle lineaments. It appears that Rousseau's real subject is not just his self as an object in history, but the imagination's own engagement with memory to create the meaning inherent in events through a language that deeply embodies human feelings. In its workings it creates worlds out of a slight gesture, a piece of a story, a sudden object of interest. We take him seriously when he makes variations of these two comments often in the autobiography: "It is impossible for men and difficult for Nature herself, to surpass the riches of my imagination" (155). And a little earlier he admits: " I do not know how to see what is before my eyes; I can only see clearly in retrospect, it is only in my memories that my mind can work. I have neither feeling nor understanding for anything that is said or done or that happens before my eyes" (114). All must be imaginatively remembered for Rousseau, and when the memory fails, embellishments invariably intervene to fill out the narrative truth of his feelings by creating an emotional verisimilitude of the past. In his radical construction of *The Confessions* he anticipates and serves as the prototype of Marcel Proust's *Remembrance of Things Past*, Sartre's work on imagination, Bachelard's writing on the elements and reverie, and Merleau-Ponty on the body. These writers are the French stepchildren of Rousseau's initial elaborate construction.

Furthermore, this deeply intimate connection between self and other reflected in the language of *The Confessions* becomes the controlling emblem of the new modern self. Language carries from the interior to the exterior of one's psychological and emotional life "the hidden reality" of themselves, according to Starobinski. Language does not represent the self, for Rousseau, but "is the Self" (*Jean-Jacques Rousseau*, 195). Language is the self embodied in the world, and not just any self but the authentic self: "The problem of language evaporates when writing is not seen as an instrument of revelation, but as revelation itself" (196). The exercise of this revelation may be the most profound contribution Rousseau makes to modern consciousness in offering up as oneself the feelings and emotions created through the remembered and written and imagined incidents of one's past. The more those experiences reveal some form of wounding, even if only initially, the more memorable they become.

THE BODY OF EXPOSED PRIVACY

A scene like the one discussed above that further develops and captures the complex nature of privacy and publicity that is the hallmark of Rousseau's consciousness is one wherein, as a young man, he began exposing himself to women (90ff.). I want to look at what we see happening and then to view it as a commentary on the embodied reality that Rousseau assigns events remembered. For his body, like his stories, is constantly unfolding. David Abram suggests that the recitation of a story itself is a sensual and visceral experience that does not just implicate the head but the entire sensate being of the person (*Spell of the Sensuous,* 120). As embodied biographies, our own biology is very much entangled in our biographies through the stories we choose to tell others. Perhaps all stories we tell others, whether about us or about others, are already autobiographical on both conscious and unconscious planes. This observation may serve to lead us into the body of Rousseau through his narrative.

He begins Book 3 with longing and desire: "I was restless, absent-minded, and dreamy; I wept and sighed and longed for a pleasure *which I could not imagine,* but of which I nevertheless felt the lack" (90, my emphasis). His desire is deep and unnamed and his language here is already an attempt to give it a form and a tangible reality. The time that he is recollecting himself, he is in his late teens and, not surprisingly, full of shame, "the companion of an evil conscience,"[5] as he calls it; unable to imagine his desire, he decides to embody it by haunting the backstreets and dark alleys of the city where he could expose himself to women from afar—much as he did with Mme. Basile earlier—"in the condition in which I should have liked to be in their company." His exposure places him on a catwalk between the realms of privacy and publicity and creates through himself a character in the narratives that are his.

Now, writing years later, which is like straddling in language the private and public realms, he reconfigures that earlier hot-blooded youth, and sees in his behavior nothing devious: "What they saw was nothing obscene. . . . The absurd pleasure I got from *displaying myself before their eyes* is quite indescribable. . . . There was only one step for me still to make to achieve the experience I desired, and I have no doubt that some bold girl would have afforded me the amusement, as she passed, *if I had possessed the courage to wait*" (90–91, my italics).

He explores a particularly dark and labyrinthine area close to where women gather by a well to draw water. This is an interesting and provocative selection of locale, for as his malformed bladder continues to oppress him in later years, his dilemma is of how to withdraw water from it as his urine wells up within him. One wonders at this point if the choice of location here is accidental, or through the rich imagination of Rousseau we are to make the connection between these two events and the one he describes earlier when as a young boy he stood over the pot and passed water into the soup Mme. Clot was brewing on the stove (21). It is an act which he performs in private but now makes public in language. Can the entirety of *The Confessions* be so uncannily contrived? Is each human life so marked? Does the body of each of us continue to play out a particular set of metaphors of the self, whose forms and repetitions, if not their multiple meanings, become apparent, and transparent, only through recollection? The suggestion has already been made in a previous chapter that our personal mythologies may have their origins in the body's interior. We will see how, for example, Rousseau's disease becomes a metaphor, even a mythology, that governs much of his later life. For through the increasing irritation and thus attention he must give to his wounded body, his autobiography captures in its remembrances.

When he feels that he has found a safe hiding place from which to expose himself and then to hurriedly retreat into its shadows, he becomes emboldened and offered to the girls who came to the well a sight that was laughable rather than seductive. For some he was transparent, for others invisible; for still others he was a disgusting obstacle:

> The more sensible pretended that they had seen nothing. Others started laughing. Others considered themselves insulted and made a fuss. I rushed into my retreat and was followed. I heard the voice of a man, *which I had not reckoned with* and which alarmed me. I plunged deeper into the passages, at the risk of losing myself; noises, voices and that man's voice followed me still. I had counted on the darkness, I saw light. I shuddered and plunged on. I was stopped by a wall and could go no further. There I must await my fate. In a moment I was caught and seized by a big man with a big moustache, a big hat, and a big sword, escorted by four or five women each armed with a broom handle. Among them I saw the little wretch who had given me away, and who no doubt wanted to see me face to face. (91)

But gathering his wits about himself, the young Rousseau, reacting with his quick wit like the later Huckleberry Finn, fabricates a self on the spot, one made to fit the contours of the situation. He claims to be "a young stranger of noble birth and to be suffering from a mental derangement. I said that I had run away from my father's house because they wanted to shut me up, and that if he gave me away I should be lost." And then even to his own astonishment, the man lets him go. "Unlikely though it seemed, my appearance and my speech produced an effect; the terrible man was touched. He gave me a brief scolding and quietly let me go without asking me any more questions" (91). Have we just been witness to what Margaret Lock calls "sickness as cultural performance" that highlights and connects private illness to public maladies? The body in its woundedness or its disability is *the* "essential metaphor" ("Cultivating the Body," 142) by which the "sickening social order" can be displayed. We notice the content of Rousseau's fabrication as well as the subjective feeling it elicits from the man.

It is not the truth of the self he exposes but the sincerity of the feeling he wishes to elicit in him. Importantly, it was the man's voice that terrified Rousseau in the labyrinth of shadows before he runs up against the obstruction of a brick wall that blocks his escape. Having then uttered his story, given himself over to a fiction, Rousseau observes how the man becomes silent. Perhaps we are to understand that man as representing in some ways we the readers, who like him are to be touched in a certain way by the narrative of the self, perhaps then to exonerate him of his behaviors and then fall silent.

Now Rousseau's recollection might have ended here, but it doesn't. He sees "the man with the big sword" (92) several days later, who now mocks him, imitating (mirroring?) the young Rousseau's voice: "I am a prince. I am a prince and a coward. But don't let his Highness come back again." Rousseau slinks away after hearing him and he "supposed" that the women had made the man "ashamed of his credulity" by believing Rousseau's ruse in the first place. Rousseau says that anyone else "would have put me to shame, if only in order to raise a laugh" (92), and therefore thinks kindly of this man every time he remembers him. What he imagines of the man, finally, is his decency; he judged him fairly, allowed him his fiction, then judged him later, making the young Rousseau cautious about his public behavior for a time, as if his private body parts, exposed to public chastisement, marked him as an exhibitionist in the town and gave him an identity that he did not have before. The body's own privacy, taking on a public audience, ends in an identity that is partly fictional, partly factual, and partly reconstructed in the older man's mocking voice. Indeed, the very model of each of our selves that we are always negotiating in its private and public aspects with the world is contained in this elaborate vignette that is one of hundreds *The Confessions* relates.

What else does this incident make evident? It begins and ends with shame, a shame that makes Rousseau cautious and grateful for a long time, he admits. It also makes more evident bodily desire in its visibility and its invisibility. To be seen publicly, or to have exposed to the world from the shadows one's private body parts in the heat of an unnamed and unfathomable desire, exhibits both the revealing and concealing quality of the body and of emotion. It reveals something else as well: the fabricated body produced to elicit a particular emotional effect in the audience. Creating the story of the runaway nobleman in order to gain his liberty, Rousseau, I believe, gives us once again a method for reading *The Confessions*. For this is what he is doing throughout his narrative: creating in an embodied narrative a narrative of his own body, his own biology and his own biography. Body and life story become one seamless gesture, one being through the contours of the language that give it its fictional power. Rousseau illustrates how his own body is the sign of his remembered life now given a narrative structure. We can see more precisely the meaning of Peter Brooks' observation that Rousseau was the first to recognize the body as a significant issue in "determining one's life story" (26).

Furthermore, this incident develops something crucial to our embodied humanness in the world. In writing of "The Reciprocity of the Senses," David Abram makes an observation that seems obvious but must be given more voice because it shifts the emphasis for a moment from self to the cultural milieu in which we are embedded; we are not bodies in a vacuum: "*We* can experience things—can touch, hear and taste things—only because, as bodies, we are ourselves included in the sensible field and have our own textures, sounds, and tastes. . . . We might as well say that we are organs of this world, flesh of its flesh, and that the world is perceiving itself *through us*" (*The Spell of the Sensuous,* 68).

Moreover, the initial effect that Rousseau establishes time and again in *The Confessions* is silence. Does he write so much, so exhaustively and at such great lengths, in order to give us nothing to respond to, so completely has he covered himself? We note here that the last scene of the autobiography ends in silence. Perhaps this silence is the gap between words wherein our own identity is allowed access.

There is in Rousseau's recollection not only the exhibitionist, but something deeper seeking incarnation. It is a profound desire to be in the world, to be affecting it and to be affected by it while at the same time wishing to remain private and secret, or to expose oneself only in the shadows, to have our presence a shock to others but to be always hidden, ready to retreat, to become suddenly anonymous, to be a non-self and to have ready-at-hand the shadows of oblivion in which to plunge if threatened. This incident, moreover, should not be looked at in isolation, for it goes directly to the heart of writing itself, the creation of *The Confessions* in its own deep desires. Rousseau admits at one point that he is content to remain in the shad-

ows in privacy and to write and to let the writing be his public acknowl-
edgment and participation in the world while he himself evaporates. In language Rousseau will expose himself in private, but always for eventual
public display; such is the double-edged quality of words—to make the private public. It is this private/public interplay, another version of being
transparent and being occluded, hidden in the recesses of solitude, but there
using language to make oneself public, that is basic to his recollections.

One other element present here needs more visibility, namely, the pleasure of the feelings gleaned from the act of remembering itself as another,
and seemingly deeper, form of living. "How I love, from time to time, to
come upon the pleasant moments of my youth! They were so sweet! . . .
Ah, their mere memory still give my heart a pure delight, which I need in
order to restore my courage and to sustain the tedium of my remaining
years" (275). Through imagined images Rousseau brings the body, with its
affective resonances, into the present, to influence the quality of life he
lives now. And so often, as with the scene to which we now turn, the memory involves an intense eros which seems lacking in his present existence;
his memories often seem to have as their intention the reanimation of eros
in his life, of feelings so intense that they "sustain him" in the present. And
within this erotic construct, Rousseau both repels and invites scrutiny, of
being under the gaze of another as a way of identifying and inventing himself. The examples above show the intensity by which he examines both
"exhibitionism and voyeurism" (*Living Eye,* 26) as paths to intimacy with
others, according to Jean Starobinski. These actions capture for him the
privacy of the public image and the publicity that surrounds his private
image of self.

THE BLEMISHED BODY AND THE IMPERFECT SELF

In Book 7, at a time when Rousseau is in his early thirties (1743–44), he
confesses that "Nature has not made me for sensual delight. She has put the
hunger for it in my heart, but what might be ineffable pleasure turns to poison in my wretched head" (262). Such a dismal self-assessment orients him
and us for his narration involving Giulietta, a beautiful courtesan whom he
visits to satisfy his desires. This incident, he confesses, "plainly reveals my
character" and must therefore be told with the courage that drives him to
write the entire text. In it we are promised unalloyed transparency. He then
constructs a curious link that becomes such a mark of modernity in its intimacy and shared conspiracy in the incident. He asks that "Whoever you
may be that wish to know a man, have the courage to read the next two or
three pages and you will have complete knowledge of Jean-Jacques
Rousseau" (300). We become at this moment fellow-conspirators in his

recollection and are ourselves defined by him as he interprets himself in the telling.

His initial impression of Giulietta is that he is in the company of a woman of perfection, "Nature's masterpiece and love" (300). His initial fascination, however, is modulated by his reflection of himself in her gaze: "she knows I am a nobody, although my merits, which she cannot know, would be nothing in her eyes. There is something incomprehensible about this" (301). She knows what he is not and cannot know what he is "in her eyes." We might say that his imperfection is seen through what appears to be her embodied perfection. Here Rousseau confesses with a certainty, but also with a sense of incomprehension, that he knows what she can and cannot know, such that both transparency and obstacles exist side by side. This is the psychology of self that will in a moment find its analogue in the body of the beautiful and seemingly unmarked, untainted, and unblemished woman, at least as he is able to comprehend her from the outside. What is underneath, what remains for the time being nontransparent and private, he cannot judge. The interior body remains enticingly hidden, which itself is the strongest source of his desire. He sets us up further by having already made two references to Nature, one describing his own person and the other describing hers. In the former reference it has to do with his interiority, and with Giulietta her exterior beauty, that which we can perceive. It is as if Jean-Jacques reveals to us that there is and is not a division between the public, seen, nature of a person and that same individual's hidden interiority.

He speculates further that either his heart deceives him, "deludes his senses," or that "some secret flaw that I do not see destroys the value of her charms and makes her repulsive" (301) to those who wish to possess her. What, the question becomes, is to be trusted? The senses themselves, which may deceive, or the intuition, or a feeling, that there is some hidden reality that needs to be exposed, but that currently remains obstructed from view? He wrestles in this preamble to her, with the invisible body and the visible body that is culturally created in our private and public selves. He goes on to describe in minute detail features of her flesh, her extreme brightness, pleasant smell, and impeccable cleanliness. [6] In his descriptions, we too are initially persuaded of her perfection and begin to feel the seduction *he feels* in her presence.

Moreover, through her Rousseau begins to question the state of his own health, which is less than perfect, and begins to doubt if he is even worthy of her. He defines his own imperfection through her perfection, as if in looking through a glass perfect and beautiful he has mirrored back to him his own ailments. When he begins to feel, through these reflections, his own inadequacy and tears begin to fill his eyes, she, whom we get a sense from the description, has begun undressing to make herself more transparent, looks to Rousseau and begins to feel "at a loss." The next observation is most revealing: "But after walking round the room and passing in front of her glass, she understood—and my eyes confirmed her reason—that repulsion had nothing to do with my freakish behaviour" (301). Ingeniously, Rousseau renders the act of understanding as a form of reflection, namely, the double image of her in the mirror seen by him. It is in this crafted double nature of a reflection that I believe the self emerges.

Almost immediately then, after comforting him in his inadequacies, she invites him to her; Rousseau, shifting from shame to desire, moves to bury himself in her breasts but suddenly discerns in her now-exposed body the sensible form of her imperfection: "she had a malformed nipple. I beat my brow, looked harder, and made certain that this nipple did not match the other. Then I started wondering about the reason for this malformation" (301). As in a mirror, where supposedly the shape standing in front of it is reflected accurately in the glass, here the doubling of the breasts do not offer a perfect reflection of one another. The doubling is distorted, in the same way his own ill health is reflected through the image of her perfect being. All is distorted here: his feelings, himself, her body, and his thoughts from his emotions. "I was struck by the thought that it resulted from some remarkable imperfection of Nature. . . . I saw as clear as daylight that instead of the most charming creature I could possibly imagine I held in my arms some kind of monster rejected by Nature, men, and love. I carried my stupidity so far as to speak to her about her malformed nipple" (301), which insults the young woman after she feels an initial shame, an emotion associated with a distorted or even malformed self-consciousness.

That he finds language or is compelled to use language to engage the distortion on her breast is what is most essential to this distorted mirroring scene. Her body is now a distorted reflection of his initial belief given through her clothed appearance; he has stripped her of her covering and exposed what is "monstrous" to him, a gross defect in Nature herself. His treatment of Giulietta is of course a reflection of the treatment he has leveled at himself—to expose all of the imperfections of his own nature and to express them in the private act of writing, for eventual public display—as he is engaged in a very private-public moment with the young courtesan.

Furthermore, Rousseau is relentless both here and in the entirety of the autobiography: "But as I still felt some remnant of uneasiness, which I could not conceal from her, I finally saw her blush, adjust her clothes, and take her place at the window, *without a word*" (301, emphasis added). She moves from being reflected to becoming transparent *and silenced* as she shifts from mirror to window. A couple of points need to be made here, not the least of which is Giulietta's shift from mirror to window, from reflection to transparency, and from speech to silence. Perhaps there is a third glass, the teared eye of Rousseau himself, full of the water of emotion, as reflector of her and recollector in the eye of memory, maybe partly embellished, of the author of the autobiography. For he is, after all, reflecting himself back in time and has promised that this incident would "plainly reveal my character" (300). This action suggests a movement that corresponds to Rousseau's own way of reading the young courtesan as a text, of her becoming transparent to him and he to her, and perhaps, as we too are part of the conspiracy, he to us. Here is a reflection, perhaps slightly distorted, of his created self in the previous two incidents we have observed. Reflection follows reflection follows transparency. What has occurred here in this creation not only of the body but of narrative itself and the life that lies behind and is given some shape in the telling?

We must remember the same shift with Mme. Basile earlier. Thus, our own embodied participation is called forth in this process; we must recollect the details of the earlier episode in order to gather more fragments of this self into a whole. Judgment, as Rousseau instructs us, is our final and formidable task.

Fed up with his antics and insulted by his presence, Giulietta gathers herself back into words and instructs him: "Gianetto, lascia le donne, e studia la matematica" (Give up the ladies, and study mathematics, 302). What is revealed at the end of this story is equally astonishing, for what troubles Rousseau about his relation with her is that "she only carried away a scornful memory of me" (302). How he exists in her memory, the image of him that lives within her, is the cause of his greatest dissatisfaction.

The entire scene ends in a grotesque distortion; he is the monster she will remember, perhaps even as a defect in Nature is her image of him; this knowledge creates great uneasiness in Rousseau and wounds him deeply, even though he is the primary instigator or creator of this image she harbors of him, for a kind of transcendent purity is his final aspiration. Instead, he has created himself in her eyes by focusing on her own defect and creating in her mind a figure of imperfection, a self-consciousness that is now ashamed of her blemished body. They have both been deeply involved in the creation of the self of the other. Both are now marked through the image the other has of them; both have been wounded by the other's reflection of them. And these wounded images are the essential nature of their respective selves. They have created one another and themselves simultaneously through their respective bodies. The meeting of Rousseau and his courtesan offers a fine illustration of an observation made by Barbara Maria Stafford in her study of the eighteenth-century body: "Thus the body was intimately tied to the establishment and upholding of ethical norms for ugliness or beauty. It could be minimized or magnified, reduced or aggrandized, cleansed or cosmeticized. It provided a surface for the play of invisible yearnings and visible emotions. It was a *site for the display of purity and pollution*" (*Body Criticism*, 16, my emphasis).

These elements of purity and pollution—cultural, moral, ethical, and originally physical qualities—are precisely what are worked on and out in the above vignette. We could say that every Enlightenment vision casts some form of Enshadowment. The surface of the body blemished is the originary terrain for exploring deeper levels of pollution, or grotesque distortion, one that will spin out to involve the systems of Paris sewers themselves as an extension of Rousseau's self-reflection offered here. To cite Stafford, certainly "body metaphors can disclose veiled human experience. . . . Beneath them lay the profound need to visualize all aspects of the invisible" (16–17), certainly one of the driving forces beyond the confessional genre that gained prominence in Rousseau's era. Later, she makes one other observation that illuminates an eighteenth-century belief Rousseau puts to use here. It was "a constant refrain in analytical or philosophical criticism that the grotesque was a fault always manifested on the surface or exterior of a body" (275). Rousseau's shadow in the form of his own self-disaffected condition, his own angst over his interiority, finds expression, I suspect, in the malformed parts of Giulieta's body. This incident is one of many on the way to Rousseau focusing directly on his own body and its blocked passages for elimination.

If, therefore, he wrote *The Confessions* to liberate himself from the images of a false Jean-Jacques that he wishes to correct, an unpolluted or untainted image of self, then in this incident with the young courtesan he is less than successful. Rousseau's elaborately detailed account shows how subtle is the movement of each of us in creating the other as we reflect ourselves through that alterity. There is almost no space between self and other, and perhaps there is an equal intimacy not only between others but the larger cultural phenomenon of the city as well.

THE BODY OF WASTE AND THE SEWAGE OF THE CITY

If the body is always a metaphor for the culture that reinvents it, then the obstructed body of Rousseau, along with the excessive supply of catheters he used throughout his later years to keep the flow of urine frequent, can be understood in a larger cultural context: body as psychological shadow. Bryan Turner points to women's disorders—"hysteria, anorexia and agoraphobia—are considered as disorders of society. . . . Any sociology of the body involves a discussion of social control" (2). Body and society are of one piece. In the same way, and a hundred years earlier in England, William Harvey's *De Motu Cordis* (1628) revealed a new body, one based on circulation. With it, as Richard Sennett asserts, "Harvey launched a scientific revolution in the understanding of the body: its structure, its healthy state, and its relation to the soul. A new master image of the body took form" (*Flesh and Stone*, 255). An entire book could be written on the reinvented body of *The Confessions* as it seeks purification, if not absolution, through the cleansing of the text.

I wish to extend the meaning of the body as metaphor to offer some suggestions here concerning the flow of Rousseau's autobiography, his malformed bladder, which was a true deformation, according to him, and which gave Rousseau no end of difficulties in his life, and the invention of the Paris sewer system. For the desire on the part of the individual to come clean, so to speak, finds its cultural expression in the body of the city. Rousseau's interior body discovers its richest analogue in the circulation beneath the skin of the city streets within the depths of its own internal and newly created plumbing. In such a relationship the old standard body, the body politic represented by the king's incarnated presence, is now replaced within the Revolution's shattering of traditional values, "by the middle class body," according to Dorinda Outram (2). She goes on to observe that the ideas of inside-outside of the body becomes a new cultural metaphor, one which is thickly secular: "the disappearance of the sacral state is in conjunction with the disappearance of the sacral nature of the human body" (12). Turner echoes this idea in observing that the body in the eighteenth century is secularized; it "ceases to be an object of sacred discourse of flesh to an object within a medical discourse where the body is a machine" (36).

Given his radical place in the rise of the individual, Rousseau is no less an important figure than Harvey for opening up the interior of the self in physiological, political, psychological, and social ways. This same exposure, with its shadow side of constriction or obstruction, is a profound metaphor for the zeitgeist of Western Europe at the time. Sennett suggests of Harvey's discovery/invention that his new understanding of the body "coincided with the birth of modern capitalism, and helped bring into being the great social transformation we call individualism" (*Flesh and Stone*, 256). It is the mobility of the individual, the circulation of his or her blood, and the concomitant flow of money and goods, as well as the breaking up of fixity and stability that surrounds the body of motion, that is included in Harvey's legacy to us. I think his metaphor also includes the free circulation of the past into the present and in a true postmodern impulse, the re-creation of the self as a fluid rather than a fixed, entity.

Rousseau is no less profound or ubiquitous in his effect, for he institutes in his *Confessions* a linguistic form of waste management, of the flow of poisons from the interior and subterranean regions to the outside of the body. His autobiography ushers in a physiology and a psychology of waste and its management, of impurities being vented, even cathected; the catheters he used to unblock obstructions is also the language of his writing—a way of making the private and interior public and exterior, much as a sewer system of a city may begin as a one-directional form of expulsion.

Rousseau offers us a phenomenology of purity, sought after through both psyche and physiology. His desire to return to the purity of Nature, to be done with the city toxins and damaging diatribes leveled at his person, to exist in the unpolluted neighborhood of his own company, a kind of purity of solitude, all marked him as one who was at times possessed with disengaging from his own incarnation, examples of which we will observe in a moment.

Alfred Ziegler's observations on Rousseau's bodily distresses center on his continual use of catheters "draining his bladder to avoid uremia, self-contamination by his own excrements" ("Rousseauian Optimism," 65). I suggest that a similar danger lurked for him in the writing of *The Confessions* and analogously in his own life. Draining much of the psychic toxins of his own existence off through language comprises one of the motives for writing the autobiography; it finds its own reflection in the sewer system itself. Both the sewers and *The Confessions* were after an unconditional purity, transparency, and honesty, unfettered by pollutants. Both develop out of a psychology of hygiene and purity, an impulse that intensifies interest in human embodiment even as it begins to divorce the psyche from it, to deodorize it of its flawed nature by flushing from it all that obstructs its perfection.

If it is true that each of us tends in our lives to develop an affinity for one or another of the four elements, then Rousseau's is certainly water. His connection to water implicates some fundamental affinities with language as liquid, as Bachelard describes it in *Water and Dreams*. There is a liquid quality to language that avoids fixity, keeping the words flowing, feeling in them a shifting and coursing of thought. Language and liquidity are the fundaments of Rousseau's psyche; it is water that he must continually discharge from himself, as well as the words of his autobiography. And the sewers need water to carry their toxins away from the bowels of the city. He admits of such a connection in writing that "I have always been passionately fond of the water. The sight of it throws me into a delicious dream, although often about no definite subject" (592–93). Something about the indefiniteness of water, its shifting shape and textured surface, are also part of the imagination of reverie. Water allows one to dream even as it has the capacity to carry away what is objectionable or impure.

There is something as well in the placement of the sewer system, underground, to which stuff falls, to be taken through sluices and deposited outside the walls of a city, there perhaps to be treated and then the waters returned, cleansed and purified, to be used again in a circulation of cleanliness. Embedded in *The Confessions* is a psychology of hygiene, of sanitary cleansing, and of expulsion; the shadows of these qualities are the poisons that, if allowed to stop up and be stored in the body, will eventually poison the organism and lead to death. The therapy of catharsis, of letting go, of allowing the impurities of psyche to find a channel of expulsion, is a newer and more technological form of what the Greeks understood as supremely valuable in witnessing the action of tragedy—a ritual and communal cleansing of pity and fear in order to guarantee or increase the probability of a healthy and sanitized polis. Body and city health were conjoined in a unity. Rousseau's own ailment, along with his confessions, is in keeping with the metaphor of the body and psyche that the Greeks imagined to be united so intimately,[7] and that today finds its most tangible expression in the client–therapist dyad.

With Rousseau is born, we could say, the democratic body, the body of the common person who as an individual wishes to feel part of and responsible for the body politic. The individual's own interiority is not separate from the external world. Language becomes the most prominent and effective mediating force for change and for personal experience. In addition, there developed also in the eighteenth century what Richard Sennett calls a "poetics of sympathy" (*Conscience of the Eye,* 100), which for Rousseau meant to be able to pity others, to become others in their suffering, and to envision the world through their eyes. Sympathy demands that one see the other clearly, unfettered, or without the smoked glass of obscurity blocking that communion that is crucial to the empathic imagination. Transparency, as we have seen in our discussion of parts of *The Confessions*, finds its analogue in the creation of transparent glass, which we mentioned earlier, becomes available in the late eighteenth century. Sheet glass is introduced through the invention of cast iron rollers for smoothing it out, which allows for larger and clearer sheets of transparent windows to be constructed. The glass house and the greenhouse, along with the glass arcade, come into existence at this time (Sennett, *Conscience of the Eye,* 107), both of which effectively collapse the distinction between inside and outside. In fact, the interiority of things takes on a new cultural position, uncovering, so to speak, the invisible quality of a thing. So when Rousseau claims he is striving to be completely transparent, he gives psychological voice to the cultural move to make the interior of things visible to the eye but not necessarily available to the senses, or to the body.[8]

If Augustine uncovers the spirit of the individual through the sensate body and its appetites, then Rousseau uncovers the psychological sludge or poison of the individual through the embodied language of sincere feeling, even as Jung's autobiography pierces beneath the basement floor of the psyche to discover the reservoir of the collective unconscious and the arche-typal contents covered with the dirt that haunt its region in their ageless design.

One shudders here when looking toward the horizon of postmodernity, for there one sees the figures who inherit Rousseau's legacy: Phil Donohue, Oprah Winfrey, Geraldo Rivera, Jerry Springer: those who create the post-modern electronic confessionals for the mass audience and promise to lay bare the offal of an entire culture through the distorted or malformed nar-ratives of today's guests. The monstrous interior of common persons with uncommon desires and manufactured sewage seeking a causeway on the electronic sewer lines is given full coverage in the shadow of the afternoon talk shows, none of which could have been imagined without Rousseau. We see on the television screen both a mirror and a transparent window, where we are served at one time a grotesque image of ourselves, however morbidly embellished, as we peek through the transparency to the transparent soul before us. And we listen, as we do with Rousseau's *Confessions*, to the sor-did narratives that are unveiled before us. Both use the act of confessing as a way to purge themselves after making clear and available the sordidness of the interior of being human. One can only speculate at this point at the connection among *The Confessions*, the television confessional talk shows, and the rise of bulimia and anorexia in our present cultural morbism to see the nature of the grotesque highlighted through its various forms.

Rousseau is able to give voice to both sides of the complex: glass and sewer, what is above ground and clear as well as what is below ground and repellent, even repressed. In this last regard, he anticipates both Freud and Jung and the invention/discovery of the unconscious, where the psy-chic sewage finds a hidden home. Part of the fascination of his *Confes-sions* is in its continual movement between these two poles of being embodied and psychologically susceptible.

Rousseau's work is also a compendium of contradictions involving the body in the eighteenth century, for it reflects the new impulse toward man-aged therapy at a time which, again anticipating Freud and analytical psy-chology, was fascinated with madness, pathology, abnormality (G. S. Rousseau, 64), as well as with the managed exorcism and remedy for these impurities. Such a movement coincided with the growing preoccupation with body hygiene, cleanliness, elimination of body odors, and a general sense of making the flesh more antiseptic and thereby more distant and fi-nally abstract in its odorless and blemishless condition. This move also sig-nals in some crucial ways the loss of the body "through body purification" in a move that Roy Porter has called a "tactics for dematerialization" where the body became an object not to be touched, especially by the great un-washed ("Barely Touching," 78).

Such emphases begin to create *The Confessions* as a body book, even a body manual, for the age. It can be viewed in one sense as a casebook on how to eliminate impurities and the use of technologies to rid oneself of pollution, be that technology written language, medical catheters, or psychological therapy.

And like the sewer systems themselves, a growing locus of great hazardous working conditions because of the vapors and viruses that floated in the air beneath the streets of Paris, *The Confessions* can be understood in part as a witness to "the dangerous potential of what comes from below or from inside to pollute the world outside" (Reid, *Paris Sewers and Sewermen,* 2). What comes from below can include the poison of urine or the feelings and actions of a shameful life finally given expression. Even Victor Hugo, whose fiction contained more sewer scenes than any other writer of the time, as well as references to sewers as metaphors for the cultural miasma he believed was poisoning culture, remarked that "the condition of the sewers of Paris" reflected "the breakdown of a society which was no more capable of sweeping away the truth than the abuses" (*Paris Sewers and Sewermen,* 18).

The Confessions is thus both an individual and a collective complex. It includes, like the mixture of body wastes themselves, a synthesis of bladder, biography, and the bilge water of the city. Rousseau is interested, as is true perhaps of any authentic confession, in coming clean, letting it out, separating himself from the offal of self, so that he may be absolved and cleansed by his own and subsequent cultures as well as by history. Autobiography becomes linguistic detox. His disease is an appropriate metaphor for his life's work, which is the redefining of liberty, of being free, and of promoting the inherent purity of the individual soul. At the end of his life, as he makes clear in *Reveries of the Solitary Walker,* written just two years before his death, he wishes to take his decree of freedom one step further, to disengage the body itself, to abandon it so that freedom may be whole and complete, as he outlines it in this declaration: "My body is now no more than an obstacle and a hindrance to me, and I do all I can to sever my ties with it in advance" (*Reveries,* 33). And again, in the third walk: "The time has come to enrich and adorn my soul with goods that it can carry with it when, set free of this body, that obstructs and blinds it, it sees the truth face to face" (61). His final liberation from the world will be in jettisoning the body completely, abandoning its pain and its odious limits for a truth that transcends the world, a kind of final leap toward absolute purity, devoid of all matter.

Having developed an intricate and elaborate poetics of waste in *The Confessions,* Rousseau gives expression to the modern split between flesh and mind in these last reminiscences: "I never found any real charm in the pleasures of the mind unless I was able to forget all about the interests of my body. . . . My soul could never take wings and soar above the natural world as long as I felt it to be tied to the needs of the body" (111), even though he used medicine in the form of a few favorite doctors to whom he "gave complete authority over my carcass" (111).

Furthermore, it is in the *Reveries* that he looks back and makes crucial insights about his autobiography, among them this declaration of disappointment in his readers: "And whoever reads my *Confessions* impartially—if ever this should happen—will feel that the actions I reveal are more humiliating and painful to confess than things which are more reprehensible yet less shameful. . . . It follows from these reflections that my professed truthfulness is based more on feelings of integrity and justice than on factual truth. . . . I have often made up stories, but very rarely told lies" (79). This last remark is a fitting legacy of autobiography, a form of expression that is interested in the experience of the past as it provokes feelings in the present, than in the facticity of what happened.

Moreover, do we read his deformed bladder, which he has had since birth (*Confessions,* 336), as a metaphor for his entire life? True, the ailments of his bladder do not assert themselves until Rousseau is in his adult years, and expresses his own imperfect nature. And do we understand the catheters—as a last-ditch effort to give himself some relief through an escape from the medical doctors "who did me as much harm as my illness" (340)—as a metaphorical bridge between transparency and obstruction? What Rousseau at this period in his life fears most is suffering retention— "of urine, gravel, and stone" (*Confessions,* 340)—of clogging up, of backing up the body poisons in his system and dying an agonizing death. His uniqueness becomes painfully apparent here when he remarks that "everything that relieves others—decoctions, baths, and bleeding—merely increased my distress" (341). His obstruction is unique; only the frequent use of catheters to alleviate a sense of fullness of the bladder allowed his distractions to abate enough for him to work. The analogy with the sewer system here is provocative.

We learn that for the engineers who authored it, the new sewer system was, in the words of one writer, an "expurgated and expurgating text in which all could read evidence of a society able to reveal and restrain its once rebellious refuse" (*Paris Sewers and Sewermen,* 44). Now while the sewer may be a text, it may also reveal a subtext, one resting below the life of order, cleanliness, and hygienic respectability. Sewers helped to clear the air above ground by moving the filth of the city through invisible tunnels, making the cities more inhabitable, less prone to disease-carrying miasmas. The irony here is that visitors to Paris as well as Parisians themselves began visiting the sewers and actually riding in boats through the dark circulatory system of the city, so fascinated were they by what was moving invisibly beneath their feet below the surface of the streets. They sensed that the city was perhaps more of an organism with provocative connections to the body itself.

So what of the text as a sewer? As Donald Reid makes clear, "The sewers remained a metaphorical locus for the baser elements of life. The late nineteenth-century interest in the unconscious encouraged such mapping of a psychological underground" (50). The wounds of the body and the city as well as their pollutions and poisons must be taken deep into its organic structure and there be disposed of. Rousseau's own embodiment as a text and his text as a body of culturally managed and controlled waste, is one of the most psychological works prior to the formal creation of the discipline of psychology.

And lest it sound as if all in Rousseau's autobiography is being passed off as nothing but waste, we notice another analogy with the sewers, namely, that the objects that were flushed down toilets, once they achieved a critical mass, began to create a small industry of retrieval, not unlike many incidents in *The Confessions*. For what was discarded as something without value by one person began to be retrieved and recycled by others working in the bowels of the city who found in them intrinsic value and use, even if that use was only monetary sales potential. So the circulation of waste into objects of value became part of the economy of the sewers and those who worked within them. There is a pressing analogy here as well in Rousseau's intentions to write his self story.

We learn that sewermen began retrieving different objects, cleaning them and selling them to junk dealers (*Paris Sewers and Sewermen*, 53). Perhaps particularly appropriate to our discussion is the retrieval of corks, because they were the most visible and plentiful of objects floating through the sewers and often most easily retrievable: "The administration directed sewermen to skim these corks off the top of the water. It then sold them to perfumers, who cut them down for use as stoppers in perfume bottles. Thus did the foul meet the fragrant" (Corbin, 53). What a metaphor for *The Confessions* generally! Body management and issues of hygiene took over the French imagination such that, as Alain Corbin illustrates, "sanitary cleansing became more specific and a daily requirement. Cleaning meant draining and movement disallowed putrefaction" (92). The idea of body management found its corollary in the impression and feeling management of *The Confessions*.

"The sewerman has been civilized along with the sewer," wrote one of the first visitors to the new sewers (*Paris Sewers and Sewermen*, 117). A close and intimate relationship grew up between the sewermen and common persons or those persecuted, for sanitation took on a large part of the cultural psyche, promising in effect not only "to improve urban sanitation, but also the material and moral conditions of the downtrodden" (117). Furthermore, as a psychological place as well as a repository for the discarded items of culture, the sewer is a place where people deposit the evidence of their wrongdoing and the byproducts of their wasted lives (129). One might even be cautioned to get her or his mind out of the sewer. Is it too much to suggest that there exists a confessional quality to our sewers; if we examine individually and as a culture what we believe is disposable, are we not giving in this expression an entire set of values that define our interior life? To look at what an individual or a society throws away gives a solid indication of what they value and what they find mundane. Our trash is a record of our values, as Rousseau's *Confessions* is not the product of one man but a reflection of an entire epoch.[9]

Within the construction of the sewer is a whole host of terms that reflect the changing values of the period, modernizing them toward our own century. Alain Corbin lists the following: "ventilating, evacuating, circulating, deodorizing, regulating, managing, draining, cleansing, privatizing" (*The Foul and the Fragrant*, 102). Private space, he asserts, promotes narcissistic reverie, interior monologues, self-examination, along with a preoccupation with self, body, miasmas, and odors (102). These elements in the construction of the self and the reinvention of the body are our legacy from *The Confessions*.[10] In conjunction with Rousseau's own physiological impediments and the sewer systems, as Paul Schilder writes, the eighteenth century is one of water, water control, hydraulics, filling in all the fetid parts of the city that were stagnant. The cultural impulse, of which Rousseau's autobiography is a critical dimension, was "to eliminate putrefaction from the city" (221). Schilder further asserts that a "new rhythm began to take hold in the 18th century, a rhythm espousing acceleration" (222) and, we can say securely, elimination. That which would destroy life with its threat to clog and deter health, had to be eliminated. "The domestication of water became a vital necessity. . . . The city became aware of its own environment, its own junk and waste" (230) and realized that, in its growing self-consciousness, it had to purge itself of its own impurities. Such cultural, physiological, and psychological activity is Rousseau a witness to; in working to purify himself, he gave to us in the character of an individual psyche exploring its own interior terrain a blueprint for the construction of the modern SELF. He held a slightly smoky mirror up to himself and asked us to judge what we saw in the reflection. In that judgment, he was certain, we would perhaps pass the harshest sentence on ourselves.

From the time of Rousseau forward into the nineteenth and twentieth centuries, the city and the body were not grand analogues to the excellence of its people: Dostoevsky's *The Brothers Karamazov* explores what value the decomposing, stinking corpse of an old monk, Father Zosima, might have on the belief of his parishoners and on the faith of his young student, Alexey Karamazov. Is there, Dostoevsky questions, something redemptive in our own body's decay? Does the flesh's decomposition in death open us to the possibility of a new faith and a deeper, less formulaic belief in the transcendent?

6

Corrupting Corpse versus Reasoned Abstraction

The Play of Evil in The Brothers Karamazov

Sound exists only when it is going out of existence.
—Walter Ong, *Orality and Literacy*, 71

One of the more interesting discoveries in literary theory during the past decade, and one that we have been exploring in this study, is that of the human body as both metaphorical reality and cultural invention.[1] Certainly Dostoevsky's works have always yielded an abundant harvest of insights for psychology, and the psychology of embodiment may be his most constant image in a thickly enfleshed world, what might be termed a poetics of the body. His final novel, *The Brothers Karamazov,* finished just months before his death, takes as its primary poetic image the corrupting flesh of Father Zosima, whose influence controls the action of the entire narrative.

Rene Girard is not alone among critics who speaks of the "harm done by the absurd postulate of a total separation between psychology and literature" (*To Double Business Bound,* 78). And more to the point of this study, in her collection of essays (*Literature and the Body*), Elaine Scarry believes that "the body is both continuous with a wider material realm that includes *history and nature*, and also discontinuous with it because it is the reminder of the extremity of risks entailed in the issue of reference" (xxi, my emphasis). She expresses the body's connection to history and nature and connects it with language, the consequences of which place us deeply within the enfleshed world of the word in *The Brothers Karamazov* and extends and refines a central preoccupation of Dostoevsky's that was fleshed out in part in *Crime and Punishment*; the body has as its locus an intimate relation to "the voice, to language" (vii), and to the creation of narrative itself.[2]

Within what could be termed a theological poetics of Dostoevsky's creative imagination, the question becomes: How do we understand the words of

John's Gospel that "the word was made flesh"? (John I: 14). Dostoevsky invites us to read the body not only as a poetic image but as a spiritual metaphor.

In the same way that there has been penetrating criticism on Dostoevsky's insights into human memory, especially by Robert Louis Jackson and, more recently by Diane Oenning Thompson's *The Brothers Karamazov and the Poetics of Memory*,[3] we have witnessed the profound effect of Mikhail Bakhtin's work on the body's relation to carnival.[4] Moreover, in *Art and Answerability* he continues to explore the social dimensions of embodiment: "the body is not something self-sufficient; it needs the other for completion" (51). Bakhtin's suggestion that to be embodied is already to be part of a larger community, that our shared incarnation initiates us into the same family, is a truth lived out directly by Father Zosima in his directive: each is responsible for all.

The central argument in *Karamazov*, then, is illustrated by way of the flesh in two central events: the ironic statement made by Father Zosima's corrupting corpse and the poetic statement uttered by Ivan Karamazov in his "Legend of the Grand Inquisitor." Together these two central expressions reflect the interplay of nature and history that Scarry illustrated earlier. Moreover, the first action, the decaying flesh of Zosima, is most important as an *ironic* illustration because it runs counter to the traditional belief held by the townspeople who visit the monastery that the dead body of a holy man will offer them miraculous moments of healing, a belief that has become too facile, if not morally presumptuous in their attitude toward faith that requires tangible proof. The second action, a poetic theological narrative that Ivan utters to his brother Alesha, expresses a divorce from the flesh in favor of a more reasoned and abstract, and therefore more distant stand toward others. There is, however, the same intensity of irony in Ivan's words as there is in Zosima's rapidly putrefying body. The irony in the relationship between Ivan's poetic word and the old priest's quickly decaying flesh is that the Word does once again become flesh, but in a fantastic, even poetic way. So it is on the irony inherent in the word/flesh relationship that I wish to concentrate. The corrupting body of Zosima is a jarring, completely unexpected witness to a faith that has decayed in its insistence on miracles on demand. The stench of the decaying body rebuffs such an insistence.

While some critics of Dostoevsky have dealt with the body and pollution in *Karamazov*, especially in the imaginative reading of Smerdiakov in Gary Saul Morson's essay (*Critical Essays*, 234–42) or in John Jones' epithet of the work as "the novel of evil smells" (*Dostoevsky*, 317), much of the criticism of the novel has tended to sidestep the flesh of Father Zosima, preferring instead to interrogate the spirit of the saintly man while leaving his body less fully attended. Jones, for example, focuses on the stinking flesh only long enough to allow a comparison with *Poor People* (301). Victor Terras remarks that Dostoevsky was fascinated by the power of fiction as well as by the human body, "the incarnational aspect of human life" (196). Ralph Matlaw begins a very interesting discussion of Zosima's corrupting corpse compared to the young Iliusha's body that, while ferociously diseased in life, gives off no odor in death (110); but he does not extend the two images beyond their suggestion of miracle or its absence. However, Sergei Hackel finds that the fullest refutation of the Grand Inquisitor's position is not through words but through image, what Dostoevsky himself referred to as "an artistic picture" (143). This image is that of Zosima, whose prototype in the narrative is Christ.

My own reading would extend Hackel's thesis to the body of Zosima, most specifically to his corrupting corpse, which ironically enough, causes the old monk to be more memorable in the minds of the people than he might have been even with miracle, as the narrator informs us more than once: "something happened so unexpected, so strange, upsetting, and bewildering in its effect on the monks and townspeople, that after all these years, that day of general suspense is still vividly remembered in the town" (*BK*, 303) And, to be sure we do not fall victim to short-term memory, he again reiterates this connection of odor to memory: "something took place which I alluded to at the end of the last book, something so unexpected by all of us and so contrary to the general hope, that, I repeat, this trivial incident has been *minutely remembered to this day* in our town and all the surrounding neighborhood" (*BK*, 308). The power of smell, especially the unpleasant odor of a decaying body, to implant in the memory an experience that might have been forgotten sooner, is the grotesque, even fantastic refutation that would cause the faithful to remember what they had anticipated but failed to receive as a sign of faith. The corrupting corpse of Zosima is an image of the wounded body that strikes the heart of complacent faith held by the faithful; it shatters their security of miracle and forces them to revision their beliefs.

Moreover, that the odor gains currency "at 3 o'clock" invites the further memory of Christ's death on the cross. Indeed, the corrupting body of Zosima becomes a mnemonic image that returns us to both history and teleology, similar in its spiritual force to the Russian Orthodox icon.[5] But here the nature and function of the icon in the lives of the faithful is parodied in Zosima's decay in order to challenge the impulse toward complacency, and with it, a ferocious literalism that denies the imagination the possibility to envision faith as something that is not to be literalized. The townspeople expect, far too comfortably, miracle from the holy monk's dead body.

In the shock of this incident, the narrator informs us, not simply does the corrupting odor unite the town and the monastery, but perhaps most crucially, its effect on the young Alesha is nothing short of an inner *transformation* even as the corpse undergoes an outer *deformation*. The unpleasant corpse extends the memory of the saint and offers an ironic twist to the flesh being made word, that is, given a language and a history. This action is itself a form of the miraculous; the irony is extended when we recognize that the faithful who come to the monastery in need of miracle, and those envious monks within the monastery who smell evil in the decaying corpse, both misinterpret the miracle set before them. Its form, however, they find offensive because it does not square with *their* image of miracle.

The narrative of the old monk lives in the memory of his corruption with the strength equal to his words of love and charity to even the most profligate in society.[6] In fact, Holquist takes this split of word (narrative) and deed (corrupting flesh) a step further when he affirms that "this confusion of the life is in contradiction with the canonical norm of the Life" (187). We might then interrogate Zosima's corruption in relation to Ivan's prose poem to understand Dostoevsky's ironic sense of faith outlined in this novel.

This deformation of Zosima's body, certainly an action in excess of nature's normal time for decomposition, and in effect a violation of time, a distortion of its normative movement, certainly invites another reading. For it is construed by the self-mutilating monk, Ferapont, as a sign of the deceased man's moral corruption, what Robert Louis Jackson has called *bezobrazie* ("Triple Vision," 304). It is, he writes, analogous to "the morally and aesthetically 'monstrous' or 'shapeless'" and is "counterpoised to *obraz* (image, form, icon)" (304). The stinking corpse of Zosima, moreover, is one of the great ironic images in literature, for by means of it the young Karamazov monk, Alexey, is transformed even as the townspeople are scandalized by its offensive odor. Zosima's body incites, as far as possible in his monastic surroundings, the topsy-turvy nature of carnival as Bakhtin develops this rich metaphor. His body "transgresses" normal natural limits, as Peter Stallybrass argues is the case within carnival (26). It is a kind of inversion of Christ's own transgressing normative limits when He rises from the dead within the Christian myth. The body's condition is out of keeping with the image of faith Zosima has been imagined to be.

When the narrator speaks of the "faithful" who have gathered around the dead body anticipating miracles, he observes, not a little naively: "they expected something quite different" (*BK*, 309). Logic, one might say, is deconstructed by the memory of the priest's logos—his teachings and his words of forgiveness. His odor is quick-forming, poignant, and intimate. Few of the body senses have the capacity or the power to stir the memory as does this overriding sense of smell.[7] And to push his offensive body a step further, Stallybrass argues that "the 'carnivalesque' mediates between a classical/classificatory body and its negations, its Others, what it excludes to create its identity as such" (26). As a consequence, "sectors of social and psychic reality are affected through the intensifying grid of the body" (26). Zosima's putrefying body gains an unprecedented power in the social and spiritual communities in its outlandish behavior that rivals any of the outrages of old Fyodor Karamazov and with more lasting effect.

What links Zosima so intimately to Christ in the exercise of one's faith is that it is a bodily activity and it is most powerful *after death*. It must be enfleshed in the world in action rather than remain in a more abstract Euclidean world of ideas, the kind of language Ivan enjoys expressing. The faithful need a radical action to offset the thinking outlined accurately if not cynically by Ivan Karamazov, who imagines so powerfully the anti-Christ in the form of the old cardinal of his poem.

Of this impulse to de-flesh the world and one's involvement in it, Ivan admits to his brother: "I have a Euclidean earthly mind, and how could I solve problems that are not of this world?" (*BK*, 216). His quarrel with God is not that He exists, but that He created a world along the lines of Euclidean geometry, which is, like God Himself, beyond human understanding. So Ivan is content to accept the idea of God, but he denies His created world: "I don't accept this world of God's, and, although I know it exists, I don't accept it at all" (*BK*, 216). If we can posit that the Word made flesh includes not only Christ but also, by way of God's incarnation, the world itself, then Ivan's denial of the world is, in effect, an attitude of mind that disincarnates it, while still wanting to believe in God. The end result of such a movement is to effectively divorce God from the world's body, which is to nullify by extension Christ's presence as an active force of love in people's lives. The stench of Zosima upsets such abstract thought. His decaying body forces on the townspeople a difficult way of imagining their faith.

The "illogic," or perhaps the "alogic" then, of Zosima's decomposing dead body is itself indeed a miracle of irony when juxtaposed to the univocal and destructive force of reasoned abstraction that, while certainly alienated from the world, nonetheless serves to breed evil in its denial of the earth's sacredness, much less that same world's existence; it is Dostoevsky's profound insight into postmodernity that when spirit is truncated from embodiment, it produces a disease of the intellect which assumes the form of figures like Stavrogin, Kirilov, Ivan Karamazov, or the old Inquisitor himself. These characters are emblems of intellect loose in the world without the grounding of bodily existence, memory of sacred traditions, or the originary ground of holy Mother Russia herself.

William Barrett has spoken eloquently of just such an intellectual move in what he terms a demonic impulse to "desubstantialize our thinking" (*Death of the Soul*, 128). He describes a form of thought whose intention is to deny the world's, and indeed one's own, embodiment. With the decomposition of self comes a corresponding deconstruction of the world. One serves as metaphor for the other. In another context I have tried to illustrate this as a move to abandon the notion of substance altogether.[8] In such an intellectual enterprise, ideas replace image and intellect subsumes the flesh of matter.

To take the consequences of such an intellectual migration one more step, I would cite in the writing of Oswald Spengler how the issue of abstraction can be symptomatic of the corruption of civilization itself. Speaking of a divorce from the soil within the confines of the city, Spengler writes in *The Decline of the West*: "Separated from the power of the land—cut off from it, even, by the pavement underfoot—Being becomes more and more languid, sensation and reason more and more powerful. . . . All art, all religion and science, become slowly intellectualized, alien to the land, incomprehensible to the peasant of the soil" (*The Decline of the West*, 228).

Such a split of intellect from the body is antithetical to what Gary Saul Morson retrieves in the term "prosaics": "a way of thinking about human events that focuses on the ordinary, messy, quotidian facts of daily life—in short, on the prosaic" ("Prosaics," 516).[9] Zosima's corrupting flesh exaggerates this messiness of the temporal world through the stench of his dead body, an action that severely disorients the people intent, even insistent, on a linear certainty of miracles at his death. In their comfortable anticipation of signs of holiness, placed outside them—indeed, disembodied from their own connectedness to the world—they are closely related to those people whom the Grand Inquisitor claims come to him to relinquish their freedom in exchange for a formulaic body of beliefs. Ivan's poetic creation is indeed a simulacrum of the Russian soul suffering the malady of literalism. Literalism as an act of consciousness would seem to occur, James Hillman has written, when the imagination fails or is no longer believed in as a valid way of knowing. The folk and the monks who slander the body of Zosima have lost the ability to personify, an act of imagination that "attempts to integrate heart to method and to return dead matter to their human shapes" (*Revisioning Psychology*, 15). Failing in this ability, the people are then exposed to the ingenious pathology inherent in Zosima's rotting body, whose sudden and rapid *deformation* is necessary for the Russian people to reimagine, through it, their faith, which itself, the action argues, has reached a morbidity that hardens into formula. The malodorous, decaying flesh fills the monastery and has a voice; it points to the rigor mortis of faith in many of those who seek him for miracles. Mimetically, the stench of his flesh mirrors the stench of their faith.

The failing inherent in such an insouciant attitude toward miracle is one of imagination itself because it suggests the *image* of Christ is insufficient for a life of active love. It is a failure of memory as well, for those who take for granted the appearance of miracles at Zosima's death are very much like Ivan Karamazov. They, too, find it impossible to enflesh the image of Christ, Himself the embodiment of the Word of God. Nor can they envision Him as a memorial image that points them to their own redemption. These two important acts of faith lived deeply Alexey, after much anguish, is able to perform. Through his struggle to continue to believe, we understand that faith fully embodied requires an act of imagination based on the image of the body as sacred emblem of the Word, whose prototype is Christ.

If Christ's presence in the world sacralizes it, then Zosima's words that "each is responsible for all" assume further urgency. The strategy to return those who would believe to such a form of faith is the putrefying body of the holy priest. His ironic image rests at the heart of Dostoevsky's poetics of the body. But warring against such an impulse in life is the play of a form of evil that promotes an abstraction of the world, and therefore its denial.

F. D. Reeves pointedly captures the metaphorical connectedness here: "Good and evil are nonrational. Evil putrefies the spirit, as if turning it into stinking flesh like saintly Zosima's body, but good purifies it" (*White Monk,* 126). His observation reflects the metaphorical nature of the body as a lived experience as well as a moral gesture.[10] In addition, one of the strengths of Roger Anderson's writings on myth is that he perceptively sees Dostoevsky's attempts to balance the mythical and the spiritual dimensions of the human imagination. While he underscores Zosima's connection with the earth, Anderson reveals that the decomposition of the old monk's body "recreates precisely what nature does each autumn. He not only decomposes in physical terms, but, like Markel, he 'fertilizes' the lives of those who follow him, especially Alesha's."[11] The connection between body and earth, between word and incarnation, constellates in the figure of Zosima to make him the fullest representative of John's Gospel on Christ as figure of both word and flesh. But in an atmosphere of spiritual complacency, doubt, or nihilism, articulating such a belief requires an image of irony, if not direct parody, to shake loose complacency.

Furthermore, Zosima's decomposing body also generates a part of the mythic cycle of birth-death-regeneration that is the soul of the Christian mystery. Harry Slochower reminds us that "in Dostoevsky's era, memory of the Pan-Slavic Earth Mother was fading" ("Quest," 254). For centuries as Mother Earth, she had served as "the maternal breast and womb: the black and fruitful soil. . . . She was thought to carry the family, the village, and the nation, which she nurtured . . . like a mother, according to Hubbs (55). Slochower suggests that Zosima and Alexey together revive the presence of Holy Mother Russia against the forces that encourage her forgetfulness "in Ivan and Smerdyakov its modern rationalistic and 'epileptic' forms" (254). We can see that the decaying corpse of Zosima remembers the Earth in her cycle of birth, growth, decay, and regeneration. His body, then, is a mythopoetic equivalent of Holy Mother Russia. Through his decay we understand how much the people have become amnesiac toward her in the ferocious intensity with which they condemn Zosima in his death. They have intellectualized the earth out of existence in their scathing indictment of him.

The body of Zosima, with its intimate odors and scandalously memorable decomposing flesh, represents an ironic incarnational witness to holiness and human transformation with the tradition of Holy Mother Russia as its foundation. His organic decomposition recalls the moist mother earth's fertility, its decay, and its rebirth. Contrary to the analytical proclivity of figures like Ivan Karamazov and the old Inquisitor, Zosima's corrupting flesh, occurring as "an excess of nature," reinforces Morson's insight into the novel: "*Karamazov* is about the inadequacy of explanatory systems to embrace the moral universe" ("Verbal Pollution," 234).

Moreover, even with such a reservation, Zosima shares a fundamental unity with Smerdyakov, old Fyodor's bastard son and epileptic, if we accept Morson's argument; for if "Smerdyakov's most effective pollution is verbal, . . . then his first crime is the betrayal of signs" (236). Zosima's foul odor at death is similarly also a betrayal of those anticipated miracles that the corpses of holy ones traditionally yield. Zosima's corruption, however, may be imagined less as betrayal than as an enfleshed response to Smerdyakov's position of aggressively narcissistic self-involvement.

For example, when Alexey confronts him in the garden singing to Maria Kondratievna and asks if he has seen his brother, Dmitrii, Smerdyakov, in a direct challenge to Zosima's "each is responsible for all," responds: "How am I to know about Dmitrii Fedorovich? It's not as if I were his keeper" (*BK*, 208). His boorish self-involvement anticipates Ivan's angry and memorable remark to Alexey less than half a dozen pages later: "'Am I my brother Dmitri's keeper?' Ivan snapped irritably, . . .'" (*BK* 213). Furthermore, Zosima's corruption is also a response to the demonic declarations coming from the *bloodless lips* of the Grand Inquisitor, whose reasoned abstractions about mankind Zosima refutes even in death through the image of decay.[12] The delightful irony of Zosima's stinking body is that it underscores what David Levin reveals in his excellent study of the hermeneutics of the body: "There is," he writes, "an ideal which is implicit in the body of radically reflective experience: an ideal I would describe in terms of its 'spirituality.' Merleau-Ponty's notion of 'flesh' moves us much closer to an understanding of the body's 'participation' in this spiritual dimension of existence" (*Body's Recollection*, 68).

Spirituality is therefore incarnational, a belief lost to many of the Karamazovs and twisted into a faith by the people who seek facile remedies, or a set of spiritual quick-fixes for complex problems. Into this moral vacuity

Zosima's stench invasively intrudes to promote an act of recollection, a way of intimately connecting body, earth, and spirit again, the fragmentation of which haunts the actions of each character in the novel. It is perhaps given fullest expression in Ivan, whom Holquist reminds us, "has lost all his ends and beginnings" (*Dostoevsky,* 185) while, ironically, his devil revels in the thought of being incarnated "irrevocably and for good as a two hundred pound merchant's wife" (*BK,* 184). The former is abstracted from his own biography, his own history, while his shadow lusts after an ample fleshly embodiment! The odor of Zosima promises to reconcile these two contradictory elements of human being.

Diane Oenning Thompson extends the idea of a split between intellect and flesh as systems of amnesia wherein "sacred memory" is slowly dismantled, a form of memory from which Zosima believes "all life has its vital principle" (*The Brothers Karamazov,* 210). The bodily stench of the old priest, a counterargument to "the bloodless lips" of the Inquisitor, at first unnerves Alexey; but soon it redeems his faith, which has already been under assault by the seductive reasoning of his brother Ivan's tempting Euclidean calculus and by his poetic rendering of the Inquisitor. In "Cana of Galilee" Alexey is literally brought back down to earth when he is challenged by and finally healed spiritually through the pungent body of his mentor.[13]

Zosima's death, occurring just before the novel's midpoint, is the central image in the narrative's action (even, I believe, above the image of Christ with the Inquisitor) in no less a profound way than the image of Lazarus rising from the tomb on Christ's command is the central salvific image in Dostoevsky's earlier novel, *Crime and Punishment* (even above the images of the two murdered women, Alena Ivanovna and her stepsister Lizaveta). Indeed, these two bodies, one rising in new life, the other decomposing in a hasty death, begin and end the major works of the writer. It is to the Word enfleshed that Dostoevsky turns in his most intense aesthetic and spiritual moments.

The ontological sickness of the faithful who question Zosima's holiness—almost as quickly as his decomposition—we have recognized before: in the tremens of Raskolnikov, the epilepsy and brain fevers of Prince Myshkin and Rogozhin, in the epilepsy of Kirilov, the diarrhea of Stepan Verkovhensky, and the epilepsy of Smerdiakov. While his body exacts a sudden transformation, the process turns on its head the transfiguration of Christ on Mount Tabor.

In an ironic way, Zosima's body does not reveal the sacrality of divinity but the stench of humanity, of *physis,* when left to its own laws gone awry and excessive. As such, his body becomes the center of our perception of invisible presences, the same the Grand Inquisitor in Ivan's prose poem denies by substituting a formulaic system of belief through the tenets of miracle, mystery, and authority—pale substitutes for an active and embodied image of Christ. His corrupting flesh allows Alexey to see what is invisible through the visible corpse; the young monk's vision, modulated by active love, returns to the flesh of the world, one intimately linked to the words of Zosima's declaration of active love. He even tells his young student to return to the world and to marry, and to embody his faith in the world.

Father Ferapont's frenetic response in denying the body as evil, however, is well documented within the monastery. He zealously denounces the corrupting flesh of Zosima as an irrefutable emblem of the priest's corrupt spirit. As such, he acts as an in-house version of the Grand Inquisitor, for both religious men deny the image of incarnation. We are not to believe Ferapont's reading of the body as text, for, driven by envy, he would prefer to engage in a map of misreading, finding Satan in the cherry jam Zosima periodically enjoyed with the ladies of the community, and sin in the tea he drank with them over conversation (*BK*, 312).

By the coffin of the dead priest rages an argument that broadens that of Ivan's through the Grand Inquisitor, for it once again creates an antagonism between a view of spirituality that is Euclidean, abstract, mathematical, and formulaic, and one that is based on love, is concrete, imagistic, Scriptural, embodied, and motivated in large measure by the image of Holy Mother Russia.

The essential question that is argued within the perspectives of incarnation might therefore be framed this way: Is human embodiment a deterrent to spirituality or a condition of it? If Zosima's corpse is emblematic of Dostoevsky's answer to the question, then there appears to be a conflation of both irony and "iconicity" in his death.[14] By this I suggest that his corrupting body is ironic, for it decays "in excess of nature"; but in its memorableness it is iconic, for it instills in the people of the town a remembrance that brings always to consciousness the words and deeds of the holy man, which certainly call to mind the prototype of Christ's life embodied and thus remembered in the old monk. The poet-philosopher Ivan Karamazov occupies, then, a moral liminal ground somewhere between the excess of nature, of which Zosima's decomposing body is emblematic, and deficiency, a denial of nature in Ferapont's harsh asceticism. Put another way, Ivan is between word and image[15] in his prose poem of the Grand Inquisitor and so remains slippery in both his beliefs and his intentions, an ambiguity Smerdyakov pounces on in misreading Ivan's words and thereby murdering Old Fyodor Karamazov.

In addition, Ivan's poetic fantasy illustrates his creation, the old cardinal's argument that people would prefer to consume miracle, mystery, and authority rather than engage in a life with Christ as their only guiding image. These elements comprise the seductive turns that deny responsibility, faith, and active love. Those who fall prey in his poem to this form of institutional life of nonspiritual worship are no less possessed than those who wait with a bland air of certainty that the corpse of Zosima will heal their loved ones or themselves. We are looking at the two faces of the same absence of faith from two perspectives.

Zosima's flesh disrupts the Grand Inquisitor's tidy world of ideological unfreedom as well as that of the followers of the holy monk. I don't believe it is too excessive to assert that Zosima's stench may be understood as the odor of freedom itself, which is why it is so acrimonious. The narrator underscores the immediacy of Zosima's death: "The elder's death came in the end quite unexpectedly. For although those who were gathered about him that last evening realized fully that his death was approaching, yet it was difficult to imagine that it would come so suddenly" (248).[16] The townspeople are now free to choose the words of Zosima from his life or the odor of corruption of his death.

Zosima's decomposing body, like Ivan Ilych's disease in Tolstoy's narrative, destroys the comfortable assumptions, the certain and too-familiar beliefs of those who would seek instant miracle from his body. It throws the townspeople and those who would defame Zosima into ambiguity and insists on their reimagining the values of their faith, which are exercised not according to a strict dogma, but in freedom. For instance, as soon as they hear of Zosima's death, the townspeople, in their certain faith, and as was the custom,[17] bring their sick to the monastery. They assume the corpse will heal them; the certainty of the dead man's holiness will emerge in miracle. They have already chosen the safe path Ivan's Grand Inquisitor has outlined and indeed promoted. In so doing they abdicate the imagination itself in favor of not simply a secular stance toward the miraculous, but the more passive role of *consumers* of miracles. Dostoevsky illustrates what a short leap it is from an act of worship to one of idolatry, from a life of active love to a life passive and consuming in its hunger for miracles.

The corrupting flesh is quickly seen from their secure perspective as proof the man was a hypocrite: "He was seduced by sweets, . . . he sipped tea, he worshipped his belly, filling it with sweet things and his mind with haughty thought . . . and for this he is put to shame" (*BK*, 314), derides Ferapont, his most relentless but by no means only critic. Ferapont's impulse is to intellectualize the body to serve his own ends; he therefore creates Zosima's body through the aperture of his own image, one fueled by envy. This image of embodiment is bestial; denying its appetites is the hallmark of a sacred life. Missed in his diatribe, however, is the miracle of incarnation, an event giving the body dignity, mystery, and sacrality. Ferapont enters Zosima's cell to exorcise the demons he assumes are hanging like spiders in all corners: "'I will cast thee out.' . . . He was wearing his coarse gown girt with a rope. His bare chest, covered with gray hair, could be seen under his hempen shirt. His feet were bare" (*BK*, 258). He accuses Zosima of not believing in devils because the monk prescribed medicines to heal the ailments suffered by some ill monks in the monastery. Ferapont's fiction of Zosima works backward from his disbelief in devils to a disbelief in God.

Zosima's corruption, however, expresses a refusal to be reduced to the literal and formulaic, but instead to remain steadfastly metaphorical and ambiguous. His is a carnival body which promotes the grotesque, the distorted, and the abnormal. Pathologized, it challenges the believers' basic assumptions about the nature of faith as an act of freedom. Zosima, however, is not to be adulated for his holiness, a stance the townspeople are only too willing to assume. They are prepared to hand over their freedom and to worship miracle (*BK*, 258) rather than struggle in freedom guided by the image of Christ.

Indeed, to wrestle with the image of Christ is to struggle with His words—for as Ouspensky argues in maintaining the position of the holy image in worship, icons are image-words, a Scripture in image (*Icons*, 113). The icon represents the human body aesthetically and spiritually already transformed in holiness and beauty, as Scripture seeks to transform the spirit in holiness. Zosima, in fact, in his decomposition, is the ironic double of Christ's transfiguration. His body is an ironic icon, so to speak, which paradoxically calls one back to the original prototype. The monk's unpleasant, offensive odor is the stench of freedom through active faith by means of the body, as well as a challenge of the imagination to forego external miracles for the true miracle of inner transformation. One of the few observations Dostoevsky writes in *The Notebooks* about the stench is worth noting: "When the cadaver began to smell, Alyosha began to doubt for the reason that Ivan had so clearly thrown out: 'The elder is holy, but there isn't any God'" (*Notebooks*, 110). On this note we are asked, I believe, to remember in Matthew's Gospel John the Baptist's words to Christ: "Are you the one who is to come, or have we got to wait for someone else?" (Matthew 11:2, 3).

Therefore, it is to the most metaphorical of the Gospels that Dostoevsky turns for his analogue to Zosima. One of the great Johannine symbols, certainly, is the body of the risen Christ (*Jerusalem Bible* 51, fn. j). And even for Christ to be viewed as a prophet in His own time, He must have "signs," or wonders worked in God's name. It was of course expected that He would repeat the earlier Mosaic miracles as a sign of His holiness. In this light, Zosima's "sign" might be called an "irony of corruption."

In its decay, therefore, and recalling John's images, the corpse of Zosima accomplishes several profound tasks: (1) as an ironic icon, we see through him to the memory of Christ for whom he is an image; (2) we remember the other stinking corpse, that of Lazarus, himself a sign of the prototype, the future risen Christ after the Passion and Crucifixion; and (3) we recall the miracle of resurrection even as Zosima's hasty decomposition is a miracle, but for reasons unlooked for—the odor of corruption is a sign of a higher reality, one in which the spirit is purified while firmly grounded in faith, the newly developing seed of which is Alexey Karamazov. We are reminded of the words of the rouge-cheeked simple holy woman, Maria Timofeevna in *The Possessed*, who when asked about God, answered: "'I think,' said I, 'that God and nature are just the same thing'" (*The Possessed*, 122). She has the wisdom of Sofya, which sees in the Earth herself the ground of divinity.

The moral point of Zosima's rapidly decaying flesh after a life of holiness is that it begins effectively to dismantle the three pillars of the Grand Inquisitor's demonic contrivance. Zosima's rotting corpse makes sense only in light of Ivan's prose poem. The dead body needs the words of Ivan's denial of God's creation—"and so I hasten to give back my entrance ticket" (*BK*, 226) in order to exist, Ivan asserts to his younger brother. But given that, the holy monk also dismantles miracle through his decay that promises no physical cure for the diseased and infirm; second, he dismantles mystery with Ferapont's declaration that the stench indicates unholiness, a clean, rhetorical, univocal declaration that denies Zosima's history through his rotting flesh, an opinion generally accepted and believed by many. Ferapont is thus the ascetic model of the Grand Inquisitor's voluptuous material life, even while he and the Grand Inquisitor create new narrative fictions to envelop and thereby reinvent their respective figures—Zosima and Christ—for mass consumption; third, he dismantles authority by having preached, just before his death, this lesson on memory: "keep the images of the Old Testament and New Testament alive, and in front of the people. Keep the *image* of Christ alive as the guide to holiness and active love" (*BK*, 245).

Zosima's own belief in life, ironically expressed in a rapid death, suggests a way of seeing that is always a conflation of body and world; both are sacred. Father Zosima reveals a bodily awareness that, as David Levin observes in another context, is an image of the body as the original metaphorical text; he claims that it is at the very source of our knowledge (*Body's Recollection* 171). Furthermore, the French philosopher, Maurice Merleau-Ponty, speaks of this connatural quality of body/world when he affirms that "the theory of the body image is implicitly a theory of perception. We have relearned to feel our body; we have found underneath the objective and detached knowledge of the body that other knowledge which we have of it in virtue of its always being with us and of the fact that we are our body. . . . The body is a natural self and, as it were, the subject of perception" (qtd. in Levin, 256). Applied to Zosima's death, then, his decomposing body is a way of seeing and living one's faith.

Understood within the poetics of the body in *Karamazov*, Zosima marries the spiritual dimension and the lived world to the flesh, signaling the juncture of spirit and world; human embodiment inhabits both realms[18] as the incarnation made history sacred.[19] For Ferapont, by contrast, all that comprises the world is unclean and must be expelled or denounced; his intention, therefore, is to exorcise both body and world from human life. He may best be described as the "spiritualized"[20] form of the Euclidean mind. In that role, his invectives against Zosima reveal a dissociation from the prosaics of the world. But without the active love described by Zosima, Ferapont's actions illustrate only the putrefaction of a faith turned in on itself and gnawing its own flesh in envy.

Ferapont's distancing self from world through vigilant and grotesque denial is actually a more modern notion in its insistence on fragmentation and divisiveness. He has succeeded, like Ivan's Grand Inquisitor, in abstracting—even bloodletting—the flesh of the world. Ferapont can only understand the corrupting corpse in the monastery through the prism of his own envy, as the Grand Inquisitor can imagine humanity only through the metaphor of his own consuming impulse to improve on God's design.[21]

The old cardinal's canon is another form of the cult of reason that also plagues Ivan Karamazov. As A. Boyce Gibson offers, "reason, as Dostoevsky for the most part understood it, was separatist and analytical; it splits up the totalities in which we live. By contracting the vision, it falsifies. . . . For Dostoevsky individualism and atheism went together, . . . both derive from the analytic outlook which destroys the unity of situations" (*Religion of Dostoevsky,* 210).[22]

Ivan reveals this side of his thinking about love just before entertaining his younger brother with the Grand Inquisitor narrative. He relates the story of John the Merciful, a saint who, when confronted by a nearly frozen beggar pleading for warmth, "took him home to his own bed, held him in his arms, and began breathing into his mouth, which was putrid and loathsome from some dreadful disease" (*BK,* 178). Ivan interprets this act not as one of love but more like "a self-lacerating penance." The philosopher believes that "for anyone to love a man, he must be hidden, for as soon as he shows his face, love is gone" (*BK,* 179). He concludes his deductive argument by stating his act of faith: "One can love one's neighbor in the abstract, and sometimes even at a distance, but at close quarters it's almost impossible" (*BK,* 179). Love remains solely in the arena of an idea, severed from the intimacy of the world's flesh, however infected or wounded it may seem; Ivan's love at this point in the novel is disincarnated, though his shocking images of evil brutality of individuals against children are all graphically enfleshed. He is therefore alienated from revelation which is always incarnated; as Arthur Trace observes, salvation finally comes "not by reason but by revelation, not by philosophy but by religious faith" (*Furnace of Doubt,* 80).

The thought of John the Merciful's active response to the bodily sickness and mortal decay of another finds its poetic analogue in two other responsive kisses: when Christ, after His long and patient silence in the face of the Inquisitor, kisses him on his bloodless lips in response to the latter's confession of ministering to Satan rather than God; and again in the mocking kiss of Alexey to his brother Ivan; the metaphor of decay swirls out to include imaginations diseased by self-preoccupation and driven by profound, albeit infirm, motives.

Yet Ivan can admit that his understanding of the world is "Euclidean" (*BK,* 184), and that the suffering of one child would negate for him the beneficence of God's world. An astute critic of Dostoevsky, Louise Cowan has noted that Ivan has never seen a child suffering, as has Alexey in the stoning and then disease of young Ilyushka; he has instead read of horrifying instances, but has never witnessed it (Lecture, "The Brothers Karamazov," 1985). If such is the case, do we observe yet another division of flesh from word, of idea severed from incarnation, of a reasoned abstraction that constitutes a move to an infernal worldview because forged from the heat of a self-absorbed imagination? If so, then Ivan's Grand Inquisitor is a logical and abstract extension of his belief in love as an intangible reality.

In such a context dwells a wonderful irony in Christ's action in Ivan's narrative when He kisses the Inquisitor. Christ's silent action (that He is wordless throughout the encounter is itself ironic!) could not have been more rhetorically powerful. At the same time, Christ's kiss to the Inquisitor, His enfleshed response to nihilism, revokes Ivan's abstract notion, shows his own confusion, and leaves the young Karamazov ambivalent toward a faith incarnated in active love. Yet Ivan's response is one of pure delight when his brother incarnates his own love by kissing *him.* Love embodied surprises, then pleases him; it has the silent force of muting the energy of his ideology as it goes beyond words to silence.

Given Ivan's response, it is clear that he may still be redeemed, especially when he tells his brother that he "loves the sticky little leaves as they open in spring" (*BK,* 211), a love that allows him to remain poetically attached to the natural world of Holy Mother Russia. Ivan's distant relation to the world is thus tempered by his affection for the moist earth. On this dichotomy in Ivan, William Lynch suggests that none of us really lives "in the universe, but in a much smaller space; we live *within the language of our bodies*" (*Images of Faith,* 98). Lynch's remark illuminates further an aspect of Ivan, who seems hopelessly divided in head and heart, but who can nonetheless sense some important contact with the prosaics of the world even as he rages for abstraction, which creates a chasm between the flesh and the word.[23]

Zosima by contrast reminds the community in word and in action not only of Lazarus but also of Christ. His is an image which embodies the words of Scripture and thus guides rather than tyrannizes belief. The poetic argument Dostoevsky proposes suggests that imagination without faith leads to a denial of creation as God's work; faith without imagination leads to a recalcitrant self-righteousness of the type enfleshed by Ferapont; and intellect without imagination leads to a stubborn despotism that the Grand Inquisitor embodies.

As Zosima in life ate cherry jam and drank tea with the ladies as a way of illustrating the integrity and goodness of appetites and bodily desires when wedded to a life of spirit—as Christ's first miracle at the Cana marriage sanctified the body in union and love—his decaying corpse reveals that the physical body is not an end in itself, but that incarnation ought to carry into the world the Word of God. It is not idolatrous when both word and image participate fully in the body of the world, with a vision of the sacred and the eternal given through the God/man's presence historically. Memory, then, serves one's vision of the future. As "The Peasant Marei" beautifully expresses it, remembering Christ while blessing oneself is the conflation of word made flesh, which has the power to transform one's vision of the world, as Dostoevsky realized suddenly during an epiphany while in exile in Siberia.

The scandal of corruption initially drives Alexey to escape the cloistered life in bitterness, "for it was justice he thirsted for, not simply miracles" (*BK,* 261). He loses his meekness in his anger and begins, with the foppish Rakitin as his guide, "to eat sausage, drink tea," and visit the lovely coquette Grushenka, even letting her sit on his knee. He begins to embrace his own embodied appetites, and by so doing, learns to love the world in all of its prosaic sacredness. The putrid flesh of Zosima in death, as well as his guiding language in life, invites his young student to oppose a modern tendency to separate body from spirit and the Holy Earth of Russia from the life of the intellect.

His impulses are quite different from Ahab's, whose scarred body and ivory leg relate him closely to the white whale he intends to destroy. Alexey, however, shares some common comic affinities with the young Ishmael, witness to the cataclysm of the *Pequod* and who lives to construct a narrative that promises to close the wound splitting body, spirit, and nature so prevalent at the end of the nineteenth century.

7

The White Whale and the
Afflicted Body of Myth

> We are told, [erroneously] for example, of a whale's *roaring* when wounded by the harpoon.
> —Melville, "Etchings of a Whaling Cruise," 531

Perhaps one of the most distinctive traits that many works of nineteenth-century American literature share with the older oral tradition of epic, especially those of Homer and the still earlier heroism of *Gilgamesh*, is an apparent self-consciousness that coats the narrative, and gives them a sense of their own self-identity. The epic work of Herman Melville, *Moby-Dick*, and the oral-written narrative of Mark Twain's *Huckleberry Finn*[1] bestow on their respective storied voices, Ishmael and Huck, an aesthetic self-reference, a benign narcissism, that keeps the story reflecting its own history as it moves forward through fictional space and time.

One might even suspect that such a narrative voice thinks itself into being both through its experienced journey and the later narrative one that remembers the intricate plot. The narratives of Ishmael and Huck recall here the voice of the poet-pilgrim Dante Alighieri who, more than most other poets of epic, gave voice as well as form to the journey of the soul coming to know itself. While certainly written stories with a memory of an earlier event, the nature of the narrative is to be compellingly oral so as to give voice to an informal, at times conversational, quality to the renderings of experience.

In slightly more mechanical language, but no less important, Mikhail Bakhtin and P. N. Medvedev suggest that "literature reflects and refracts the ideological environment of which it is a part" even as it "anticipates developments in philosophy, ethics, in an intuitive form." Their belief is that the artist senses these developments "in *statu nascendi*," in the early birth stage (*Formal Method,* 16). What this refraction illumines for us today, as more attention is rightly given to both ecology and biology, is a series of relationships among language, human embodiment, and inscriptions, including markings, etchings, writings, tattooings of experience, in order to make visible in some permanent language or image what has remained hidden to ordinary perception. Such cultural activity becomes extremely acute in the nineteenth century, as writers like Donald Lowe, Peter Brooks, and Peter Gay have observed,[2] when the desire for privacy collides with communal curiosity, giving further credence to the novel as a form that both stimulates and satisfies these urges.

Melville, operating within the epic tradition of Homer, Dante, Milton, Faulkner, and Toni Morrison, incorporates in his American narrative, one that is both a modern novel and a patterned epic of America's myth of industrialism in the form of whaling, what I wish to call " a poetic physiology" that is intimately tied to the imaginative act of creating story.

Body and inscription are inseparable metaphors in Melville's work, which has as one of its many-layered meanings to explore the word and the flesh as they intertwine about a central hunt. Lynda Sexson reminds us that the word "text" originally referred to "weaving," suggesting perhaps that the loom was the locus of storytelling (*Ordinarily Sacred*, 46).[3] Such a word puts at least a dual spin on the title of the first chapter, "Loomings," which stitches together almost immediately a sense of foreboding about the future, whales appearing on the horizon, and the tight weave of the plot's intrinsic design. The weave, the skein, the line, the wound or body marking—all of these inscribed forms invite us into the hermeneutic space of the novel, one which has as its central action the interpretive journey by Ishmael to know himself through the world's body; his great voyage of discovery is one of understanding the wound, the scar, the inscription and even to explore in depth the deep fathom of what interpretation itself is.

I wish therefore to explore in this chapter several possible intertwining lines connecting the world, the flesh, and the whale as it bears on both reading and writing as well as on the larger concern of how meaning is arrived at, even in the most tentative way. For stories, as Sexson continues, are the narratives that often recapitulate the great archaic originary stories of, for example, The Fall, Transformation, or the labyrinthine Journey into Self-Consciousness (47). Now even while stories will not explain the workings of memory, Sexson offers the interesting insight that "stories remembered may be parables for memory itself" (45). How these stories are embodied will reveal, particularly through a study of Queequeg, Ahab, and the white whale—all of whose bodies are marked in some way—how a fuller and less fragmented way of perceiving can develop that collapses the Cartesian split so prevalent in our own time, and was altogether open for business in the nineteenth century. Ishmael is fond of referring to such a condition as "Descartian vortices" (*Moby-Dick,* 140), an attitude not sus-

ceptible of abatement under conventional ways of seeing. Through the figure of Queequeg primarily, Ishmael the whaler/writer undertakes another
expedition, a retrieval of soul or spirit, and with it a form of the sacred that
has fallen into the shadow cast by the new term, "self," a social science version of identity that indeed replaced the notion of soul in modernity.[4] Such
a distinction includes a form of existence in which body and soul are separate, yet there exists a unity between them. What is at stake in each is a vision of language's place in culture. Sharon Cameron's helpful insights
further reveal how *Moby-Dick* explores a poetics of anatomy that is tied to
a modern sense of the body, including its fragmentation (*Corporeal Self,*
24).[5] Perhaps in this novel is born the myth of the modern body—codified
in its markings to reveal a worldview of separateness, as well as an older,
mythic body in the figures of Queequeg, Ahab, and Moby-Dick that retrieve a primordial cosmology as well as the markings left from the myth of
industrial capitalism.

The primary business of whaling is wounding; its success depends on
harpooning creatures from the depth of the ocean, pulling them onboard,
and fragmenting them into marketable commodities. In *Moby-Dick*, two
predominant myths collide onboard the *Pequod*, a moveable psychic container for the entire world: that myth which Queequeg wears on his body as
the son of a Polynesian king, and the myth of the maimed Fisher King who
is wounded and incapacitated, as Harry Slochower observes (*Mythopoesis,*
240). Ahab's flaw is his wound; he needs a young knight to save him, perhaps in the form of Starbuck or Ishmael. While Starbuck fails, I believe Ishmael uses the destruction of Ahab and the *Pequod* to save the entire world
by marking the story of the hunt. The act of writing itself becomes the great
elongated scar on the face of the white page that redeems the community,
but only through the violence of the three days' chase in which the white
whale dives and is reborn three times. The final resurrection is of Ishmael
himself, borne on the coffin-life buoy whose outer skin replicates the tattooed cosmion of Queequeg's ornamented flesh.

While I make no profession of discipleship as a Lacanian, I find useful
his observation in *Ecrits*: "what the psychoanalytic experience discovers in
the unconscious is the whole structure of language" (147), out of which
evolves a whole theory of semiotics, a formidable finding that allows one to
speculate perhaps that the white whale of this novel is an emblem for the
origins of language issuing out of depth, discourse, speech, storytelling,
from the bottom, so to speak, of silence itself. What Lacan does more safely
permit is a consideration of *desire* and its connection to ancient knowledge
(301), an observation conducive to understanding the most interesting and
enchanted forms of embodiment in the novel: Ahab, Queequeg, and the
white whale, each of which represents a radically different world. While for

Lacan this desire is at its foundation sexual, I include as well the unfailing human desire, as embodied beings, to enflesh and "text" ourselves into the world—formulating images into phrases, as Lynda Sexson expresses it (*Ordinarily Sacred,* 31) in order to make ourselves into embodied beings with a history in the world.

Moby-Dick, perhaps more fully than any other American novel, develops a poetics of inscriptions that invites a healing of body and soul that has been so effectively divorced by the rise of science and philosophies that, beginning in the seventeenth century, would proclaim most vehemently the ascendancy of intellect over matter. As a philosophical and physiological movement, it was not given its fullest expression until the onrush of nineteenth-century novels of America, Europe, and Russia that explored the constant dream of improvement and growth. The forms that this inscription takes, though varied, focus most dynamically on the nature of story, narrative, and the birth of desire as impulses that call us back to human embodiment. For even as "our cultural history is encoded in our bodies," as Wilhelm Reich has argued (qtd. in Berman, *Coming to Our Senses,* 22), so too there exists a semiotics of story that undergirds *Moby-Dick* as it apprehends the lineaments of the American epic spirit. Such a story calls us home, as Rollo May believes any powerful myth has the capacity to do. There is a healing of a cultural wound through myth that aids us in repatterning our existence based in the home of the myth. It is, May argues, "our interior structure" (*Cry for Myth,* 33). I assert that the myth of America is inscribed with variations through the bodies of Queequeg, Ahab, the white whale and the etchings of the book itself that comprises Ishmael's original mark in the world.

The question I propose, then, is this: How do these elements that implicate both the human and the world's body, writing and whaling, wound and words, conjoin in *Moby-Dick* to outline in general form the prevailing myth of America? Is there something distinctly American in the action of this epic novel that seems to be intrinsic to us as a new nation, a mixture of tribes and peoples that intertwine several world myths and gather round the activity of industrialism (specifically hunting the whale) and commerce as the central action we share? Perhaps we are less a melting pot or a mixed salad than a confederacy of myths that swirl around the psyche of America with an undeveloped unifying image that will give them all a coherence. And what place do we give the scarred, scored body of Ahab? Is he our emblem of the cosmic wound, the originary wound that each of us carries inscribed on our own souls? As a marked and wounded Titan, Ahab gathers all of us around him, to share in his obsession.[6]

Melville's patterned awareness of this relationship is present in many sections of the novel; he invites us to link the inscribed bodies of Queequeg, Ahab, and the white whale to the notion of story. They are equal in their signification, for each one of them invites a different act of interpretation; each is a text to be deciphered; they are hieroglyphs that need a varied hermeneutic attitude so that what is mysterious can be grasped through Ishmael's inscripted markings.

We notice that the three bodies mentioned share two qualities: (1) each of these bodies is "storied" into being *before* they actually appear in the narrative, and (2) each of them is already marked and/or wounded when they appear in the narrative. They carry the scars, markings, or tattoos of their own respective histories and cultures: Queequeg is introduced in a joking way to Ishmael by Peter Coffin before he appears to share Ishmael's room and bed; Ahab is introduced by Captains Peleg and Bildad and narrated to Ishmael ("The Prophet," 86) before he appears on the Quarter Deck of the *Pequod*; and Moby-Dick is storied into being by numerous narratives of Ahab and by members of other ships during several gams, before he finally surfaces to confront Ahab and his crew directly. With the ocean as his text, "there the encounters with the whale had taken place; there the waves were storied with his deeds" (173). Perhaps it was insights like the one here that led Carl Jung to call *Moby-Dick* the greatest American visionary novel: "I would also include Melville's *Moby-Dick*, which I consider to be the greatest American novel, in this broad class of writings." He goes on to specify why a work like Melville's is such a rich field to mine. He senses that "such a tale is constructed against a background of unspoken psychological assumptions, and the more unconscious the author is of them, the more this background reveals itself in unalloyed purity to the discerning eye" ("Psychology and Literature," 88). What Melville consciously realizes in marking the bodies of his major figures in the novel is less important than that we discern what the visible wounds and markings tell us about the action and the meaning of the plot. There is, I believe, a significant mythic sensibility surrounding the body in its markings that ritualizes in a cosmic and communal way our own unique incarnations. A deep mimesis is explicit in the markings of the words on the page and the lines in the flesh.

That each of these inscribed bodies is made present in story first, what might be called "phantom bodies," eventually to become actual corporeal bodies in the narrative, invites a discussion between language and flesh, the semiotics of things and their actual referents. For the book Ishmael creates makes what is absent to us, fully, if fictionally present. Through him we sense a deeper "carnal relation to the world" (*Prose*, 139), according to Merleau-Ponty. The markings on these three figures are emblems of vastly different cultures or worlds if we consider that Queequeg's body is marked by a tribal seer and prophet with the myths of nature and an entire cosmogony;[7] Ahab's body is marked as if by a lightning bolt, that flash of whiteness out of the heavens that begins on his forehead and carries itself jaggedly the full length of his body. He is also marked by the whale bone leg. He is therefore seeking vengeance on the beast who he is already becoming. And Moby-Dick is marked by the harpoons of Ahab, twisted and fastened to his back, visible traces of his most relentless pursuer. Finally, Ishmael himself is not unmarked, for to keep in his mind the dimensions of a whale, which "are copied verbatim from my right arm, where I had them tattooed" (376), he marks the trace of the whale on his own flesh.

In discussing other literary texts, Peter Brooks sets the foundation for his approach by observing the place of the marked body in narrative. He pulls the two elements of writing and the body together through the prism of semiotics when observing that "the sign imprints the body, making it part of the signifying process. Signing or marking the body signifies its passage into writing, its becoming a literary body, and generally also a narrative body, in that the inscription of the sign depends on and produces a story. The signing of the body is an allegory of the body become a subject for literary narrative—a body entered into writing" (*Body Work,* 3). Part of the necessity for inscripting the body into culture, to which Brooks appends the rather clanking phrase, the "epistemophilic project," namely, one that involves knowing the body and knowing *through* the body (278), is that from the eighteenth century forward there is no shared sense of what it means to be corporeal, no communal body of beliefs that would ensure a given meaning for being enfleshed in the world.[8] So redefining the body's meaning is as much Ishmael's hermeneutic project as is learning the craft of whaling; both enterprises, as he suggests, demand a great attention to detail.

THE MARKED BODIES OF MYTH

The bodies of Queequeg, Ahab, and the white whale are to be approached as three different narratives, or three unique ways of experiencing the world and making meaning out of it. Each body bears its own inscription of meanings: Queequeg's tattoos, Ahab's "rod-like mark, lividly whitish" (110) running the length of his body, as well as his ivory leg; and the ubiquitous white whale's body, with its "peculiar snow-white wrinkled forehead and a high, pyramidal white hump . . . , his deformed lower jaw" (159), and buried in his hump, "the tall but shattered pole of a recent lance projected from the white whale's back" (447), which marks and wounds him through artifice. The markings on his white back as well as the lines in his white forehead are the analogues to Ishmael's marking the white page with his own penetrating mini harpoon, his pen.

The corporeality of Queequeg, as an inscribed body, can hardly be separated from Ahab's dismembered and scarred flesh and Moby-Dick's deformed and marked corpus.[9] Clark Davis speculates that Ahab's relation to language is one of "human instrument to be employed against the instruments of the unknowable, . . . It is a substitute for his lost body" (*After the Whale*, 12), making language and the body for him inseparable shipmates who need to be studied together. And all of these "encultured" bodies make possible and resonate constantly with the last marking, that of the text itself, which Ishmael marks not with harpoon or lance, but with the ink of his pen. The most completely inscribed body becomes the epic we journey through as readers, creating, during our journey, our own myth which we weave together with the mythopoetic construction of Ishmael. Different from the harpoon, which is less able to inscribe but only to penetrate the white page of the whale's skin, Ishmael's pen is able to inscribe surface with depth, a deepening of understanding that language allows for and promotes through the tropes of fictional narrative. The inscribed bodies of savage, captain, and whale make the inscribed narrative possible at the same time that they conjoin the myths of industrialism, primitive presence, and animal vitality, all dominant forces in the American psyche. In his prose that reconstitutes the world, Ishmael's act of writing echoes the insight offered by Merleau-Ponty about the relation of embodiment to world: "There is a universality of feeling—and it is upon this that our identification rests, the generalization of my body, the perception of the other. I perceive behavior immersed in the same world as I because the world I perceive still trails with it my corporeality" (*The Prose of the World*, 137).

His observation grazes the deeper issue of mimesis through the body, a way of blending and relating to the world through the corpus of my own being and its shared analogue in the body of the narrative. Furthermore, Brooks' insight above offers a rich and crucial avenue into speaking of the body and inscription in story that *Moby-Dick* poetically explores throughout the whaling journey. That it begins with the section, "Etymology," consciously places words and their histories, or their own linguistic stories, squarely at the origin of the work and already invites a meditation on the origin of one word, "whale," which serves linguistically as a "phantom" presence of the body that is as yet absent.[10] First the story of the word, then of its presence in stories ("Extracts," 2–11), before the actual bodies of whales are hunted, harpooned, anatomized, sliced, eaten, drained, tried, barreled, and stored for consumers on land.[11]

Melville begins his epic in such a manner in order to call attention to the storied bodies of the whales offered first by inscription, which then eventually shifts to the inscribed body of Moby-Dick. When Ishmael proclaims "I celebrate a tail" (314), he voices this connection between body and story (tale) that carries us to the central meaning of the novel itself, namely, that the word and the flesh are not to be separated any more than are body and soul. Here Brooks introduces another fitting element to this vision of Melville's novel and perhaps to nineteenth-century fiction generally, the act of *desire*.[12]

He speculates that beginning with Rousseau and Balzac, a modern semiotics of the body is born; *marking the body* is its way of being formatted, capable now for the first time of receiving the imprint of messages. It has been signed (*Body Work,* 46). As a cultural construct, the body comes into being through its markings, specifically through the impulse of desire. Said another way, the body takes on its story through writing, whose central inspiration is desire. This "epistemophilic project" of knowing the body and knowing through it (278) is enfleshed most forcefully, therefore, in Queequeg, Ahab, and Moby-Dick. It may be that the nineteenth-century novel generally, "with its plots of education . . . and its presentation of reality as enigmatic, requires an inquest into the nature of its signs in order to decipher them," a hermeneutic act that leads to the search for "a certain body that takes on special meaning, as goal, origin or both: a body that becomes the signifier of signifiers" (*Body Work,* 48).

In a more intensely sustained form, then, *Moby-Dick* illustrates that the physical, tangible body is a second-order or narrative presence, indeed even a phantom presence: first words, then presences. Words can conjure an absence into presence; the trace of such presence is the novel itself, inscribed with enigmatic meaning always around the body of Queequeg, Ahab, and the whale. We could say that the words re-member what is absent into a presence because the words allow us to imagine what is not there through their verbal simulacra.[13] These three bodies bear witness to a narrative whose message is that "the body is the referent of reference itself . . . The body is the ultimate field from which all symbolism derives and to which it returns . . . the primary source of symbolism" (*Body Work,* 6). *Moby-Dick* is an exemplum of the novels of the nineteenth century which appear to underscore an active desire, one in which "we are forever striving to make the body into a text" (7). This desire is what Ishmael grows into but only after having confronted a text that *is a body,* namely, the body textualized in Queequeg's figure.[14]

And yet he is not alone. To recapture the past through memory and to story them, to inscribe these memories imaginatively is at the same time to interpret our own lives, to understand ourselves, as Sexson writes, "symbolically" (*Ordinarily Sacred,* 46). Narcissus is such a predominant myth underlying the action of *Moby-Dick* because it conveys, perhaps, better than all others, the act of reflection through image; one sees oneself clearly, first as some "other"; then slowly, as a figure that begins to float mysteriously toward the surface of our awareness, we see that it is ourselves.

These varied forms of embodiment might therefore be labeled in the following way: the tattooed skin of Queequeg as the cosmic, ritualized, or mythic body, the body of imagination's presence itself; the dismembered and scarred flesh of Ahab as the abandoned body,[15] the body split within itself; the corpus of Moby-Dick as the phantom body, the commercial body, the body of nature, the spiritual or cosmic corpus. As wounded or tattooed or marked bodies, they are the cardinal emblems of an absent presence. It is Ishmael's task to remember these varied forms of embodiment and to render them in language through their stories; his task is to make them representational. By remembering these textual bodies, Ishmael incorporates into his writing the text of the world. In such an action he makes a text of his own life, one that is intertextual. As Ahab is supported by the whale bone for a leg, a kind of impotent pen with no ink, Ishmael is supported at the end of the novel by the carved coffin of Queequeg. His mythic-memorial coffin keeps Ishmael afloat; he survives by riding the myth of Queequeg's inscribed body, which has been transferred to the coffin through the islander's own artistic efforts. Artifice saves Ishmael. Queequeg's myth is rendered in image; Ishmael's in words. He floats on the miniature ship crafted by Queequeg, who is present through the carvings on the wood that mirror his own body's ritual and mythic markings. He has created in the wood and in the design of the footlocker/coffin/lifebuoy a replica of his own body, as Ishmael creates in his narrative a replica of his own embodied psyche through what he remembers. In this sense, Ishmael and Queequeg are linked closely. Merleau-Ponty points out that "the other's body is a kind of replica of myself, a wandering double which haunts my surroundings more than it appears in them. . . . Every other is a self like myself" (*Prose,* 134). It is this deep sense of communal relationship with others in the world that allows Ishmael to dwell within a comic and not a tragic space, buoyed by the memory of his exotic double.

The movement of narrative that implicates both body and inscription, that is to say, to make them as bodies culturally and poetically formatted to enter language as signifiers, requires three translations: (1) from absent body to a body present in narrative; (2) their actual presence *in* narrative; (3) their remembered presence *through* narrative.[16] The idea of a phantom presence appears in the three bodies in the form of memory that is both incarnated and linguistic. For example, in "The Chapel" appear the cenotaph inscriptions (39–40). As words about those who have died at sea without being recovered, they are substitutes for the absent bodies, all of which are lost to their families forever. Words replace the absent body and are able to make them present through linguistic substitution. Signing the body, Peter Brooks suggests, "is an allegory of the body become a subject for literary narrative—a body entered into writing" (*Body Work,* 3). In "The Chapel" episode these bodies are inscribed with a memory *as a result of their absence.*[17] Words are carved into stone. What is absent becomes present, and in a way the temporal is made eternal through the stone memorial inscription. Much like Ishmael's will, or Ahab's charts that he marks so meticulously in his search for the absent whale, these cenotaphs are inscriptions to fill the absence; they promise the presence of what is yet to be made tangible. And, like scars left by wounds, they re-member the *original* event or person.

Such an absent presence appears later in the novel with Ahab's phantom limb he discusses with the carpenter.[18] Ahab claims that he feels the phantom limb that Moby-Dick severed from his body and offers the sensation of a dual body: "When I come to mount this leg thou makest, I shall nevertheless feel another leg in the same identical place with it; . . . my old lost leg; the flesh and blood one, I mean. Can'st thou not drive that old Adam away?" (391). And then to his observation that there is in the world an invisible presence that this reality shadows, he responds: "How dost thou know that some entire, living, thinking thing may not be invisibly and uninterpenetratingly standing precisely where thou now standest; aye, and standing there in thy spite?" (391).[19] As if to desire suddenly a visual aid to augment such a metaphysical reflection, Ahab has the carpenter place his own real leg against the captain's own artificial limb, doubling the phantom limb with real flesh and bone in a futile attempt to make authentically present what has been taken from him by Moby-Dick. His phantom limb, a crude double of the original, does not quite "measure up." His measurement is to no avail, for the wound remains.

In fact, throughout the novel, wills, charts, affidavits, inscriptions of many varieties attempt to make present, indeed to embody, what is absent. In this respect the narrative opens up to a psychological story. Writing becomes an act of mirroring, a movement toward self-reflection. Such a gesture is given added mythic power through Narcissus's presence already in the first pages of the novel. In addition, as Robert Romanyshyn observes, "language is a glass on which or through which the image of self is reflected" (*Psychological Life,* 8), which observation furthers the image of Narcissus, who suffered from an excess of reflection.

John T. Irwin's remarkable study, *American Hieroglyphics,* echoes this idea when he writes specifically of Moby-Dick: the qualities of the whale, he suggests, "are the projected attributes of his pursuers, and in particular, the chief of his pursuers, Ahab" (287). While more than a simple univocal projection is at stake in the novel, nonetheless Irwin is correct in citing how the "white whale swam before [Ahab] as the monomaniac incarnation of all those malicious agencies which some deep men feel eating in them till they are living on with half a heart and half a lung" (*Moby-Dick,* 160). Does the malignancy of Ahab begin, then, when he wounds the body of the whale with his own marking utensil, the harpoon? Does Ahab not commit the same linguistic, or semiotic, simulation that Ishmael later dramatizes in writing the text? The bodies of the whale and Queequeg are also marked by a language, and in fact are desired by language; they are marked by mythologies of which they are a part.

Spread more generally throughout the novel, the hieroglyphic nature of the text Irwin interprets as a thick action of doubling the world when he links it to language itself: "The blank background on which the novel's hieroglyphic shadow selves are projected is either the sea or the whiteness of the whale hidden beneath the sea's surface, or a conjunction of these two" (290). Blackening the page with ink highlights or foregrounds blackness over the white blank page.[20] Brooks eloquently propels this observation forward in observing that "the semioticization of the body and the somaticization of story" are so intimately linked because the destinies of the body so marked tend to play out the narrative plot (*Body Work,* 86–87). This semiotic imprint on the body is not only a prevalent theme in nineteenth-century literature, but is central to modern narratives generally (87).

By examining for a moment the body of Queequeg as a poetic, inscribed body that precipitates and even promotes the creation of narrative, we glimpse more profoundly the psychological story of our American myth.[21] And much as the legend of *Faust* became a heroic story of a collective myth which, Jung writes in his autobiography, "anticipated the fate of the German people" (*Memories, Dreams, Reflections,* 210), so may our own American myth be intertwined in the inscribed bodies of *Moby-Dick,* an alchemical try-pot or cauldron in which the bodies of many cultures are melted into a new transformed liquid.

QUEEQUEG AND THE RITUAL BODY

Few characters in literature incite the imagination as provocatively as does Queequeg. He appears to befriend, guide, and save the uninitiated orphan, Ishmael, who wishes to leave the land in order to enter the world more fully as a whaler. What he has lost, in his proclivities toward violence and death, is a presence to the world that is communal or loving. He has also lost or misplaced his relation to stories, particularly his own *mythos,* as well as a sense of belonging to place. He is one of America's archetypal orphans, an individual who in his initial aimlessness and anger, is without a narrative; he has become unmoored from his story and with it, from any analogical connection to the world and to others.[22] His gift on this journey is Queequeg, who will allow him later to retrace the narrative in order to capture in writing a cultural story through an intricate and inexhaustible web of interconnected images. This tattooed "other" from an island that appears on no map, is an image, I believe, for story itself.

We may remember at this late date, some of the facts about Queequeg. Son of an island king, he sells shrunken heads in New Bedford; yet his own decorated body is covered with "large, blackish looking squares . . . with black squares on his cheeks" (28). In contrast to these heads, which have been "twisted smaller" in comparison to human heads, will appear the colossal wrinkled head of the sperm whale, which seems to double the wrinkled brow of Ahab.[23] But contrary to the heady captain, Queequeg is of the body, and so his heads are miniatures. Ishmael pens a wonderful pun at this point when he describes the savage's body: "they were stains of some sort or other. At first I knew not what to make of this; but soon an *inkling* of the truth occurred to me. *I remembered a story* of a white man" (28–29, emphasis mine). Two elements surface in Ishmael's initial description: first, the connection between inscriptions and the body, with the pun on *ink*; second, the provocation of memory in Queequeg's presence through which Ishmael recalls a narrative. It is a first impulse toward reweaving himself back into his own narrative design and into a human community, even while Ahab, tangled in his hemp line, will be snatched by Moby-Dick and pulled onto his back in a delicious reversal of men hunting and snagging the whale. While the written lines of Ishmael will create a community which he can participate within as the only survivor of the whale hunt, the tangled lines of Ahab's hemp ropes will wed him forever with the body of the white whale as it plunges deep into the Pacific waters.

The only memory Ishmael relates of his own personal history, moreover, occurs when he sleeps with Queequeg. It suggests that Queequeg is a guide for Ishmael's soul; he relates to him as the god Hermes relates to us as a guide to dreams and the underworld. As Hermes, Queequeg, being the only one in the novel who dives deep into the ocean to save others, "brings the message of destiny; *hermeneuein* is that laying open of something which brings a message" (Palmer, 13). In his mythically tattooed skin, he enacts the symbolic function "of transmuting what is beyond human understanding into a form that human intelligence can grasp" (13). He is the imaginative process twisted larger.

Queequeg's presence is so powerful for Ishmael that he prompts a recollection of story; it is through stories and storytelling, as Jung has noted in his own work, that an individual can reconnect with the human community (*Memories, Dreams, Reflections,* 130). The thread of a story is a beneficent hemp line that leads one back into a shared sense of humanity, to a ground of healing his wounded nature, and to a reconnection with the world's body, as the "monkey rope" will later intensify his connection to Queequeg.

Through him and lying with him, Ishmael recollects in "The Counterpane" the story of his stepmother putting him to bed early on the longest day of the year, June 21. Queequeg's presence provokes this childhood memory that profoundly affected Ishmael, for in his sleep, "half-steeped in dreams," Ishmael relates how he felt "a supernatural hand [which] seemed placed in mine. . . . the nameless, unimaginable, silent form or phantom, to which the hand belonged, seemed closely seated by my bed-side" (33). Immediately thereafter he draws striking similarities between the visit of this phantom and Queequeg himself, a close encounter with "the ungraspable phantom of life" he observed earlier in relation to the Narcissus story ("Loomings," 14), which is the originary myth of self-reflection wherein one sees deeply through water to the image of soul. This vision, Ishmael believes, harbors "the key to it all" (14). And I believe it is our clue to the myth through which to read the entire narrative, the archetypal action of Narcissus and Echo.

We learn at about the same time that this elaborate tattooing on the primitive's body was the work of a departed prophet and seer of his island who, by means of those hieroglyphic marks, had written out on Queequeg's body "a complete theory of the heavens and the earth, and a mystical treatise on the art of attaining truth" (399). He is not only an embodied text of images and words, but a "living parchment whereon they were inscribed, and so be unsolved to the last" (399). An inscribed body, Queequeg yet remains an enigma to those who would tease out his meaning. As Hermes, his full meaning remains Hermetically sealed. He remains to the end an inscrutable and unscribable presence to his shipmates.

I don't believe he can be "solved" any more than the narrative *Moby-Dick* can be solved, because he is a presence, indeed the force of transformation itself; in Queequeg's presence, transformation takes place. He is the force of transformation, transmutation, and translation, an imaginative presence that turns the experiences one has into moments of epiphany. As such, the native enfleshes one of two ways that the soul, as Thomas Moore observes, can abrupt itself into the world: in creativity and in mythic enactment (*Care of the Soul,* 135) or in the form of violence, which Ahab would embody most monomaniacally.[24] In this sense, Queequeg is the signifier of the deepest act of being human, becoming or allowing for transformation, transition, or a passing from one state of consciousness to another. He is a psychopomp who is essential for the soul's journey of the hero. If we think for a moment of the mythic journey of the hero that Joseph Campbell outlines, then Queequeg, in his hieroglyphic presence, assists Ishmael across the first stage of the mythological journey "which we have designated 'the call to adventure'—and [which] signifies that destiny has summoned the hero and transferred his spiritual center of gravity from within the pale of his society to a zone unknown" (*Hero,* 58). This ritualized body of Queequeg is a mythical flesh, marked by the sacred and carrying the cosmogonic origins of the created order on its surface. His myth is mercurial.

In color he is brown (51), a transitional color between his ebony black idol, Yojo, and the white world to which he has signed on. His value lies in his being a mediator, an in-between figure who gives imagination depth and allows the ordinary things of the world to be remembered fully and experienced deeply. In fact, during the novel's entire action, and like the actions of the whales themselves, he spends more time diving deeply than any other figure and saves different individuals from drowning or helps in the birthing of one of the crew. His movement is therefore as vertical as it is horizontal.

As a body covered with "grotesque figures and drawings . . . , tattoos from a departed prophet" (399), Queequeg is, as we mentioned, closely associated with the dream state, a shadow, so to say, that lingers on the threshold of waking consciousness, on the edge of dreams themselves, which may be understood as the stories of the soul's becoming; he is a liminal figure and functions in ways similar to language itself. With his tattooed body he might best be conceived as an emblem of the imagination itself, or even a particular way of imagining that is mythic and symbolic in its nature. He is like the mysterious and ineffable presence of soul that nonetheless has its own existence, if only seemingly phantom-like. He is, as Toni Morrison describes others of this lineage in American literature, the "deep dark other" (*Playing in the Dark*, 47).[25]

As one who inhabits the liminal state of consciousness, he is between boundaries but not of them. For him boundaries are permeable; he moves through them as might a god or a daimon.[26] I don't believe it is sufficient simply to call him Ishmael's shadow, as John T. Irwin does (*American Hieroglyphics*, 256), or the partner in a "homosexual relation," which Sharon Cameron believes (*Corporeal Self*, 43). Such narrow restrictions simply arrest this rich mythical and poetic relation and suffocate that part of the creative process that Melville explores throughout the whaling hunt.

Ishmael refers to Queequeg, shortly after remembering the phantom in his youthful dream, as "a creature in the transition state—neither caterpillar nor butterfly" (34), and places him in touch once again with his own narrative, with his own myth, but on a level more deeply felt and imagined than simply remembered. That Ishmael uses the transforming life of a caterpillar into a butterfly to describe Queequeg is subtle, for the noble primitive is closely related to the animal world as well. When Ishmael, for example, first observes him in the room at the Inn, he watches Queequeg pull from his bag "a seal-skin wallet with the hair on," and then takes off "a new beaver hat" (29). Even Yojo, his wooden idol, is also a liminal figure, inhabiting a place somewhere between human and animal: Queequeg "fumbled in the pockets and produced at length a curious little deformed image with a hunch on its back, and exactly the color of a three days' old Congo baby" (30).

In addition, Queequeg represents that connection between body and text that couples language to incarnation and soul to body. Later in the voyage, having had the carpenter make him a coffin for his ailing flesh, he suddenly recovers and, instead of leaving the coffin empty, he transforms it into a sea chest and begins carving the lid "with all manner of grotesque figures and drawings" (399), striving, in his refined aesthetic manner, to copy parts of the twisted tattooing on his body, twisting them smaller to fit the confines of the box. His ritual action is central to the entire scheme of embodying stories—both personal and mythic. In one sense, Queequeg writes his embodied text into the world as artifact; as an artist, he takes something crafted for function and ritually inscribes it, transforming its mythical presence onto an object that will save Ishmael in his absence. The central attribute of his being is one of transformation, for he continually changes what he embraces in the world.

His coffin is transformed into "a symbolic duplicate of himself," as Edinger argues (*Melville's Moby-Dick,* 141). His effect on Ishmael is primarily alchemical *and* symbolic; his central presence in the action is to recover soul in the world, especially if the body is understood as its tangible trace; the body's expressions have their "cunning duplicate" in the soul's activity. Ishmael underscores this relation between the body of Queequeg and the inscribed coffin rather neatly. Early in the novel, when he dives to rescue the young man who has just moments before insulted him, he is described like a whale breaching: "Shooting himself perpendicularly from the water, Queequeg now took an instant's glance around him, and . . . dived down and disappeared" (61), finally to bring the man safely to the surface. In like manner, in the "Epilogue," Ishmael writes that the coffin, "owing to its great buoyancy, rising with great force . . . , shot lengthwise from the sea, fell over, and floated by my side" (470). Once again, and even in death, Queequeg saves the life of another young man so that he may inscribe his own *mythos* onto the pages of the journey we have just completed. So the coffin, inscribed with images deep into the wood, is Queequeg's text, a floating and buoyant one, that makes possible Ishmael's own bookish creation, not in images but in words that carry the images on themselves. I like Clark Davis' observation that "it is the body and its relation to language, the 'cosmic' body of the sea's creatures and the flesh of the book itself that energize and inform Ishmael's text" (*After the Whale,* 19) because the observation grasps in another way this intimacy, or tangled lines of body, writing, and world that culminate in the confrontation with the white whale.

The savage's artistry further dreams his myth into existence through his body images duplicated on the coffin; such a poetic action has its correlate in Ishmael's grander design: to textualize all these disparate bodies into one "epistemophilic" unity, as Brooks called it. His desire is to create a world text that reflects the world soul, the *anima mundi*. Queequeg's request, therefore, to make the coffin in the first place as he feels his impending death has its linguistic analogue in the action of Ishmael who, after almost drowning in the ocean after the *Pequod* bears down on them to smash their whaling boat in the chapter, "The Hyena," goes below to write his will: "Taking all things together, I say, I thought I might as well go below and make a rough draft of my will. 'Queequeg,' said I, 'come along, you shall be my lawyer, executor, and legatee'" (196), after which he feels resurrected, like Lazarus, when "a stone was rolled away from my heart" (197).

In both cases, creation and inscription develop directly from a confrontation with possible death, with a feeling of one's vulnerability through disease or one's fragility in the sea. That reality raises to conscious awareness each man's respective mortality. Ishmael's will is a miniature story of his life insofar as it relates what he owns and what he will part with. His will is the prototype of the larger story that will become the book about the whale. I believe Ishmael first inscribes himself through his will as preparation for the creation of his more eloquently epic task of writing the book. The will is a form of his inscribed presence even when he will be bodily absent. The will is the cenotaph of his absence; it is a languaged presence of his embodied absence. As such, it is a witness to how one has indeed passed on into writing; this is in the larger scheme of things the "cunning little duplicate in mind" of the larger text, *Moby-Dick*, the book about the body and soul of the whale and the world.[27] Furthermore, Brooks makes reference to the intimacy between writing and mortality in suggesting that "mortality may be that against which all discourse defines itself, as protest or as attempted recovery" (*Body Work*, 7).

Walter Benjamin has written insightfully on stories and storytelling: "the storyteller's gift is the ability to relate his life; he could let the wick of his life be consumed completely by the gentle flame of his story" ("Storyteller," 108). And if one's will is a way of remembering one's life, then wills are indeed stories of one's own history, always with the backdrop of death as the phantom, absent but at any moment capable of being present, that haunts it. "Death," Benjamin observes, "is the sanction of everything that the storyteller can tell. He has borrowed his authority from death" (94). So as Queequeg and Ishmael are united in life and in the act of whaling, they are also united in their awareness of death, which prompts in both of them a desire to create artifacts—one written, the other crafted in image, as traces of their lives. This recognition of death is the deep wound of our humanity; the affliction of mortality is embodied in this consciousness and serves to prompt one to record or to leave a trace of one's mortalness in some more permanent or fixed form. The wound of death leads to our creating the words or images that will fix us in the world.

In addition, they both share a series of experiences that are regenerative because they involve forms of death and resurrection, archetypal actions of verticality, diving deep, and breaching suddenly to the surface. When Ishmael, "buoyed up by that coffin" sails for a day and a night "on a soft and dirge-like main" (470), we are witness to how Queequeg's artistry saves the text of Ishmael and his journey aboard the *Pequod*. Their individual inscriptions achieve, even retell through reflection, the guiding myth of Narcissus as he reflects his own image through water. On reflection, the myth records our double in the depths of the world.

Creating a double of oneself in the world through inscription occurs within the conscious limits of being human. Language and inscriptions of all kinds generally allow one to double oneself in the world. Desire itself may begin with this urge to double oneself through creation, shrouded always with the consciousness of mortality. Lacan's observation on language is instructive: "It is a subtle body, but body it is. Words are trapped in all the corporeal images that captivate the subject. . . . And words themselves can undergo symbolic lesions and accomplish imaginary acts of which the patient is the subject" (*Ecrits*, 87, 89).[28]

I believe Queequeg's act of first inscribing his coffin with body images to make of it a double of his tattooed flesh is a mythically calculated response to Ahab's vision earlier when he addresses "The Sphynx" (Chapter 70), the bloody, dripping head of the sperm whale severed from its body and hanging on the hooks to one side of the *Pequod*. Contemplating the whale's descents to the depths of the ocean, deeper than any living thing had gone, he speculates: " O Nature, and O soul of man! how far beyond all utterance are your linked analogies! Not the smallest atom stirs or lives in matter, but has its cunning duplicate in mind" (264). Perhaps he would have received a more satisfactory response had he addressed the same remarks to his savage crew member.

Queequeg imagined as a living text underscores the body and story or narrative as one image, analogically related and ritually inscribed. In a sense, as a human form of the monetary doubloon, he is a public presence for all to read but for none to successfully interpret or find a single meaning in; he is the reverse image but with a structure similar to the text Ishmael is to write, one in which no single meaning will hold all the water. The imaginative, indeed mythopoetic force that Queequeg's textual body exerts on Ishmael is reversed in the latter, for Ishmael's creation will fully contextualize the body, most specifically the body of the whale, as an analogue no less profound than the doubloon which Ahab puts up as reward for whoever sights the white whale first and which he struggles to decipher: "this round globe is but the image of the rounder globe . . . which to each and every man in turn but mirrors back his own mysterious self" ("The Doubloon," 359). If, as Ahab remarks, "Starbuck is Stubb reversed, and Stubb, Starbuck," then the same is equally true of Ishmael and Queequeg. If we were to compare him to Ahab for a moment here, then Ahab-consciousness is concerned more with finding *meaning* in the whale through dominating or destroying it, whereas Queequeg by contrast is a figure who embodies *presence*.

Queequeg places his own mark on the world, first through his signing onboard the *Pequod* with a signature of a cross to represent himself, and then by imitating the cosmic or mythic structure of his body on to the coffin, which will be sealed airtight by the carpenter and so become its reverse, a life buoy destined to breach from the whirlpool to save Ishmael, to remember and tell his story. Perhaps we can say that if Ahab's support is physical whalebone that replaces his phantom limb, then Ishmael's support is cosmic coffin that replaces the phantom, mythic son of an island king.

AHAB'S NARCISSISTIC WOUND

Moreover, in his painted, textual nature, Queequeg is the antithesis of Ahab, whose fragmented, split, or abandoned body has already been partly transformed through the ivory leg he wears. As he commands the *Pequod*, the white whale has already begun to reclaim him. But Ahab has left his harpoons in the wounded side of the whale and is able to identify him through the sightings of other whalers who relate to Ahab these irons in the whale's skin. Now if Queequeg's coffin allows the resurrected Ishmael at the end of the novel to float into the arms of the Rachel as she searches for her captain's lost son, Ahab appears to Ishmael as "a man cut away from the stake, when the fire has overrunningly wasted all the limbs without consuming them" (109–10), a man stricken, who stands initially before his crew after they have sailed into the Atlantic, "with a crucifixion in his face" (111). His titanic obsession to find and murder the white whale depicts a rage that seems limitless; the "lividly whitish" wound that marks him from scalp to foot is an elemental lightning's trace or marking that signals a deep splitting in his bearing, a mark made by nature; in addition, his leg has been amputated by a force in nature. In contrast to Queequeg's mythically inscribed tattoos depicting a cosmos, on Ahab's wounded and dismembered body are wounds and markings that come from a battle with the elements themselves. As a wounded, narcissistic figure, Ahab embodies the figure that Ishmael introduces in the first chapter, "Loomings." As he reflects on the mythic importance of water, he returns to the story of Narcissus, "who because he could not grasp the tormenting, mild image he saw in the fountain, plunged into it and was drowned. But that same image, we ourselves see in all rivers and oceans. it is the image of the ungraspable phantom of life; and this is the key to it all" (14).

What "key" is meant we are not able to grasp until we have journeyed through Ishmael's narrative. Then we see that this passage describes Ahab's maniacal quest for vengeance. Ahab's shattered body is the emblem of this narcissistic rage as well as the source of its seemingly limitless energy. His exterior, visible bodily wounds mask deeper afflictions that finally surface shortly after he offers the Ecuadorean doubloon as reward to him who sights the white whale. Onto the whale Ahab has appended "all those malicious agencies which some deep men feel eating in them, till they are left living on with half a heart and half a lung. That intangible malignity which has been from the beginning" (160).

Ishmael speculates, as he studies Ahab as a text, with the same focused intensity with which Ahab studies his charts or the captured whale heads that hang on either side of the *Pequod* later. He surmises that his "monomania" probably did not infect the captain "at the precise time of his bodily dismemberment" (160). Ahab "probably felt the agonizing bodily laceration, but nothing more." Only later, as he was forced to turn back, and as he lay brooding on a hammock, helpless and infirm, "then it was, that his torn body and gashed soul bled into one another; and so interfusing, made him mad. . . . In a strait-jacket, he swung to the mad rockings of the gales" (160). Later, coming into sunnier and more serene waters, Ahab emerges from "the dark den of his cabin" seemingly better, but "in his hidden self, raved on" (161). His rage eventually becomes titanic and subsumes all of the crew as the captain persuades them all to swear an oath together to pursue the white whale. Behind this obsession of Ahab is one desire: to return to the site of the original affliction and to wound again or be wounded in a compelling repetition.

Heinz Kohut, writing profoundly on narcissistic rage, makes the following observation: Human aggression is most dangerous when it is attached to the two great absolutarian psychological constellations: the grandiose self and the archaic, omnipotent object. Underneath the narcissistic wound is the rage for revenge, "for righting a wrong, for undoing a hurt by whatever means, and a deeply anchored, unrelenting compulsion in the pursuit of all these aims" (637–38) in which the one who has been injured allows himself no rest until vengeance has been carried out. Kohut suggests that there exists almost superhuman power around this form of woundedness. The one seeking vengeance has no regard "for reasonable limitations" and feels a "boundless wish to redress an injury and to obtain revenge" (639–40). Reasoning faculties sharpen, calculation becomes more acute, and the sense of being wrongly injured is heightened. The wound is the emblem of a severe loss which must be avenged. His next insight helps us to envision the metaphysical level of Ahab's monomania: "The enemy who calls forth the archaic rage of the narcissistically vulnerable, however, is seen by him not as an autonomous source of impulsions, but as a *flaw in a narcissistically perceived reality*" (644).

It is, according to Kohut, that the enemy of the narcissist offends him by its independence and autonomy because then it does not fall easily under the narcissist's control. The independence of the object increases the rage, which we see expressed by Ahab as he ponders the mystery of Moby-Dick through the filters of his own wounds. In his imagination, and through his rage, he asserts, "the white whale is that wall" which separates the "pasteboard masks" of visible objects from "some unknown but still reasoning thing" that "puts forth the mouldings of its features from behind the unreasoning mask. If man will strike, strike through the mask!'" (144). Wound what has wounded by pursuing the invisible through the visible, and then wound it by puncturing through to it, Ahab affirms: "That inscrutable thing is chiefly what I hate; and be the white whale agent, or be the white whale principal, I will wreak that hate upon him. Talk not to me of blasphemy, man; I'd strike the sun if it insulted me" (144).

Ahab's language is full of images of wounding to avenge his own deep afflictions.[29] While Queequeg's markings remember cosmic and unitive designs of the psyche, Ahab's markings, dismemberment, and language express a tyranny of chaos in the soul. Nothing can stop him as he follows his charts, compass, and quadrant until all of them are exhausted and he moves into the uncharted waters of the Pacific. In the uncharted regions he confronts once again the source of his afflictions. Nothing, not even the mournful pleas of Captain Gardiner of the *Rachel* to help him find his twelve-year-old son in the uncharted waters (435), dissuades Ahab as he remains fixated on deck with the end of his ivory leg firmly planted in the deck's niche so that he can pivot while remaining fixed in place. His rage and desire for revenge will not be altered by any act of generosity, so fixed is his purpose, so obsessive his design to return to the exiled waters of his original wounding.

Chapter 130 ("The Hat") begins with this description:

> And now that at the proper time and place, after so long and wide a preliminary cruise, Ahab . . . found himself hard by the very latitude and longitude where his tormenting wound had been inflicted; . . . Now it was that there lurked a something in the old man's eyes, which it was hardly sufferable for feeble souls to see. (437)

All the crew members feel the transformation of place as they enter the primordial waters of Ahab's dismemberment. Ahab sizes up the crew: "So Ahab's purpose now fixedly gleamed down upon the constant midnight of the gloomy crew" (437). They have entered the space in which Moby-Dick has revealed in the past "the demoniac indifference with which" he "tore his hunters, whether sinning or sinned against" (437). Ahab's destructive force here reflects again the narcissistic desire to control and to destroy the agent of its wound. In so doing, as Herbert Rosenfeld writes of the narcissistically wounded person, that is often like working with "a powerful gang dominated by a leader, who controls all the members . . . to see that they support one another in making the criminal destructive work more effective and powerful" (249).

We recall that this archetypal action of returning to the location of an original wounding was familiar to Odysseus, to Oedipus, to Hamlet, as it will be to Ruby Turpin, O. E. Parker, as well as to Sethe and Paul D. and the entire community of *Beloved*. It seems a psychological necessity in being wounded to revisit the origin of body/psyche woundedness and there in some cases to reenact the original affliction. What mythology is expressed in returning to the wound's origin, to where one has been marked, afflicted, or dismembered by the other? Does the wound open afresh? Is through it remembrance given space? Is something retrieved by revisiting the wound?

We are offered a partial answer in Ishmael's reflections in Chapter 7 ("The Chapel") when he reads and muses on the cenotaph tablets "with black borders, masoned into the wall on either side the pulpit" (39), "frigid inscriptions on the wall" (40). He observes the women in their "unceasing grief" reading the inscriptions of those loved ones they have lost at sea. Ishmael enters their grief: "Here before me were assembled those, in whose unhealing hearts the sight of those bleak tablets sympathetically caused the old wounds to bleed afresh" (40). What they experience in remembering their lost loves and so opening the wounds again is analogous to what Ahab experiences as he enters the space of his original wound; it begins to bleed afresh. The phantom limb feels the original flesh taken by the whale. The phantom limb is an absent but powerful memory of the original wounding.

Perhaps, then, the site of Ahab's wound is a place where consciousness itself or feeling is reawakened. Ahab may need to inflict a deeper wound on the whale that has wounded him to begin to reclaim himself from his own narcissism and to reclaim a feeling of being a whole and intact human being. The wound's need to be redressed is an archetypal action of retrieval and revisioning, of revelation and transformation. Ahab's deepest self unfolds in the wound, in the memory of his loss; it opens up all over again. We might call it here an alchemical wound, or opening where the original pain bubbles up. The entire action of the novel is to get back to this place, an originary ground of being and pain for Ahab. The novel spiralizes down, whirlpools down, sucking everything with it into the gaping maw of Ahab's wound. The sea's skin itself is wounded by the breaching whale. The wounded white whale also returns to wound its wounder again. For both, the wound is a place of opening, of vulnerability, an orifice, an aperture. As the white whale breaches from the sea's depth, Ahab wants to go below, into its terrain, to fathom the white whale's mystery and to slay that mystery. The opening of the ocean's skin by the whale may be the primal wound of the world, a wound we all experience through the act of simply being born.

We see Ahab, moreover, earlier envisioned in Father Mapple's sermon of Jonah. Tormented in his suffocating cabin room, Jonah is full of self-torture; he feels "the chambers of my soul are all in crookedness" (47), like the crooked lower jaw of Moby-Dick. But more than that, Jonah and Ahab share something of the same wound. Jonah knows he is hiding from God's command; as it settles into him, he feels a "deep stupor" take possession of him, "as over the man who bleeds to death, for conscience is the wound, and there's naught to staunch it" (47). In his restless sleep, according to Mapple's imaginative narrative, Jonah heeds not the "far rush of the mighty whale, which even now with open mouth is *cleaving the seas* after him" (48, italics mine). Jonah's whale and Ahab's whale both wound the sea, splitting it open; their wake is the memory of the wound. Both woundings are the memory of what they must perform in order to heal the wound of conscience, with one difference. Jonah's denial of God's command is in direct contrast with Ahab's making his own woundedness his God and it is that cry of vengeance that controls him.

The place of the original narcissistic wound is also the location of compulsion, according to Mary Watkins (interview, 1998). The one wounded returns to the site of the original hurt, with one possibility: to reenact the original conflict again, and again, fixated in the rage of the suffering the wound first brought on. But psychologically, it is the place where an authentic breakthrough can also occur. In the sore space of the wound a transformation can occur, another narrative can breach to counteract the stuck story one is in. Where the wound originally resides, therefore, is the site of a possible cure. Gaining control over what has wounded one is another reason for returning to the original site, as it is true of Ahab here. To let go of the wound is to first journey to it and there to metabolize it. Such a move requires intense courage. The scar that grows over the wound contains the memory of the first experience. We could say the scar is the mask that hides the original affliction. Ahab's wound marks an original initiation in him. So to return to it is to return to a safe place, according to Watkins, for there no new terrors exist to wrestle with. No horizons are shifted. Only the old familiar tale is to be lived through again. Yet the wound's location is the promising place of healing as well, by going back through the original wounding and being wounded. The archetypal wound is also the container for an archetypal healing; for Ahab it is not to be. But Ishmael, whose rage at the beginning of the novel is akin to Ahab's but "twisted smaller," is given Queequeg to guide him toward a healing that eventuates in the writing of the narrative.

In contrast to Ahab's rage, Queequeg is the poetic embodiment that expresses a oneness of flesh and soul; he is both substance and shadow, civilized and savage, pagan and christian, a presence that is comfortable with both surface and depth. He also finds himself occupying both regions even after his death, for as his body is deep within the waters of the Pacific, his "cunning duplicate" in wood is on the surface to save the life of Ishmael. As a transitional body, Queequeg has more affinities with the whales and with Moby-Dick specifically than any other figure. As a transitional figure of soul, he participates in both the cultural world of ritual and whaling and the animal world or animal soul of the world.[30] One incident early in the novel will help illuminate this last observation.

Ishmael finds himself in the bedroom with all of Queequeg's belongings, but without his presence; Ishmael discovers the former's poncho, which has "a hole or slit in the middle" (27), so he tries it on to see if it will fit. But Ishmael's language is careful here, for how he states this action further associates Queequeg with the whale and with an incident involving a part of the whale's anatomy later: " I put it on, *to try it*, and it weighed me down like a hamper, being uncommonly shaggy and thick" (28, my emphasis). When he ventures in front of a mirror and sees his own reflection, that once again underscores the story of Narcissus, Ishmael is horrified and pulls it off so quickly and forcefully that he gives himself "a kink in the neck" (28).

Implicated here through the intertwined bodies or skins of Queequeg, Ishmael, and the whale is a witness to the reality that soul and eros are always together and that soul and spiritual worship are also of a piece. In "A Squeeze of the Hand," the spermaceti is the active ingredient of eros and community by which Ishmael begins to feel the hands of the other whalemen. Their task is "to squeeze these lumps back into a fluid. A sweet and unctuous duty!" (348) which has the same effect as melter, "mollifier, . . . softener," on Ishmael as does Queequeg when he says earlier that in his presence "he melts." Certainly the action is an alchemical one which changes Ishmael's soul through Queequeg: "I felt a melting in me. No more my splintered heart [a reference more appropriate to Ahab] and maddened hand were turned against the wolfish world. This soothing savage had redeemed it" (53), immediately after which Ishmael turns the pages of a book with Queequeg and tries to explain the meaning of the print and the pictures to him. Illiterate and an ineffable text himself, Queequeg can only count the pages in packs of fifty.

Such reveries as Ishmael has in Queequeg's presence and around the sperm pot on deck, conjured by squeezing all together and musing over images of community in "the wife, the hearth, the bed, the table, the saddle, the fire-side, the country," reveal the convert Ishmael's desire to squeeze the whale's fluid eternally, for "In visions of the night, I saw long rows of angels in paradise, each with his hands in a jar of spermaceti" (349).

Queequeg's presence is the power of the life force. He is analogous to the whale, an emblem of the world soul, the *anima mundi*. It is to this force or presence that Ishmael reconnects when he dons the poncho of Queequeg, as it is the soul of the whale that the mincer assumes when he sports the foreskin. Granted, the mincer is less involved in a mythic ritual than he is in a commercial function; nonetheless, Ishmael makes apparent that the commercial hunt still retains a powerful ritual underlay even if it is driven primarily by capitalism and consumption.

In this process of the body's textualization, to which Queequeg, Ahab, and the white whale are most semiotically relevant, all three become most fully textual through the imagination of Ishmael as he writes the novel, a structure, according to Brooks, which takes on a new form of textualization in the nineteenth century. Here marking the body as a text, as we have been exploring Queequeg's tattooed body, is a new way of inscribing the world with one's narrative.[31] The signed body points to the deep implication of the flesh in narrative; the body is the place where central narrative meanings are inscribed or branded such that incarnation becomes the key narrative signifier (Brooks, *Body Work,* 73). The ritual nature of tattoos and the painted body itself reveal how Brooks' observations are applicable to the inscribed, scarred, and wounded bodies of the novel.

As studies in anthropology have made more apparent, it was indeed the skin, the "parchment" of the body, that received the first designs, and they were designed with greater complexity, according to Michel Thevoz, in order to create symbolic structures by which man wrenched himself free of animality (*Painted Body,* 13). The human body was "the prototypical surface for any ritual inscription " (16) and led Freud to call it "a disturbing strangeness," for body painting "provoked in the Western imagination a resurgence of archaic phantasms" (24).

Body painting and tattooing also collapsed any distinction or distance between our own "corporal unconscious and that of primitive man" (28); matter and mind, body and soul are united through the painted or tattooed body. Victor Turner adds that "tattooed men and women wear on their bodies subtle and beautiful expressions of a continuous tradition that links deity, nature and humankind" (272). I believe this is Queequeg's legacy to Ishmael. He returns to the orphan a form of mythically imagining the world that allows him a poetic vision that is deep as well as broad. He also guides Ishmael into a sense of ritual or ritual presence to his world. We have noticed earlier that Queequeg's body tattoos were inscribed on him ritually; such a ritual had as its purpose a "reminder of human origins, like myths and in accordance with myths," as Thevoz makes clear (30). Such body markings were part of a ritual of establishing "a communication with the unlike beyond; they are meant to make man unlike his usual self" (34) to help him on his journey, even to assist him in a rite "to become inhuman, to become animal, to become other" (34).

The process of tattooing I believe bears on the harpooning of the whale as well as "the metal dents" with which Ahab punctuates the deck of the

Pequod, or pokes at the head of the sperm whale in an impotent attempt to force the animal's head to speak of the seas' deep mysteries. His ultimate desire has been to "strike through the mask" of visible objects in a raging that seeks vengeance for his dismemberment.

For Ishmael, ritual marking or tattooing takes the form of inscribing both his own arm with whale measurements and the blank page that will create these bodies semiotically in the words of the novel. Ishmael's "tattooing" of the page I would call the poeticizing of desire, for in his relatedness to Queequeg and his connectedness to the world, especially in "The Squeeze of the Hand," he makes public and linguistic the private realm of desire in the same way that Queequeg's tattooed body ritualistically allows him to enter culture as a public figure sedimented with the images of his ancestry; his body not only *is* a history, but *bears* a history. The marking of Queequeg's body is like the stamping of a coin, tattooing metal, in a way, in order to prepare it to enter the flow of culture ornamented with images and language that unfold a history of meaning for that people. The body marked assumes "the positive significance of a social integration." As Thevoz writes of primitive tribes, "a body unmarked is a stupid body" (50).

In conclusion, I have tried to grasp the experience of this white whale with my own tangled lines in the following poem:

Whiteness

In you, whiteness is the still flesh of
The circling globe,
Magnet and lodestar.
Fluke, head, hump, spout.
Deeply silent in the slippery sibilant of
Ocean.
Fluid-like:
Sperm, oil, blood, spray of mist.
Just beneath the surface you glide,
Reservoir of energy and shadow of depth.
Breaching between two worlds, you are
For an instant upright—
And so you speak the words of depth
And infinity.
We are washed in the after-spray
Of your cosmic foam; then
In the slow bathe of white jissum,
Put on your cloak of whiteness
And steal, ourselves, into
The chambers of History
(*Wild Turkey: A Literary Review,* 11)

8

Rebellious Things and Deepening Wounds in the Life of Ivan Ilych

The gods have become diseases; Zeus no longer rules
Olympus but rather the solar plexus, and produces curious specimens for the doctor's consulting room.

—Alchemical Studies, 37

With all of the various criticisms that have explored Tolstoy's masterpiece, *The Death of Ivan Ilych*, it is surprising that very little attention has been paid, for example, to the incarnational dimensions of the
story, especially to the technically functioning body of Ivan Ilych and to the
transformative power of wounding that blossoms into a deadly disease.

Not only human embodiment as a poetic image, but the images of the
ordinary and quotidian things of the world as extensions of one's embodiment in the world, Tolstoy interrogates according to their inherent poetic
qualities. Ivan Ilych lives in a world cluttered with schedules and objects,
things that cluster and litter the world of social success. We might think,
for example, of the pouffe that sends the young bureaucrat, Peter
Ivanovich, skyward as he visits with the newly widowed Praskovya Fe-
dorovna at Ivan Ilych's funeral, where the lace of her shawl "caught on the
carved edge of the table" (100); or the room "full of furniture and knick-
knacks," and of course the newly purchased drapery that Ivan is adjusting
when he slips from the ladder and catches himself, but not before knock-
ing "his side against the knob of the window frame" (116). The wound itself, inflicted on Ivan when he is busy improving his material lot in the
world by hanging new embroidery and managing still further his surroundings, is the aperture we pass through to explore more closely the interior life of Ivan as his wound opens him to a way of being he has
steadfastly drawn a curtain across in his life.

In the act of being wounded, however, the world invades him, calls
out to him by name, and addresses the contours of the curtain that has

successfully insulated him from suffering on any deep psychological or spiritual level. In examining his woundedness, we attend carefully to the source of that wound in order to hear the voice of the world wanting to be witnessed speaking through it, resonating his deepest authenticity.

Ivan Ilych may be understood as a modern wounded poetic version of Oedipus, an earlier prototype of high official and public stature who, as Ilych will follow this same path, is returned to his infancy and childhood through the remembrance of the painful wound inflicted on him shortly after his birth when his father shackled his ankles. Sophocles and Tolstoy both sense in the act of being wounded an archetypal movement back to origins, to the beginnings of being. The wounds offer a peripety, a way of "turning about," so that what had been concealed in the past is now revealed forcefully through the wounded present. Imaginatively guided by the wound's voice, part of its painful expression, one is forced to turn about, to recognize and to reflect on what has gone before but has been forgotten, buried, and made voiceless under the scars of the original site of being wounded. Wounds ask us to remember the origins of our lives and to bring the story of our being into a coherent form so we may identify and accept our full and authentic existence.

Such an exploration of Ivan Ilych's wound and disease would therefore also include the place of his faithful servant Gerasim in Ivan's illness, especially as this robust employee, present at the funeral in Part I and active throughout the ill man's suffering, seems to be the only one to whom Ivan will turn for help or to express the interior life of feeling in affection during his critical condition. He is as well the only healthy soul Ivan Ilych in his illness is not repulsed by.

Order, arrangement, systematic, agreeable, decorous, pleasant, correct: these words comprise the verbal calculus through which Ivan Ilych lives his life; yet the narrator continually cuts through these conventions in a very understated tone that carries the terror of Ivan's normal life: Ivan Ilych's life "had been most simple and most ordinary and therefore most terrible" (104). Is such a judgment leveled at him because his thoughts and actions have always been on the side of the world, with little attention paid to the interior life of spirit? Certainly Ivan Ilych is covetous of material things, and of continually improving his professional position; but these actions in themselves are not terrible. Accumulation does not in itself lead to alienation; there must be something more afoot here to understand how his minor wounding becomes the condition for his dying, and, further, how such an affliction of his being can be considered a gift, in fact, a most prized possession because it allows a life fully lived, if even briefly.

What he finds most repulsive in his life is an illness that he learns to covet as most responsible for a moment of authentic being, but only after what he has found most comfortable is first threatened, then completely disrupted. His disability illustrates to his family and friends how powerful "a threatening presence" (43) disabilities can become, writes Rosemarie Garland Thomson.

Tolstoy suggests in the structure of the plot itself a way of reading the action of Ivan's life. It begins with the *words* of his death, which Peter Ivanovich reads from the obituary column of the daily newspaper to a group of fellow clerks during an "interval in the Melvinski trial": "Gentlemen: Ivan Ilych has died" (95) and ends with the *action* of his death ("He drew in a breath, stopped in the midst of a sigh, stretched out, and died" [156]). From the story's structure we begin to grasp the fact that Ivan has lived his life backwards. This reversal becomes even more apparent when we learn that he lived through his childhood and youth "without [their] leaving much trace on him" (105), but through the wound of his disease he revisits his childhood and discerns its impact on him in the last days of his life. He becomes increasingly conscious—by means of his illness—that the only time in which he experienced any form of happiness was during his childhood. As his disease progresses, it opens up his imagination, allowing him to envision not just the world of officialdom, which is increasingly dissatisfying, but that of childhood, when the number of divisions and curtains in his life were minimal and when his joy was greatest.

However, as the demands of professional power and authority over others increase over the years prior to his wound, Ilych's life becomes more fragmented and functional, more concerned with the outer trappings of things and less with any rustlings of interior truths about his own identity. A curtain is drawn between soul and world and this division locates itself within his body. In this lies the terribleness of his existence. All of his moves become formulaic (108), all according to a plan: to move as society dictates with as few interruptions as possible. Ivan Ilych learns to master, and then prides himself on following, the proprieties of external forms which are "required by public opinion" (111). To avoid "inconveniences" and to "secure his own independence" (110) is the guiding value of his life, all the while maintaining the illusion of decorous and agreeable behavior as he expands his position and his professional power. He neatly and cleverly draws a screen between his home life and his professional world. When unpleasantness at home, in the form of his new wife's inconvenient pregnancy, yields to arguments and strife that rupture decorum, he draws a blind between domestic troubles and his social life of playing bridge and behaving "agreeably." His curtain takes the psychological form of the attitudes he insists on to keep his worlds neatly divided, antiseptically managed and under orderly control. In such a manner Ilych is able to control his world through the metaphors of technical functioning and efficiency, the qualities of his rigid mythology. These attributes are also how he lives his own embodiment, and Tolstoy suggests poetically that such is the genesis of his dis-ease.[1] The disease gestates in the form of his fixed life outlined above; when it heats up sufficiently, it bursts into the world through his possessions.

THE BODY OF TECHNICAL FUNCTION

In his powerful collection of essays on the body, Jan Kott offers in "The Memory of the Body" a distinction that Tolstoy gives poetic form. In writing about a succession of heart attacks he experienced over a few years' duration, Kott reflects on pain:

> We can separate other experiences from ourselves. If my leg hurts, it is as if that leg were a separate part of me. I feel the pain, but I am not the leg that hurts me. I can separate from that part of myself. The profound experiences of sex and death, however, no longer divide the 'I' from the 'not-I'. (114)

His observation is important for our exploration of the body in pain and then its progression, so to speak, to suffering. If only pain has to be confronted, then separation between self and body and even self and world can be maintained. But if the pain moves to wound us deeply such that our own existence is suddenly called into question, then the separation collapses, the curtain is rent asunder, and the divisions in our life and from ourselves dissolve.

The wound, which begins as a bruise on Ivan Ilych's body, marks him deeply; it becomes the locus of his pain, a pain in his side that, at first localized, grows and metamorphoses into suffering. Suffering may be understood as the spiritual analogue of physical pain; it is pain of soul; but it may first enter the body or inscribe itself on the body as a mark of woundedness, as the boar marked Odysseus' body or the shackled feet of the infant Oedipus marked him for life or the mutilated back of Sethe marked her relation to her painful past. We move then, from a body that is technical to a body that is experienced soulfully.

Kott goes on to say of his heart attacks that "the heart is not just a sack that pumps blood but one that bears the scars of our loving and our dying until that final day. . . . The pump and Eros are one and the same" (117). There is in the flavor of Ivan Ilych's life a desire to technologize his existence by means of the same image that contains his work in the form of technical function. Robert Romanyshyn's insights into this peculiarly modern split in consciousness and embodiment help us see more profoundly this deadly technologizing tendency. Ivan Ilych's disposition to control, arrange, and curtain off one area of life from another—an action that he sees as a virtue!—might best be described as the creation of "distance." This "modern self" (90), as Romanyshyn refers to such a character, may be a new species of humanity, which he calls "homo astronauticus." Like the literal astronaut of our space age, he moves vertically to distance himself from the earth, narrows his focus, becomes the specialist, and in the process loses a sense of the whole of experience. Ivan Ilych, in fact, as the narrator informs us, "became such a new man" of the reformed judicial system, a new examining magistrate, a bureaucrat of officialdom. He begins in this role to embody the calculating attitude of "efficiency [which] wedded to indifference is a cold abstraction of a human being," according to Romanyshyn (*Technology*, 91).

He further suggests that the "mind that is addicted to the literal," which has no room in the imagination for the ambiguous in its striving for purity (100), develops a "habit of mind" that recoils from uncertainty, is in fact "a self without a shadow, a self, then, which is disincarnate" (101) and, I would add, lacks any deep sense of self-knowing. From his observation, we sense that on one level, Ivan Ilych has left his body and has embraced only the body of the world. From such an attitude, his being is defined exclusively by things behind which he hides, the curtain that he hangs in his home signals his striving for decorousness through decorations so that where he lives can reflect the banality of normalcy: "In reality, it was just what is usually seen in the houses of people of moderate means who want to appear rich, and therefore succeed only in resembling others like themselves" (116).

Try as he must to upholster his life with luxury, Ivan Ilych is only able to attain the mediocre; his life is most terrible because of what he sacrifices to achieve such tawdry ends. Or perhaps it is truer to say that one symptom of his disease is a way of thinking that he has surpassed all others in his status and acquisitions; he has, however, done no more in his striving than achieved their level of commonplaceness. But the cost is far greater than even he thought he would have to pay. He suffers from the same moral blindness that attacks Willy Loman, Ivan Ilych's workday alter ego, at the end of his life in Arthur Miller's *Death of a Salesman*. At his father's funeral, Willy's son observes of his father: "'he never knew who he was," a man, the neighbor Charley informs his son and us, was one "way out there in the blue, riding on a smile and a shoeshine," and rebels at the son's belief that his father had no clue as to what his identity was, as Joseph Campbell understands this tragic figure (qtd. in *Power of Myth*, 43).

In a very similar way, Ivan Ilych's disease may also direct him to areas of his life that have been left untended. Tending to the material and social realms, Ilych has ignored the deeper, more spiritual and psychological dimensions of being. The bruise in his side contains a complex metaphor for

Ilych's one-sided way of living, a one-sidedness that festers into disease. Disease then becomes a way of being one-sided, even of crossing over to the other side, the one that is now ailing. This unbalanced or one-sided attitude toward life he will shed, however, as the bruise in his side festers in him; it soon loosens or dislodges his imagination such that an awareness of his more deeply located diseased condition begins to be heard. From a curtained and cordoned life, Ilych moves through his wound to an openness, to facing what he has left hidden. And, as an examining magistrate, *evidence* is what he spends his professional life examining, sifting through, judging, and finally taking action on. Like his prototype before him, Ilych moves through the same pattern of awareness as Oedipus, the great riddle-solver who remains for most of his existence a riddle to himself, a being shrouded in the mystery of his past, which the oracle dislodges and sends him on the road to self-discovery through a remembrance of his original wounds.

Such a skewed life, if we might return to the beginning of the story for a moment, is not restricted to Ivan Ilych; his co-workers share the same habit of mind, though perhaps in a more inchoate form. For example, the attitudes toward death itself that each tries to deny under the aegis of inconvenience and irritation that Ivan's death brings them, is highlighted not only in Peter Ivanovich, whose last name carries the sobriquet "son of Ivan," but also of the figure of the dandy Schwartz, whose obsession with bridge saves him from even entering and gazing at the dead body of Ilych: "the mere fact of the death of a near acquaintance aroused, as usual, in all who heard of it the complacent feeling that, 'it is he who is dead and not I'" (96). Tolstoy's irony is pellucid in the subtle tone he uses here and throughout the narrative, for indeed these men are developing corporate clones of Ivan Ilych, who in their own "usualness" and complacency already suffer from a disease of spirit that can also be labeled "terrible." Certainty is what must be maintained so that no sense of not being in control and not managing all aspects of one's corporate and home life are allowed any seepage in.

At the funeral itself, where all seems arranged and proper, what unbalances Ivanovich in the ambiguity of his facing death though the corpse of his longtime friend, is how to behave properly, how to perform appropriately, which is another way of never moving toward the *experience* of death. The odor of death, however, unnerves him and sends him into awkward gestures of uncertainty. The presence of death and his anxiety in the face of it is a micro drama of Ivan Ilych's entire narrative from disease to death. By analogy, Peter moves through the same experience as Ivan. Whether he learns anything from it is doubtful, as the game of cards waiting for his arrival seems to cancel out this distasteful experience by promising once more a cocoon of certainty that wards off any taint of mortal limits.

When he enters the funeral parlor, however, one of the first persons he sees is the robust servant Gerasim "strewing something on the floor. Noticing this, Peter Ivanovich was immediately aware of a faint odor of a decomposing body" (98), which draws him to the dead body of his friend, in front of whom he gestures awkwardly in blessing himself: "when it seemed to him that this movement of his arm in crossing himself had gone on too long, he stopped and began to look at the corpse" (98).

When he gathers his courage to gaze directly at his dead superior, Peter notices that "the expression on the face said that what was necessary had been accomplished, and accomplished rightly. Besides this there was in that expression a reproach and a warning to the living. This warning seemed to Peter Ivanovich *out of place*, or at least not applicable to him" (98–99). For just an instant, he feels something penetrating him, wounding him by the image of death. It is the possibility of a psychic wound that would open him to death's fatal reality. But instead of dwelling with it, and rather indecorously, Peter flees from the room to find the reassuring eyes of Schwartz, who promises a life of entertainment and diversion from such unsavory and mysterious activities like dying.

However, the image of the dead body begins to work on Peter's imagination so that soon after, while listening to the financial woes of Praskovya, "he again saw that brow, and that nose pressing down on the lip, and felt afraid for himself" (102); but such existential horror is buried quickly under "the customary reflection . . . that this had happened to Ivan Ilych and not to him" (102). Customary behavior might be called an attitude which allows Peter to distance himself from the reality of mortality in this scene with Ilych's wife, a miniature version of Ivan's own denial and distancing that the wound in his side insisted by its presence of collapsing so powerfully and unconditionally.

She in turn uses her economic woes to keep at arm's length the dead body lying content in the room nearby. She exhibits no change as a result of witnessing his suffering, screaming, and dying; she reveals no inkling of the transformation that such a rite of passage wrought in him in his last hours. In the same attitude as Proskovya's, containment is essential in Peter's response; like her, he must keep the curtain drawn between life and death and thereby keep both comfortably corralled within the boundaries of the objective, the official, and the customary. Covered with such armor, Peter and his colleagues are able to maintain their innocence. James Hillman suggests that "the wound that is necessary to initiation ceremonies ends the state of innocence as it opens in a new way at another place" ("Puer Wounds," 113). The fixing of conventions and customs provides casings that keep the skin from being vulnerably exposed to possible woundings. But memory is difficult to control and has within its structure both the autonomy and the capacity to wound deeply.

Only when the image of the dead body of his friend reminds him of their growing up together, the memory of their playing together, and now as his death enters his imagination, does Peter feel the horror of mortality, which breaks through convention and decorum to become both specific and localized. He begins to suffer, if even for a moment, his friend's death as a real occurrence. The dead body offers Peter a way of seeing his own mortality that officialdom and specialism seek to obfuscate, perhaps even to cheat him out of, in much the same pattern of action that allowed Ivan, in his official capacity as magistrate, not to see the people who came before him every day as unique and subjective: He was proud of his capacity of "reducing even the most complicated case to a form in which it would be presented on paper only in its externals, completely excluding his personal opinion of the matter" (107). Such is the attitude of technical functioning, invented, like the body, for a particular cultural purpose,[2] keeping the ambiguity of existence at arm's length.

But as Peter Ivanovich draws away from its emotional and lived power, he simultaneously distances himself from himself; such an action is part of the malady that the story diagnoses. The dis-ease is buried in the attitude of distancing and thereby fabricates everything in the same pattern, without, however, the irritating ambiguity that attends distinctions. Distancing erases distinctions and in its operation reflects the body of technical functioning. Carl Jung describes such a distancing as a consequence of the "cult of consciousness" (*Alchemical Studies*, 36) that has infected modern sensibility, one which especially in the West has lost sight of the existence and value inherent in the unconscious. From such a movement results, not surprisingly, a desire to literalize the world, to strip it of its metaphorical resonances, and to keep things on the surface and superficial. Such a safe disposition promotes consumption of material things. All of these attitudes become full-blown in the actions of Ivan Ilych himself; all of them play their part in the creation of his dis-ease; in fact, they *are* the disease.

Two questions Robert Romanyshyn raises in his study of technology and the body are worth repeating here as we prepare to look at the wound of Ivan Ilych, the wound as metaphor which Peter Ivanovich perceives and feels in the emotional horror attendant upon looking at his dead friend. Romanyshyn writes:

> Symptoms ignored . . . do not disappear, and thus the death we would deny only appears elsewhere, perhaps in more virulent forms. For example, are our diseases, especially those of epidemic proportions, symptoms of cultural denials? . . . . Do we not know-

ingly or unwittingly arrange for our diseases to carry the shadow of our culture, and, more to the point here, do we 'choose' and designate victims to suffer our cultural symptoms? (*Technology as Symptom and Dream*, 29–30)

It is in the structure of wounds to cast a shadow on what may be unmarked. The wound is a shadow, a rupture or violation on a surface. It calls into question one's invulnerability, focuses attention on it, and raises questions that need never be asked prior to a wounding. Wounds are violations of conventions and the ordinary; they call forth what is remarkable and uncover what is mysterious in the life of each person. As such, the effect of the wound is to elicit wonder where before there was none. Prior to his wounding, Ivan Ilych feels no sense of the numinous haunting human life.

THE BODY OF THINGS

Ivan Ilych's literal fall from the ladder in his new home when he is adjusting the drapery of the new curtains is the second "fall" in the story. The first fall or stumble occurs when he suffers the injustice of being passed over for a judgeship he was sure was going to be offered to him: "In the country, without his work, he experienced *ennui* for the first time in his life, and not only *ennui* but intolerable depression" (113). But then, after a short time, and through a series of unexpected meetings and seemingly fated turns of events, Ilych finds himself back in a position in his former ministry with more salary and with more power. His excitement over his new post and renewed harmony with his wife prompts him to buy a new home and to personally supervise the decoration of its interior. His center of gravity shifts once again, this time from work to home, or from the outside social world to the inside world of his personal existence. Yet he remains on the surface of his life, never questioning any deeper issues than those of consuming. His own interior decorations remain dismally normal.

Adjusting the curtains *within* the home is an appropriate stage for the bruise, which begins outside on his skin and then moves inside his body, embellishing it in a new and fatal way.

Content with his progress and his possessions, Ivan Ilych surrounded himself with the things he has purchased, "chose the wallpapers, supplemented the furniture . . . and supervised the upholstering" (115), activities that allow him to move more closely to "the ideal he had set himself." He sees himself in absolute control of all his things: "he could see the fireplace, the screen, the what-not, the little chairs dotted here and there, the dishes and plates on the walls, and the bronzes, as they would be *when everything was in place*" (115, my emphasis). This strategy that rules his life, his controlling myth, so to speak, of fixing everything in the right place, is the cornerstone of Ilych's relation to the world of things, his work, his family, and himself. Being out of place brings with it *ennui*, depression, and alienation. Out of place, things are soiled; in place, they exhibit a purity that reflects his own imaginal way of being. Place—home, courtroom, bridge club—each neatly cordoned off, curtained, screened, hides the alienation; all is surface without a corresponding depth. Another way of saying this is to say that the "cult of consciousness" has made everything in Ilych's life superficial with a thin veneer of *prestige* coating it. Being wounded will be the first serious interruption of this new life; receiving the wound will plunge him from surface into a depth of being that forces him to question the value of his virtues. Suddenly, not things but *he* is out of place; the disease displaces him from the commonplace.

James Hillman tracks the word *prestige* to its etymological root: "prestige comes from *praestigia*, delusion, illusion like a juggler's trick, leading to the meanings of deception and imposture. We have the illusion of power without substance" (*Kinds of Power,* 122). The etymology of this word fits with the desires of Ilych, for the illusion or the appearance of things allows him to feel status and importance based on surface. So Ivan Ilych lives through and for things; not so ironic then that things themselves bring him down. Through this fall he suffers his bruised side physically, one that has actually been festering for some time in him and blocking his vision of the deeper sense of things, the "stuff" of the world. It is as if what he desires as growth moves within him and becomes disease.[3] We might say that the wound is what his superficial soul longs for, to be kidnapped and taken deep into depth, into the underworld, and into a level of consciousness that he has successfully avoided. He is Persephone seeking to be kidnapped into depth.

So we need to look closely at the origin of the wound as an experience of exposure that brings him down off the ladder he has been climbing for years and into the underworld of himself.

The fateful incident occurs when Ivan Ilych is hanging drapes in his new home. Having once again purchased a new place to reflect his new status, he assumes particular delight both founding it and finding a place for everything in it, putting everything in its place in an attitude of managed efficiency. As he shows the upholsterer how he wants the drapes hung, "he made a false step and slipped, but being a strong and agile man, he clung on and only knocked his side against the knob of the window frame. The bruised place was painful but the pain soon passed, and he felt particularly bright and well just then" (116). He even goes so far as to mention that he felt "fifteen years younger." And so long as he has things to "adjust," "arrange," and "order," he is happy. But something is now amiss. His contentment is dislodged, moves out of place. Now it is only when things have all found their place that irritation sets in, expressing itself as annoyance over any impurity, stain, or blemish on things. In effect, if anything he possesses carries even the slightest wound or marking from use or abuse, he recoils in anger. Nothing must show the wounds of the world, the nicks and scars of their being in the world; they must maintain the same kind of unwounded purity he has successfully designed for himself and his family.

While Ilych has wounded himself in placing things in the home, the irritation initially finds its locus in things outside himself: "Every spot on the tablecloth or the upholstery, and every broken window-blind string irritated him" (117). In fact, every "disturbance" distresses him even while he clings to the watchwords of his existence: "decorous," "pleasant," and "easy."

Now we might think it coincidental that his initial fall involves both the drapery of his windows and the window knob, and that he feels irritation over the soiled or broken fixtures mentioned above. I believe, however, that the narrator wants us to think of the image of the curtain, upholstery, and tablecloth as coverings of other things. They hide the surface of things with another surface, and in the case of the curtains, they block vision as they hang over the windows, preventing vision from inside to outside or from one room to another. Even though windows physically divide one place from another, they do allow visual access between worlds. In his singleness of vision, Ivan Ilych is not able to see beyond where he is; he does not, we might say, have a "window vision" which allows him access to more than one place, one world. Such is the structure of his consciousness. In order to see more, therefore, he must be wounded, a reversal of Oedipus' own internal vision, his insight, which precipitates his own self-wounding when he blinds himself.

I also find it important that the knob of the window is what knocks the side of Ivan Ilych and inaugurates the wound, even as the ladder itself may have played an active role in his falling as it cooperated with the invisible force of gravity to bring him down. For the knob of the window allows more than ocular access from one space to another; it allows physical access as well, a movement from place to place but always with the possibility of closing that access off when movement is to be discouraged. In other words, things themselves are conscious in this story; they have a movement, a part to play, a motive for their actions, even. Things have more than characteristics here; they also have character, a life of their own. This is another way of stating that things are ensouled, are part of the *anima mundi* and as such invite respect and attention.[4]

Let me return for a moment to those frisky, even aggressive pieces of furniture mentioned in the introduction of this chapter, things that populate the home Ilych so enjoys managing well but that seemed nonetheless to attack and wound him for his efforts. Full of a desire to maintain decorum even under these unsettling circumstances, the clerk Peter Ivanovich leads the widow Praskovya into the drawing-room "upholstered in pink cretonne" (100), and Peter sits "on a low pouffe, the springs of which yielded spasmodically under his weight." The room is so full that it seems difficult to move about, and as Praskovya tries, "the lace of the widow's black shawl caught on the carved edge of the table. Peter Ivanovich rose to detach it, and the springs of the pouffe, relieved of his weight, rose also and gave him a push." When he sits down after assisting her, Peter once again suppresses "the rebellious springs of the pouffe under him"; when he rises yet again, "the pouffe rebelled and even creaked" (100).

It is as if the things Ivan Ilych worked so aggressively to manage and place so carefully in life are now seeking their own intentions and now speak out in his death. The hand of management has lifted, but the rebellion is not new, for things that he sought to own and keep in place have gotten out of place and now, almost mischievously, intend to exercise their own life. And as Ilych's disease, whose genesis was in falling from the ladder onto the knob of the window, increases and overwhelms him, so does the image of the black sack, a cloth like the curtains themselves that lured him up the ladder in order to bring him down in disease. Punching out through the bottom of the black sack will mark the first time in his life that Ivan Ilych is actually free. We might understand the black sack as a symbol for the unconscious of Ivan Ilych. First he must make contact with it; then he must pass through it to an awareness that is both heightened and sacred. Then, by means of this new consciousness, he must act, for enhanced awareness alone is insufficient.

Again his freedom, like his disease, comes through things. Touching, arranging, managing, ordering, and adjusting things has kept Ivan Ilych out of touch with his own family, his own spirit, his own soul. Therefore, through the energies and actions of ensouled things, he is put in touch with what he has avoided or been unconscious of. It is through things that he recovers from an atrophy of consciousness. Things form a conspiracy to plunge him deep into himself. But the effort is costly and violent as it moves from a harmless bruise to a terminal disease.

Here I would mention Vladimir Nabokov's utterance of what he calls the "Tolstoyan formula: Ivan lived a bad life and since a bad life is nothing but the death of the soul, then Ivan lived a living death" (434). True enough, but such a pronouncement is a bit simplistic. It is not Ilych's soul that is dead; he has, however, divorced himself from it by living exclusively through things consciously but with no self-consciousness. Things in their behavior, then, act as the consciousness he lacks and then they project it into the world. They rebel; he does not. They are his consciousness in revolt. And in their insurrection they wound him, the end result of which puts him in touch with what he has ignored.[5]

THE WOUNDED BODY OF DISEASE

Climbing the ladder of prestige and success, if not power, forever active with diversions of adjustment, and always living outside himself with no contemplation of his interior drapery, Ivan Ilych slips and is suddenly pulled out of the mainstream of life and into an eddy of quiet suspension. What was before hidden now in disease surfaces: things become "distasteful"; he has a queer taste in his mouth (120) and his wife's "hidden" exasperation increases "his irritation" (120). Now, as he begins to experience a breakdown in arrangements, he finds most repulsive what he had before worked so diligently to shore up, promote, and worship: the arrangement and containment of things as well as his own life.

Believing that another professional person will rectify by putting back into its rightful place what has been knocked out of its familiar terrain, he visits a specialist. "The doctor indicated that there was so-and-so inside the patient, but if the investigation of so-and-so did not confirm this, then he must assume that and that" (121). Ilych is chagrined that there is no efficient, easy solution forthcoming; he falls into ambiguity and uncertainty as no two doctors can agree on his "condition." All arrangements and containments are off and Ilych begins to sink deeply into himself, into the underworld of himself through the aperture of his wound. We cannot and ought not be able to diagnose the illness of Ivan Ilych because part of Tolstoy's poetics of dis-ease here is to make it nameless, going only so far as to refer to the disease through the pronoun "it," with a purposely vague antecedent. Nonetheless, Russell Lockhart's diagnosis of cancer is illuminating here. He writes of the disease as "growth gone wrong" (6), a response to "something of one's psychic and bodily earth that is not allowed to live" (2). Such a diagnosis seems plausible within the context of Ilych's previous life and the onset of illness. Growth gone wrong is an apt description of his personal life as the bruise ripens into disease. Furthermore, we can see how his response after being infected with this virus of modernity gives credence to Lockhart's observation.

To maintain order and to continue to manage all aspects of his life poison Ivan Ilych's attitude toward his disease. He continues to hope "to adjust what was wrong, to master it and attain success, or make a grand slam. But now every mischance upset him and plunged him into despair" (123). Moreover, the disease links his interior life with the exterior existence of his family: any "unpleasantness" at home, any "lack of success" at work, or even "bad cards at bridge" make him "acutely sensible" of his disease (123). The crust or shell or curtain that he has used successfully to protect himself from irritation and annoyance dissolves in disease and exposes him to his illness, even while the medical model of anatomy and physiology tyrannically pushes everything about his malady into a specialized container. For just as the things that surround Ivan Ilych and rebel against him in the exercise of their own consciousness, so too do his body organs take on a frisky life of their own: When the specialist visits him to take unequivocal charge of the disease, he brings up the question "of the kidney and appendix, which were not behaving as they ought to and would now be attacked by . . . the specialist *and forced to amend their ways*" (143, my emphasis). In other words, the specialist draws a curtain around the body of anatomy and physiology and treats it as Ivan Ilych once treated things— through management, adjustment, division, and control. The anatomical body that is the specialist's medical model, however, is a safe refuge, for it does not go beyond stimulus-response behavior. Thus through what we today call "managed care," the doctors attempt to cordon off his kidney and appendix in order to isolate the issue. Ivan Ilych feels the full power of crisis management leveled against his condition but gains paltry reassurance in this knowledge. James Hillman suggests that in wounding, "each organ has a potential spark of consciousness and afflictions release this consciousness" ("Puer Wounds," 116). This deep body consciousness does not allow the neat containment Ilych has found most familiar and comforting. He feels the weight of another knowing presence deep in his flesh; it becomes more disconcerting for him to listen to its voice.

Even in his condition, however, death is far too ubiquitous and refuses, like an obstinate patient, to be isolated; instead, the consciousness of "It" pours through the opening of his woundedness and assumes the face of his disease. Thus, rather than saying that Ivan Ilych has a wound or is diseased, perhaps it would be truer to say that his wound and his disease have possessed him. As he struggles initially to shape his disease, his disease turns and begins to shape him; he begins to be refashioned by his illness and through it, by his relation to his own life, most especially his past. His disease shakes loose his imagination so that he imagines his life with a keener eye, one with a more penetrating gaze. His disease, in other words, is a way of seeing and judging the quality of his existence. Through it, what was critically important for him becomes trivial, and what was insignificant for him takes on a profundity that is terrifying.

As he plays cards and tries to ignore the initial stages of the disease, he makes a grand slam and feels the queer taste in his mouth "and it seemed ridiculous that in such circumstances he should be pleased to make a grand slam" (126). Through his woundedness he begins to wonder, and this wondering reveals to him the trivial nature of his existence. The game he has been playing grows less and less satisfactory. The queer taste in his mouth may be likened to the alchemists' *prima materia*, the base matter which they would begin with in order to refine it into a more valuable metal. Writing on "The Alchemy of Illness," Kat Duff cites Paracelsus' belief that "each disease 'bears its own remedy within itself. . . . Health must grow from the same root as disease'" (47). Her description of the process is relevant here: "The alchemists insisted that two things must happen before the cure can be extracted from the disease: the problem must be kept in a closed container, and it must be reduced to its original state through a process of breakdown" (47).

Russell Lockhart follows the word "cure" in disease to its origin and discovers there that the root *cura* also gives rise to "curious" and "curiosity" (21). He speculates that in patients with terminal diseases, a cure begins when one does not flee from the wound, "when someone is motivated by curiosity to go into the pathology rather than away from it" (21).[6] This soft spot in Ivan Ilych's side, locus of the bruise that is also the genesis of disease, is a break in his surface, a place on his body where he is forced to focus his attention. It becomes a breach or perhaps even a window, into the life of spirit through reflection. The body calls him back and in through the wound. Writing of wounding in another context, Hillman suggests wounds may have a spiritual quality. A wound "is a learner and a teacher both . . . and has a message" ("Puer Wounds," 108). It is a place, as in other "handicaps" one suffers, that "give[s] soul" (109). The irony of Ivan Ilych's disease that grows from the wound is that it may be his most prized possession, far surpassing in value all of what he has materially acquired, and it was given to him *through the things he believed he possessed*. It is a gift that wounds, "the gift of a wound" ("Puer Wounds," 107).

Ivan Ilych's questions continue to expand out from the place of the injury therefore to bear less on questions of disease and more on whether he will live or die. Left alone, he gains a "consciousness that his life was poisoning the lives of others and that this poison did not weaken but penetrated more and more deeply into his whole being" (126–27). Clearly he begins to see the world through the metaphor of his illness, the filter of his suffering. His wound as a gift begins to parent him, especially as his childhood begins to play a more significant role in his reflections on his life. Going deep into himself, which is a journey he never allowed himself when he lived on the surface of life, he feels and touches his disease and slowly begins to suffer, that is, "to bear it" with acceptance.

Let us say that the wound's voice begins to be heard; disease then has a speech. It gathers its own language and voices itself into the world when the normative activities of everyday life begin to be displaced and silenced. His wound opens up parts of his personal myth that otherwise would remain mute. Wounds are callings; they are voices insisting we do or become something we have avoided. They also have their own energy and it is felt as the wound deepens. Something in the wound echoes as well another condition or state of being. In the hollowness of the wound, the disease, in the gap, is an echo; something is returned, like an echo's return of words spoken, to us in the wound or disease. We question what Ivan Ilych's has echoed back to him through his bruised side.

As he has spent a great part of his adult life touching, arranging, adjusting things, now he is in turn touched by things; they initiate a touching change in him. It is as if what he has sought to control becomes in some ways his therapist and touches him back, thus initiating a deep transformation in his soul, a place within his own landscape that has no decoration, no embellishment or antique furniture. It is space cleared of debris. His soul is not dead; it is simply barren and voiceless. By touching his side, the window knob slows this activity-driven man so that he might hear the barren room of his own soul pleading for some decorum in his life. His soul suffers and he does not know it until some of the world's stuff violently knocks him down and off the ladder of success.

We might at this point recall that almost insignificant detail Tolstoy offers us when he describes the hearty Ivan Ilych dancing with Princess Trufonova,"a sister of the distinguished founder of the Society 'Bear My Burden'" (119). To bear one's burden would suggest a "suffering with," and a being with one in his suffering; this act of generosity and selflessness only two characters in the story are capable of embracing: Ivan's young son and the servant Gerasim, whom I will introduce more fully in a moment. Ilych's dis-eased life takes on both psychological texture and spiritual depth. Hillman suggests that in woundedness a "new spirit" has an opportunity to emerge; "through our holes the unexpected comes out. A wound has this spiritual logos quality" ("Puer Wounds," 110) and can teach. Richard Gustafson supports such a reading in observing that it is Ilych's suffering "that begins its teaching task" (463), although he does not outline the lineaments of such an important tutorial.

GERASIM: THE BODY OF EARTH AND SERVICE

Touching, arranging, readjusting, fixing, getting into place, cordoning and curtaining off, dividing, isolating: these terms describe Ivan Ilych's existence prior to his wound and his subsequent disease. Accompanying his malady is a dissolution of the boundaries and compartments of his life. What is added to his suffering is another image of cloth, like the curtains: the black sack, which appears for the first time to signal a shift in Ivan's rebellion against the generalized, vague malady. It is an underworld image that Ivan must pass through; his guide or support in this journey is the servant Gerasim, a figure like Hermes who guides souls through the underworld. We need to look closely at this unassuming figure who so generously aids Ilych in his illness, for he is the embodiment of service and an emblem of Christian love and sacrifice. He is also, like the figure of the Peasant Marey in Dostoevsky's powerful recollection during the years of his penal servitude, an icon of Mother Earth herself.

The metaphor of the black sack is an important one in Ivan's move to a more spiritual level of human being, for it signals a rite of passage essential in order for him to recover from his spiritual illness: "It seemed to him that he and his pain were being thrust into a narrow, deep black sack, but though they were pushed further and further in they could not be pushed to the bottom. . . . He struggled but yet co-operated. And suddenly he broke through, fell, and regained consciousness" (147). This is perhaps the third fall Ivan Ilych experiences in the story; when he awakes, the first thing he becomes aware of is Gerasim at the foot of the bed, "dozing quietly and patiently" with Ivan's "emaciated stockinged legs resting on Gerasim's shoulders" (146).

This robust, generous servant is the only figure in the story who is without a home; he is the only one as well, according to Gustafson, "shown without a family or friends," yet he knows "how to live because he accepts the facts of life and death" (464). He is more than simply a character who accepts the facts of human mortality. If, as Tolstoy has insisted throughout the reading of this story, we pay close attention to the things populating the narrative—furniture, clothing, curtains, ladders, cloth, sacks—then we notice in his peasant presence that his "heavy boots emitted a pleasant smell of tar and fresh winter air" (135).

In addition, one of the first tasks that he readily accepts is cleaning the excrement of Ivan Ilych and disposing of it, the odor of which torments Ilych because it underscores his soiledness and his decaying mortality. We remember how in his daily life earlier every little stain would upset him; now his own soiled nature he finds disgusting, as the odor of the dead Ivan lying in his coffin Peter Ivanovich notices and which draws him in fear and uncertainty to the corpse. The soiled things of the world have transformed themselves into a soiled self. The stain is no longer just part of the tablecloth; it is now part of Ivan himself.

But Gerasim's strong, pleasant outdoor odors pacify, even soothe Ilych, as the servant's odors mix with the excrement of the ill man. His waste is out of place. The "special arrangements" made to contain Ivan do not work. Now, words like "uncleanliness" and "unseemliness" replace "decorum" and "arrangement"; but Gerasim moves through this muddied world with an unselfconsciousness that persuades Ilych to trust him and even to ask for his forgiveness for the sordidness of his condition: "I am uncleanliness and disorder" (139), Ivan thinks at one point, as all decorum dissolves to make more room for a spiritual life of caring not for things but for others. All through this transformation is the presence of Gerasim, who as a "natural" force in service to Ivan guides his spirit both through the black sack and back to his childhood by serving without patronizing as an icon of charity and generosity.

My sense is that Gerasim, like Ivan's disease, teaches him something valuable: how to respond in love and selflessness to another without thought or desire for reward.[7] The curtain between his adult life and his childhood parts, like a wound, exposes something through its aperture; Ivan Ilych begins to realize through his disease that the period of his earlier life, a time in which "all the enthusiasms of childhood and youth passed without leaving much trace on him" (105), he now apprehends was the only time in his life when he was truly happy, when the curtains and divisions of his existence had not yet been constructed.

He also understands another reversal of his allegedly successful life: "It is as if I had been going downhill while I imagined I was going up. And that is really what it was. I was going up in public opinion . . . but life was ebbing away from me" (148). His recognition reverses, to some extent, the definitions of health and disease; they are both redefined through the orifice of woundedness and as such actually parent the dying man. Gerasim participates in this parenting through his actions of cleaning up the now helpless child. The body of disease becomes the body of memory which transports him back to his childhood; the body of resistance must pass completely through the black sack and into a new attitude, one of forgiveness.

The robustness of Gerasim's own body is indeed an important metaphor in the story, for as Ivan Ilych's own spiritual malady emerged through the aperture of his wound and ensuing disease, so does Gerasim's healthy body, "grown stout on town food" and complete with "a clean Hessian apron, the sleeves of his print shirt tucked up over his strong bare young arms" (135) and with his face showing the beginnings of a young beard, correspond to his spirit of unconditional service. He serves Ivan in his journey toward spiritual cure and renewal. The interior of Ivan growing toward cure through care is embodied in the healthy physique of Gerasim. It is an imaginal body in the sense that a developing spiritual robustness in Ivan Ilych is given its equivalent bodily metaphor in the figure of the young peasant servant who is the incarnation of Holy Mother Russia herself.

That he elevates the feeble legs of Ivan Ilych in order to give him physical relief from his pain, and in so doing reverses or inverts the body of the dying man, reveals how Gerasim's acts of generosity offer Ivan Ilych another way of being in the world, one that redeems his neglect of family. Gerasim's generous actions exhibit a love that needs to be passed on, and this Ivan Ilych is able to do through his son. Gerasim, like the wound itself, is a gift to Ivan Ilych; what he has cursed or treated with only the most peripheral attention now become his most valuable possessions.[8] Wounding has transformed his consciousness. The gift of touch and comfort passes from the body of Gerasim to Ilych and from the body of Ilych to his son, the only one who seems to be in deep mourning for his death.

Lewis Hyde's powerful reflections on gift-giving should be at least mentioned as they relate specifically to this passing on of a gift of caring through the body. Hyde observes that any culture still alive and healthy will have "transformative gifts as a general feature. . . . It will have spiritual teachings available at all levels of maturation and for the birth of the spiritual self" (47). But one must have developed sufficiently in order to gain the capacity to pass a gift on, and this is the point of gift giving from Gerasim to Ivan Ilych to his son that I quote at length:

> With gifts that are agents of change, it is only when the gift has worked in us, only when we have come up to its level . . . that we can give it away again. Passing the gift along is the act of gratitude that finishes the labor. The transformation is not accomplished until we have the power to give the gift on our own terms. (47)

With Ivan Ilych, the opportunity that suddenly arises when his son enters the room of the screaming man is itself a gift; at this moment Ivan Ilych passes the gift along that was given to him from Gerasim: "His hand fell on the boy's head, and the boy caught it, pressed it to his lips, and began to cry. At that very moment Ivan Ilych fell through and caught sight of the light, and it was revealed to him that though his life had not been what it should have been, this could still be rectified. He then gestures to his wife and son that he forgives them and himself, though instead of 'forgive' he says 'forgo'" (155). When he hears someone almost immediately say to the others in the room, "It is finished," he repeats to himself, "Death is finished" (156); I believe such a recognition comes to him in large measure because he has reached a sufficient level of spiritual awareness to pass the gift given him by Gerasim along to his family. He becomes, in an important way and for the first time, a gift to them and they to him. At the last moments of his death he lives fully for the first time.[9] Instead of things, the family members become valuable gifts to one another.

Tolstoy's understated narrative, with its fidelity to the world of matter, the body, and selfless service, which seems to be the locus of subdued but effective power, renders poetically the search for wholeness in one soul who in his quest for decorum and ease discovers through the experience of woundedness and disease the fulfillment of a life when it is directed both deeply into oneself and outward to the care of others. Ivan Ilych's true cure comes through the action of care, a gift he learns that, only through his woundedness, was still a possibility for him moments before dying. In his end is his true beginning; in his death is his birth. Being wounded opens him to living fully while it marks clearly the trajectory of his death.

In the next chapter, we will explore two short stories by Flannery O'Connor. First we will witness another character who suffers a wound, this time from a book thrown at her in a doctor's waiting room, with some of the same jarring shifts of vision incurred by Ivan Ilych. The second story explores a tattooed body, full of the markings of nature and history; this same marked body will be called to an image of Christ that finds its way on to the back of a man who believes deeply in mystery.

9

Wounds and Tattoos

Marking the Mystery in Flannery O'Connor's "Revelation" and "Parker's Back"

> Does cancer enter us or do we, in falling ill, enter the revelation of the universal cancer?
> —Guido Ceronetti, *Silence of the Body,* 29

MYSTERY AND WOUNDED MATTER IN "REVELATION"

Disease was no stranger to Flannery O'Connor, who wrote every day at the same time when her lupus would slumber quietly enough in her to allow a few short hours of creativity. In her relation with her own malady, she came to believe that disease is less a thing or an objective reality than it is a place, a terrain that one goes to and dwells in body and imagination (*Habit of Being,* 132). No wonder, then, that so much of her fiction is concerned with characters who feel ill-at-ease in the world and who often suffer physical wounding. For matters of the body, the flesh and certainly incarnation are constantly important to her poetic and theological worldview.

One of her characters who fits this portrait, Ruby Turpin in "Revelation," whom O'Connor created late in her writing career, might even be called, at least in her outward appearance, a character in search of a wound, gash, or blow that will awaken her to the deeper mysteries of divinity and the sacred matter of the world as well as her place in such a numinous level of being. Her story is about lifting the veil of blindness so that through the presence of mystery itself one glimpses the invisible presence of the sacred in ordinary life. But given that half of the story takes place in a country doctor's waiting room where the Turpins await an examination of Claud's bruised leg, we might ask of Ruby: Is she ill or diseased? And what is the difference between these two conditions?

In *The Psychology of Chronic Illness,* analyst Robert Shuman, himself afflicted with multiple sclerosis, has turned to the inner experiences surrounding disease, which is a way the body is wounded or lesioned by viruses. He makes an interesting distinction between disease and illness relevant to my discussion of "Revelation." Shuman suggests that "disease usually refers to the observable damage or malfunctioning of organs, tissues, or systems of the body. . . . Disease can exist with no previous signs of illness" (97). We will see from this brief description that Claud is diseased. But Ruby warrants a different diagnosis: "Illness, on the other hand, captures the meanings and biopsychosocial outcomes of an anticipated or identified disease. People may feel ill when no disease is present in their bodies. . . . Illness may linger once disease is gone" (97–98). But here the malady thickens in what he states next: "Since most chronic conditions are not curable and their symptoms and course fluctuate, it is very difficult to distinguish between disease and illness" (98). We can, I believe, offer a prognosis early on: While Claud may be diseased, Ruby is chronically ill. But her illness requires an antidote that is harsh, quick-acting, and permanently transformative. O'Connor's story is a working out of this prescription, especially when the illness is deep in the spirit rather than simply on the body's surface as a biological bruise.

O'Connor was concerned throughout her writing about an attitude or habit of mind that denies the matter of the world. Not unlike the Russian writer, Fyodor Dostoevsky, O'Connor saw the inherent danger in abstract ideas and in their power to efface the given condition of the world, to disincarnate the flesh of things so that the world could be reshaped to mirror one's own prejudices, obsessions, and self-image. The seemingly pious and devout Ruby Turpin harbors within her attitude toward others a distinctly bold challenge: to question the value and worth of the world's body. Ruby's deeply ingrained intolerance of those aspects of the world that do not reflect her own image is a moral and cultural symptom of a deeper, perhaps morally pervasive cultural illness, which includes a disdain for creation itself, and for the Creator who seems bent, she is convinced, on offending her sensibilities. Ruby's denial of matter itself, even of *mater*, the earth, can be understood within O'Connor's poetic theology as a pervasive metaphor for the incarnation of divine presence.

Through Ruby Turpin especially, O'Connor asks that we consider fully what we generally only glimpse through the lens of crisis—what may rightly be called a theological poetics of corporeality—in order to understand the inherent tyranny embedded in an imagination that denies the world its substance. Implicit in such tyranny is a voice that says the material world, especially in its sacred lineaments, does not matter, or that it matters only insofar as it reflects one's own image. Perhaps such an attitude develops from the hybris of moral superiority, a narcissism of the imagination that suggests the world is actually only a matter of mind. Within such a frame of reference, it is easy for one to put the matter of the world, its own finite and definite reality, out of mind.

The cultural critic, Ivan Illich, has persuasively argued the antithesis of Ruby's attitude by describing what he calls "vernacular dwelling," which is a style of inhabiting the world deeply and materially so that we leave behind traces or tracks of our presence—odors, stains, residue—the muck—of our own imperfect, aging, and soiled bodies. Vernacular living allows us to maintain a history of ourselves in our habitation.[1]

Through the figure of Ruby Turpin, O'Connor's poetics of corporeality has its own revelation: to reveal the tyranny embedded in an imagination that denies the stuff of the world its being, at the same time that it denies the world and those in it their history. Both visions of the world's denial twist and exaggerate belief, according to O'Connor. The story, she believes, "has a purpose, and the whole structure of the story or novel has been made what it is because of belief. This is not the kind of distortion that destroys; it is the kind that reveals, or should reveal" (*Mystery and Manners*, 162). Written just months before she died, "Revelation" actually fulfills this revelatory quality of belief through a soul that has lost touch with the soiled and sullied qualities of the world's imperfect and often unpredictable unfolding, even as she and her husband raise pigs, an animal that certainly has no history of denying the world's matter. Her pigs live in conditions as antiseptic and sterile as her own; they reflect in their sterile habitation a mirror image of Ruby's pure vision of the world. The antiseptic and tidy pigpens, which she prides herself in keeping in such a condition, is a perfect simulacrum of her trim vision of the world that forestalls ambiguity or unpleasantness from entering. Her pigs are raised on cement floors; their feet never touch the earth. They are fed and hosed down in that same sterile condition.

A close reading of the body in "Revelation," given its setting in a doctor's waiting room, a space as clean and antiseptic as the pig parlors, will nonetheless allow to enter the body ill, the body wounded, and the soiled quality of everyday life. The second part of the story, which takes place on the Turpins' pig farm, implicates the natural animal world and the attendant mysteries that it contains. But this animal world, specifically in Claud's wound from a cow's kick, has already had its influence in bringing Ruby to a place where what she has failed to see because of a narrow vision can be revealed to her. One might think that the animal wound to Claud's leg is insignificant to the larger action, which gathers itself around Ruby's character. But another angle might reveal that the animals know her condition and inaugurate the beginnings of her cure, which must begin with a wound to the head, for that is the source of her skewed seeing. We remember Oedipus' own wounds to his feet as he turned back to see the nature of his past actions. Some Sophoclean energy drives Ruby forward into her past.

The blow to the forehead " just above the left eye" that Ruby receives from the young college student, Mary Grace as she, too, waits to see the

doctor, will awaken Ruby through the shock of her wound to what I sense
is first an animal imagination back on the farm, where some of her tidy and
decorous attitudes will surrender to another sense of knowing the world—
the old sow's farrowing presence. By means of this deeply panting animal,
Ruby will see through her to the divine presence and the mystery of salvation, a vision that her own antiseptic and perhaps even totalitarian vision
prohibits. O'Connor's deft imagery places animal and sacred presence at either end of the moral spectrum, with Ruby, Mary Grace, and the assorted
patients sporting drippy noses, snuff-stained lips, sack meal dresses, and fatigued, drowsy eyes, in the middle.

I suspect that her "disposition," as pleasantly acceptable as it might appear to those characters with whom she finds a kindred soul in the doctor's
waiting room, is actually much more perilous than simple small town bigotry. Rather, Ruby's attitude fundamentally denies the world in its particular and polluted condition. The irony of denying it, the story suggests, rests
in realizing that salvation comes precisely through such messiness. Said another way, whenever Ruby's clear vision of the world as she designs it turns
muddy or cloudy, or becomes infected by ambiguity, she responds by imaginatively exterminating those obstacles that threaten the creation of the
world in her own image. As such, she successfully holds at arm's length the
finite and sullied qualities of ordinary life as having a place in the divine
plan of redemption.

Critics of the story, like Norman McMillan ("Dostoevskian Vision in
Flannery O'Connor's 'Revelation'"), explores the crisis of spirit through the
body in this story, and Sura Rath's "Redemption: Thomistic Resolution in
O'Connor's 'Revelation'" focuses on the senses. Rath, for example, cites St.
Thomas' belief that "man as a knower must be such that he can give existence, within his knowledge, not to abstract, but to sensible beings. That is
why man as a knower *needs a body*" (2, my emphasis). W. R. Martin, who
in "A Note on Ruby and Revelation," does not sustain the image of the
body, does point convincingly to the colors red and purple as analogies of
specific moral stances, reflected in the red or purple faces of Ruby herself or
her nemesis of revelation, Mary Grace. She is also Ruby's mimesis in that
she mirrors back to her Ruby's own intense landscape.

Perhaps it is less an angle of vision than it is an epistemology that
needs a corrective for Ruby to inhabit her world in a more instinctive and
embodied way. She may need to acquire not simply the small, black eyes of
the pig, but its full sense of being, even as she embodies something of that
animal's physiology: "The doctor's waiting room, which was very small,
was almost full when the Turpins entered and Mrs. Turpin, who was very
large, made it look even smaller by her presence. . . . Her little bright black
eyes took in all the patients as she sized up the seating situation" (191).

Not an attitude of largesse but a biology of bigness characterizes her presence. Her body is less a "site of political struggle" (16), as Susan Bordo argues for the female body in a postmodern frame, than it is a moral lightning rod for knowing. Bordo is accurate in asserting that the body can be one of the apertures into the divine, sexuality, and appetite (3). For Ruby, her own body, which retrieves something of the animal presence in things, leads her into a vision of salvation in the story's ending. We intuit the profound position of corporeality as the aperture through which one enters into mystery, especially the mystery of divine judgment. This same opening is possible to enter only, as O'Connor herself believes, through what can be called an anagogical imagination. "It is this kind of vision," she maintains, "that is able to see different levels of reality in one image or one situation" (*Mystery and Manners,* 72). She then offers in "Writing Short Stories" a fine illustration of this deepening reality in her character, Hulga Hopewell of "Good Country People," who possesses, in descending order, both a Ph.D. and a wooden leg. O'Connor observes that the physicality of the artificial limb *has its analogy* in the moral terrain of her soul: "we perceive that there is a wooden part of her soul that corresponds to her wooden leg. Now this of course is never stated" (99). Something of Ahab's disposition haunts Hulga's artifical limb. For both Ahab and Hulga the "phantom limb" is a meeting of psyche and physiology (Merleau-Porty, *Phenomenology of Perception,* 77).

The most important part of O'Connor's observation is the phrase "never stated." The poetic image carries the invisible and powerful moral temper through the palpable image of the hardened leg. The body's condition, if not its gestures, carries with it, deeply embedded in its flesh (or in this case its wood) an analogue of that person's moral condition. The body as metaphor is a conduit for conversion. The invisible condition, the psychological demeanor, is revealed in and through the visible state of the body. Flesh, then, is always a metaphor, always pointing in its gestural relation to the world to endow it with a moral or ethical or psychological status. O'Connor's poetic imagination gives us sharply and crisply the interior of the character through that character's physicality. Physical condition is moral predisposition *by analogy.* What is not stated is perhaps then the best place to begin to explore Ruby's narrow vision.

What O'Connor has observed of another character, Sarah Ruth Cates in "Parker's Back," which we will take up later in this chapter, she might well level at Ruby: "Sarah Ruth was the heretic," O'Connor writes, because of her "notion that you can worship in pure spirit" (*Habit of Being,* 594). Spirit divorced from flesh breeds a moral tyranny toward the world of matter. Separated from the fully embodied being of animals, from instinct and sense, one can become victim of a diseased vision distinct from matter.

Possessed of such a disposition, Ruby shares more with Ivan Karamazov than she does with his monastic brother, Alexey.

The analogy of Being, for O'Connor, seems present most fully through the mystery of flesh and just as often through the condition of violence. "Revelation" is perhaps the finest expression of such a denial of the body and the flesh, and by extension, the moral responsibility shouldered by any soul who accepts the reality of divine incarnation. Of course there exists in the physicality of Ruby one of O'Connor's fine comic ironies: She who denies the world its body is herself oversized, plump and abundantly enfleshed.

The story begins when Ruby and her husband Claud enter the doctor's waiting room in order to have Claud's injured leg examined. The description around Claud's leg is also revealing; Ruby insists that he roll up his trouser leg to expose his wound, which is hidden from view, as is her own more deeply embedded malady. This incidental action of opening up or exposing one's hidden or veiled wound, acts as a leitmotif of the entire story, beginning small and building toward a profound act of violence. His leg "reveals a purple swelling on a plump marble-white calf" (192). Through these two images, of cow and calf, coupled with Ruby's own "little bright black eyes," (191), like those of her pigs, we sense already that the animals, which are fully embodied in their sensate presence to the world, are already vibrantly alive in the doctor's office. They will become not only more plentiful in their variety, but more outspoken in their being when the story shifts to the farm. Part of Ruby's revelation also discloses the intimate connection between divinity and animality, an insight the young college student, Mary Grace, with her carbuncular complexion, will open Ruby to when she hurls a book entitled *Human Development* at her from across the room. Hit and wounded by the book,[2] Ruby is for the first time dislodged from her angle of vision on the world, which treats it as a specimen, as a matter of mind. She begins to experience it as both profoundly enfleshed and deeply sacred in its imperfect incarnation. Her vision will be led finally to what has been hidden in plain view; the mystery of the sacred will be embodied in the image of her own sleeping sow waiting to farrow on their pig farm. The large and perhaps grotesque heaviness of the sow is an image of amplitude, of new life within her waiting to be born in all of its magnificent messiness. This largesse is what Ruby lacks.

Perhaps Ruby's revelation is less about divinity's presence in matter than it is a discovery of the flesh as our web of connectedness to all other life. It is one thing to be enfleshed consciously; it is quite another to sense that such a condition is what unites, however imperfectly. Merleau-Ponty's writing on the body and world claims that "the Flesh is an intertwined and actively intertwining, lattice of mutually dependent phenomena, both sensorial and sentient, of which our own sensing bodies are a part" (qtd. in

Abram, 84). This sensate presence, as Abram continues, links us to the "whole of the sensuous world that provides the deep structure of language. As we ourselves dwell and move within language, so, ultimately, do the other animals and animate things of the world. . . . It is no more that *we* speak than that the things and the animate world itself, *speak within us*" (85). Body, language, self, and divinity or the sacred realm of being all constitute an eco-community; denying any one part collapses the order of the entire structure. Ruby's denial of what she cannot grasp in her simple and abstract vision of the world is therefore very destructive of creation. Her language continues to give her away because it is most intent on silencing the voices of others.

The smooth-skinned ample woman without blemish, bruise, or wound, whose skin is more like a baby's than a mature adult's, and who is by all appearances a picture of health and jollity, has unknowingly, in accompanying her husband, come to have her own sight surgically altered, by being wounded. It becomes apparent, however, that as Claud is there as the patient, he is accompanied by a woman who is very impatient with almost everyone she sizes up in the waiting room. At first she uses her size to ingratiate herself to the one figure in the room with whom she identifies, a woman stylishly dressed:

> Mrs. Turpin eased into the vacant chair, which held her tight as a corset.
> "I wish I could reduce," she said and rolled her eyes and gave a comic sigh.
> "Oh, you aren't fat," the stylish lady said.
> "Oooooo I am too," Mrs. Turpin said. (193)

As they continue to get acquainted, Ruby and the stylish lady agree that one cannot go far wrong if one has a good disposition and clear skin, two assets guaranteeing one's being liked and respected in the world. One speaks of an inner attitude, the other of an external condition.

Like Hulga, the Ph.D. student with a woman leg in "Good Country People," Ruby's soul has its overt and palpable analogue, less apparent in Claud's bruised leg, but much more pronounced in the carbuncular face of Mary Grace, which is pock-marked and ablaze with pimples that cause Ruby to recoil from her: "Next to her was a fat girl of eighteen or nineteen, scowling into a thick blue book which Mrs. Turpin saw was entitled *Human Development*. . . . The poor girl's face was blue with acne and Mrs. Turpin thought how pitiful it was have a face like that at that age. . . . Mrs. Turpin herself was fat but she had always had good skin, and though she was forty-seven years old, there was not a wrinkle in her face except around her eyes from laughing too much" (194).

In the physiognomy of Mary Grace dwells an image that embodies the fury and limitless energy of Ruby's bigotry, which is aggravated and enflamed further by the various wounded, sick, and low-class figures waiting with her in the doctor's outer office. Most of the characters are there in hopes of being diagnosed and healed. But Ruby's disease cuts deeper, and so her surgery needs to be more profound and radical. She must suffer the body's pain in the form of a violent wounding by Mary Grace's college text rather than by medical care. The book is her prescription, its weighted wound her beginning cure. Through the wound over her eye, her vision alters and her ears are cleared so that they can receive the words uttered by Mary Grace when she physically attacks the large woman.

O'Connor suggests that what makes Ruby Turpin's disease more serious and frightening is that she believes, in a pattern of thought that reminds us of Oedipus Rex, that she is both unpolluted *and* innocent. She will begin to see, however, through the wound, what her diseased vision has kept her from noticing. Her wound will in fact be curative; it will teach her the extent of her illness and her state of dis-ease in the world, and it will open her to another way of seeing the animals on her farm. Her sight will begin to include the numinous through the fertile sow panting softly in the stye.

O'Connor is not squeamish about violence and about her characters being wounded by the world. Her own insight includes, as she tells us, the necessity of violence in certain instances: "I have found that violence is strangely capable of returning my characters to reality and preparing them to accept their moment of grace. Their heads are so hard that almost nothing else will do the work" ("On Her Own Work," 112). But lest she be misunderstood, she adds this caveat: "Violence is never an end in itself. It is the extreme situation that best reveals what we are essentially" (113). Perhaps her observations offer a way of understanding the place of violence in world mythologies; the violent act breaks down conventions and normal patterns; they allow us to see what would otherwise remain hidden, tucked into the recesses of habitual living. Violence, perhaps in "extreme situations," as O'Connor calls it, may be the necessary way for divinity to intrude itself into a life that has hardened in its vision. Violence, as a mythological and archetypal action, has its own necessity that abrupts the sacred fully into a life that has created the world out of its own cloth. Grace itself has a violent side to it; it gains the attention of the recipient like no other presence is capable of achieving.

Put in more psychological language, Ruby is a representation of what Lionel Corbett understands as a mythic theme in the brittleness of the psyche: "the remarkable frequency with which psychosis reveals mythical themes . . . suggests that the disintegration of the self uncovers deeper structural elements which have long been depicted by the objective psyche in mythical forms" (*Religious Function*, 92). Not that Ruby is to be turned into a case study as a psychotic, but rather that the "disintegration" of her neat worldview abruptly allows an uncovering of "deeper structural elements" that open her to divinity on a level that is new and more profound for her.

However, there is already in her vision a symptom of her disease working its way to the surface, for Ruby is preoccupied with obsessively examining people's feet and what kinds of coverings they wear. At every opportunity, she glances down to discern what seems a mystery to her. Looking down on people is her normal attitude toward those she meets, one that finds its literalization in her obsession. I believe it also carries the gesture of humility through which, after looking down on the large sow later, she has a vision revealed to her that is profoundly humbling. But here in the doctor's waiting room, she gazes toward the floor: "Without appearing to, Mrs. Turpin always noticed people's feet" (194), an action that occurs just after the gospel hymn playing on the waiting room radio proclaims: "When I looked up and He looked down," a song the last line of which Ruby finishes in her head: "'And wona these days I know I'll we-eara crown'" ("Revelation," 194). Her hierarchical way of envisioning everyone, with herself at the top, will be shattered when Mary Grace indeed crowns her, with a book.

O'Connor also prepares us for Ruby's final and most important downward gaze into the sow's pen at the end of the story, where she experiences the mystery of the old sow herself pulsing with mystery. Ruby's fascination with feet prepares her for the final vision in the story when she witnesses the movement of souls up Mount Purgatory after death. Her sight at this moment takes in what might be termed an imagination of movement as well as an initiatory vision of eternity. O'Connor's irony surfaces when we learn that Ruby defends her raising hogs against the objections of a "white trash" woman whose lips are stained with snuff. She insists to Ruby that hogs are "Nasty stinking things, a-gruntin and a-rootin all over the place" (198), to which Ruby responds: "Our hogs are not dirty and they don't stink. . . . They're cleaner than some children I've seen. Their feet never touch the ground. We have a pig-parlor—that's where you raise them on concrete" (198). Her hogs mirror her own disposition, one which winces at impurity, pollution, or the messy vernacular quality of animal or human life: "Cleaner by far than that child right there,' she thought.' Poor nasty little thing.' He had not moved except to put the thumb of his dirty hand into his mouth" (198).

Ruby's wish is for the animal world without any of its nasty body residues; her desire contains a large metaphor for her accent toward matter itself. Within her own created hierarchy there exist no odors of mortality, bestiality, or the imperfections of the flesh; her own smooth, wrinkle-free skin is a testament to such an attitude, as Mary Grace's purple, chaotic complexion reveals the underside of the blemish-free attitude that Ruby incarnates. In her control of the farm animals, Ruby successfully denies them their animal life as she denies her own embodied nature of imperfect and easily corrupting flesh. But the incarnation of God in the figure of Christ she appears to have created again in her own image.

Convinced that she believes in and loves Jesus, Ruby engages him in fantasy conversations late at night lying in bed and speaking to the ceiling. She considers the following scenario: "If Jesus had said to her before he made her, 'There's only two places available for you. You can either be a nigger or white-trash,' what would she have said?" (195). After pleading with him to "'make me a nigger then—but that don't mean a trashy one,' he would then have made her a 'neat clean respectable Negro woman, herself but black'" (195). One notices the shift from the vernacular and demeaning word "nigger" to the more respectable "Negro" in Ruby's fantasy. She senses that the only metamorphosis she can believe in is one that duplicates herself in its present disposition. Clean and neat and respectable, in a tidy world like Ivan Ilych's earlier, define the contours of her respectability. It is a moral high ground from which she eagerly gazes down to condemn others who are much more soiled.

Furthermore, Ruby considers herself already redeemed. She also devoutly regards herself as a good, generous person with a kind and friendly disposition who authentically does good works. And though she feels a bit too ample, as when she squeezes herself into one of the chairs in the waiting room, she believes, like Job, that she is blessed beyond the ordinary, with Claud, a respectable, antiseptic pig farm, and unblemished skin. Both she and her pigs are beyond filth and pollution, even beyond corruption, in her eyes. For O'Connor, given this portrait of the woman, Ruby may also be beyond redemption, unless her disposition is violently altered.

She believes as well, in a self-satisfied way, that she has the world and everyone in it in the right order, in a rigid and self-created hierarchy free of contamination. All inhabit the right place that she has designed for them because Ruby has succeeded in her own mind in reinventing the world in her own image, free of contradiction, ambiguity, and confusion.

When the messiness of the world in its ambiguity repudiates her blueprint or her moral grid of how the hierarchy should be, she has an uncanny ability to level out any such mystery: "Sometimes Mrs. Turpin occupied herself at night naming the classes of people. On the bottom of the heap were most colored people, not the kind she would have been if she had been one, but most of them" (195). All is orderly until exceptions to the rule begin to seep into her clean space; then Ruby "would dream they were all crammed in together in a box car, being ridden off to be put in a gas oven"

(196), thus eliminating any surrender to the opaqueness and mystery inherent in the world's body by simply enacting the Nazis' "final solution."

She has the capacity, then, to solve immediately and permanently the world's inherent inferiority and ambiguity by creating it in her own image or by incinerating the disparities. Ruby's solution bespeaks a distancing from the world, like her pigs, which never touch the ground. So long as such distance can be maintained through a seeing that is limited and clouded, Ruby is safe from mystery and from the numinous presence of divine knowing. In such a sterile and bright way of knowing where there are no uncertainties, however, exists the shadow that it casts: "A grotesque revolving shadow passed across the curtain behind her and was thrown palely on the opposite wall. . . . The door opened and a colored boy glided in with a tray from the drug store. . . . He was a tall, very black boy in discolored white pants and a green nylon shirt. He was chewing gum slowly, as if to music" (200). The shadow side of Ruby's thinking, its embodied dark reality, has its analogue in her dream of the Jews being shipped off to be exterminated. The delivery boy's dark racial presence contains another image of what she finds to be distasteful and disagreeable in the world. That he appears first as a grotesque shadow puts him in the company with Mary Grace, indeed all forms of life that Ruby's shadowless mind would like to see eliminated, burned to ashes, and forgotten.

The diseased or wounded people in the waiting room pale, therefore, before the grotesquely deformed disposition of Ruby herself, which embodies an attitude toward matter that is inflated, twisted, bruised, and even pock-marked in its intolerance, while her own flesh denies any world-woundedness or pollution. Claud's ulcerous leg and Mary Grace's ulcerous face together take in the entire body and suggest a vision, through their physical concreteness, into the ulcerous disposition of Ruby herself, blue with acne.

Distortion, or blemish, is indeed a way of seeing; it is already a vision. The bodies of the two characters host outward blemishes of Ruby's interior life, which is itself split, to reveal a wound of which she is unaware. She seems unable to see how her outward disposition and her interior life of racial hatred and ethnic cleansing are separated by a psychic wound, an infliction of prejudice and self-importance. They are the ulcers of pride and social hierarchy as well as moral superiority, revealed through the mysterious metaphor of flesh. It is therefore her ulcer that needs medication; the first step in her diagnosis and treatment will be the shock of recognition inaugurated by Mary Grace, whose anger and outrage from across the room may manifest the interiority of Ruby's judgments of most of the patients in the room and alarms the jovial woman who cannot see *or hear* her own intolerance through the visage of the carbuncular young woman.

She is nonetheless unsettled by Mary Grace's scowls: "All at once the ugly girl turned her lips inside out again. Her eyes were fixed like two drills on Mrs. Turpin. This time there was no mistaking that there was something urgent behind them" (203), a response that confuses Ruby and makes her ability to control the conversation in the room more difficult. She is puzzled as well because just a moment before she expressed her gratitude to Jesus, who had "given her a little of everything" (203). Her feeling of euphoria at her own good fortune she experiences in a very fleshly way: "Whenever she counted her blessings she felt as buoyant as if she weighed one hundred and twenty-five pounds instead of one hundred and eighty" (203).

With her book opened on her lap, gripped "with white fingers" (202), and with a face that looks "as if she would like to hurl them all through the plate glass window" (204), Mary Grace embodies a distorted and grotesque image of the Blessed Virgin in the Annunciation. We are told, for example, that when the archangel Gabriel visited Mary, she was reading silently and alone. Many of the medieval and Renaissance paintings of this popular theme depict her in the act of reading words which she will eventually fulfill when it is revealed to her that she is to become the mother of Jesus. So the angel's greeting, "Ave," is language uttered, while Mary reads the words spoken. What the angel brings to her is the word of God that she will help to incarnate in Christ. She will be the mortal vehicle through which the word of divinity will indeed become flesh. Human development, one might say, will be more fully increased thereby.

O'Connor's use of the book on "human development" is therefore an appropriate pun as it replicates in distorted form the original Annunciation. But in Ruby's case it carries no less weight, for grace comes to her violently, without reservation. Its violent nature bespeaks how deeply set Ruby is in her own prejudices such that it takes a force as acute as Mary Grace's attack to break through its crusted barriers.

This "mimetic distortion," so to speak, of the original Annunciation, an "ave" of grace through a violation of the ordinary, assigns Mary Grace the role of the angel announcing a sudden change in destiny to the woman who has just called up Jesus' name in her gratitude. The Virgin Mary and Ruby differ, of course, in the wounds they are visited by the grace of God because Mary, in her humility and openness to God's word, is very receptive in her disposition to receive Gabriel's announcement. Ruby is not. She therefore requires a force powerful enough to override her deeply seated negation of the world. O'Connor suggests that a distorted and grotesque vision of ordinary life split from one's idea of perfection and superior status within it requires an equally valid distorted or excessive response by divinity. Such an initiatory response of violence carries within it a corrective—even an antibody—to change the flow of one's life. It maneuvers her toward redemption through a vision of salvation in which the grotesque, the lame, and the marginal members of society lead the procession.

Mary Grace is no less effective, for in her violent wounding of Ruby after hurling the book at her followed by her flying across the room to attack her physically, she announces in clear but whispered speech, "'Go back to hell where you came from, you old wart hog'" (207). Her annunciation shifts forever the destiny of a woman who believes she has "a little of everything" and who readily swoons in a public display to illustrate her ecstatic gratitude to Christ: "'Thank you, Jesus, for making everything the way it is! It could have been different. . . . Oh thank you, Jesus, Jesus, thank you'! she cried aloud" (206) to her sentimental and very domesticated image of Jesus, a figure she has fashioned into a safe, even innocuous presence as safe and clean as the hogs on the farm.

Ruby, however, has forgotten something about animals in Christ's coming. Implicit here is the connection between Christ's birth in a stable, surrounded by animals, and the way through the sow on her farm to a vision of earthly life and eternity. In both Christ's beginnings and in the destiny of Ruby, toward which she begins to travel, humility is the virtue that pervades both. But first Ruby needs to see the path she is to take with a clarity of vision unknown to her before her attack. The timing, then, is impeccable, for it is just at this instant that the book rifles across the room to strike her above the left eye and alter her vision instantly and dramatically: "All at once her vision narrowed and she saw everything as if it were happening in a small room far away, or as if she were looking at it through the wrong end of a telescope. . . . and Mrs. Turpin's vision suddenly reversed itself and she saw everything large instead of small" (206). It is as if the lens of her moral vision seeks its own proper way of seeing, so it adjusts itself radically in both directions. It also illustrates the fundamental assertion that salvation begins and develops through incarnation. The lens by which she sees is jarred and begins to distort the appearance of things as it recovers from a sacred slam to the head. And perhaps what is needed to be revealed to us is present always, but to see it authentically, our focal plane needs adjustment in order to bring it into our nucleus of sight.

Ruby is struck by Mary Grace's book at the height of her own hubris, which expresses, in other words, what William Lynch has labeled the "univocal imagination, one which has no respect for reality; [s]he is either contemptuous of it, or destroys it, or distorts it or flattens it—or [s]he refuses to take up responsibility in the face of it. . . . The univocal [person] is not free. [S]He is rigid, unbending, fixed" (*Christ and Apollo,* 118). Breaking through this fixity is a moment of grace for Ruby that announces itself in violence. Coming through the angry young woman is the invisible hand and voice of divinity that shatters her totalitarian hold on the world. It is a

heady if not godlike habit of being that can easily foster what James Hillman has called the great scourge of modernity—"literalism" (*Revisioning
Psychology*, 149). Literalism is a form of moral tyranny that contributes to
Ruby's holocaust imagination, one that finds solutions in the incineration of
mystery. The world in all of its particulars has no voice, no equivocity.
Mary Grace's attack places Ruby in touch with the earth, forcing her to experience the powerful sway of gravity so that her large body and inflated
sense of her own place in the world finds the ground of being. Her distant
vision collapses under the weight of gravity; the appearance of things is no
longer fixed; instead, it dissolves into wavering shapes and sizes.

A transformed vision has its genesis, therefore, in and through the
body; she is hit above the left eye, precisely where Ruby lacks physical vision, the outward correlative of knowledge and insight. Her fixed focus
contains no visionary knowledge. Ruby has no awareness that her thought
uttered to herself before Mary Grace's charge, that "you had to *have* certain
things before you could *know* certain things" (199), is directly self-indict-
ing. Because her vision is so distorted, she is most in need of a medication
prescribed by the nature of her disease. She, like Oedipus, carries forward
an archetypal action of a cure that discovers on what appears to be a legit-
imate road to healing that it is in truth the disease. Massimilla and Bud
Harris have written that "Where we are wounded and where we have stumbled is where we will find the psychological gold that holds the key to our
new development and renewal" (*Like Gold through Fire*, 94). This insight
Ruby embodies when she and Claud return to their pig farm with Mary
Grace's words echoing deeply in her. It is the words she utters to Ruby, not
the book hitting her, which is the deeper wound.

THE CORPSE AS A WAY OF SEEING

The power and the deadly seriousness of Ruby Turpin's imagination might
be described as one having the power and ability to transform the world
into a corpse (Romanyshyn, *Technology as Symptom and Dream*, 215),
into lifeless matter, so powerful is her idea of the world's true hierarchy,
without the paradox of the Beatitudes. The disease of her own denial of the
world's body reveals itself analogically in her turning things into corpses,
into things that are denied their history and therefore incapable of a destiny.
Given the image of the holocaust in the train taking souls to the gas ovens,
Ruby's imagination is particularly pernicious in its impulse to murder life
itself.

Perhaps her gaze or vision of the world is more like that of a spectator,
one who is able to see the world without being intimately connected to it, a
vision distant and detached, one which then allows the world to be re-

formed into one's own making. The body in a real sense is abandoned, divorced from any lived sensate experience. Such a disposition forsakes the world's matter by removing it from a lived context, much as Ruby's imagination divorces things and people from their vernacular dwelling.[3]

Emerging in such a world is a perspective which, in focusing on the body itself as a spectacle for observation, *isolates* the body from its living context or situation and *fragments* the body which it sees. Romanyshyn underscores this assertion when he observes that the world formatted by distant vision has no history, and therefore no real life and can therefore be fragmented and dissected without a full sense of its humanness (*Technology*, 127). Ruby's disposition toward the world transforms it into an idea to be changed and then facilely manipulated at will. Until Mary Grace's attack, what seems missing in Ruby's attitude of seeing is any quality of intimacy and human contact, a condition Mary Grace remedies in her hands-on assault which leaves its markings on the surface of Ruby's skin as well as deep in her psyche.

Ruby's greatest insult, and perhaps her deepest fear, is to be marked and wounded, bruised in fact by something she finds repugnant and blemished in the world; only by being marked, stained, polluted, and knocked to the ground, however, can she be brought into the world of imperfection and then open to the ground of mystery, which she experiences most deeply through the animals on her farm. Her linear vision of the world must be attended to so that she can see that the messiness of the world matters. Its matter too is sacred and not to be spurned, denied, or incinerated. Within all matter, the story's poetic logic suggests, are the shadowy realities that point to and include mystery, the transcendent, the soiled and stained, and the ineffable origin of the world.

The second half of the story takes place on the farm when Ruby and Claud return after the doctor has treated Ruby's wound. They are once again surrounded by animals: the pigs, cows, Ruby's new self-image of a wart hog leveled at her by Mary Grace, the snake that takes the form of the streaming hose Ruby uses to clean off the pigs (215) as she challenges God's design for the world that is inferior to her own, and even the lowly chirping crickets in chorus after her final vision. After creating the world so cleanly in her own mind, she wonders now how God could disagree by mixing up realities that she had firmly installed into a logical hierarchy of her own making. "'Why me?' she rumbled. 'Its no trash around here, black or white, that I haven't given to. . . . And do for the church. . . . If you like trash better, go get yourself some trash then,' she railed'" (215–16). And out of her words and her action emerges the following startling image: "She shook her fist with the hose in it and a watery snake appeared momentarily in the air" followed by her roaring challenge to God: "'Who do you think you are?'" (216).

She is greeted only by the echo of silence that follows her dispute. Ruby sees then the marvelously mysterious movings of the sun's colorations as it descends into dusk. She stands there in dumb muteness, her body altered by the intimate violence of Mary Grace, a kind of initiation into mystery when she grabbed and squeezed her neck: Ruby now wears "two little moon-shaped lines like pink fish bones . . . indented over her windpipe" (208), she has been called a wart hog from hell (207) and "the dark protuberance over her eye looked like a miniature tornado cloud which might any moment sweep across the horizon of her brow" (213–14). Her transformation makes pale by comparison the "purple swelling on a plump marble-white calf" (192) of Claud's injury. Her body as well as her attitude has been violently removed from a condition of unblemished purity that typified her angle of vision earlier, with a body that was flawless. Now it is bruised, wounded, and marked by images of the natural order: moon and tornado.[4] And in her hand she holds the lowliest of God's creatures, the snake.

Is this a body being drawn toward the earth, the sea, with the fish image, and the heavens at one and the same time? And are the moon, with its reflected quiet light, and the tornado, with its chaotic dismantling of order, images of her transition? Her body is now clearly earthbound; she continues her journey toward incarnation through a more sacred image of the world, free of the veil of shadows, but only after passing through a kind of satanic pride of creating the world in her own image.

Crucial to Ruby's beginning transformation after being wounded is that she comes to this movement through her animals, especially through the "old sow a few weeks off from farrowing. She was lying on her side grunting" (214). Close to her animals, she challenges divinity with the hose she uses to scoot down the pigs and at the same time tries to penetrate into the mystery of God's design: "'what do you send me a message like that for? . . . How am I a hog and me both? How am I saved and from hell too?'" (215). In her questioning "she gripped the hose blindly, pointing the stream of water in and out of the eye of the old sow whose outraged squeal she did not hear" (215) because her own squealing drowns it out.

At the same time, her stream of words and accusations leveled at God reveals the full gush of all her prejudices, stereotypes, and bigoted assumptions. It is a torrent of words and water mixing, jumbling, moiling, and roiling together as the world's ambiguous body comes bearing down on her. Her last and final attempt to stave off mystery bursts forth in the challenging question mentioned above, followed quickly by another kind of holocaust image. Claud's truck suddenly appears on the highway looking "like a child's toy. At any moment a bigger truck might smash into it and scatter Claud's and the niggers' brains all over the road" (217). Such a violent image shatters her vision of having the best the world offers, for in spite of their well-groomed farm and neat possessions, their value is diminished in this image, which promises to scatter into dust what she holds most valuable. Before the sacred mystery can be grasped, all that she has held as most valuable to her life must first fall away from sight. Now her own possessions must be incinerated.

As her vision clears, she looks down at the hogs, as she has looked down at people's feet "and gazed, as if through the very heart of mystery, down into the pig parlor" (217). A glow suffuses the grunting old sow, who with the others "appeared to pant with a secret life" (217). This moment of epiphany allows Ruby to see through the world in its animal nature to some invisible but palpable presence. In one way she becomes the sow to see how the sow sees, to be present to mystery as a natural part of the world's design. She has in an important way moved to the ground of mystery itself through the softly panting life of the sow.

These stationary animals prepare Ruby's vision to accept the dancing, clapping, shouting, rejoicing sounds of the souls saved; she senses, in a fully sacred and abundant image, an understanding that all are to be included in salvation, and that, true to the paradoxical poetry of the Beatitudes, the last indeed shall be first. Ruby's gaze now matters for she has been initiated back into the world of matter behind which pants the magnificent mystery in things. Her literal mind now dissolves in the face of an anagogical vision. She sees behind the veil; what is revealed to her is that the inscrutable silence and dominant justice of God's grace gives priority to "the battalions of freaks and lunatics, shouting and clapping and leaping like frogs" (217) that populate her epiphany. The crickets join in the hierophany at the end as Ruby treads "the darkening path" back to the house; it is not the crickets she hears in their literal chirping; they have been transformed into "the chorus of souls climbing upward into the starry field and shouting hallelujah" (217). Once again, the mystery of divine presence comes through the small, finite particularity of the world's things, even as seemingly insignificant as a cricket's chirp.

Ruby now senses that the world matters, even in its seemingly lowliest life forms; the presence of grace suffuses all that exists both in this life and in the one thinly veiled behind it. In the divine scheme, more generous and tolerant than her own, there is room for all rungs of life on the railing. We are reminded dramatically of the last words of the Book of Revelation when Christ makes clear: "See, I am coming soon; my reward is with me, to repay according to everyone's work. I am the Alpha and the Omega, the first and the last, the beginning and the end" (22:12).

Her bruised and wounded body has been baptized into the world and marked by grace. She now carries, as images of initiation, parts of the natural order on her throat, origin of speech, and her forehead, origin of thought. Both thought and word have been initiated into a sacred mystery through the violent intrusion of grace. Grace has the capacity to be violent and polluting; but in the process this gift from God prepares one for the final cleansing, one which includes pollution and the messiness of the world to underscore its transcendent mystery. The focal plane shifts to accommodate the images of Purgatory, not Paradise, as our true earthly condition.

In "Parker's Back," another image, gained once again through a violent experience, initiates the tattooed husband as he seeks an image to override his prickly wife's refrain that all the world is nothing more than vanity, and that the images tattooed on her husband's body reflect the mind of a fool.

EVIL AND THE SUFFERING TATTOO ON "PARKER'S BACK"

O'Connor's story takes up the place of human embodiment in the individual's pilgrimage toward salvation. "Parker's Back" is a colorful meditation on being incarnated and marking the flesh with a series of disjointed, tattooed images. The central conflict is one that pits a rigid set of Old Testament pieties against the New Testament image of incarnation. In the process, "Parker's Back" reveals powerfully and comically the profile of a deformed soul coming to know itself through an image it is called to have inked onto its back. It is also a story about heresy and prophecy, about ideas divorced from image, and about faith rooted in abstract ideas against a belief grounded in sacred images.

The controlling figure that unifies the entire narrative, and is in some ways its protagonist, is a Byzantine icon of Christ the Pantocrator tattooed, part by part, on O. E. Parker's back. O'Connor's story assembles a modern understanding of evil against a tradition of faith rooted in the flesh of the world. Written at the end of her life, the story embodies one of the boldest examples of her own aesthetic sense that when fiction is made according to its nature, it should reinforce our sense of the supernatural by grounding it in concrete, observable reality. That the image of Christ is tattooed, like a magnificently colored wound, onto the back of Parker attests to the concrete and incarnational reality of Christ's presence in the world. In effect, Parker suffers Christ into the world through the painful plotting of His image on his own body. The desire, even obsession, for such an image, grows directly from a moment of violent revelation in which he is called.

In fact, not unlike the dilemma raised in "Revelation," this story reveals that the issue of evil may swirl around the issue of the flesh's denial itself. By this statement I mean that the kind of religious enthusiasm that we witness in both Dostoevsky and O'Connor leads us to suspect that literalism, which might best be understood as abstractionism stood on its empty head and hard heart, is at the core of demonism in the postmodern imagination. Such a suggestion is implicit in Margaret Whitt's observation when she addresses O'Connor's vision of life: "Religious enthusiasm is part of the South's grotesque profile" (Religion").

Like so many of O'Connor's stories, "Parker's Back" also explores how, by means of grace, an individual learns to focus his or her moral vision on the visible creation in order to apprehend, if even for an instant, the invisible presence of the Creator. But on a grander, though no less theological level, it also depicts the narcissism of evil, which will not surrender self-will to the things of creation. The most compelling and grotesque seduction of all may be the individual's own reflection, which magnifies the will beyond its boundaries. Here resides the condition of Sarah Ruth Cates' soul.

On the literal level, O'Connor's story concerns a man, O. E. Parker, and his wife, Sarah Ruth, whom he marries seemingly against his will after courting her and her family with food. He does so in the face of her disapproving attitude toward his colorful body. After they have married, he takes on as his mission in life to find an image of God that will persuade her to believe in God incarnate, in the image of the Redeemer. He is impatient with her denial of the panoply of images inscribed on his skin. Her self-will and hard heart protect her, however, from softening and accepting an image of salvation. In this spiritual agon between them exists a curious confrontation between God and Satan, between concrete images of creation and abstract ideas about the world's vanity. In this battle, God remains for Sarah Ruth a concept safely distanced from any enfleshed authenticity. Put another way, for Sarah Ruth, as for any literalist, accepting the *fact* of God's existence does not in any way mean that one surrenders to the *flesh* of His being in Christ. Evil in this story involves, consequently, a denial of the world's body, the willingness that keeps one from submitting to a higher authority by castigating all images as vain. In her beliefs, therefore, Sarah Ruth is a self-centered stepsister to Ruby Turpin.

Within the contours of this story, we cannot speak about evil in the world without at the same time acknowledging the presence of grace. My question then, is: In what way does the tattoo of Christ serve as an embodied image of Parker's experience of grace when he is thrown from a tractor while cultivating the earth and then later receives the image on his back from a tattooist in town? To answer this question is to make sense of the relationship between the New Testament *image* of Christ and the Old Testament *names* of this less than compatible couple. There exists in this transformation of Christ's image from a book, in the tattooist's office, to a man's back, that assigns the body as a book on which the divine may inscribe and thus incarnate its images and its story. The body has, then, a mimetic quality in its being. As Cain's body is marked by God as a protection as he journeys to a new land, the tattoo artist is an instrument of God's design, who then marks the body of Parker, as Mary Grace's violent attack marked the body of Ruby Turpin in "Revelation." The body becomes "a template," writes George Elder, "in which we may perceive larger meanings" (*Body,* viii). Living in this action is a deep mythical element in the body marked, identified, and pained by the presence of the sacred quality of being. Parker's name is therefore as important and as initiatory as the image he is prepared, as one chosen, to receive—however reluctantly. Which of us, the implicit question asks, willingly seeks the wound that may prepare us for receiving grace? The icon of Christ is Parker's own initiation into the sacred on a level which penetrates more than simply skin deep. The tattoo as an image from the New Testament completes and fulfills the ancestors of his names originating in the Old Testament. Parker is then a complete Biblical study.

O. E. Parker has the first name of Obadiah, which means "servant of the Lord." Obadiah is the protector of God's prophets (1 Kings 18:3–18); Elihue, whose name Parker also carries, is an ancestor to Elkanah, father of Samuel. Both Obadiah and Elihue share one quality—their very commonness. These names appear frequently throughout the Old Testament, and we know that O. E. Parker was "as ordinary as a loaf of bread" (509). Sarah Ruth, by contrast, is a woman distrustful of the world's matter. She carries the name of the wife of Abraham and mother of Isaac. Known for her beauty (Gen. 20–21), the Biblical Sarah is hardly reflected in Parker's wife, a fleshless woman, whose facial skin "was thin and drawn as tight as the skin on an onion, and [whose] eyes were gray and sharp like the points of two icepicks." In other words, "she was plain, plain" (510). She also has the name of Ruth; however, the Biblical Ruth, described by one source as "a model of family loyalty and trust in God, and of the fidelity of God who reveals himself as the protector of the defenseless to those who place their hopes in him" (*Concordance,* 584), is hardly an accurate prototype of the Ruth in this story. The modern Ruth of O'Connor's imagination inhales the odor of sin everywhere and exhales the dirge of Ecclesiastes, "Vanity of vanities," with her icepick eyes rooted scornfully on her husband's generously tattooed body. The action is therefore as much about identity, about the history of these figures from the Old Testament as it is about the transforming quality of the New Testament, which offers a more incarnated logos of divinity.

The essential contrast is therefore between Parker, whose body is resplendent with images, though admittedly without form or anything approaching a controlling theme, and Sarah Ruth, who is a woman not only without images, but who outwardly scorns them. She is also a woman without imagination. The loss of the imagination may be at the heart of the demonic impulse in our postmodern world; for if the demons can no longer be imagined, they may then exist only under the clinical rubric of psychological symptoms, or worse, social problems, which in their empty language, distances them still further from our experience.

But the intrigue goes even deeper than simply Sarah Ruth's aversion to images. For in her denial she negates the fleshly order of the world's body itself. In her confusion of images in the form of the tattoos that abundantly cover Parker, she mistakes one animal for another. Her powers of discerning the things of the world are poor, but that does not prevent her from quickly condemning these things as foolishness, whatever they are trying to represent:

> "All that here," the woman said, pointing to his arm, "is no better than what a fool Indian would do. It's a heap of vanity." She seemed to have found the word she wanted. "Vanity of vanities," she said.
>
> "Well, what the hell do I care what she thinks of it?" Parker asked himself, but he was plainly bewildered. "I reckon you like one of these better than another anyway," he said, dallying until he thought of something that would impress her.
>
> He thrust the arm back at her. "Which do you like best?"
>
> "None of them," she said, "but the chicken is not as bad as the rest."
>
> "What chicken?" Parker almost yelled.
>
> She pointed to the eagle.
>
> "That's an eagle," Parker said. "What fool would waste their time having a chicken put on themselves?"
>
> "What fool would have any of it," the girl said and turned away. She went slowly back to the house and left him there to get going. (515)

The larger concern of the story begins with this exchange, for it focuses on the imagination itself, what I would call the theological imagination,[5] which begins with the things of the world but sees through them in faith to the reality of the incarnation of God that rests through and behind them. For Parker, the image of his own faith will be revealed to him in the form of the tattoo of Christ that mysteriously calls to him from an assortment of tattoos in a book. So the friction between them is set. Sarah Ruth has found the right word to describe him and his tattoos—"vanity"—so that he must now find the right image to counter her judgmental vision.

Of course, as his body bears his history, even before he is led to the icon, Parker has lived his life smothered in images; each has marked the crucial moments in his life. He wears his autobiography just under his shirtsleeves. For example, his body is steeped in eagles, cannons, serpents, tigers, panthers, hawks, "even portraits of Elizabeth II and Philip over where his stomach and liver were respectively" (514). But taken together, all of his images show no order or overall design. Rather, the effect is, as the narrator affirms, "botched." Taken as they are, his embodied images have no form, no coherence, and no overall meaning. Left to themselves in their current placement, they are meaningless. Nonetheless, he is a man who believes in the power of the concrete, in the images of the world that embody the invisible presence of the numinous. And while Parker professes no faith—"hasn't got religion"—the story suggests that he is *susceptible* to redemption because he does not divorce spirit from flesh, and indeed searches religiously for the right image to unite them in his own mind. In fact, as he experiences the image of God, there descends on him the tincture of a mystic, a visionary, a holy man on a pilgrimage to the truth of divinity's presence. As such, he takes on qualities that Victor Turner suggests traditionally have been found in leaders of "historical religions" in which "founders, prophets, saints and notable teachers of the faith are sometimes associated with supernaturally generated bodily characteristics" ("Bodily Marks," 274), including tattooed markings.

Moreover, he is not without a strain of generosity. When courting Sarah Ruth earlier, for example, he brought baskets of apples and peaches to the hungry Cates family and fed all of them. His abundant largesse is imaged already on his tattooed body, which tries to include as many illustrations of the world both natural and historical as is possible. He is the image of generosity toward others. We recall the Book of Ruth, which begins in famine and moves through to harvest. Parker's harvest with Sarah Ruth, however, is destined to bear little savory fruit.

By contrast, she is the modern voice of Ecclesiastes, which laments that all of the world and man's action is vanity.[6] She does not like automobiles (510), believes churches are idolatrous (518), and finds the tattoos on her husband's body repulsive. Further, she allows him to be naked only in the dark; in fact, she prefers him "dressed with his sleeves rolled down" (519). She likes him best, therefore, when his body, along with his images, is obstructed from view so that he is reduced to little more than a concept with a voice. She prefers the shadow of Parker over his enfleshed and highly imagistic reality. It is also her vision of how she prefers the world as well. The analogy at work is that only in this manner can she accept her God; that is, when He is without an image, without flesh, without incarnation, when He lurks in the shadow as a being without concreteness. She will accept His word but not His embodiment. Therefore, Sarah Ruth regularly gives Parker premonitory warnings, such as, "'At the judgment seat of God, Jesus is going to say to you, 'What you been doing all your life besides have pictures drawn all over you?'" (519). She denies images and with them the very nature of the concrete, temporal world as God's creation. To deny the images on her husband is to deny a larger order that his own body represents.

In a letter O'Connor refers to this denial as a heresy, especially in one who professes belief in God: "Sarah Ruth was the heretic," O'Connor writes, because of her "notion that you can worship in pure spirit" (*Habit of Being*, 594). I want to go a step further than O'Connor and say that Sarah Ruth's denial of the body, of the incarnate dimension of humanity, is part of evil's expression which may be both heretical and diabolical. Here she is in sharp contrast to her husband, whose colorful presence is referred to by his employer on a neighboring farm as "a walking panner-rammer" (519). The central concerns of the story—embodiment versus spirit, grace versus evil, as well as the power of image—appear to find a reconciliation in the image of the icon, the image of Christ, which is, in effect, a representation of two forms of embodiment. The icon depicts the intrusion into time and space the sacred image of divinity and suggests at the same time a body (Parker's) already transformed.[7]

As the story develops, Sarah Ruth accelerates her search for sin; at the same time, Parker doubles his resolve to find a holy emblem, a tattoo that she "would not be able to resist—a religious subject" (519). It is at this juncture—when Parker's obsessive search for a compelling image prepares him for an experience of grace that allows him to see more—that I wish to illustrate the icon's importance. But we should not miss the irony in Parker's heroic quest, for the image he seeks is not for his wife but one that *he needs* in order to give harmonious form to his varied body images, the external emblems of his own spirit. Victor Turner reminds us that "the etymological link between *cosmos* and *cosmetics* . . . both derive from the Greek term meaning 'order, ornament, universe'" ("Bodily Marks," 274). Finding an order through a cosmetic design, here a tattoo, is the unseen and unexpressed mission that Parker engages in his quest.

As a plan for countering Sarah Ruth's litany of rebukes directed at his "idolatrous" concern for tattoos, Parker first visualizes, as the subject of his tattoo, a replica of the Bible opened to a particular verse. Here he chooses *the word* of God but can already hear his wife's rejoinder that, since she has a Bible, why would she want to read the same verse over again? For her, words are empty; they do not incite images, only vanity. For Parker, on the other hand, all experiences are imagined. He has what might be called an archetypal imagination; his world, his way of seeing as well as the content of his seeing, is through and by means of images.[8] Further, he possesses what William Lynch has called an ontological way of seeing because his experiences are rooted in the world, not only in concepts or ideas, as are hers. The ontological imagination allows images to develop, to shift, to deepen and change with the alterations of lived experience (*Christ and Apollo*, 48). Quite literally, his images are deeply embodied, going below the surface of the flesh.

Equipped with such an imagination, both archetypal and ontological, Parker seeks the image he believes will change the heart of his wife and ground her in the sensate world; in his obsessive concern he begins to lose both sleep and flesh. His transformation has its genesis deeply in the body. His eyes even assume the shape of those he will have revealed to him; they take on an iconic form: "As he continued to worry over it, his eyes took on a hollow, preoccupied expression" (520). Before he has settled on the icon or even thought of it, Parker assumes the image of mystic, and his eyes hollow out to express an iconic gaze. He develops both an ascetic posture as well as a mystical reverence for the world. He is being prepared, unbeknownst to himself, for a moment of violent grace to enter his life that will permanently mark him. And it will arrive, in the same way everything important in Parker's life makes its appearance, through an inky image.

But we have not understood completely Sarah Ruth's denial of Parker and his tattooed images. It is one thing to say she has lost the ability to imagine the world, to see in the images the face of the world; it is quite another to say she is evil. But may she not be living out a demonic denial of the world in its substantial nature? And is there not a connection between narcissism and evil that is expressed in her attitude toward Parker's images and in her attitude toward the image of the Byzantine icon on his body, the image that will be part of his own flesh and will bear a bloody and beaten witness to his faith at the story's end? What I am calling evil here is the propensity or impulse to separate body from spirit, a modern malady that promotes abstractionism and absolutism and that often assumes the guise of liberalism (to add one more "ism").

In his study of narcissism, Alexander Lowen illustrates that the self is possible through a sensed presence of one's own embodiment. Insanity, he goes on to argue, may be the consequence of that split between the image one has of oneself and the actual body one is (*Narcissism,* 56). Ernest Becker, in his perceptive study, *Escape from Evil,* also draws several compelling connections between evil and the body. His claim is that the devil has historically been represented by the body, by body-boundedness. To be part of the demonic is to realize the "absolute determinism of man's earthly condition. . . . He reveals the reality of our situation, the fact that we can't really escape our earthly destiny" (123). Therefore, to rid ourselves of the devil is, at the same time, to rid ourselves of our bodies, of the sensed presence of our own finiteness and mortality. Given such insights, we might then ask: Has evil done a somersault from the traditional view to the modern one? Or are we in fact viewing what Becker refers to as the driving force behind evil inhuman affairs: the paradox that man is in the flesh and doomed with it, yet is simultaneously out of the flesh in a world of symbols, trying to continue on a heavenly flight? To lose the image is to deny the body, while to lose the symbol is to be caught in the flesh with few if any options.

Sarah Ruth Cates, then, represents a modern, rural deconstructionist, one who desubstantiates the world of flesh. May evil today be taking the form of decomposing the self, as William Barrett speaks of deconstruction in *The Death of the Soul*, of "desubstantializing our thinking" (128) into the energy of a sound byte or a computer blip? Is this a movement to abandon the notion of substance altogether? I am not saying that deconstruction as a philosophy is evil; but the impulse to disintegrate the world's body is.

I want also to mention another writer whose work has proven helpful in understanding Sarah Ruth more fully. M. Scott Peck's *People of the Lie: The Hope for Healing Human Evil*, offers a suggestive angle on respectability, fastidious decorum, and narcissism as tenets of evil. His claims touch on those of both Becker and Lowen. Particularly, Peck connects evil to narcissism: "we see then, that their narcissism makes the evil dangerous not only because it motivates them to scapegoat others, but also because it deprives them of the restraint that results from empathy and respect for others. . . . [The evil needs] victims to sacrifice to their narcissism; their narcissism permits them to ignore the humanity of their victims as well" (137). Wounding her own husband by denouncing his images is, however, one of the ironic mysteries of faith that puts Parker on his own quest for a cosmic image of wholeness.

Tied closely to evil and narcissism is the issue of power, which may be used to destroy the spiritual growth of others in order to defend and preserve the integrity of the sick selves of the evil (Baker-Miller, 67). Through the language of sickness, I wish to focus on Sarah Ruth's denial of the world's flesh, even if it is offered to her through the images on the body of her husband, images that represent several worlds[9] but are not finally harmonized until they gather around the image of the icon. But first he must be called to its place.

While plowing the earth in the tractor furnished him by his neighbor employer, Parker loses sight of a large tree in the middle of the field when he becomes distracted watching the sun shift from his front to his back as he turns the tractor in a spiral: "he appeared to see it both places as if he had eyes in the back of his head. All at once he saw the tree reaching out to grasp him" (520). Suddenly he is hit and thrown off the machine "and he heard himself yelling in an unbelievably loud voice, 'GOD ABOVE!'" (520). Both he and the tractor land on their backs and flames quickly engulf the machine; he feels from the shock of the accident a change come over him, one that propels him immediately to the town's tattoo parlor, where he has had other images embossed on his body. Parker then feels compelled to page through a book of tattoos of God, starting from the back and coming forward, until he heard a voice from one: "it said as plainly as if silence were a language itself, GO BACK" (522). He orders the tattooist to put that precise image on his back, a process that, because of the image's ornate design, will have to be done in two stages: first, the tattooist gives it its full shape to include everything but the face: "the eyes had not yet been put in" (523).

The next day, after spending the night on a cot "at the Haven of Light Christian Mission" (524), Parker returns to have the face completed. He adamantly refuses the tattooist's pleas to look at the completed image and turns away from the face on his back that "continued to look at him—still, straight, all-demanding, enclosed in silence" (526). After a skirmish in town, he heads toward his home, but the image has taken him out of himself: "His head was almost clear of liquor and he observed that his dissatisfaction was gone, but he felt not quite like himself. It was as if he were himself but a stranger to himself, driving into a new country" (527).

This new image on the raw, sore skin of Parker's back unites body and spirit, inseparable and consubstantial. In it is contained a faith that weds the world to the spirit in sacrifice and selfless love and insists on a transformation of consciousness that is now deep in the flesh. Parker's early tattoos have been insignia of more secular changes in his life; they have paved the way, so to speak, for this grand and harmonizing figure. The pain of these tattoo applications implicates a death of Parker and the birth of a different being as he is initiated deeper into the mystery of incarnation.

George Elder traces the pain incurred in receiving a tattoo: "it is symbolic of the 'death' of an old status making way for the 'new being.' . . . And that new status is as indelible as the tattoos themselves" (*Body,* 60–61). The deep transformation of spirit and the tattoo share the legacy of permanence for the individual. A rich analogy takes shape wherein the inside of Parker finds its aesthetic correlative on the inky surface of his skin. His appearance modifies as he prepares for the new image that he will carry, like a heavy but harmonious burden, into the world. This image, ironically, is one which Parker does not have access to unless he holds up mirrors that reflect it. It is an image that demands reflection to be envisioned. If it is true, as Michel Thevoz asserts, that "man's first adornment was in fact body painting" (12), a process that developed the body to a symbolic level of being, than Parker's preparation to receive the image is a primordial and mythic ritual whose archetypal roots extend back and down to the origins of the species. In addition, Parker is also prepared to be wounded deep within him by the image, a symbolic form of wounding by the tattooist's needles.

Sarah Ruth, however, cannot accept this image of faith and will violently reject it because it suggests that God has a face and a form in the figure of Christ and that this image in action is incarnational of authentic love.

Nor does she even hint at any empathy for either Christ or his carrier; rather, she is content to repeat the refrain that "all is vanity" in order to secure her defenses from the assault of her husband's sacred, scarred flesh. Her empty words protect her from the sacred mystery of divinity's embodiment. She is extremely willful and determined to have her own way, although Parker himself is not without his own heated, persuasive flourishes.

The difference between them is that as the story progresses, he is transformed by the icon; he suffers its burden upon his flesh. Its multicolored, inky presence seeps below the surface of the skin to mark his soul as well. He is now marked by Christ, as the word *tattoo*, from the Tahitian word *tattau*, means "to mark," according to Victor Turner ("Bodily Marks," 270). His flesh and the flesh of Christ mark one another; they exist connaturally in the miracle of one flesh. The back of Parker carries the front of Christ's. Through the addition of Christ's image on his body, Parker discovers and feels an instant harmony between all of the other images that have previously existed wildly, without connection, conjunction, or unity. It is as if the cacophony of the animals and people had no aesthetic form until the icon's completed image appeared to create a unified effect from the previously "botched" panoply. Harmony exists only through the icon, which literally transforms Parker's body, marking him in an aesthetic unity. How radical is the contrast between Sarah Ruth's and Parker's dispositions is apparent only when the husband returns home, having finished the tattooing and having gotten into a barroom fight with a group of men intent on seeing his new creation.[10]

Angered by Parker's sinful behavior, Sarah Ruth locks the door so that when he returns from town early in the morning he will be forced to plead with her to let him in. In her impatience, even meanness toward him, she tells her husband when he knocks that she knows no one by the name of O. E. Parker, to which he pleads:

"O. E. Parker. You know me."

There was silence. Then the voice said slowly, "I don't know no O. E."

"Quit fooling," Parker pleaded. "You ain't got any business doing me this way. It's me, old O. E. You ain't afraid of me."

"Who's there?" the same unfeeling voice said.

Parker turned his head as if he expected someone behind him to give him the answer. . . . Then as he stood there, a tree of light burst over the skyline. (539)

And then she forces him to utter the ineffable: his full name, which he has told her he has said aloud only twice in his life: "Parker bent down and put his mouth near the stuffed keyhole. 'Obadiah,' he whispered, and all at once he felt the light pouring through him, turning his spider web soul into a perfect arabesque of colors, a garden of geese and birds and beasts. 'Obadiah Elihue!' he whispered" (539).

Several important events take place simultaneously on either side of the door separating them. First, we notice how disembodied Sarah Ruth has become. She is only a voice, like the voice of Echo to Narcissus in the myth. She has become in this meeting with her husband a wife with a voice but no flesh. We also see how the body and soul are one in Parker's life, for the arabesque-colored body is also the soul with its perfect harmony of natural objects. His name surges deep into his being and finds there a spiritual harmony that is a metaphor for the harmonious body, one that has found its controlling image in the face of Christ. The images of the body give us the body imagined in images. These images are not idols but rather presences of the world in their most colorful arabesque forms. We recall Queequeg's hieroglyphic body with the signs of the zodiac on it, a constellation of creation and cosmic presences that gives his being a solid and mellifluous magnificence.

Even if we agree with William Thompson, that evil is in the nature of things (*Evil and World Order,* 59) and that the closest evil thing to the comic hero is his own impotent and limited body, we may still choose to celebrate the imagination, and through it, human freedom. It is this attempt to exercise his freedom that brings Parker to reveal the new image on his flesh. However, as his body is not complete and united through this last image, in like manner he initially elects to speak just the initials of his full name. Only after does he dare utter the full force of the names borne by those historical figures. He achieves his fullest identity at this moment when the image on his back is consubstantial with the words of his identity. His history meets his teleology in the body.

In such a complete state of harmony, Parker is quick to forge this difficult entry into the house because he wants to reveal to Sarah Ruth his image. When he begins to remove his shirt, she knows immediately that he has colored his body again:

> "Another picture," Sarah Ruth growled. "I might have known you was off after putting some more trash on yourself."
>
> Parker's knees went hollow under him. He wheeled around and cried, "Look at it! Don't just say that! *Look* at it!"
>
> "I done looked," she said.
>
> "Don't you know who it is?" he cried in anguish.
>
> "No, who is it?" Sarah Ruth said. "It ain't anybody I know."
>
> "It's him," Parker said.
>
> "Him who?"
>
> "God!" Parker cried.

"God? God don't look like that!"

"What do you know how he looks?" Parker moaned. "You ain't seen him."

"He don't *look*," Sarah Ruth said. "He's a spirit. No man shall see his face."

"Aw listen," Parker groaned, "this is just a picture of him."

"Idolatry!" Sarah Ruth screamed. "Idolatry!' Enflaming yourself with idols under every green tree." (529)

She follows her harsh words by picking up a broom and beating the raw, tattooed back of her husband until "large welts had formed on the face of the tattooed Christ" (529). He flees from the house and collapses under a tree in the back yard, perhaps the one she had in mind when she accused him of finding "idols under every green tree" earlier. Sarah Ruth glares out at him from the kitchen door: "She looked toward the pecan tree and her eyes hardened still more" (529). Parker, wounded deeply and bleeding by the tree, reenacts the posture of the crucifixion, with Christ too undergoing once again the initial scourging by one who claims to know and worship God. Sarah Ruth attacks the incarnation of God through the image of Christ by wounding the majestic Byzantine icon, bringing it once again to the cross, to suffering, and to the words of Christ at the time of His first crucifixion: "Forgive them, Father, for they know not what they do."

As she did not recognize that the eagle tattooed on his arm was not a chicken when Parker first courted her, so again at this point Sarah Ruth is so severed from the life of sacred imagination that she sees the icon only as another of her husband's vain idols. Her faith, like her vision, is diseased by abstraction, making her incapable of any images of faith. O'Connor has suggested something of the split that Sarah Ruth represents: "When the physical fact is separated from the spiritual reality, the dissolution of belief is eventually inevitable" (*Mystery and Manners*, 62). By contrast, those welts on Parker's back—welts that cover both the flesh of Christ and his own—reveal the inseparability of spirit and flesh in the incarnation and the suffering attendant upon one who dares to witness the mystery of the Word made flesh. His faith is now connatural with the suffering of the incarnated Christ.

They also reveal again how the wounds he receives from this new, more powerful tattoo place him again on the margins as an outcast in his own home. Woundedness seems to occur to those already marginalized, yet singled out in a calling (Elder, 376). Their wounds are the emblems of the special vocation; each of us carries some form of wound that is at the same time our calling. For Sarah Ruth, however, "evil is in the nature of things," as William Thompson writes (59). *Things* are evil. No imaginative leap within it sanctions human freedom.

At the very same instant Parker sinks deeply into the mystery of transfiguration offered through the icon seared into his flesh, wounding him raw, and then has it beaten by his wife into a bloody, painful pulp. Sarah Ruth, who is without imagination, denies the flesh, denies the world as well as the reality of Christ's embodied presence. Her trumpet call of "vanity" is demonic. Her vanity is such a strong force that it is capable of denying the image of Christ's salvific nature. Obsessed with the presence of sin, Sarah Ruth does not allow for the possibility of grace. God is insubstantial, not consubstantial. She has deconstructed and denied God's incarnational presence. William Thompson offers that "the Satanic principle is the abhorrence of existence. It is a hatred of everything that is other than the rich darkness of the void. . . . The horror of existence is so extreme for the Satanist that he must strive to pervert all forms. In raising the horrible to our eyesight, he tries to show us the hidden horror that is, for him, the true nature of existence" (*Evil and World Order,* 84).

On a grander scale we have in this description the memory of Ivan Karamazov's abstract Euclidean mind that is more secure among ideas than among images. But worse than Ivan, Sarah Ruth possesses no compassion or generosity in her vision. She hardens even more in her willfulness as her husband weeps in suffering for the again-wounded Christ. The new powers and principalities, of which Paul reminded us, have taken the form of the power of abstraction. And from this will to the abstract, no tenderness is active, for no body is present. None, that is, but the wounded back of her husband, carrying the burden of the incarnated Christ on it once again to the tree of sacrifice. On this last point, Sarah Gordon, writing of Flannery O'Connor's interest in Edith Stein and Simone Weil, reminds us of O'Connor's idea that tenderness separated from the source of tenderness leads logically to the concentration camps of the Third Reich and the mass cruelty of mankind (lecture, 1987). Sarah Ruth's lack of generosity and even her aggressive violence toward her husband illustrate the force of this evil even as it attempts to justify itself through the condemning voice of "vanity."

In Toni Morrison's *Beloved,* scarring the back of one who suffers for her freedom is a central image of woundedness that is assuaged by the love of a man who accepts Sethe's scars and wishes to lay his own story beside hers in mutual love. It is a novel about the powerful wounding yet redeeming quality of memory. Not leaning against a tree in suffering, like Parker, Sethe has a tree's design whipped into her flesh, a tree that both wounds and buds from that same affliction.

10

The Narrative Body and the Incarnate Word in Toni Morrison's *Beloved*

> Moreover, it is not the brain nor the heart that is the
> organ of recollection. It is the skin! For to gaze upon the
> skin is to bring to life the past.
> —Richard Selzer, *Mortal Lessons,* 115

F ew American novels possess the mythic range and depth of Toni Morrison's *Beloved.* The large themes of slavery, human embodiment, the haunting specter and then presence of the murdered Beloved, language, especially the Scriptural language that is embedded throughout the action, the powerful force of the community in an act of saving one of their own, the place of human suffering, homelessness, shame and guilt, as well as the saving act of imagining grace and the ubiquitous presence of "rememory" make it an essential fictional creation to read in our time. The novel moves under the weight of a great and deep collective wound of a people—slavery. One is born into it, suffers the wound at birth, and tries to keep it from bleeding open too much as a life of bondage and travail outlines the lives of individuals. Loving thin rather than too thickly is the credo embraced by many who are worn out grieving loss.

Slavery as a national and communal wound marks all the characters in the story, white and black, with the taint of shame. Slavery had the power, as did the Holocaust for the Jews, to wound an entire nation, a wound that runs so deep that its scar tissue will, like Ahab's "lividly whitish" marking, never disappear. Toni Morrison planned this epic work as the first part of a national trilogy, with *Jazz* constituting the second installment and *Paradise* the third.

Researching material as she prepared to write the Pulitzer Prize winning novel, Morrison confessed: "I certainly thought I knew as much about slavery as anybody. . . . But it was the interior life I needed to find out about" (*Contemporary Authors,* 325). Slavery, and the countervalent force of freedom through the acts of remembering and imagining, present first in the flesh and then in the spirit of Baby Suggs, Holy, after she has died, reverses the consuming power of the murdered Beloved, who appears first as spirit haunting the house of 124 Bluestone Road; after Paul D.'s appearance and his exorcising the spiteful specter, she later returns out of the water, fully embodied. These two forces, love and shame, give the narrative its direction as well as its tragic and comic thrusts.

Three dominant themes will comprise this chapter: the human body, especially in its embattled and scarred condition; the presence and nature of Beloved herself, since she has quarried such a vast and varied number of readings among critics; and Baby Suggs, Holy, especially in her relation to both the language of Scripture and the life of the black community that prays and feasts with her, but then rejects her generosity, which takes the form of a feast she prepares for them. These three themes, I believe, cannot be separated; together they form the mythic bulwark of this haunting and tightly woven epic of suffering individuals as well as a deeply scarred people. The body, memory, and language comprise what Henry James called the "stout stakes" of a work, those qualities, themes, and images that give a work form and direction, that make it, finally, cohere into a crafted and integral work of art.

Toni Morrison has given us a gift in this novel that repays close and repeated readings. She has also given us in *Beloved* perhaps her fullest expression of comedy, for this novel, in its lineaments and in its final scenes, portrays a communal presence of largesse and generosity growing out of the memory of Baby Suggs' generosity; such action places it in the tradition of *The Divine Comedy* and Dostoevsky's *Crime and Punishment*. I would offer that *Beloved* may be Toni Morrison's *Crime and Punishment*, and is in many ways equally as complex and far-reaching as Dostoevsky's masterpiece. Like Dostoevsky, Morrison explores with great tenderness the shaping and the cultural consequences of the incarnate word, how the flesh is languaged into existence, given shape, and how our individual incarnations are the place of both human and divine inscription and signification.

THE MARKED BODY

Morrison's novel illustrates repeatedly the quality of human embodiment first as a lived metaphor because it continues to be explored in literary criticism in unique and provocative ways. For example, the body has been understood as a cultural metaphor and invention (Romanyshyn, 23), and is connected with the force of "desire, . . . the drive to know, and narrative" (Brooks, 5). Within the action of *Beloved* especially, the flesh assumes a greater and deeper role in interpreting culture.[1] Human embodiment in Morrison's fiction would benefit from an exploration of the Christian myth and its connection with sacred language, utterances that serve to bind a community tightly together through a shared body of beliefs and images; this gap in the criticism of Morrison seriously overlooks some of the force implicit in her poetic insights. I mention at this point only a few examples of a more secular interpretation of the body in Morrison's novel. Hortense Spillers, for example, suggests that Sethe remains "a body whose flesh . . . bears . . . the marks of a cultural text" (qtd. in Wyatt, 478), while Jean Wyatt herself focuses on the "readings" of Paul D. who scans the body of Sethe through touch, "quickly becoming a participant in Sethe's discourse of bodily connection" (479). Morrison suggests early in the novel that we are to link words and body together as conditions, even meanings, of the same reality, for language is one critical and communal way the body gestures its meanings and intentions into the world.

In many of her works, including *Beloved*, Morrison tends especially to mark her female characters' bodies as kinds of tangible insignia of their physical and emotional suffering. Deborah Horvitz observes that "In *Song of Solomon*, Pilate has no navel; in *Sula*, Sula has a birthmark over her eye; in *Beloved*, Sethe's mother is branded with the cross in the circle and Sethe is permanently marked from the whipping on her back" (167). Of course, Beloved herself is marked with the gash across her throat, the edge of which Denver espies with fascination, as well as by "three vertical scratches on her forehead so fine and thin they seemed at first like baby hair" (51). Furthermore, Ella, who was tied up and abused for almost a year by a white man and his son, remembers painfully that "the scars from the bell were thick as rope around her waist" (258) when she was imprisoned by the inhuman pair she refers to as "the lowest yet." In *Paradise*, as the caretaker, Connie, receives each of the women who drift into the convent for respite, she sees one of them "secretly slicing her thighs, her arms. Wishing to be the queen of scars, she made thin red slits in her skin with whatever came to hand: razor, safety pin, paring knife" (222).[2]

Each of these body markings is in fact a shorthand narrative that painfully remembers the carrier's respective histories. A narrative line is attached to each etching of the flesh—be it an image, a symbol, or a gash—so that language and incarnation are continually yoked to form a physical and spiritual meaning that each separately is incapable of rendering. This connection between word and flesh, word and wound, language and memory, word and incarnation comprise the substance of the novel, especially as it implicates and defines not just Sethe, Beloved, and Paul D., but more poignantly, Baby Suggs, Holy. What we see through the body marked and violated is that memory itself is deeply wounded, scarred, and in need of a counternarrative that heals.

There exists a profound relationship between the word and the flesh that implicates and further defines the Christian mystery of the incarnate word which places Baby Suggs, Holy, at the center of the novel's prominent action, both in life and as forcefully after her death. More important, it aligns Baby Suggs in significant ways with the figure of Sophia in the Eastern imagination, a mediating figure between divinity and humanity. I want to explore this connectedness shortly because through Baby Suggs, a modern emblem of the more ancient Sophia, the word and flesh congeal, finally, in both the individual and communal memory of the characters. She is a figure whose memory has the capacity to begin healing the wounds of injustice. Such a congealing occurring in the individual and collective memory of the thirty women in the community who descend on 124 Bluestone Road to save their own, saves Sethe and her daughter Denver from the destructive and devouring impulses of Beloved.

WRITING THE FLESH

To understand the body in its wounded, enslaved, and liberated possibilities in the novel, it is necessary to make a short excursion into the body in history and literature, in order to highlight the heritage Morrison is working within. Such a short historical description of the place of the body in recent literature, but one unfortunately that is devoid of any mention of how the body is made sacred in language, is the subject of Peter Brooks' *Body Work: Objects of Desire in Modern Narrative* mentioned in the preceding chapters. His work offers an intriguing account of the way the flesh is introduced into nineteenth-century narratives through markings. In his study he suggests that Rousseau in his *Confessions* was the first writer consciously to inscribe the body with individual meaning. The body then becomes the "scene of discourse"; logos and the body must be then shown to be inseparable (47). Body and autobiography, one's individual life story, are seamless. It is not that the body in fiction is new; instead, as a cultural invention it must be reconfigured, or reassigned meaning through language. The notion of the modern body, Brooks continues, is now tied to the notion of personal identity, where it is "newly emblematized with meaning" (53).

I suggest that *Beloved* goes well beyond this preoccupation with personal identity to embrace a much larger concern: how the body and logos are most fully realized through the action of grace, through generosity and through the memory of an oppressed people, most specifically through the image of Baby Suggs. There are two figures that constitute the polarity in this novel: the haunting, enfleshed body of Beloved herself, and the Logos-centered utterances of Baby Suggs. Perhaps we might understand better the place and role of the young white woman, Amy Denver, who is on her way to Boston in search of velvet cloth. She meets the pregnant and abused Sethe in the bushes beside the road to Cincinnati, when she is about to deliver her daughter Denver, and in her kindness toward the lacerated woman, serves as the bridge between Sethe and Baby Suggs in her generous acts of healing the wounded back of Sethe and in assisting at the birth of the child, who will then be named in memory of her generosity.

Brooks continues by summing up the point of his study as well as an important insight for initiating this discussion: "the process of semioticization of the body . . . results in an impressive somatization of stories because the destinies of the body so marked tend to play out the narrative plot" (86–87). He reveals through this insight the enfleshed nature of narratives and even hints at their purgative possibilities for the teller and the listener.

Given such an intimate connection between body and story, I believe that with Paul D., Sethe, and even the enfleshed figure of Beloved herself, desire aims at recovering a story that has been stripped of their bodies, but which their bodies hold in trust, so to speak, through their markings. The markings are the memories of their stories which must be faced, submitted to, and accepted if any interior freedom is to be gained. Each of their bodies, as emblems, implicate always the great enveloping narrative of the traffic in slavery through the Middle Passage and the muting of individual freedom, identity, and even the simplest enjoyment of sensual pleasures for the black race, which Morrison in her studies estimates to be "60 million or more." On this larger scale we sense that there is a major epic story that has not found its voice, but that, as John Leonard passionately observes, "Without *Beloved* our imagination of the nation's self has a hole in it big enough to die from" (qtd. in *Contemporary Authors,* 325). The novel includes a powerful set of voices as well as wounds, and the wounds want to voice their own origins through those who carry these violations, so they will be heard by the national ears of our country.

Attitudes like the white schoolteacher's on the plantation, who in the service of pseudoscientific calculations, aligns the plantation slaves' characteristics with those of animals in order to illustrate their subhuman nature to his two rapacious nephews, is a perspective that dispossesses a people from an intimacy with their own flesh. His measuring the traits of animals and aligning them with the traits of black slaves is a process that dirties the self, as Sethe describes it. No one, she is determined, will ever have a chance to perform on her own children this act of soiling the self; she therefore attempts to murder all of them before the schoolteacher has the opportunity to retrieve them back to "Sweet Home" to ensure, Sethe believes, that their life of slavery is as miserable as her own. Under such inhumane treatment, one becomes divorced from one's own flesh. Morrison's profound insight here is that when one loses the body to technical function—either by being viewed as a unit of labor, as an exchange value, as an analogy to an animal, or as a link in a chain gang—one simultaneously loses one's own narrative. To abandon the body is also to abandon one's history and one's biography. To retrieve one's own embodiment, bit by bit and piece by piece, and to stitch the parts back together is at the same time to reclaim the history of that embodiment, for incarnation always insists on a context—a history and a future. The body is therefore embedded in language as deeply as words are enfleshed, a revelation Morrison renders through Sethe primarily, a woman who has closed the door on her past and on the body that she brought from that tragic region to 124 Bluestone Road. But she offers as well a way to freedom through the image of Baby Suggs, whose relation to language and to human imagination offers an opportunity for freedom that shame itself is incapable of destroying.

James Hillman writes astutely on this attitude held by the schoolteacher and those like him; he claims that modern forms of theories and therapies, scientific experiments, all seek to deaden "the most human of all faculties—the telling of the tales of our souls. . . . A mark of imaginal man is the speech of his soul" (*A Blue Fire,* 29). Embedded within human flesh, we might say, is the story of that same incarnation's coming to be. Behind this action in *Beloved* haunts the existence of the Incarnate Word, invisibly present, but realized through memory. Baby Suggs herself becomes what I would call the controlling metaphor of the Incarnate Word's presence, even while "Beloved" is the single word that Sethe purchases through the violation of her own body, one she must distance herself from as the stone engraver sexually satisfies himself in payment for carving the word on the pink speckled gravestone of her murdered daughter: "Ten minutes for seven letters. With another ten could she have gotten 'Dearly' too?" (*Beloved,* 5). Abusing her body, the stone engraver wounds Sethe once again. Sethe is wounded for one word, an act she submits to and is determined to spend the rest of her life forgetting. In the novel's action, bodies and words both carry price tags and will be marketed to the highest bidder.

To take this idea of the distant body one step further, the body under the deadening gaze of the schoolteacher, who manages the slaves at Sweethome, is *only* an object of interlocking systems; but as Robert Romanyshyn argues eloquently against such a reduction, he suggests that the body is less an object than it is a *situation* (*Technology as Symptom and Dream,* 17). It is less a given natural fact than it is a human cultural gesture. The body is a cultural matter and so it *matters.* And through its matter, the rememories of its history are brought back into consciousness to shape the future. But only insofar as they are articulated stories can they gain significant preeminence for both an individual and an entire community. Rosemarie Garland Thomson underscores the marked body's history in writing that "both Sethe and her unnamed, enslaved, rebellious, hanged mother have markings that map their histories upon their bodies, at once imposing identity and differentiating them from the unmarked" (121). Their wounds are their names, the words of their biographies. But Thomson takes the body one step further: "As with each marked female character, Sethe's bodily reconfiguration is paradoxical, embodying simultaneously the terrible price demanded and the extraordinary character produced by her history and identity" (121). The body the school-teacher denied as a person has become, through the whippings, a body individually and uniquely marked by the image of a "chokecherry tree," as Amy Denver describes it. It is Sethe's witness to her drive for freedom; the tree on her back blossoming with dots of blood and pus is her signature of freedom, as are the blossoming trees that Paul D. is instructed to follow north to freedom when he escapes the brutality of those in charge of the chain gang. Within the scars and pains of our wounds is the blossoming flower of freedom; the wound has the capacity to open up to liberation, even when the origin of such freedom is so tender and vulnerable.

Those rememories, as Sethe speaks of them, situate the body in place and give it a home, as she describes it so decisively to her daughter Denver, who is named after both place and a person: "Someday you be walking down the road and you hear something or see something going on. And you think it's you thinking it up. . . . But no. It's when you bump into a rememory that belongs to somebody else." Denver quickly deduces from her mother's observation: "If it's still there, waiting, that must mean that nothing ever dies." To which Sethe responds: "Nothing ever does" (36). Memories, like the wounds of one's own or others, even those of others, continually haunt the space of the present; and in Sethe's description, which is lyrically poetic and reveals the deep, mythic sense of her being, one acknowledges that memories are embodied, substantial, have a shape and a form to them. Further, memories, like wounded people, may always be seeking a home, like the ghost of her murdered daughter. Rememories are ways that the past gestures itself into the present; remembering itself is an imaginative gesture that intertwines past with present, the souls of the dead with the living, those who have perished through deep suffering and their offspring, in a seamless confluence. Much of the novel's action as well as those who are marked, wounded, scarred or tattooed circulates around this possibility.

SETHE'S WOUNDED BODY

Denver relates the story of her own birth to the embodied Beloved shortly after the latter, in the form of a "fully dressed woman, [who] walked out of the water. She barely gained the dry bank of the stream before she sat down and leaned against a Mulberry tree" (50). She then makes her way to their home at 124 Bluestone. Hungry for stories, Beloved asks her sister to relate how Denver came to be and to be named as she is. Denver gathers up the parts of the story she knows within herself and prepares for the telling, in order "to construct out of the strings she had heard all her life a net to hold Beloved" (76). We have learned before Denver's picking up the part of the story that she knows, that Paul D. and Sethe have been gathering this story, now eighteen years old, between them several pages earlier. The story evolves, grows, and matures slowly in the telling by various voices. I would call it a deeply wounded and dismembered story, one that fell apart, or was blown apart in the suffering and separation of those who participated in its making. Now, in re-membering, the members of that story finally begin to find one another to stitch the painful strands of the narrative back together. Perhaps no one, finally, has the full story of their lives, but must rely on others to stitch the various pieces together, like a quilt. If it takes a village to raise a child, then it might take an entire people to reclaim the painful suffering narrative of their past.

Sethe, pregnant with Denver and fleeing "Sweet Home" and the punishments of the schoolteacher, is raped of her milk by his rapacious nephews as he looks on and takes notes. His pen is full of ink that Sethe herself has made. Her husband, Halle, looks silently down in horror from the hayloft where he is hiding; she escapes to meet with her children and others who have planned a run for freedom as Halle, insane with keeping silent, smears his face with butter and loses all desire to live.

Exhausted and dying, Sethe falls into some weeds beside the road to Cincinnati and into a deep, painful sleep, only to be awakened by a young white woman, Amy Denver, journeying to Boston in search of blue velvet. Amy takes Sethe to a lean-to by the river and massages her swollen and cracked feet, then removes her dress to examine the split skin on her wounded back. Startled at first, she begins to breathe regularly again as she describes the marks she discerns on Sethe, who can feel but not see the design of her beating: "'It's a tree, Lu. A Chokecherry tree. See, here's the trunk—it's red and split wide open, full of sap, and this here's the parting for the branches. You got a might lot of branches. . . . Your back got a whole tree on it. In bloom. What God have in mind, I wonder'" (79).

She tells Sethe that the only thing she can do is find spider webs in order to relieve some of the pain from the raw wounds and to promote its healing: "'Maybe I ought to break them blossoms open. Get that pus to running, you think? Wonder what God had in mind?'" (80).

Amy seeks out spider webs and returns to dress the wound. She cleans the webs "and then draped [them] on Sethe's back, saying it was like stringing a tree for Christmas" (80). She ministers to Sethe, first singing to her, then comforting her wounds so that she can survive through the night. Only then, Amy believes, will Sethe have a strong chance of surviving and delivering the child. Amy knows she has talents—"'I'm good at sick things'"—and makes from two strips of Sethe's shawl filled with leaves two wrappings for her feet. Amy Denver, for whom the child about to be born will be named, is a midwife for Sethe and ministers to her through both words and touch. She serves Sethe on the level of the individual in the same way that Baby Suggs, Holy, serves her entire people—through the gestures of stitching up and through the Logos of healing in which soothing words are used along with the webbing for her wounds. The wounded body of Sethe is the occasion for the two women to come together in such an urgent and deep communion; Amy offers her gifts to Sethe in the form of a laying on of hands to the scarred tree that is ready to bloom, as her other side, distended with child, is ready to burst with new life. With milk dripping from her breasts, her back in bloom, her womb about to give birth, and her feet wrapped in nature's substance, Sethe is reminiscent of the great goddess of fertility, of the earth goddess, of life itself insisting on finding an aperture into the world, regardless of what form; it is insistent and powerful in its desire to find a place and to be recognized.

In addition, Amy has made the analogy of putting on Sethe's oozing tree the spidery filaments being similar to "stringing a tree for Christmas" (80), which makes of Sethe's body a narrative of the entire life of Christ, from birthing to crucifixion. Sethe embodies the birth of Christ as well as His suffering on the tree for all the injustices of humankind. Baby Suggs, Holy, will voice the word of this Christian mythology throughout the community. Deep within the wound is the power of healing; the wound is then a paradox because it contains within it the impulse to bring the parts back together—to rememory them. The birth of Denver occurs just as Sethe enters the waters of the Ohio River to freedom.

Amy, in turn, in her gestures of kindness, is the antithesis of the schoolteacher with his technological reduction of his black charges; he is the kind of technician of human life that in David Levin's view embodies "the reductive nihilism of our present historical epoch," who subjects everyone and everything to a permanent availability and total control. Our technologically conditioned ontology is a reflection of hands that are motivated by the will to power: the will to dominate and control, the need to hoard and secure" (*Body's Recollection*, 133–34). Amy Denver, however, is witness to another form of embodied gesture; she is one who "cultivates gestures of tenderness and caring, so that some of the rage and some of the violence in our world might be transmuted into energies of better purpose" (134), as Levin suggests. To concentrate on the former while ignoring the latter, *Beloved* asserts, is to doom an entire people and perhaps the entire planet to a poverty from which none of its members may escape.

Amy's generous gestures of healing promote the birth of new life; she is its shepherd and steward. In the morning Sethe moves herself to a small rowboat on the shore of the river; as soon as she approaches it "her own water broke loose to join it" (83). In a birth both painful and desperate, so many of the memories of Beloved's own death and rebirth out of the primordial waters bear in on her. Her water breaking by the river reminds us of how an overwhelming urge to urinate like a horse comes over Sethe when she draws close to Beloved waiting for them on the tree stump in front of 124 Bluestone (51). In addition, here in the leaking boat, struggling to give birth to Denver, Sethe "reached one arm back and grabbed the rope while Amy fairly clawed at the head" (84), another action that remembers the three fingernail marks on the forehead of the infant Beloved as Sethe pulls her head back to slit her throat in the shed. Birth, death, and regeneration all conspire in this wonderfully complex and cosmic scene of the birth of Denver, a birth in which all of nature seems to resound in complicity of the life force itself exploding into the world. Amy wraps a skirt around the infant "and the wet sticky woman clambered ashore to see what, indeed, God had in mind" (84). Now the natural order, prompted almost by this birth, responds with its own bursting new life: "Spores of bluefern growing in the hollows along the riverbank float toward the water in silver-blue lines . . . , seeds in which the whole generation sleeps confident of a future. And for a moment it is easy to believe each one has one—will become all of what is contained in the spore: will live out its day as planned" (84).

Life itself, with its perpetual and nonsurrendering yearning to be born and to fulfill itself, is the gathering strength that overwhelms the evil beatings and dominating power of the force of the schoolteacher and of slavery itself. There is a myth more powerful than that of shame and beating back the pain of the past. It is the mythic energy of life itself. Even the beating of Sethe takes on the shape of a tree in full bud. It is a dual tree that she wears as a blooming wound on her back. On one hand it is the "cross of the redeemer" that each of us carries, "not in the bright moments of his tribe's great victories, but in the silences of his personal despair," as Joseph Campbell ends his book bearing witness to the heroic (*Hero*, 391); but it is also the tree of life, a mythological image of the life force that has the capacity to redeem the dismembering energy of nihilism and cruelty. With its buds ready to burst on its branches, the great wound on Sethe's back is a primordial mythic presence of the world soul's suffering as well as the budding possibility of creating new life out of such travail; imagined as a cross, her wound contains within its mutilation the death of Christ and a regeneration in the resurrection. Perhaps that is what is contained in the refrain throughout this scene in the novel, to see "what God had in mind."

Sethe's back carries the wound of an archetypal tree which embodies, paradoxically, both the suffering and the new life embedded in its nature. It is precisely what Baby Suggs, Holy, has offered to her people in life and continues to inform them of through her memory in death: the image of hope itself, which can only be gained through the courage to imagine, in spite of one's oppression. Are we to imagine, then, that it is through being wounded that the numinous in the form of the sacred has the opportunity to enter our lives? Woundedness is intimately connected to divinity, and is perhaps the aperture through which divinity may enter the immanent realm from the transcendent expansiveness of eternity. Does God have in mind woundedness as a necessary part of human being? The images in this section would assert such a possibility.

Furthermore, Morrison's genius here is captured in a nutshell, as James Hillman writes in discussing his acorn theory, "to use a natural image in an unnatural way" in order to reveal "the very kernel of our archetypal point of view, which aims to turn the organic, time-bound developmental view of human life backward on itself" (*Soul's Code,* 274). As Baby Suggs recalls the incarnate word, Sethe's brutalized body, full of new life, bears witness to the incarnate wound. The wound contains in its markings the tree of new life that moves restlessly in her belly waiting to be born out of the primal waters of her and into the primal waters of the river, a dark expanse that separates her from freedom.

Beloved herself, emerging from the primal waters to enter her mother's life again eighteen years after being killed by her, is a visible witness of the power of memory to incarnate itself in the world. Memories may be understood as ways of imagining our stories; we retrieve those moments from the past that actually shape and define our identity. The body enslaved, scarred, beaten, abused, the memories attendant on those experiences, memory and narrative, are of a piece in the individual; one cannot be dealt with without the others. It is a multicolored quilt with individual and unique patches conspiring together in a harmonious unity. Baby Suggs, Holy, as we will see, is the sacred instrument of such a confluence.

THE HAUNTING FLESH OF BELOVED

The house on 124 Bluestone Road is the central site in the novel and the resting place of memory, a point of its coalescence and confluence. As an archetypal crossroads, it has undergone many transformations in the community and has received a wide range of characters residing there. It is like a memory theater, a local habitation of memory. Memories inhabit this house with the same substantiality as its human occupants. Suggesting something of this idea, Toni Morrison remarked in an interview that Sethe "is remembering by having her house haunted" (2). Perhaps a far too literal reading is offered by Melvin Dixon, then, when he writes that "Sethe's narrative of infanticide is disrupted by the actual presence of memory in the form of the dead daughter's ghost" (23) because Beloved seems more, even in her venomous spectral heat, than simply memory.

At first only a haunting and disembodied presence, Beloved assumes the flesh of a grown woman with new skin, almost translucent in its texture, but with the scar ringing her neck from her mother's knife. Her marked body carries the rememory of her death. We remember with this image Sethe's relation to her own mother, a memory prompted by Beloved's question as she, Denver, and Sethe return home one evening. Sethe relates to her two daughters her own mother's marked body: "Right on her rib was a circle and cross burnt right in the skin. She said, 'This is your ma'am. . . . If something happen to me and you can't tell me by my face, you can know me by this mark'" (61). When Sethe remembers asking her mother to be marked in the same way to connect them as mother and daughter by the brand, her mother slaps her face, an act she does not initially understand, "Not till I had a mark of my own" (61). Sethe, however, does mark her own child, Beloved, with the knife that slices her throat and with the three scratchings from her fingernails as she yanked her head back to expose her neck; all four markings are visible on her even while the skin on her body is new. The scars marking the original place of violence link her to her mother in a way that Sethe did not experience with her own. Both wounds or markings, however, are signs of recognition; they mark the relationship as well as the individual nature of each woman. They are rememories of their lives burned into their flesh. Mark Ledbetter persuasively argues that "the imposed mark of ownership" worn by Sethe's mother "becomes a welcomed mark of distinction, painful and necessary in a world of oppression" (162). The wound becomes a bond, knitting together rather than separating mother and daughter. Through it, anonymity is shed and individual identity becomes painfully apparent.

Beloved emerges from the water, however, only after Paul D. has exorcised her ghostly presence in the house. Such an exorcism allows him room to become the third family member with Sethe and her daughter, Denver. Possessed of a grand presence wherever he travels, Paul D. is, as Sethe describes him late in the novel, blessed: "She looks at him . . . and sees it—the thing in him, the blessedness, that has made him the kind of man who can walk in a house and make the women cry" (272). He learns her suffering past initially through the clumped scars on her back; he reads her body with his own wounded and loving mind and face: "He rubbed his cheek on her back and learned that way her sorrow, the roots of it; its wide trunk and intricate branches. . . . He saw the sculpture her back had become, like the decorative work of an ironsmith too passionate for display" (17). Paul D. sees no tree on her back ("because trees were inviting; things you could trust and be near, talk to if you wanted to" [21]); rather, he sees only "a revolting clump of scars" and as Sethe tells him, she has no feeling in them. Her back is as numb as her history to her; she loves Paul D.'s presence and fears that through him her back might begin to feel again.

Against Paul's blessedness, however, Beloved recoils; she is driven by appetite and vengeance, both of which are too great to allow any other person to be part of Sethe's world. As the missing "3" in the address, "124," Beloved has far too many stories to devour. Stories are her main subsistence. As the hands of the three figures—Paul D., Sethe, and Denver—begin to cast shadows as they interlock on their shared journey home from the circus (49), the spirit of Beloved incarnates and emerges from the water to enter the house on Bluestone Road, "a fully dressed woman" (50). Who or what this figure is has initiated a wide range of interpretations.

Terry Otten, for instance, echoing Morrison's own observation, believes that Beloved is "not just Sethe's dead child come to exact judgment, but also the representative of the 'Sixty million and More [who died even before reaching America] to whom Morrison alludes in her headnote" (qtd. in Segal, 60). Deborah Horvitz suggests Beloved "is the haunting symbol of the many Beloveds—generations of mothers and daughters—hunted down and stolen from Africa. . . . She represents the spirit of all the women dragged onto slave ships in Africa" (157). But more specifically, "Beloved generates a metamorphosis in Sethe that allows her to speak what she had thought to be the unspeakable" (158). Jean Wyatt proposes that Beloved is "a spirit in search of a body and a preoedipal child who desires a merger with her mother" (480). All of these responses, however, while attesting to the epic breadth of the novel, assiduously avoid the spiritual reality of the reincarnated figure named by the single word, and miss the larger story of the Christian myth that supports the entire narrative as it moves communally to save Sethe from the grip of Beloved's vengeful hunger. Few of these critical voices even mention the important presence of Baby Suggs as a redeeming figure of the Word. She is as crucial in her relation to the word uttered as is her prototype, Sonya Marmaladov in Dostoevsky's *Crime and Punishment*. Both of these women not only embrace the wound of the other, they work to heal it through the orality of the word, the Word embodied.

On the other hand, and suggesting that "the metaphorical focus of *Beloved* is incarnation, the embodiment of spirit in the things of matter" (293), Louise Cowan offers a more penetrating and far-reaching reading of Beloved: "this invading spirit was not simply the baby's ghost but a creature that, in the words of the traditional prayer to Michael the Archangel, 'prowls about the world, seeking the ruin of souls'" (*Classic Texts and the*

Nature of Authority, 294). Cowan develops this idea further by suggesting that "Beloved is a false creation, engendered by a wrong idea upon nothingness, greedy to enter into existence. . . . Something like Beloved took over the mind of Nazi Germany when a pseudo-ideal was taken as genuine" (296). Larry Allums, rightly giving a tragic cast to the character of Sethe, believes that Beloved may be the reflection of excess, mirroring in some deep ways Sethe as the "excessive maternal in action, revealing the limits of the maternal vision, its reluctance . . . to envision the whole, or the world outside the space of its mothering role" (275). These last interpretations take the figure of Beloved out of sociology and Freudian psychology and situate her figure within a deeper and more cosmic texture of meaning. Beloved's cast shifts to include more. Michiko Kakutani writes: "*Beloved* possesses the heightened power and resonance of myth—its characters, like those in opera or Greek drama . . . , strike us as enactments of ancient rituals and passions" (qtd. in *Contemporary Authors,* 325). This deeper and fuller mythic sensibility takes us further into the heart of the action of a narrative that seems to join older mythic presences with New Testament images of forgiveness and generosity.

Certainly the figure of Beloved embodies the excess of appetite that feeds insatiably off of stories, of narratives that she has missed being a character in. The growth of her appetite occurs only *after* she is enfleshed. As such, she begins in her incarnation to continue to dissolve Sethe into edible pieces which she can then devour at will, eventually to destroy both her and Denver. Her desires are driven by pulling apart, deconstructing and dividing into small segments what she devours. Initially, Beloved appears to be a benevolent force who has the gift of opening up stories in Paul D., Denver, and Sethe. But she systematically overwhelms them with her hunger and breaks apart their newly formed community, one that for the first time in eighteen years promises Sethe, however tentatively, the image of a future. Walking home from the carnival with Denver and Paul D., she notices that their shadows are holding hands but they weren't: "Nobody noticed but Sethe and she stopped looking after she decided that it was a good sign. A life. Could be" (47). In feeling this hope, she begins to heal enough not to suppress her memories by keeping them back; her desires are now shadowy, not having reached fully enfleshed reality, but she begins to feel hope and desire.

Beloved perhaps can be understood as a correlative image of Sethe's shame embodied, pinning her to a stony place, like Prometheus. The body of Beloved may be read as the incarnation of Sethe's denial of her crime, a fantasy image that bloats and expands as her returned daughter inhabits more and more of the house, which is not only cursed but isolated from the entire community after Baby Suggs' death. Explored through the angle of tragic excess, 124 Bluestone Road shares a similar fate as the House of Atreus in Greek tragedy, a dwelling that is cursed, condemned, and left to the fated actions of family violence and wounded bodies that continue to repeat the same destructive impulses, and whose toxic actions spill over to infect the entire polis. Only Baby Suggs, *remembered* for her generosity and in her relation to the Word, promises to redeem in a communally forceful way the inevitable trajectory of tragic suffering and wounded selves Sethe and Denver embody.[3]

The corporeal and fleshy body of Beloved feeding on words and stories as well as on food is transformed bodily from being fully clothed early in her appearance to being "a pregnant woman, naked and smiling in the heat of the afternoon sun" at the end of the novel when the 30 women confront her on the porch: "Thunderblack and glistening, she stood on long straight legs, her belly big and tight. Vines of hair twisted all over her head" (261). She is like the internal jungle placed in the soul of the black people by the white slaveholders. Later a little boy fishing claimed that he saw "cutting through the woods, a naked woman with fish for hair" (267). Paul D., sensing some force pushing him from the house and Sethe's bed, tangibly feels her increasing power and actually sanctions it when Beloved visits him in the shed behind the house: "a life hunger overwhelmed him and he had no more control over it than over his lungs." Later, full of shame, he would also feel some gratitude "for having been escorted to some ocean-deep place he once belonged to" (264).

The primordial depth out of which she emerges, and the depth that Paul feels on reflection, illustrates how originary is the energy and the presence of this newly formed and practically storyless creature. As a presence, Beloved offers to those in her midst what they desire but feel the need to repress. And if she is in fact the image of their repressed desires, she carries always with her the promise of satisfying those same yearnings in an excessive way. As an image, she emerges from the deepest levels of the human psyche in all of its primordial holdings. She is a fully enfleshed archetype, a powerful image of one of those deep and eternal patterns of psychic functioning that has the power and capacity to arrest one on that exclusive level of being. As with all archetypes, Jung reminds us, she is a "complex of experiences that come upon us like fate" (*Archetypes and the Collective Unconscious*, 30).

Sethe's own frustrating image of her own "rebellious brain" reveals in its inward qualities those that Beloved outwardly embodies: "Like a greedy child it snatched up everything. Just once, could it say, No thank you? I just ate and can't hold another bite? . . . But my greedy brain says, Oh thanks, I'd love more—so I add more. And no sooner than I do, there is no stopping" (71). The passage gains intensity as brain and child are drawn even closer together: "But her brain was not interested in the future. Loaded with the past and hungry for more, it left her no room to imagine, let alone plan for, the next day" (71). Beloved will snatch her future from Sethe as her brain refuses to say no to "enough." The stories her brain is intent on stuffing into it finds its enfleshed analogue in the bottomless appetite of Beloved for stories.

How different she is, therefore, from Baby Suggs, Holy, who does not take but gives back the Word as a healing gift to her people; she gives them the word of Scripture to feed on, to be nurtured by, and to gain a cohesion through, while Beloved pulls the words out of Sethe and Denver, starving them to death by siphoning their diminishing energy.

Beloved's intention grows clearer when she gains a footing at 124 Bluestone. She plans to separate out Sethe, Denver, and Paul D., to alienate them from one another, to undo the knots of their familial affection and scatter them so she may dominate and devour their individual narratives. Initially she represents a provocation to remember the past and to speak it only to her. She has the capacity as well to shape the past so that it becomes in its full terror a paralyzing rather than a liberating force for those who remember. The body of Beloved, as it grows and bloats in excess, becomes more primordially part of the natural order, eventually to merge with earth and water.

We could consider Beloved a kind of byproduct of rememory, a monstrous rememory that needs to be forgotten communally. In lines that serve as an Epilogue to her presence, the narrator confesses that the entire presence of Beloved " was not a story to pass on" (275). What Peter Brooks observes about the monstrous makes sense in this context: the monstrous, he concludes, "is an imaginary being who comes to life in language and, once having done so, cannot be eliminated from language" (218). Beloved gains her purchase and her life in the world through language, specifically through stories remembered, beginning first with Denver, who is only too anxious to share those stories passed down from her mother, of her own birth. "'Tell me,' Beloved said. 'Tell me how Sethe made you in the boat'" (76). "Now, watching Beloved's alert and hungry face, how she took in every word, asking questions about the color of things and their size, her downright craving to know, Denver began to see what she was saying and not just hear it" (77).

Later, after ice skating with the two daughters, Sethe prepares them hot milk and honey, and then shuts the door on the world. But in a turn she does not anticipate, she feels herself slowly and methodically drained of her life stories by the constantly feeding phantom of her daughter. Beloved's initial ghostly presence, followed by her incarnational reality, behaves as an eighteen-month-old infant would. This is her age when Sethe cuts her throat. Like an infant, she is practically barren of stories and a history; her monstrousness gains in stature through the stories she devours in order to gain an identity her mother sacrificed. She is, in fact, the vengeful body of remembered stories; Brooks offers an important insight into such an idea when he combines words with flesh: "language is marked by the body, by the process of embodiment. We have not so much a mark *on* the body as the mark *of* the body: the capacity of language to create a body, one that in turn calls into question the language we use to classify and control bodies. . . . We know it is not easy to get rid of the monstrous body linguistically created" (220).

Beloved may be perceived, therefore, as the psychic life of guilt and shame of Sethe as it becomes enfleshed, becoming incarnated through the words of her mother.[4] As she admits in her soliloquy about her Beloved: "'Paul D. ran her off so she had no choice but to come back to me in the flesh. . . . When I explain it she'll understand, because she understands everything already. . . . I'm here. I lasted. And my girl come home. Now I can look at things again because she's here to see them too'" (200–201). Such a tragic misreading of the embodied daughter opens Sethe to be brutalized by her. The trap of explaining to Beloved why she murdered her is the fullest form of incarceration Sethe could ever impose on herself. She is willing to trade her stories to Beloved, but in so doing unwittingly becomes a slave to her own remorse and shame. Her dominant desire seems to include talking her way out of her past actions.

To Denver then initially falls the central responsibility of saving her mother from the swelling demands of Beloved; her increased needs are reflected in her bloating body: "Listless and sleepy with hunger, Denver saw the flesh between her mother's forefinger and thumb fade. Saw Sethe's eyes bright but dead, alert but vacant" (242–43). With her "basket-fat stomach" (243), Beloved is described in her destructiveness as "wild game" (242) who "whined for sweets although she was getting bigger, plumper by the day" (239). Barbara Ann Schapiro accurately assesses one of the central images "at the psychological base of the book: it is the picture of a lost, greedy child whose ravenous hunger/love is out of control" (*Relational Self,* 139). Nurturing has been victimized by appetite in a distortion of desire keenly reminiscent of the suitors in Homer's epic. Although perhaps itself a distortion as well, Baby Suggs, Holy's feast prepared for her people, while labeled by them as nothing more than "reckless generosity," is essential to counteract the monstrous hunger of Beloved's power in the world.

As Beloved balloons, language itself within the house becomes muddled; voices multiply amid garbled words and sentences. Language bloats in confusion as the body swells. Bloating body merges with a confused excess of words. Stamp Paid, attempting to visit one day, but finding the door locked even to him in direct violation of his free access to the community's homes, leaves after hearing the rumblings within and "believed the undecipherable language clamoring around the house was the mumbling of the black and angry dead" (198). Words and stories surrender to a massive angry force of all the black people who have died, not in a bed like Baby Suggs, and are few in number who had not even "lived a livable life" (198). Left to themselves in 124 Bluestone, Sethe and Denver will eventually be starved by the ferocious avenging appetite of Beloved.

The house is cursed; it can be redeemed only by action from the larger community. The importance of Baby Suggs makes sense only if we see her presence against the backdrop of the figures that have been condemned to feeding the life stories to Beloved. Baby Suggs seems to hold the entire community together when she was alive; her memories in the minds of the community prompt their generous assistance when she is dead. In life and earth she served her people as a container of their grief, loss, and joy. In her death, far from being forgotten, she is felt as a presence even more deeply through the folks' felt act of remembering. The war for the soul of Sethe then, rages between the two poles of remembered figures, the holiness of Baby Suggs and the embodied vengeance of Beloved.

THE REDEMPTIVE WORD OF BABY SUGGS, HOLY

Given Beloved's excessively destructive appetite for remembered stories, there may initially seem little hope for Sethe and Denver. The contrary impulse in her action and her language, characterized not by the quality of excess but by abundance, generosity, and largesse, is the presence of Baby Suggs. Unlike Beloved, Baby Suggs does not isolate individuals but promotes their individual involvement in community; she works as an anodyne to the devouring power of Sethe's murdered child. In her generosity and her intimacy with the Word, she is the antithesis of the devouring impulse of shame represented by Beloved, who has descended on 124 Bluestone. Baby Suggs, Holy, is undeniably, as Louise Cowan has suggested, "a sybil, the prophetess of the novel, seeing everything, finally fallible herself, though her 'calling' of others serves to keep them alive as a community" (*Classic Texts and the Nature of Authority,* 298).

Furthermore, as a "figure of the mother-goddess" (299), Baby Suggs is an originary presence, an archetypal counterweight to the primordial and destructive impulses of Beloved. Only as such a presence—mythical and primordial as Beloved herself, yet as Christian in her wedding Scripture to incarnation as is Christ—does Baby Suggs offer the community both the words and memory necessary to expunge Beloved from the communal body. While Beloved prefers to isolate Denver and Sethe in order to feed on their stories in isolation, Baby Suggs is the communal icon of generosity and bounty who stitches the various members together through largesse. By so doing, she wars against an inclination that the blacks of the community have been conditioned by a harsh and meager life to judge as shameful, so accustomed have they been trained to loving small and living little. The words she *utters* are for public consumption and nourishment; the words Beloved *hears* are for her consumption alone. Because abundance in anything seems an outrage, especially in the feast she prepared for them, which made them feel small in the presence of so much bounty, they respond by avoiding the inhabitants of Bluestone Road.

After the feast prepared by Baby Suggs and Sethe, the people become furious. "They swallowed baking soda, the morning after, to calm the stomach violence caused by the bounty, the *reckless generosity* on display at 124" (137, my emphasis). Growing from two baskets of berries picked by Stamp Paid, "it grew to a feast for 90 people . . . who ate so well and laughed so much, it made them angry" (136). We remember through this instant feast the New Testament parable of the loaves and the fishes, where from a few baskets of fish and bread there was more than enough for all. Envy mingles with their own sense of shame to birth powerful discord toward Baby Suggs: "Where does she get it all, Baby Suggs, Holy? Why is she and hers always the center of things? How come she knows exactly what to do and when?" (137). Receivers of largesse, their one unanimous response is to wound with ridicule the efforts of a woman who calls up in them their own best and magnanimous self.

Her feast is an effort to allow them to imagine more fully and with greater abundance; it is an alchemical meal in this respect. But they are initially unable to rise to such a level, so beaten down and habituated by their own suffering and condemnation by the white race have they become, that they only know how to live small. When they step back from her, Baby Suggs takes to bed to die, believing she has failed the community she served so faithfully with the Word during their prayer meetings in the clearing. What she cannot know in the last days of her life is how she will, as in Christ's words to His disciples at the last supper, "Do this in memory of me," be an even stronger presence to her people in memory than she was in life. Wounded deeply by the community, she is nonetheless permanently part of their communal memory and will rally them in the greatest time of need.

Baby Suggs is therefore more than a mythic presence; she is the midwife of not any words but of *the Word*, the sacred utterance of Scripture whose stories redeem the narratives of all those living who struggle to remember and accept their narratives, as well as all those who have not had stories told of them. She is in such a capacity an embodiment of the figure of Sophia, the bearer of the redemptive word, and it is this dimension of Baby Suggs that needs a fuller voice than she has been given.[5]

After Baby Suggs' death, Beloved seems to accelerate her free rein to devour Sethe completely, much to the horror of Denver. In her soliloquy on her sister Denver muses: "'I'm afraid the thing that happened that made it all right for my mother to kill my sister could happen again. I don't know what it is, . . . but maybe there is something else terrible enough to make her do it again'" (205). Feeling the terror nascent in Beloved, Denver prepares to launch herself from the front porch of Bluestone Road into the world, to seek helpful voices in the community, beginning with her former teacher, Miss Jones. On the brink of being consumed, along with her mother, by Beloved, Denver hears the voice of Baby Suggs, guiding her as Beatrice guides Dante, or Athena Odysseus: "Then what do I do?" to which the voice of her grandmother responds: "'Know it, and go on out the yard. Go on'" (245). She tells her granddaughter that there ain't no defense against the past; accept that and move into the world before she is devoured by Beloved.

It is also the powerful presence of the *memory* of Baby Suggs in the minds of the women that prompts them first to leave baskets of food for Denver and her mother, to repay the largesse of an earlier feast by providing in abundance where there is scarcity in excess at 124 Bluestone: "Two days later Denver stood on the porch and noticed something lying on the tree stump at the edge of the yard. [This same tree trunk is where Beloved perched and slept immediately after coming out of the water to find her mother.] She went to look and found a sack of white beans. Another time a plate of cold rabbit meat." And all through the spring "names appeared near or in gifts of food. . . . Many had X's with designs about them. . . . All of them knew her grandmother and some had even danced with her in the Clearing, a communal space of prayer and fellowship. Others remembered the days when 124 was a way station" (248–49), a confluent place where the community gathered, traded gossip and letters for travelers, and passed on to other territories. It used to be a central communal place, like the Haymarket in *Crime and Punishment*. The voices heard there were communal, varied, joyful, and equal.

These same women who feed the starving Denver and Sethe eventually gather to descend on 124 Bluestone armed with forceful and vivid memories of Baby Suggs' generosity to free Sethe from this "low down thing" that plagues her life. Baby Suggs gains a force in death through the memory of her words and acts, a force she felt she had lost in life. In this respect, she shares with Father Zosima in *The Brothers Karamazov* the same powerful memorial presence for a people. The presence of her memories heals the wounded, shameful souls who are bitter and defeated in their condition. In rememorying her, the women gain something of their rightful freedom back and choose to act generously toward one of their own enslaved in their midst. In being remembered by the women in the settlement, Baby Suggs truly expresses the Incarnate Word through the image of Sophia.

THE IMAGE OF SOPHIA

The other connection worth noting here between Sophia and Baby Suggs is that the former, according to Erich Neumann, has the power to nourish what has been spiritually transformed and reborn. His language is interesting because it links Sethe with Baby Suggs in their shared concern for nourishing others: "on the level of spiritual transformation the adult human being receives the 'virgin's milk' of Sophia" (*The Great Mother*, 329). Sethe's love takes the metaphor of milk as well when she tells her two daughters: "There is milk enough for all" (222), which recalls the milk she was actually raped of by the schoolteacher's two nephews.

However, as she is associated more with the heart "that sends forth the spirit-nourishing 'central' wisdom of feeling, not the 'upper' wisdom of the head" (330), Baby Suggs/Sophia connects nourishment with language as well as with food. She is, in addition, one who in her inclusiveness brings the disparate and disjointed elements together into a unity. Sergei Bulgakov reminds us that Sophia "embodies the attributes of eros, of love, of binding together"; in her capacity as a mediator, Sophia "also restores the feminine element to creation and the divine. . . . Through her begins the process of resacralizing nature and the cosmos, of reconnecting humanity to God" (xviii). She embodies in her spiritual being "the Word of all words" as it is spoken: "This Word spoken constitutes part of the hypostatic life of the Logos. . . . The Logos comprises the ideal content of Sophia" (*Sophia*, 44–45).

Caitlin Matthews adds that Sophia is "both World-Soul and bride of the Logos" (*Sophia*, 296), who, though pursued, beaten, and ravaged, nonetheless takes all of the world into her. Her relation to matter, to language, and to the earth "shows us that ourselves [separate] from the Earth is a delusion" (323). Robert Sardello describes Sophia as a figure "who stands as the world soul, she through whom everything in the outer world has qualities of interiority. . . . She is ever faithful to the world's matter and works for renewal and regeneration of the material world" (*Facing the World with Soul*, 16).

Shamed and rejected nonetheless by the way the community treats her for creating a feast for them, which they believe is motivated by a "reckless generosity," Baby Suggs feels the fatigue as a consequence of fighting, loving, and giving unconditionally for over sixty years. But when she prepares to withdraw to her bed, wounded by their response and feeling defeated, Stamp Paid knows what valued presence the community will lose if Baby Suggs divorces herself from the Word. She has been chosen, he knows, to carry the Word to the people by witnessing its truth. He pleads with her as they walk in the street: "'Listen here, girl,' he told her, 'you can't quit the Word. It's given to you to speak. You can't quit the Word, I don't care what all happen to you'" (177).

Visibly shaken by her treatment at the hands of the people, she equivocates when Stamp Paid asks her if she is going to call the Word on Saturday in the clearing, a sacred place of worship that is their outdoor church, free of the jungle entanglements that the whites have created in them. She hesitates over his question, which perhaps sounds more like a command: "'If I call them and they come, what on earth I'm going to say?'" To which he responds: "'Say the Word!' He checked his shout too late. . . . Bending low he whispered into her ear, 'The Word. The Word.'" (178)

The Word is that of incarnation, of living joyously in the body as part of the incarnate word; Baby Suggs' calling is to incarnate the Word. She is able to give the Word flesh so that the Word matters and so that the people carry the Word in their memories to aid them in healing the suffering of their lives.

She is the converse of Beloved, who wants the words without body, even thinking aloud at one point: "All of us are trying to escape the body" (210). It is the body of Sethe that Beloved wishes to steal, a final violation of her mother's life. As the young nephews of the schoolteacher robbed Sethe of her physical nourishment, meant for her baby Denver, so is Beloved intent on robbing her of her emotional life in the form of her remembered narratives. The remembered narratives of the thirty women who recall the goodness of Baby Suggs will be like the grace that redeems Sethe from Beloved.

Baby Suggs' intimacy with the Word, moreover, extends back to when she rented 124 Bluestone Road before the murder. For a time it enjoyed the central place of commerce and communication, but it has now been pushed to the margins of society. The house was both a dwelling for the Word as well as a crossroads for communal language to be exchanged, passed on, and folded back. It is also the place close to the clearing where Baby Suggs would pray in the center with the community, looking on until they were called for.

Her observation to the people clothes her in the voice of both memory and imagination; together they are necessary for the reception of grace. They must desire grace for it to be present to them. The act of imagining big is an act of courage that shame deadens if it is allowed to rule. Shame has the uncanny power not only to beat back the past, but to beat down the future, making both not just *inaccessible* but *inexpressible*. Such is the powerful presence of shame to enslave the human spirit. It is Baby Suggs' calling to break this slavery.

Just as important, then, she also connects individuals back to their own bodies so that the Incarnate Word is literally realized. She gives them a way of seeing that part of themselves they have been taught by the whites to be ashamed of, to disown, and to alienate themselves from but which they may retrieve through *imagining it,* in much the same way Sethe can have a future only if she allows herself to imagine it, an action that terrifies her. Later we are offered an image that helps us to see the importance of this clearing space. It is the antithesis of another place, this one deep within the black people: "Whitepeople believed that whatever the manners, under every dark skin was a jungle" (198). It is an image that grows more dense and entangled the more

> colored people spent their strength trying to convince them how gentle they were, how clever and loving, how human. . . . But it wasn't the jungle blacks brought with them to this place from the other (livable) place. It was the jungle whitefolks planted in them. And it grew. It spread. In, through and after life, it spread, until it invaded the whites who had made it. Touched them every one. . . . Made them bloody. (198–99)

The suffocating space of the jungle deep within the black people needs the clearing of Baby Suggs to give them a space to believe and imagine within and to find a communal home that is theirs exclusively.

In the clearing and through her generous language, Baby Suggs connects the people back with their bodies; through her words they once again become incarnated and are able to disentangle themselves from the jungle image imposed in and on them by the whites.

> "Here," she said, "in this here place, we flesh; flesh that weeps, laughs; flesh that dances on bare feet in grass. Love it. . . . Love your hands! Love them. Raise them up and kiss them. . . . This is flesh I'm talking about here. Flesh that needs to be loved. Feet that need to rest and to dance; backs that need support. . . . And all your inside parts, . . . you got to love them. The dark, dark liver— love it, love it, and the beat and beating heart, love that too." (88)

All the images of scattered parts, shattered pieces of the home, of one's life, all congeal and coagulate here to form a unified body—an embodied wholeness through the force of Baby Suggs who, in her soulful presence gives the members back their bodies by asking them to re-member the Word. She reunites them to their own flesh through love; in this action the great epic wound of their ordeal as a people finds a salve that begins to heal their collective shame, for to be shamed is another form of being wounded and enslaved. She is the one, we recall, who stitches Sethe's dress, who anoints the whipped flesh on Sethe's back to heal it. Her action is one of pulling things back together. We might say Baby Suggs is the great "re-memberer" of the communal soul, She reorders it, in the same spirit in which Sixo's 30 mile woman does for him when he tells Paul D.: "'She gives pieces back to me all in the right order. She gather me, man'" (273). A gathering up is what the communal soul of the people requires. Without a communal act of remembrance, the dividing and devouring force of Beloved will grow more excessive and destructive, wounding even more deeply the vulnerable soul of the black race.

Moreover, Baby Suggs gives stories and people a sense of home; she unites place to narratives and bodies to place so that a communal order that takes root and grows emerges from a deeply shared set of memories lodged in the Word of Scripture. Her love, like that of Sethe's, is excessive, but with an essential difference. While Sethe's excessive misguided love of her children prompts in her a desire to destroy them because she is able to imagine their future that simply repeats her own suffering condition, Baby Suggs' excessive love of the community implants in them memories that will bear fruit in acts of generosity long after she is gone. While Sethe fights for years to "beat back the past" from seeping into the present, for the wounds resting there are too raw and open, Baby Suggs, Holy instills in her people memories of the Word that they may call upon when crises become overwhelming. As the former's memories are denied, the latter's memories are desired, even necessary.

Such a residual effect grows stronger in time. Memories of her after she is dead prompt strong and decisive action on the part of Stamp Paid and the larger community of thirty women. Remembering the image of Baby Suggs prompts the old man to knock on the door of 124 to check on its inhabitants. How different from Sethe's response when she slams the door with herself, Denver, and Beloved inside and proclaims: "'I don't have to remember nothing'" (182).

What Baby Suggs insists on from others are powerful acts of generosity and love that individuals must achieve in themselves and in one another if the cruelty and inhumanity of the slave traders and slaveholders—indeed if the world's suffering—are to be vanquished. As carrier and witness of the sacred text, Baby Suggs offers an image of redemption through remembrance. Lynda Sexson, writing about sacred texts, makes the trenchant insight that the "Sacred text is the palpable imprint of the divine, which can be traced over again, renewed and reimagined. . . . A sacred text is a means of divining one's inner self and one's relationship to the world of meaning.

A sacred text reveals to us our own identity" (29). Saying the Word to the community, a gift she has that Stamp Paid forbids her to abdicate, constitutes her salvific force in the community. And this presence remembered is the only forceful and effective antibody to the isolating, destructive presence of what Paul D. senses in Beloved is "a no good thing" (216).

Given this alliance of Baby Suggs to the sacred texts, I find it interesting that much criticism on *Beloved* is quick to repeat the epigram at the beginning of the novel, "Sixty Million and more," which Morrison believes conservatively is the number of slaves who perished in the Middle Passage. But the Scriptural passage that follows it is often overlooked, and with it, any connection to the theme I have been developing: the Word's relation to the flesh, or language to incarnation. It bears some study.

The passage reads: "I will call them my people, which were not my people; and her beloved, which was not beloved" (Romans 9:25). This sacred text is in some ways a response to the first epigram because it suggests an all-inclusive quality of God's mercy; *all* are elected, not just a select people or tribe. Moreover, Romans 9 focuses sharply on several crucial elements in the novel, namely, the flesh, the word "Beloved," as well as the word of God in the form of a promise of redemption to His people. More important, in reading what immediately precedes the scriptural quotation, one notices that St. Paul is actually quoting from the Old Testament Book of Hosea. I believe it is important that Paul *is remembering* a text of the Old Testament as he writes within the New Testament, thereby giving his words in Romans a resonance through a context within another sacred text.

Such a scriptural exchange between Old and New Testaments is important for the way *Beloved* itself unfolds—in memory; perhaps stated better, it is the way the characters eventually provide for themselves a context in the present through a remembrance of past stories, much as St. Paul is negotiating here between the two books of the Bible. We are then invited to link St. Paul to Paul D. in that both contain a sense of blessedness that allows them to move within and between their respective communities to offer solace and love to those in need of spiritual support.

And what is the central idea of Hosea, a short book in the Old Testament of some fourteen brief chapters? It concerns itself primarily with the sins and infidelity of a people, Israel, the punishment of God, and his promise to bind back his people: "Come, let us return to the Lord,/for it is he who has torn, and he will/heal us;/he has struck down, *and he will/bind us up,*/After two days he will revive us" (Hosea 6:1–2, my emphasis).

The message of the harsh world of the Old Testament is that God will be compassionate despite Israel's ingratitude; Paul in Romans takes up the same theme and also promises inclusion in God's love. I believe Baby Suggs, Holy, is the vehicle for this unconditional generosity and love, a human figure doing the same binding as the people in Hosea anticipate. She is abandoned by her people for so believing. Language, more specifically the Word uttered and then remembered, is the thread that stitches together the community, especially that of the thirty women. And they in their number have an affinity with Sixo's 30 mile woman who "gather me, man. The pieces I am, she gather them and give them back to me in all the right order" (272–73). This latter description of Sixo's woman might be an appropriate profile of Baby Suggs' influence on her people.

The moment quickly arrives at the novel's conclusion when the people have an opportunity to redeem themselves with Baby Suggs by coming to the rescue of Sethe and Denver. In fact, as Denver teeters on the porch of 124 in an attempt to muster the courage to enter the world's community in order to save her mother, it is the voice and spirit of Baby Suggs that returns to her imagination and with whom she converses: "Remembering those conversations and her grandmother's last and final words: Baby Suggs' voice admonishes her to make the leap without any defenses, simply to accept that fact and move: "Know it, and go on out the yard. Go on" (244).

The voice of Baby Suggs remembered, with its companion images of stitching together, gathering up, re-membering, all through language and image, word and flesh, Word and Incarnation, comprise a persuasive redeeming force that rescues all who participate in it. Denver, with the help of her grandmother's words, launches herself into the public clearing and discovers there a generosity and assistance that astonishes her. It is the power of rememory of this gracious and generous carrier of the sacred word that breaks up 124 Bluestone Road and frees Sethe to allow her own story, perhaps truly the best part of her, to rest against Paul D's. His goal is to weave their stories together: "He wants to put his story next to hers" (273), so that the word expands into story; words gathered together and stitched up like a quilt create a story; it is their storied memories of Baby Suggs that bring grace to 124 Bluestone Road in a plot that, while moving inexorably toward a tragic ending, is deflected, saved, and redeemed in the spirit of a comic and communal impulse. In this sense, the novel is not "more about Beloved than Sethe," as Barbara Ann Schapiro believes (142); it is about the individual or communal act of laying on hands in a gesture of love and generosity, beyond guilt, beyond shame, and beyond injustice. And it is more than about a "free autonomous self . . . rooted in relationship" (143). The large mythic movement in the novel is toward a communal sense of generosity in which the words of Father Zosima in *The Brothers Karamazov* come to haunt all of our lives: "Each is responsible for all."

With the inauguration of her place in the world as a woman with the one word, "'baby'" (248) uttered by Lady Jones, Denver launches her own narrative into the community. It begins, through Denver, to return the largesse of Baby Suggs as they remember her and the benevolent place of Bluestone Road when she lived there. As they walk toward 124 and look into its yard, they step into a powerful rememory: "they remembered the party with twelve turkeys and tubs of strawberry smash. . . . Maybe they were sorry for the years of their own disdain" (249), or perhaps they were ready to let go of meanness when another in trouble needed help. They are now ready to accept Sethe and 124 back into their midst, to stitch her back into the fabric of the community as whole cloth, or to add her to the quilted fabric of them all. The stitch is the scar that remembers the wound of separation but "goes on."

But not before gathering together, in the memory of Baby Suggs, and with Denver carrying on the name of this holy woman through Lady Jones' inaugural renaming of her. The name of Baby Suggs once again assumes flesh and dwells in the world. Is this not the antithesis of the one word, "Beloved," that through her sexual payment the stonecutter scars into the pink granite headstone? The thirty women are now prepared to exorcise whatever demon is holding Sethe in check and smothering her life: "The bigger Beloved got, the smaller Sethe became. . . . She sat in the chair licking her lips like a chastised child while Beloved ate up her life, took it, swelled up with it, grew taller on it" (250). And this exorcism is not about them, as Trudier Harris suggests when she writes that "exorcising the demonic part of the self so that all women are not judged to be demons—that is what the women are about in getting Beloved to leave" (164). They have, rather, gone beyond a preoccupation with themselves, with their own shame, and have joined in the spirit of imagining grace, which is gained through sacrificing for another, a spirit that the rememory of Baby Suggs instilled in them. Theirs is a larger vision of largesse than Harris would allow.

Beloved in turn is intent on retribution until Sethe herself dies. She is like a devouring Greek Fury, demanding an eye for an eye, a life for a life, and a story gained for a story denied. Such a standoff is the mark of tragic action, for neither opponent is willing to yield or to release one's grip from such a rigid position: "It was as though Sethe didn't really want forgiveness given; she wanted it refused. And Beloved helped her out" (252). Their trajectory thus heads inexorably toward a tragic end.

Yet within this community which remembers the generosity of Baby Suggs, Sethe is not destined to die while they have their recollections of good and wholesome images of the house at 124 Bluestone. As Baby Suggs nourished in abundance the entire community, both their souls with the Word and their bodies with the feast, through the power of these remembered images the women are called to action.

Janey Wagon's response to Denver's pleas for assistance is typical of the women who gather to help Sethe even as they re-memory Baby Suggs:

"'You know what? I've been here since I was fourteen, and I remember like yesterday when Baby Suggs, Holy, came here and sat right there where you are'" (253). Their help, however, exacts a price from Denver. She must first relate her story of the events taking place in her home. And when the women gather and march on 124, the first sight they see is the rememory of themselves as young women:

> Younger, stronger, even as little girls lying in the grass asleep. Catfish was popping grease in the pan and they saw themselves scoop German potato salad onto the plate. . . . Baby Suggs laughed and skipped among them, urging more. . . . But there they were, young and happy, playing in Baby Suggs' yard, not feeling the envy that surfaced the next day. (258)

Communally, they walk right into the thicket of rememories that give them new energy and a renewed purpose.

From here, led by the abused Ella, the women collectively move farther back in time, through a kind of memorial aperture of happy youths eating and dancing, to the beginning, to a place "where there were no words. In the beginning was the sound, and they all knew what that sound sounded like" (259).[6] That sound represents a primordial state necessary to confront "the devil-child" Beloved, herself an image of aboriginal retribution who rustles from slumber in the underworld to demand a vengeful payment from Sethe for her infanticide. At this moment in the novel the action has returned to the origins of time, to a place where sound was expressed prior to words; here an originary sense of justice is poised once again to be enacted mythically.

Only after Ella is able to subdue Sethe when she attacks Mr. Bodwin, who has come to pick up Denver for work, and certain in Sethe's own mind that he is the schoolteacher once again coming on to her property to claim her children, can the community give the events a comic twist through remembering them and speaking them publicly. Stamp Paid and Paul D. begin to joke about the incidents, shortly after which they are able to imagine them within the terrain of comedy: "As the scene neither one had witnessed took shape before them, its seriousness and its embarrassment made them shake with laughter" (265). Because they can imagine it as a comic and not a tragic event—though the tragic possibility always hovered around the lip of the action of Sethe's attempted murder of Bodwin, the language they are able to give it lessens its importance and, by extension, the power of Beloved herself.

Baby Suggs' memory and her words to her people finally gather them all back up into a communal whole to save Sethe and to rid the town of a force that could potentially enslave them all. Baby Suggs is like an icon for her people, whose prototype is Christ/Sophia, the Incarnate Word. She is the emblem of forgiveness, grace, generosity, and healing. Furthermore, she is witness to both the Word and the flesh, the two attributes that can stitch people together, "bind them up," as Hosea relates, and offer, through remembered images of generosity, an image of completeness that prompts the action of grace toward others. Baby Suggs' occupation of stitching shoes gives her action a mythic quality in its binding the feet of her people.

The word "Beloved" might be better written, "Be loved," shifting it from a noun to a verb. As such, Beloved is the word that makes sense only when it is coupled with the word used to describe Paul D., "blessed," and Baby Suggs, "Holy." Left to itself, it is best not remembered. Through their presences is Sethe freed from the deeper slavery of her own shame and guilt. Real freedom is to love "thick" (164), to love anyone as much as one wished. Such is the promise of the Christian mystery, of the Incarnate Word as a way of understanding and accepting life's deepest wounds.

11

Concluding Reflections

A fly wounds the water.
—Jane Kenyon,
"The Pond at Dusk," 73

No one way of speaking about the body, wounded or otherwise, can hope to include even a large measure of its complexity. What I have used is a framework, a frame of reference as a way of imagining the body wounded, marked, initiated, and how this wounding speaks outwardly to culture and inwardly into the psyche. I leave it to the reader to consider writing the prequel to this book. Entitle it something like: *The Unwounded Body: Disowning the Markings of Flesh*. For the body marked is one expression of incarnation. Wounds are both literal and analogical; the chapters of this study interrogated, however incompletely, the phenomenology of these analogies with an eye to the archetypal nature of body inscriptions in various forms.

In completing this study, I step back and gaze at the scaffold, the frame in which it took place, and see its shortcomings, its own blemishes. I take solace in Emerson's forgiving language of "The Over-Soul": "How dear, how soothing to man, arises the idea of God, peopling the lonely place, effacing the scars of our mistakes and disappointments!" (589).

Certainly some outside presence or force is needed for all of us to forgive the wounds and the wounding we do in the world.

Each work I read on the body was driven by a particular *mythos* as well as by a poetic sense of the body marked. What I have learned in the process is that in every book I read, as well as in this one I wrote, the theory used to guide the study was itself wounded; growing from wounded lives, both personal and collective. Freud reminded us that our theories are our myths; I would append his observation by asserting that our theories also carry our wounds. The nature of the wound may vary, but one thing they have in common is the recognition that no theorist, psychologist, philosopher, theologian, critic has a complete or unsullied purchase on the meaning of embodiment, scarred or unblemished.

My understanding of all theory through which we assert our own vision of a human order is embodied in large measure in D. H. Lawrence's felt sense of life: "I am ill because of wounds to the soul, to the deep emotional self and the wounds to the soul take a long, long time, only time can help" ("Healing," 113).

How these wounds are embodied is what the creative works under discussion here have shown us. I believe the artist takes us further under the skin of scars and returns us to the original experience. Lawrence addresses in the lines above the wounds to the soul, of which our bodies are pale simulacra, expressions of the soul's design, and a mimesis of our marks in the world.

The condition of embodiment situates us in space and time in a daily struggle for meaning, so that our wounds are worthwhile, suffered in a context that allows us not to reject them or wish them away, but actually to embrace them as opportunities. Our great challenge, it seems, is not to rush to heal all of the violences done to us, or to talk away those we have committed, but to bear our markings with a generous grace so that we may, through them, aid others, if only through recognizing the imperfect lives in need of forgiveness. While our wounds may separate us out and highlight our individual story, these same knotty narratives may also initialize us into a larger communal field. They allow us to be part of a communitas, retaining our individuated being, as Victor Turner suggests, while intertwining our lives with others (*Dramas, Fields, Metaphors*, 237). Our wounds can be a pathway to "open and unspecialized realms, to a spring of pure possibility" (239). Our blemishes, diseases, wounds, scarrings all mark our pilgrimage through this life and, for those who accept it, from this life to the next.

The wounds that find us or that we inflict on the world, even in the verbal "*vowels of affliction*" (qtd. in Nye, 5) that Denise Levertov suggests is an attempt not to feel ourselves by wounding others through speech, eventually return to find us out. Our wounds point to or remind us what we can so easily disremember: that our lives are always unfinished, in need of repair, imperfect, and will remain so. Our wounds are deep memories in time; they find our being in its psychosomatic unity and reveal our vulnerable underside. They pierce through our armor of immortality and remind us constantly of death.

This study of wounded bodies has offered, I hope, some apertures, several fissures in psyche and soma, a few ways into imagining our markings that transport us finally into the mysteries of being itself. I have seen more fully how wounds are full of wonder; they can inspire awe in anyone who gazes on them for they open the imagination into unique corridors of seeing how beautifully imperfect is being human; they also reveal to us how wounded is the world around us, the earth herself as she is violated by the indifference of commerce. Like the white whale, she has the capacity, if pursued too obsessively for her treasures, to breach suddenly in front of our bow to exact a revenge that becomes more warranted with time.

My one abiding hope is that something in this discussion helps you, reader, the next time your journey takes you across a cracked sidewalk or close to a building with deep fractures on the side facing the sun. I end this study with my own remembrance of a former student.

When the Wound Itself Wonders

How is it that the disease
Thinks it has the right to spread, like
When it was just yesterday
I began to feel my life as a
Wrap-around.
A wrap-around life,
like a saran wrap
even a serene rap,
One that makes me feel all the
Knuckles at once—

"In disease is divinity."
Really?
Then let us cure this curse with
a sacred syrup, an oily liquid that
tells the affliction:

"Game called because of Darkness."

In Memory of Carolyn Eide

Notes

1. INTRODUCTION

1. Robert Romanyshyn has had a forceful influence on my work on the body. I have followed his thought for the past twenty years and owe him a debt of gratitude. He has been my Virgil, a faithful guide on the slippery slopes of body phenomenology.

2. While not disparaging these approaches, I find that more often than not they do not trust the imagination of the work, but prefer instead to launch a diatribe *through the work* that very quickly leaves the figures in the literature stranded, abandoned, and unable to speak for themselves. Often they are fundamentally disrespected as autonomous figures in need of their own voice. I have found occasional insights in Jane Gallop's *Thinking Through the Body* (11–20). Sidonie Smith offers a specialized and relevant study of autobiography that brings together writing and the body (*Subjectivity, Identity, and the Body: Women's Autobiographical Practices in the Twentieth Century* [1993]), and a little earlier *The Michigan Quarterly Review* published two consecutive volumes on *The Female Body* (Fall 1990 and Winter 1991) which offer a fine range of essays on the body social and political. Body books become increasingly more specialized, as, for example, Robert R. Desjarlais' *Body and Emotion: The Aesthetics of Illness and Healing in the Nepal Himalayas* (1992) and Linda Lomperis and Sarah Stanbury's (eds.) *Feminist Approaches to the Body in Medieval Literature* (1993). *Troubled Bodies: Critical Perspectives on Postmodernism, Medical Ethics, and the Body* (ed. Paul A. Komesaroff) is one of a growing number of studies on the medicalization of the flesh. Also of interest for my study are Clinton R. Sanders' *Customizing the Body: The Art and Culture of Tattooing* (1989), and Marilee Strong's *A Bright Red Scream: Self-Mutilation and The Language of Pain* (1998). Other studies have appeared that are more interested in the body in a wider cultural and phenomenological, if not archetypal, field.

241

Two particularly useful books for anyone studying human embodiment are the three-volume *Fragments for a History of the Human Body* (1989), edited by Michel Feher with Ramona Naddaff and Nadia Taze, and the more recent excellent compendium of body parts and their mythic and cultural significance in a wide range of cultures, George Elder's *The Body: An Encyclopedia of Archetypal Symbolism* (1996). Of course today the number of body books, both specialized and general, virtually pour off commercial and university presses. There exists no end of fascination with our own incarnational reality.

3. Pulling together the body and mythology, J. Nigro Sansonese's study, following on the work of Carl Jung and Joseph Campbell, convincingly argues that myths are biologically rooted; the body is the primary genesis of myths and mythic imaginings. The body is mythic in its physiology and in its psychology, something that the poet intuitively understands and gives expression to (*The Body of Myth: Mythology, Shamanic Trance, and the Sacred Geography of the Body* [1994]). I would here underscore the important work of Marija Gimbutas, who has shown through archeological discoveries and her own readings of these findings how earlier peoples "created a deity who was a macrocosmic extension of a woman's body" (*Language of the Goddess,* xxii) and how the earliest symbology grew directly out of the female body primarily and initially.

4. In *The Soul's Code: In Search of Character and Calling,* James Hillman advances the idea that each of us "enters the world called. The idea comes from Plato, specifically his Myth of Er" (9) and develops the idea of a daimon who guides us here. "The Platonic myth of growing down . . . says the soul descends in four modes—via the body, the parents, place, and circumstances" (62). This first element, the body, suggests that the wounds we receive are absolutely necessary to fulfill the calling in our lives. The body that is marked or wounded or the wounding one does to other bodies, while not condoned, is tied mysteriously and inextricably to one's destiny and, because of our origins, to divinity, to the numinous part that is essential to our full being. Every body wound is a mark of memory and a sign of one's destiny.

5. Although he does not treat the body from any literary framework, nonetheless Anthony Synnott's *The Body Social,* especially Chapter 9, "Bodies and Senses" (228–64), offers a very thorough and helpful survey of key books on body studies over the past thirty years. His chapter nicely outlines three approaches: phenomenological, structural, and poststructural angles on body meanings.

6. Edward S. Casey makes the interesting assertion that when the body came to mean the hard physical body of anatomy, place was transformed into space: "as body came to designate the hard physical body of *res extensa,* so *place* came to mean a mere segment of infinite space" (*Getting Back into Place,* 45–46).

7. For further study of the relation between the body and place, especially in light of the city, see Peter Brown's "Body and City" (5–32) in *The Body and Society* (1988); also Richard Sennett's *Flesh and Stone: The Body and the City in Western Civilization* (1994), especially "The Suffering Body" (82–86) and "Modern Arteries and Veins" (324–37); also, Morris Berman's *Coming to Our Senses: Body and Spirit in the Hidden History of the West* (1990), especially "The Gesture of Balance" (297–318); and Bryan S. Turner's *The Body and Society: Explorations in Social Theory* (1988), especially "Disease and Disorder" (204–26).

8. Some form of wounding seems to be part of any major epic action. Louise Cowan, writing eloquently of the qualities of epic, believes that its function is one of "*cosmopoesis*, its making of a cosmos wherein the other genres find their place. . . . A cosmos is a self-enclosed state of order which must be intuited" (10). She goes on to make an observation that bears on the wounding quality discussed above: "A primary feature of the epic cosmos is its penetration of the veil separating material and immaterial existence, allowing an intimate relation between gods and men and a resultant metaphysical extension of space" (11). My own sense is that this penetration comes about through a wound, an opening, a break in the fabric of being that allows one to step through, even in imagination, to discern another sense of being.

2. NATURE AND NARRATIVES

1. For an original treatment of how history, anatomy, culture, and the city have tight psychological connections, see Richard Sennett's recent book, *Flesh and Stone: The Body and the City in Western Civilization*. He studies six cities, from Periclean Athens to present-day New York.

2. Sansonese's book is very provocative in connecting myth and biology as well as in illustrating how in Homer's world the body "is both material and spiritual" (34) and that it is always speaking metaphorically, such that in Homer's lexicon, one would not say that Hector "was afraid" but rather, "his knees were loosened" (*Body of Myth*, 34).

3. Gaston Bachelard's *Fragments of a Poetics of Fire* is appropriate in this discussion of Odysseus. He writes convincingly that "real freedom comes through imagination" (6); one way to understand Odysseus' own lack of freedom to return home, if looked at imaginally, is that he is not yet sufficiently free from the enslavement of the appetites of war to return home. He needs time to develop into his own freedom, which he does through creating the images that populate his stories to the Phaecians. Relatedly, Bachelard writes that "a poetic image speaks to one if one accepts it as a psychologically privileged moment of exaltation, a transformation of one's Being through language" (12).

4. Glen Arbery has written with passion and finesse on this bodily aspect of *The Odyssey*, especially Odysseus' own appetite for fame that brings on his worst troubles. "Against the Belly of the Ram: The Comedy of Deception in *The Odyssey*."

5. I want to bring up the whole idea of the animal imagination later, but here animal presences seem to circumscribe both hunt and identity through stories of them.

6. Tom Absher rightly suggests that Odysseus' weeping in several places on the way home reveals "his efforts to recover from the petrification of war" and how much of his life "since leaving Troy has been reshaped by the sacred feminine" (*Men and Goddesses,* 34–35). This psychology of softening, of yielding to feelings, is in line with the texture of fabric that characterizes the nature of stories themselves. Stories have a capacity to wrap us in them.

7. Casey's section on "The Body in Place" (41–106) is a fine study of spatiality and identity. We can then think of the Odyssean body, in all its proprioceptive permutations, attempting to find place, origin, and identity as he journeys home. His scar brings him back home. See also Martin Heidegger's fine insights in his essay "Building, Dwelling, Thinking," in *Poetry, Language, Thought.*

8. Noel Cobb points out that for the Greeks, "the head was the beginning, the source of generation. The seed of life was in the head. The head was packed with seed, like a pomegranate. It was the seat of the soul; it contained psyche, which alone survived death, appearing as an *eidolon*, or image, in Hades" (*Archetypal Imagination,* 254). Jean Vernant refers to the word "sphincter," in Greek, meaning "seed of fire" (*Mortals and Immortals,* 57).

9. Sansonese illustrates how the name Menelaos derives from *mens* and *manas*, both of which mean *mind*. As Odysseus is breaking free of Calypso's island, Telemachos is being put in mind of the Trojan War and its difficult, often treacherous homecoming, by Menelaos, his most impassioned teacher.

10. No doubt Athena is the grand architect, great fabricator, and wily deceiver in this epic. But Hermes is her brother and therefore plays an integral role in the nature of storytelling itself. A trickster, he establishes fiction, and one's self as a fictional creation. Perhaps we could call him the patron saint of *poiesis* itself. Not only is he guide of psyche, but represented as a phallus with a head at the top, he is the power of the procreative seed, which is formed in the head and then moves downward to "the male testes through the cerebrospinal column" (Strathern, 47).

11. Lawlor goes on to note that "walls, doors, and other building forms are the means by which our thoughts are extended into the environment, the Word made architectural flesh" (12). Perhaps we could extend his fine insights on physical structure to include poetic structure, a dwelling with a different set of stories. See also Gaston Bachelard's classic work, *Poetics of Space,* for excellent reveries of space.

12. Roberts Avens gives a fine account of Hades and the bodies of the shades in his *Imaginal Body: Para-Jungian Reflections on Soul, Imagination and Death*. He is particularly insightful on Henri Corbin's idea of "the *mundus imaginalis*, a distinct field of imaginal realities" (215), which is analogous to the world of archetypes (*mundus archetypalis*). "The forms and figures of the imaginal realm subsist on an ontological plane" (215). His description here might typify the reality of Hades that Odysseus enters in order to converse with the imaginal bodies there.

13. I would mention here, without dwelling on it, the work of Depak Chopra on what he calls "organ memory," wherein transplant patients, say of a human heart, begin to have dreams that are the stories of the life of the donor, one whom they knew nothing about. Could Homer, then, have sensed this intimate relation, in an originary way, between the body's interiority and the interiority of our stories? Parmenides had suggested, according to Strathern, that "*nous*, or mind, was present in all the limbs of the body" (53). Odysseus's scar contains in a mindful way, therefore, the story of its original wounding.

14. I would point the reader to the vast array of words corresponding to different dimensions of embodiment that Vernant offers in his study. It is as if Homer is turning over the body's possibilities with as much frequency as Odysseus' stories turn over the possibilities or the variants of home to reveal the outside world through the body's interiority. Vernant, for example, offers *soma* as corpse; *demas* as individual stature, size, and build; *chros* as bodily members in their suppleness; *melea*, or limbs as bearers of force; and *kara*, the head, used metonymically for the entire body (*Mortals and Immortals*, 28–32). His study underscores how important the body was to the Greek imagination. Richard Onians' *Origins of European Thought*, which I cite from in this chapter, is the other crucial book for the study of the Greek and Roman anatomy in antiquity.

15. Eric Auerbach's seminal essay, "Odysseus' Scar," from his *Mimesis: Representations of Reality in Western Literature*, does not look deeply enough into this epic, or the texture of Odysseus' nature, or the subtlety of Homer as a poet. When he states that "in Homer everything is expressed, put on the outside" (25) and that "delight in physical existence is everything to them, and their highest aim is to make that delight perceptible to us" (28), he misses the invisible connection between scar and story, body and narrative, that I believe is subtly interwoven into the main action, indeed *may be* the main action. Norman Austin is more sophisticated and nuanced in his assessment of the classical poet when he claims that "in Homer's *Odyssey* landscape and mind seem almost coterminal: the changing landscape and the changeable mind mirror each other back and forth" (206). He further claims that Odysseus is the first hero "to glimpse that the most seductive of all romances is the journey of the mind outward into the world and then inward

into self" ("Odysseus/Ulysses," 207). See also the excellent essay by George Dimock, "The Name of Odysseus," for a subtle reading of both the narrative and the name of Odysseus and the divinities who guide him.

16. See her excellent discussion on storytelling (83–86) and Hermes' power. Also see William Doty's "Hermes Heteronymous Appellations" in *Facing the Gods*, 115–34. Also, Norman O. Brown's *Hermes the Thief: The Evolution of a Myth*, especially Chapter 3, "The Age of Homer." In *The Homeric Hymns* he is portrayed as a chronic troublemaker, always throwing the established order out of balance, causing strife by breaking boundaries, much like Odysseus himself.

17. R. Lopez-Pedraza's fine book, *Hermes and His Children* (1977), associates this god with a rumbling stomach and, following Onians, with sneezing. The rumbling stomach Jung associated in his seminar on dreams with Hermetic omens (40). So Hermes is not only with Odysseus here in his cursed stomach; Hermes also links father and son through the only sneeze in the entire epic, executed by Telemachos, which makes his mother laugh soundly through the halls of their home. Andrew Strathern writes that "sneezes, proceeding suddenly from the head, could be taken as prophetic, since they were a sign of disturbance, in the *psyche* within the head" (*Body Thoughts*, 47).

3. WANDERING WOUNDS AND MEANDERING WORDS

1. Sennett's study offers valuable historical, but not deeply psychological, information on the growth of the city in the West and its metaphorical equivalent in human embodiment that easily promotes further fruitful study of the body and tragedy.

2. A fine article on place, "Getting Placed: Soul in Space," by Edward S. Casey, suggests an intimate connection between "place-heart-memory: here is a genuine *mysterium coniunctionis*, which yields heart as the place of memory; memory as the place where heart is . . . heart as what is left of remembered place"(7). His essay opens up further insights into place and the body.

3. The entire Fall 1993 issue of *Parabola: The Magazine of Myth and Tradition* is devoted to the theme of "Crossroads" and offers in the various essays ways to deepen the possibilities contained in this critically important image of the play.

4. SPEAK DAGGERS BUT USE NONE

1. In a revealing article on Dionysus, Robb Pocklington observes that "Dionysus' mythical history of death, madness, and rebirth provides a template for all tragedy. . . . Viewed in this way, Hamlet, like Dionysus, begins his story of being thrown into a particular world and then denied his own

authenticity" (22–23). He does not, however, look at the movements of incarnation, murder, and chaos as part of Dionysus' presence, one who disrupts and then renews a world order.

2. Richard Sennett's recent study, *Flesh and Stone: The Body and the City in Western Civilization* (New York: Norton, 1995), pays particular attention to the polluted body of the Jews living in the ghettos of Venice. The Venetians, he notes, were haunted by "the impurities of indifference" (215) regarding the Jews, who were associated with prostitutes and the filthiness of money in usury.

3. Joanna Hubbs offers a wonderful study of the connection among mother, matter, and language in her study, *Mother Russia: The Feminine Myth in Russian Culture*. See especially her discussion of Mother Earth in Chapter 6.

4. An especially rich psychological reading of the ear, orality, and performance in *Hamlet* is offered by Patricia Berry in "Hamlet's Poisoned Ear." Her reading tracks the orality of language as the dominant motif of the play as well as locates the psychic nature of the original pollution.

5. A more modern version of this action is explored by Nathaniel Hawthorne in his short story, "The Birthmark." Here the scientist Aylmer seeks to create a perfect being by removing the tiny pigmy hand birthmark on the cheek of his new bride, Georgiana, and in the process of purification, kills her.

6. The French philosopher and phenomenologist Gaston Bachelard is well worth studying, especially his treatment of lived space. His work, *The Poetics of Space*, offers a rich and deep way of reading this and other scenes in *Hamlet*. See especially Chapter 9, "The Dialectics of Outside and Inside," 211–31.

5. ROUSSEAU'S *CONFESSIONS*

1. Here I would include the following works: Thomas Moore's *Care of the Soul: A Guide for Cultivating Depth and Sacredness in Everyday Life*; Carl Jung's *Memories, Dreams, Reflections; Aion: Researches into the Phenomenology of the Self*, volume 9, Part II of *The Collected Works of C. G. Jung*; James Hillman's *Healing Fiction* and *The Soul's Code: In Search of Character and Calling*; David Levin's *The Body's Recollection of Being: Phenomenological Psychology and the Deconstruction of Nihilism*; Robert Sardello's *Love and the Soul* and *Facing the World with Soul*, to name a few that bear directly on Rousseau's psychology. Rousseau continues a tradition that is passed on to the phenomenologist Maurice Merleau-Ponty as well as to an original explorer on the imagination of the natural elements, Gaston Bachelard.

2. An entire chapter could be written on the theory of the acorn brought forth beautifully in James Hillman's *The Soul's Code: In Search of Character and Calling* (1996). Rousseau's autobiography is an early and full reflection on how the capacity inherent in one soul can be found in the early maneuverings of desire in childhood. Hillman's book gives many pertinent examples of this genie in the bottle of our souls wanting out. See also Jung's discussion of the *daimon* or *daimonion* in his chapter, "The Self," in *Aion* (23–35).

3. I will say more later, but three books that should be mentioned here that deal with this tight intertwining of body and city are Richard Sennett's *Flesh and Stone: The Body and the City in Western Civilization* (Norton, 1994); Robert Romanyshyn's *Technology as Symptom and Dream* (Routledge, 1989); and David Abram's *The Spell of the Sensuous: Perception and Language in a More-Than-Human World* (Pantheon, 1996).

4. Peter Brooks' *Body Work: Objects of Desire in Modern Narrative* is very helpful in outlining the new body inaugurated by Rousseau. He observes that Rousseau's concern with the "aesthetics of embodiment—invents the modern body" (87). The terms of this newly minted body is what this chapter is most interested in exploring. See also Judith Butler's chapter, "Rewriting the Morphological Imaginary," in *Bodies That Matter* for a thorough discussion of Lacan, the body, and narcissism. She cites Lacan: "There is something originally, inaugurally, profoundly wounded in the human relation to the world" (72)—which refers back to the underlying pain one senses in Rousseau's autobiography.

5. I don't wish to mention this observation in the body of the work, but it does warrant a place here. In a *New Yorker* article on the British filmmaker, Mike Leigh, the discussion at one point focuses on the word "shame." Some scholars claim it has its roots in the Indo-European word for "cover." One psychoanalyst has "recently linked the word for camera," a protective chamber within which sensitive film can be exposed to light, to this same root. The author ties this insight into Leigh's films, whose own camera "seeks out and dissects those sensitive moments of humiliation and antagonism which are the byproducts of a class-ridden society" (52). The preoccupation with the eye, with ocularity in Rousseau's world, with the constant interplay of mirroring, reflection, transparency, and blocking of vision, opens *The Confessions* to a discussion of the camera eye, illustrating once again another quality of modern consciousness. "This Other England," *The New Yorker*, September 23, 1996, 50–54.

6. Much could be written on this passage and others in *The Confessions* involving smells, hygiene, and cleanliness, especially considering Corbin's work, *The Foul and the Fragrant: Odor and the French Imagination*, where issues of body smells became a dominant cultural concern in

making the flesh more antiseptic. See also Ivan Illich's *H2O and the Waters of Forgetfulness* for a discussion on body odors and waste.

7. Other "treatments" of Harvey and the city as metaphorical place of the body include Robert Romanyshyn's *Psychological Life: From Science to Metaphor* (107–13) and *Technology as Symptom and Dream* (136–38); Ivan Illich and Barry Sanders, *The Alphabetization of the Popular Mind*. Two other books on the body and culture are *The Body Imaged: The Human Form and Visual Culture Since the Renaissance*, ed. Kathleen Adler and Marcia Pointon, and *The Making of the Modern Body: Sensuality and Society in the Nineteenth Century*, ed. Catherine Gallagher and Thomas Laqueur. Also relevant to this section of the book is Thomas Laqueur's *Making Sex: Body and Gender from the Greeks to Freud* and James J. Lynch's *The Language of the Heart: The Human Body in Dialogue*. For a collection of classic essays on the body, see *The Philosophy of the Body: Rejections of Cartesian Dualism*, ed. Stuart F. Spicker. Also, the multivolume *Fragments for a History of the Human Body*.

8. Barbara Maria Stafford illustrates in her book how the eighteenth century opened the body's interiority to scrutiny not seen with such intensity before in history so that it gains a thick, metaphoric value in the process. She uses the term "metaphorology" to describe her book as an attempt "to open up horizons for new, significant, and egalitarian connections" (3), a process that I am attempting to add to in this discussion of the body and the sewer system. Joel Schwartz's study, *The Sexual Politics of Jean-Jacques Rousseau*, implicates the foul and the ideal in his chapter, "Sexual Dependence and the Individual." His thesis is that *The Confessions* underscores Rousseau's "propensity to imagine ideal societies" in order to "transcend his actual society . . . , to make him independent of society" (101). This move to purity and away from the polluted quality of everyday life is part of his autobiographical cleansing.

9. Eric Auerbach's important and enduring study, *Mimesis: Representations of Reality in Western Literature*, offers this psychological observation that apprehends *The Confessions* as a cultural artifact: "Rousseau helped to launch the awakening of a new sense of the individual merely through the revelation of his own unique individuality" (466); and later: "The Rousseauist movement and the great disillusionment it underwent was a prerequisite for the rise of the modern conception of reality" (467). Rousseau not only invented, with great elaboration, the modern sense of the self; he also constructed around it a reality that we continue to live out today.

10. For additional reading on the concept of cleanliness, see George Vigarello's *Concepts of Cleanliness: Changing Attitudes in France Since the Middle Ages* and Leonard Barkan's *Nature's Work of Art: The Human*

Body as Image of the World, as well as Dorinda Outram's *The Body and the French Revolution: Sex, Class and Political Culture.* See also L. J. Rather's fine study, *Mind and Body in Eighteenth-Century Medicine,* as well as Paul Schilder's *The Image and Appearance of the Human Body: Studies in the Constructive Energies of the Psyche.* Alfred Ziegler also offers an intriguing observation regarding this new fascination with cleanliness. He coins the term "morbism" to convey the idea that "the human species is by nature morbid and can escape its fate only in death" (64). He also connects its growth at this time with the dissolution of the idea of original sin, which resurfaces as "morbism, in medicine for instance in the notion of indigenous pathological tendencies "that include anxiety, depression, envy, grief and guilt feelings" ("Rousseauian Optimism," 64). On the body polluted and diseased and the acceleration of pollution in London and Paris during the eighteenth century, see Barbara Maria Stafford's excellent study quoted above, *Body Criticism,* especially Chapter 4, "Marking" (281–340). Her entire study exposes graphically the deep cultural pathologies of disease and a fascination with the morbid, the freakish, and the deformed in this society.

6. CORRUPTING CORPSE VERSUS REASONED ABSTRACTION

1. Some of the more noteworthy books on this subject include Robert Romanyshyn's *Technology as Symptom and Dream* (1989), and his earlier *Psychological Life: From Science to Metaphor* (1984), as well as Morris Berman's *The Reenchantment of the World* (1989); David Michael Levin's *The Body's Recollection of Being: Phenomenological Psychology and the Deconstruction of Nihilism* (1985); the issue entitled "The Body," *Parabola,* Fall 1985; *The Philosophy of the Body: Rejections of Cartesian Dualism* (1970); George Elder's *The Body: An Encyclopedia of Archetypal Symbolism* (1996).

2. Especially helpful books dealing with body imagery in literature include *The Making of the Modern Body: Sexuality and Society in the Nineteenth Century,* ed. Catherine Gallagher and Thomas Laqueur (1987); Merleau-Ponty's *Prose of the World* (1973); *Eroticism and the Body Politic,* ed. Lynn Hunt (1991); Jane Gallop's *Thinking Through the Body* (1988); James Hillman's *Healing Fiction* (1983); and Peter Brown's *The Body and Society: Men, Women, and Sexual Renunciation in Early Christianity* (1988).

3. I have dealt with this theme in two previous articles, the first influenced in part by Robert Louis Jackson's article on "The Peasant Marei."

The first is "Is Memory Metaphorical or Is Metaphor Memorial? Dostoevsky's 'The Peasant Marei,'" *Ambiguities in Literature and Film*, ed. Hans P. Braendlin (1988), 23–32; the second is "The Icon and the Spirit of Comedy in Dostoevsky's *The Possessed*," *The Terrain of Comedy*, ed. Louise Cowan (1984), 195–220.

4. Mikhail Bakhtin's *Problems of Dostoevsky's Poetics*, ed. and trans. Caryl Emerson (1984), and *Rabelais and His World*, trans. Helene Iswolsky (1984). In addition, see Bakhtin's remarks on the novel as genre and the body in "From Notes Made in 1970–71," in *Speech Genres and Other Late Essays*, trans. Vern W. McGee (1986), 133–58.

5. Obviously this topic is too complex to address here, but I want to make its importance known for the image that is guide for one's spiritual quest.

6. On this point David Levin cites Nietzsche, who believed the body even more mysterious and more astonishing than the soul. "Perhaps the entire evolution of the spirit is a question of the body; it is the history of the development of a higher body that emerges into our sensibility" (qtd. in *Body's Recollection of Being*, 36).

7. Here it might be well to mention a new idea in eighteenth-century France, namely, the power of odors to stir the affective memory in a search of "the memorable sign," as Rousseau put it. Alain Corbin writes of the belief that "a violent confrontation of the past and present was engendered by recognizing a particular odor" (*The Foul and the Fragrant: Odor and the French Social Imagination* (1986), 83.

8. "Evil and the Negation of the Body in Flannery O'Connor's 'Parker's Back.'" *The Flannery O'Connor Bulletin* 17 (1988): 69–79.

9. Morson pulls this idea of prosaics into the work of Tolstoy especially, in order to emphasize the messiness of human life.

10. I have tried to reveal in a discussion of "The Peasant Marei" how memory alone is insufficient for meaning. If memory is indeed metaphorical, then it is through metaphor that one can glimpse what is absent, what is not readily visible: "memory's metaphorical aspect allows a vision of the invisible" ("Is Memory Metaphorical?" 30).

11. "Mythical Implications of Father Zosima's Religious Teaching." *Slavic Review* 38, no. 2 (1979): 280. This decay-rebirth cycle also implicates the sense of the comic in that new life is always promised through decay. Especially helpful is Roger Anderson's "The Meaning of Carnival in *The Brothers Karamazov*," *Slavic and East European Journal* 23, no. 4 (1979): 458–78. Also relevant here is D. H. Lawrence's commentary on harvest in "The Grand Inquisitor," in *The Brothers Karamazov*, ed. Ralph Matlaw (1976), 829–36.

12. I would disagree here with Nathan Rosen's observation that the first miracle is Aleksi's bowing and kissing the earth after Zosima's death as the first response to the Grand Inquisitor ("Style and Structure in *The Brothers Karamazov*," 850). I would say the first response to the Grand Inquisitor is Zosima's odor of putrescence. It is a miracle out of the carnival tradition.

13. I like the discussion on "Decay and Rebirth" in Piero Camporesi's *Incorruptible Flesh*. He writes of how the corpse is still alive as it decomposes: "seed turned to foam, blood coagulating in the [body] which by increasing in volume becomes flesh, melts into pus . . . and dissolves the fine 'machinery of the body' into horror and stench, ferments flesh inside the tomb like wine in the bottle. . . . The process of putrefaction therefore grows and liquifies and reduces the human frame and makes it smell, for the smell is none other than a gross and hotly immoderate exhalation that overwhelms our spirit" (88).

14. The issue of the Russian Orthodox icon is vast. Those key works that treat the icon in a way that allows one to see its use in Dostoevsky's poetic imagination include Leonid Ouspensky's *Theology of the Icon* (1978); Leonid Ouspensky and Vladimir Lossky's *The Meaning of Icons* (1952); St. Theodore the Studite, *On the Holy Icons*, trans. Catharine Roth (1981); and Peter C. Phan, *Culture and Eschatology: The Iconographical Vision of Paul Evdokimov* (1985).

15. As Scripture proclaims the words of the divine image, so the icon is an image of the divine word (Ouspensky, *Theology of the Icon*, 134). The icon is a crucial image of embodiment for it shows the inextricable connection between flesh and word, image and Scripture, a union that abstraction seeks to foil.

16. *BK*, 248. I would challenge the rigid reading of Mark Kanzer, who would have the odor of decay trigger cannibalistic drives: "The disgust aroused is familiar to analysts as a defense against the desire for oral incorporation; in this light, the unspecified excitement with which the followers were filled must be interpreted in relation to the cannibalistic phantasies which follow upon the death of the father and play such an important part in shaping the mourning process that ensues." "A Psychological View of Alyosha's Reaction to Father Zosima's Death," in *The Brothers Karamazov and the Critics*, ed. Edward Wasiolek (1967), 103–7. When the spiritual dimension of Dostoevsky's work is circumvented, then psychoanalysis seems to want to rush in to fill the void.

17. I believe this break with tradition is meant to shatter the complacency of a faithful who have begun to expect miracle too facilely, another example of the impulse to idolatry. I owe credit to Edward Wasiolek's essay, "*The Brothers Karamazov*: Idea and Technique," 118–44.

18. Rene Girard's discussion of "Sacrificial Substitution" is important for recognizing Zosima's uniting two realms in his death. Girard writes that "the surrogate victim dies so that the entire community, threatened by the same fate, can be reborn in a new or renewed cultural order. . . . Understanding this process, we can also understand why death should be regarded as the elder sister, not to say the mother and ultimate source, of life itself." *Violence and the Sacred*, trans. Patrick Gregory (1972), 255.

19. Paul Evdokimov's observation is relevant here: "Only true eschatologism will be able to discover all the value of history because it looks at it from the viewpoint of the 'telos,' the perfected. It is not a Buddhist flight from the world; rather the whole Christian paradox lies in the fact that the Kingdom of God is accessible only through the chaos of the world." qtd. in *Culture and Eschatology*, 61.

20. I borrow this term, as well as the general idea of "idol," from one of the most comprehensive studies of the term, Owen Barfield's *Saving the Appearances: A Study in Idolatry* (1962).

21. Ferapont may also be Dostoevsky's representative of thought held by the heretical Cathars in the twelfth century, who believed food evil, body decay disgusting, putrefaction as the devil's work. As Carolyn Bynum writes, the twelfth century was obsessed with decay. "Heretics (say the orthodox) think the body is filth. They equate fertility with decay . . . ; they deny that body is self" (219), hence their abhorrence as well with food and with the organic life of the flesh. True miracles of the body expressed triumph over decay (*Resurrection of the Body*).

22. Gibson addresses the all-inclusiveness of Dostoevsky's vision: "He developed almost a fixation on the 'Vsechelovek,' the 'all-man' who can encompass the whole of human experience, discrepancies included" (*Religion of Dostoevsky*, 33).

23. Robert Romanyshyn has accurately assessed this distancing of the body from the world, an amputation that began in the fifteenth century with the discovery of linear perspective vision among Italian painters and codified with Alberti's *De Pictura*. Romanyshyn writes that in "breaking the bond of gravity we have broken more than a physical restraint. We have broken the spiritual condition of humanity" (*Technology as Symptom and Dream*, 5). His argument implicates the heart of the split in Dostoevsky's vision.

7. THE WHITE WHALE AND THE AFFLICTED BODY OF MYTH

1. Two of the most original discussions on the cultural and linguistic dimensions of *Huckleberry Finn* are Toni Morrison's *Playing in the Dark: Whiteness and the Literary Imagination* and Ivan Illich and Barry Sanders' *The Alphabetization of the Popular Mind*.

2. Donald M. Lowe, *History of Bourgeois Perception*; Peter Gay, *The Bourgeois Experience: Victoria to Freud*: vol. 1, *Education of the Senses*; Peter Brooks, *Reading for the Plot: Design and Intention in Narrative*.

3. Only because Melville puns throughout the text do I wish to suggest the double meaning here of both weaving and foreboding. Both implicate the future intricate network of the narrative lines of story.

4. Thomas Moore's excellent treatment of this shift is found in his influential *Care of the Soul*, especially 267–72.

5. Sharon Cameron's *The Corporeal Self: Allegories of the Body in Melville and Hawthorne* is immensely helpful, especially her reading of Ahab. Her interpretation is, however, too narrow in that she limits her discussion to the "self," as if the notion of soul were not even present in the novel.

6. Girard offers a way of understanding Ahab's vengeance as perhaps an attempt to be beyond desire. "The demystifier constructs on top of all the death myths the greatest myth of all; his own detachment, to be completely autonomous—to be beyond desire." *Deceit, Desire and the Novel: Self and Other in Literary Structure*. It is my reading of Ahab that he wishes to suffer no desire by abandoning his body, and with it his narrative history. But as an embodiment of literate ego consciousness that abhors mystery, Ahab is trapped in his despotism. See also Robert Romanyshyn's excellent essay, "The Despotic Eye and Its Shadow: Media Image in the Age of Literacy," in *The Hegemony of Vision*, ed. David Levin.

7. In writing of "the dark other," and the African especially in the imagination of white American writers, Toni Morrison believes that this "other" became the means of thinking about body, mind, chaos, kindness, and love, always with the backdrop of the alien, dark outsider. (*Playing in the Dark: Whiteness and the Literary Imagination*, 51). See also Paul Brotkorb's chapter on "The Body," 42–50, *Ishmael's White World: A Phenomenological Reading of Moby-Dick*.

8. Brooks credits Rousseau as the first writer to consciously recognize the body as problematic in that no common ground of understanding corporeality existed after the eighteenth century. "Marking Out The Modern Body," 54ff., *Body Work: Objects of Desire in Modern Narrative*.

9. In fact, whiteness, the white culture, according to Toni Morrison, cannot fully understand terms like freedom, power, and assertiveness without "being shaped by the racial other." *Playing in the Dark*, 46. Morrison's observations on racial interfacing offers another angle on why Ishmael needs the presence of Queequeg if he is to effectively define his own being in relation to Ahab and to the world generally.

10. Bainard Cowan's work on Cetology has prompted my own thinking on this same dance between the presence of language and the absence of

the body. "From Cenotaph to Sea: The Turn." (*Exiled Waters: Moby-Dick and the Crisis of Allegory*, 60–89). In addition, Elizabeth Renker's chapter, "Fear of Faces: From *Moby-Dick* to *Pierre*," explores in depth Ahab's exasperation and outrage over those things that are "bodiless" and "the 'phantom' status of the white page" (48).

11. D. H. Lawrence intuits this understanding of the flesh when he calls Moby-Dick "the deepest blood-being of the white race; he is our deepest blood-nature. . . . We want to hunt him down, to subject him to our will . . . our blood self subjected to our will" (*Studies in Classical American Literature*, 160). The force of Ahab as intellection, "heady will," is an impotent witness to the force of the world's body that is the corpus of the white whale. Lynda Sexson writes that "memory, or story, is the dressing up of the invisible, masquerading of the ineffable" (*Ordinarily Sacred*, 53).

12. Russell Lockhart has likened Melville's novel to "an alchemical oven" wherein our souls are made to desire deeper imaginings when the normal answers for our collective psyche are no longer adequate. "What Whale Does America Pursue?" *Words as Eggs: Psyche in Language and Clinic*, 79–84.

13. Lynda Sexson reminds us in her study that "the consequence of memory's gift is the knowledge of death. . . . The past throws up a mirror before our own forgetting which we call death" (*Ordinarily Sacred*, 54). This reminder of death is part of the legacy of the whale journey that hovers throughout the action of whaling and writing.

14. Merleau-Ponty has written that "the world is made of the same stuff as the body . . . and vision happens among or is caught in, things." He goes on to observe that "the soul has its own knowing; it thinks with reference to the body, not with reference to itself" ("Eye and Mind," 163, 176, *Primacy of Perception*). Such activity of the soul is what Queequeg's presence offers to Ishmael.

15. I borrow this term, "abandoned body," from Robert Romanyshyn, who discusses its implications in relation to technology in his highly original cultural study, *Technology as Symptom and Dream*. See especially Chapter 5, "The Abandoned Body and Its Shadows."

16. Peter Brooks connects his thesis here to the growth of the private realm. *Body Work*, 54ff. See also Lowe's *History of Bourgeois Perception*, 85–109.

17. Drew Leder's study offers fresh insights into ways of understanding the body, especially in its absence. See Chapter 4, "The Immaterial Body." *The Absent Body*.

18. Sharon Cameron's insights into Ahab in his conversation with the carpenter are very perceptive. She writes that Ahab's great question is: Can

things be embodied? He grapples with the flesh's inability to define identity in any substantive or satisfying way (*Corporeal Self*, 61).

19. Cameron writes perceptively of Ahab in observing that there exists a discrepancy "between Ahab's desire to *have* palpable embodiments of things and, when they are present, his finding of them inadequate" (*Corporeal Self*, 61). Furthermore, in speaking of a "literate consciousness" that seems to me very applicable to Ahab, Robert Romanyshyn suggests that linearity, part of an absolute literate consciousness, has as its impulse to destroy *matter* and with it, mystery. And Charles Olson believes Ahab to be a conjurer in the tradition of Faust, who invokes his own evil world (*Call Me Ishmael*, 53).

20. I have written about the liquid quality of language and the writing of Ishmael in "Watery Worlds/Watery Words: Ishmael's Write of Passage in *Moby-Dick*," 62–66.

21. Toni Morrison acknowledges the place of the outsider in American literature when she writes: "As for the culture, the imaginative and historical terrain upon which early American writers journeyed is in large measure shaped by the presence of the racial other" (*Playing in the Dark*, 46). Russell Lockhart cites Edinger's study, *Melville's Moby-Dick: A Jungian Commentary*, in which *Moby-Dick* is referred to as America's alchemical oven ("What Whale Does America Pursue?" in *Words as Eggs*).

22. In a very similar fashion, and one which links Ishmael to Ahab as father and son, is this sense of alienation from community. As the hunt for the white whale draws closer, Ahab, according to Cameron, loses his sense of analogies as he becomes a more complete victim of his own ideas. (*Corporeal Self*, 53).

23. The text focuses often on the wrinkled or protruding foreheads of three figures in the novel: Queequeg, Ahab, and the white whale. Perhaps one could argue for three forms of knowing with this trinity: Queequeg as mythic or imaginative knowing; Ahab as technical knowing, and the white whale as the wisdom of nature herself.

24. Two works that amplify this notion of violence and regeneration as Ahab embodies his desire to destroy are Rene Girard's *Violence and the Sacred*, and Richard Slotkin's *Regeneration Through Violence: The Mythology of the American Frontier, 1600–1860*. Slotkin writes that "In American mythogenesis, the founding fathers . . . were those who . . . tore violently a nation from the implacable and opulent wilderness" (4), beginning a legacy that I believe Ahab is a stark inheritor of.

25. John Conger writes of the shadow body and suggests that "all the gods are in our body; the body is a cosmion" ("The Body as Shadow," *Meeting the Shadow*, 84). Queequeg is the fullest expression of this cosmic body in that he is most manifestly a full mythic presence.

26. Morrison's interpretation of Melville is that he "uses allegorical formations—the white whale, the racially mixed crew, . . . the white male captain who confronts impenetrable whiteness—to investigate and analyze hierarchic difference" (*Playing in the Dark*, 68–69).

27. See John Conger's argument that while our bodies are the deep friend of our soul, yet body awareness and spiritual awakening have had an unnatural separation in the West (*Jung and Reich*, 189). I believe that language, the act of writing, is in Ishmael's imagination, through Queequeg's influence, the path back to a unity of body-soul by retracing history and the *Pequod*'s passage through the work of narrative passages he writes.

28. I have written elsewhere that perhaps the myth of Narcissus and Echo is the imaginative paradigm for the act of writing itself ("Speaking, Reflecting, Writing: The Myth of Narcissus and Echo," 217–20).

29. Bainard Cowan has written persuasively that Ahab is necessary as epic hero to help bring down an old order based on competitive and rapacious acquisitions. He is like the god Apollo who enters and clears away old debris so that something new can be built ("America Between Two Myths: *Moby-Dick* as Epic," *Epic Cosmos*, 217–46).

30. Carl Jung makes several relevant observations on the animal soul in his *Memories, Dreams, Reflections* (1963), especially that the animal soul, the individual soul, and the world soul, are all mythically intimate in their being. See also the chapter from Morris Berman's study, "The Wild and the Tame: Humans and Animals from Lascaux to Walt Disney," (*Coming to Our Senses: Body and Spirit in the Hidden History of the West*, 62–101).

31. Ishmael reminds us that his body is also tattooed with "the skeletal dimensions" of the whale so that he will remember its body accurately. He also tells us that he "wished the other parts of my body to remain a blank page for a poem I was then composing—at least what untattooed parts might remain—" (376). He is, in the flesh and in action, the inscriber inscribed.

8. REBELLIOUS THINGS AND DEEPENING WOUNDS IN THE LIFE OF IVAN ILYCH

1. I have written of this quality of disease in making a distinction between pain and suffering as the fundamental crisis of Ivan Ilych's life ("*The Death of Ivan Ilych*: A Distinction Between Pain and Suffering," 185–94).

2. There exists here an entire discussion that Carl Jung opens up in the beginning pages of *Alchemical Studies* when he interrogates the modern tendency to live a one-sided existence, which he calls "a mark of bar-

barism" (9). Such a condition occurs when consciousness becomes independent, to the detriment of the unconscious, which is then "thrust into the background." Consciousness then extricates itself from the unconscious archetypal patterns and moves toward a state "of instinctual atrophy" (12). I suggest that Gerasim is the fullness of conscious and unconscious forces, a man of the Russian soil who stays in touch with perhaps the greatest archetypal actions of all— birth and death as two impulses in the act of regeneration.

3. This idea of a physical and psychological space of inner and outer is a rich image in Tolstoy's story. Following some of Hillman's writing, we could speak of surface and depth, upper world of appearance and underworld of psychological experience, with fruitful results. For my purposes, deepening is what the wound does to Ilych, and this is one of the forms of growth that Hillman explores in his work, *Kinds of Power: A Guide to Its Intelligent Uses,* especially 45–66. I would also recommend Robert Shuman's study of his own disease in *The Psychology of Chronic Illness: The Healing Work of Patient, Therapists, and Families* (1996), especially Chapter 4, "Time Out of Joint" (47–56).

4. Hillman follows Jung in developing the idea of a world soul, which puts the notion of ensouledness back into things. When things are ensouled, they demand care. Psychological pollution stems in part from putting all soul into self and leaving the world as an inanimate dead thing. This one-sided consciousness Jung believes is the disease of the modern psyche. It allows for no consciousness except in the heads of human beings. The whole world then becomes a corpse. See especially the chapter, "Maintenance," in *Kinds of Power.* For an in-depth discussion of the idea of *anima mundi,* see Robert Sardello's *Facing the World with Soul: The Reimagination of Modern Life.*

5. Consciousness can become so tyrannical, so one-sided, believes Jung, that the individual can get "so far out of touch with primordial images that a breakdown ensues" (*Alchemical Studies,* 13). The "cramp of consciousness" (16) can develop or grow into disease.

6. Lockhart cites Jung's belief that "the only real disease was normality, that man's illnesses and his neuroses were his riches and that by going into them, one would find the completeness that is so missing in what we consider normalcy" (21).

7. While Y. J. Dayananda's essay, which matches the stages of Ivan Ilych's journey through his disease to the steps outlined by Kübler-Ross is interesting, it actually sidesteps the real poetic force of the story by literalizing it too much. In fact, it does to the story what the medical model does to Ivan's illness: it sets it into a container (*Tolstoy's Short Fiction,* 423–34).

8. The Japanese version of Tolstoy's story is told in a profound and moving way in Akira Kurosawa's *Ikiru.* There, the chief clerk, Kanji Wat-

anabe, functions as a cog for thirty years, pushing paper and deflecting any disruptions in his daily routine until he discovers that an upset stomach is in fact gastric cancer, with a prognosis of only six months to live. His disease, like Ivan's, prompts him to confess to himself: "I don't know what I've been living for all these years." After a night of debauchery and then hanging on to a young woman in his office, a counterpart to Gerasim in her health and vitality, he realizes that it is not too late to do some good. He becomes in his last days a courageous proponent of a park for children, constructed out of a swampy piece of land under a busy city bridge. His wound, his gastric cancer, serves him as his greatest strength; it finds its analogue in his decision to serve others, wherein great power resides. His diseased body impels him toward real meaning. His wound guides him to good work for others that is tangible and concrete. In his small way, he changes the world. For a brief moment, he serves as an icon of courage for the other anonymous men serving an indifferent bureaucracy who grieve over his passing.

9. John Bayley's very limited and unimaginative reading of Tolstoy's story, which he finds not real enough, shows a failure of insight on his part, especially when he claims that our "expectations" are "surely disappointed when we read it again. The description is too weighted, the power too authoritative" (421)—a comment for which he offers no clarity or support. Kathleen Parthe's observation that the structure of *Ivan Ilych* "leaves a unified impression" (420) I find closer to the truth of the story, especially as the generous act of Ivan Ilych at the end is the perfect antibody to his life embroiled in material possessions.

9. WOUNDS AND TATTOOS

1. This idea underpins a comparative study of mine dealing with the imagination of matter: "Imagining the Stuff of the World: Reflections on Gaston Bachelard and Ivan Illich," *New Orleans Review* 12, no. 3 (1986): 81–87.

2. Of course, this book of Mary Grace's asks us to recall the New Testament Book of Revelation, the parallels of which are numerous. For example, John commands: "write in a book what you see and send it to the seven churches" (1:9). And earlier he proclaims: "Grace to you and peace from him who is and who was and who is to come, and from the seven spirits who are before his throne" (1:4). It would be of great interest to study the animal imagery that permeates the biblical text. O'Connor seems to distort the particulars of Revelation to bring poetically forward its central meanings.

3. I owe gratitude to Robert Romanyshyn, whose book *Technology as Symptom and Dream* has been very instrumental to this discussion.

4. I would mention Dudley Young's exciting and provocative study, *Origins of the Sacred: The Ecstasies of Love and War*, which offers some fine insights into the nature of pollution, especially its connection with divinity. At one point he observes: "To discover that everything that disorders our lives may be systematically understood as divine pollution is potentially liberating" (237). There are, he continues, forms of pollution sent by divinity to disorder the mind and transform vision. I believe his entire study would open up further discussion of O'Connor's stories. James Hillman also writes persuasively from a psychological perspective on the action of wounding. He writes that "mythological figures show limping, bleeding, crippling. What deep ground of soul does it point to metaphorically?" Wounds, he continues, have the capacity to parent and can be a gift. "A new spirit emerges in weakness, and through our holes the unexpected comes out. A wound has this spiritual logos quality" ("Puer Wounds," 105).

5. William Lynch treats this form of imagining in two perceptive works: *Christ and Apollo: The Dimensions of the Literary Imagination* and *Images of Faith: The Dimensions of the Ironic Imagination*. More historically situated, but not as accessible as Lynch's work, is David Tracy's *The Analogical Imagination: Christian Theology and the Culture of Pluralism*, especially II, 9–10.

6. "Vanity" meant originally the emptiness and inconstancy of things that can neither help nor save; it deludes those who set their hopes on such things (*Concordance*, 559). This faith without image that Sarah Ruth embodies, leads to just such a lament.

7. Just a few of the texts on iconology that have influenced my thought include Leonid Ouspensky, *Theology of the Icon*; Leonid Ouspensky and Vladimir Lossky, *The Meaning of Icons*; Peter Phan, *Culture and Eschatology*; Constantine Cavarnos, *Orthodox Iconography*.

8. James Hillman questions what it is that makes up an archetypal image. He suggests that it has to do with value. "Rather than pointing *at* something, 'archetypal' points *to* something, and this is *value*. By attaching 'archetypal' to an image, we ennoble or empower the image with the widest, richest and deepest possible significance. 'Archetypal,' as we use it, is a word of importance . . . a word that values' ("Inquiry into Image," 82). Parker's world is one of value and valuing, not condemning or judging, such that images in his life guide his way of seeing everything in the world.

9. The body as the first canvas is also discussed in Prudence Glynn, *Skin to Skin: Eroticism in Dress*.

10. Clinton Sanders points out that while tattooing had "religious and magical purposes, often providing a means of identification or protection in

the afterlife" (*Customizing the Body*, 11), most people in tribal or urban communities get tattoos in order to show some close affiliation with a group. Parker's intent seems to be contrary, fighting with others rather than joining any group through his images. He remains alone to the end.

10. THE NARRATIVE BODY AND THE INCARNATE WORD IN TONI MORRISON'S *BELOVED*

1. Some other relevant and useful studies of the lived body as metaphor and as cultural construction include *The Body Imaged: The Human Form and Visual Culture Since the Renaissance*, ed. Kathleen Adler and Marcia Pointon (1993); Morris Berman, *Coming to Our Senses: Body and Spirit in the Hidden History of the West* (1990); David Michael Levin, *The Body's Recollection of Being: Phenomenological Psychology and the Deconstruction of Nihilism* (1985); *Giving the Body Its Due*, ed. Maxine Sheets-Johnstone (1992); *The Making of the Modern Body: Sexuality and Society in the Nineteenth Century*, ed. Catherine Gallagher and Thomas Laqueur (1987); and a collection of essays in *The Philosophy of the Body: Rejections of Cartesian Dualism*, ed. Stuart F. Spicker (1970).

2. With this description of Seneca's behavior in mind, I mention for further exploration an article entitled "The Thin Red Line," by Jennifer Egan which explores "self-mutilation as the latest expression of adolescent self-loathing" practiced by scores of young women nationally. Egan suggests that one reason this is done is "to make them feel better; they use physical pain to obfuscate a deeper, more intolerable psychic pain associated with feelings of anger, sadness or abandonment" (23). She cites one of those she interviewed who said this of her body markings: "I've got physical scars. . . . It shows that my life isn't easy. I can look at different scars and think, yeah, I know when that happened, so it tells a story" (24). The psychic narratives that body markings enunciate bear directly on my discussion here. See also the series of interviews conducted by Marilee Strong in her *A Bright Red Scream: Self-Mutilation and the Language of Pain* where one woman reports: "watching the blood pour out makes me feel clean, purified" (10).

3. By comedy and the comic here I do not mean what is laughable or funny, but rather a particular response to life that has as part of its texture forgiveness and joy. Comedy, in its three "moments," as Louise Cowan delineates them—infernal, purgatorial, and paradisal—offers us three conditions or states of being that give rise to different values governing human life. Of her three moments, I understand *Beloved* to occupy that third instance, the paradisal, where "its mood is merriment and joy, its motive pleasure and freedom. . . . Here love is supreme; one is not required by one's

own efforts to save the day—the natural tendency of things is upward" ("Comic Terrain," 14).

4. I believe James Hillman's insights into language are relevant here. He writes that words, like angels, have power over us for they can carry soul between people. He even dares to suggest that words "are personal presences which have whole mythologies," including "guarding, blaspheming, creating, and annihilating effects. *For words are persons*" (*Revisioning Psychology*, 8–9). The figure of Beloved is the negative and paralyzing impulse of the incarnate word, whose effects lead one tragically to isolation and destruction.

5. Trudier Harris is one of many voices who I believe diminish Baby Suggs' power after she has died: "By abdicating her creative role, Baby Suggs descends from the legendary status that has defined her to become just another victim of slavery, a victimization all the more tragic because she clearly had the power not to adhere to such a fate" (*Fiction and Folklore*, 175). I contend that she gains in power through her remembered image. In the minds of the communal memory, she gains a level of glory denied her in life. On the other hand, Harris offers fine background material on the African folk tradition that opens other areas of exploration in Morrison's novels. See especially 151–84 on *Beloved*.

6. Jean Wyatt writes that "the women's communal groan recalls women's creation of life, not God's, and overthrows the male authority of the word" (487). I think such an attitude of women's one-upmanship misses entirely the place of Sophia in relation to the word. Nor does it help illuminate any important element in the text that is not already obvious.

Works Cited

Abel, Lionel. "Is There a Tragic Sense of Life?" *Moderns on Tragedy.* Ed. Lionel Abel. Greenwich: Fawcett, 1967. 17–86.

Abram, David. *The Spell of the Sensuous: Perception and Language in a More-Than-Human World.* New York: Pantheon, 1996.

Absher, Tom. *Men and the Goddess: Feminine Archetypes in Western Literature.* Rochester: Park Street, 1990.

Adler, Kathleen, and Marcia Pointon, eds. *The Body Imaged: The Human Form and Visual Culture Since the Renaissance.* Cambridge: Cambridge UP, 1993.

Alighieri, Dante. *Inferno. The Divine Comedy of Dante Alighieri.* Trans. Allen Mandelbaum. New York: Bantam, 1982.

Allums, Larry. "*Beloved*: Remembering the Past." *Classic Texts and the Nature of Authority.* Eds. Donald and Louise Cowan. Dallas: The Dallas Institute, 1993. 268–82.

Anderson, Roger. "The Meaning of Carnival in *The Brothers Karamazov.*" *Slavic and East European Journal* 23, no. 4 (1979): 458–78.

———. *Myths of Duality.* Gainesville: U Florida P, 1986.

Arbery, Glen. "Against the Belly of the Ram: The Comedy of Deception in *The Odyssey.*" *The Terrain of Comedy.* Ed. Louise Cowan. Dallas: The Dallas Institute of Humanities and Culture, 1984. 19–40.

Aristotle. *Poetics.* Trans. Leon Golden. Commentary O. B. Hardison Jr. Englewood Cliffs: Prentice-Hall, 1968.

Auerbach, Eric. "Odysseus' Scar." *Mimesis: Representations of Reality in Western Literature.* Trans. Willard R. Trask. Princeton: Princeton UP, 1973. 3–23.

Austin, Norman. "Odysseus/Ulysses: The Protean Myth." *The Odyssey and Ancient Art.* Bard College: The Edith C. Blum Art Institute, 1993. 201–7.

Avens, Roberts. *Imaginal Bodies: Para-Jungian Reflections on Soul, Imagination and Death*. Lanham: UP of America, 1982.

Babbitt, Irving. *Rousseau and Romanticism*. New York: Meridian, 1959.

Bachelard, Gaston. *Fragments of a Poetics of Fire*. Trans. Kenneth Haltman. Ed. Suzanne Bachelard. Dallas: The Dallas Institute, 1990.

———. *On Poetic Imagination and Reverie*. Trans. Colette Gaudin. Dallas: Spring, 1987.

———. *The Poetics of Space*. Trans. Maria Jolas. Boston: Beacon, 1969.

———. *The Right to Dream*. Trans. J. A. Underwood. Dallas: The Dallas Institute, 1983.

———. *Water and Dreams: An Essay on the Imagination of Matter*. Trans. Edith Farrell. Dallas: Pegasus, 1983.

Baker-Miller, Jean. *Toward a New Psychology of Women*. Boston: Beacon, 1976.

Bakhtin, Mikhail. *Art and Answerability: Early Philosophical Essays*. Eds. Michael Holquist and Vadim Liapunov. Trans. Vadim Liapunov. Austin: U. Texas P, 1990.

———. "From Notes Made in 1970–71." *Speech Genres and Other Late Essays*. Trans. Vern W. McGee. Austin: U Texas P, 1986. 133–58.

———. *Problems of Dostoevsky's Poetics*. Ed. and trans. Caryl Emerson. *Theory and History of Literature*. Vol. 8. Minneapolis: U Minnesota P, 1984.

———. *Rabelais and His World*. Trans. Helen Iswolsky. Bloomington: Indiana UP, 1984.

Bakhtin, M. M., and P. N. Medvedev. *The Formal Method in Literary Scholarship: A Critical Introduction to Sociological Poetics*. Trans. Albert J. Wehrle. Cambridge: Harvard UP, 1985.

Barfield, Owen. *Saving the Appearances: A Study in Idolatry*. New York: Harcourt, 1962.

Barkan, Leonard. *Nature's Work of Art: The Human Body as Image of the World*. New Haven: Yale UP, 1975.

Barrett, William. *The Death of the Soul: From Descartes to the Computer*. New York: Anchor, 1987.

Barthes, Roland. *S/Z*. Trans. Richard Miller. New York: Hill and Wang, 1974.

Bayley, John. "*Ivan Ilych*." *Tolstoy's Short Fiction*. Ed. and trans. Michael Katz. New York: Norton, 1991. 420–23.

Becker, Ernest. *Escape from Evil*. New York: Macmillan, 1975.

Benjamin, Walter. "The Story Teller." *Illuminations*. Ed. Hannah Arendt. Trans. Harry Zohn. New York: Harcourt, Brace, 1968. 83–109.

Berdyaev, Nikolai. " The Eschatological and Prophetic Character of Russian Thought." *The Russian Idea*. Trans. R. M. French. Hudson: Lindisfarne, 1992. 208–32.

Berman, Morris. *Coming to Our Senses: Body and Spirit in the Hidden History of the West*. New York: Bantam, 1990.

———. *The Reenchantment of the World*. New York: Bantam, 1989.

Berry, Patricia. "Hamlet's Poisoned Ear." *Echo's Subtle Body: Contributions to an Archetypal Psychology*. Dallas: Spring, 1982. 127–46.

———. "What's the Matter with Mother?" *Echo's Subtle Body*. 1–16.

Berry, Wendell. *The Unsettling of America: Culture and Agriculture*. San Francisco: Sierra Club Books, 1977.

Bethea, David. *The Shape of Apocalypse in Modern Russian Fiction*. Princeton: Princeton UP, 1989.

Billington, James. *The Icon and the Axe: An Interpretative History of Russian Culture*. New York: Random House, 1966.

Boer, Charles. "In the Shadow of the Gods: Greek Tragedy." *Spring: An Annual of Archetypal Psychology*. Dallas: Spring, 1982. 133–50.

Bordo, Susan. *Unbearable Weight: Feminism, Western Culture, and the Body*. Berkeley: U California P, 1993.

Brandon, David. "Nowness in the Helping Relationship." *Awakening the Heart: East/West Approaches to Psychotherapy and the Healing Relationship*. Ed. John Welwood. Boston: Shambhala, 1985. 140–47.

Brooks, Peter. *Body Work: Objects of Desire in Modern Narrative*. Cambridge: Harvard UP, 1993.

———. *Reading for the Plot: Design and Intention in Narrative*. New York: Knopf, 1984.

Brown, Norman O. *Hermes the Thief: The Evolution of a Myth*. New York: Random House, 1969.

———. *Love's Body*. Berkeley: U California P, 1966.

Brown, Peter. *The Body and Society: Men, Women, and Sexual Renunciation in Early Christianity*. New York: Columbia UP, 1988.

Buci-Glucksmann, Christine. "Catastrophic Utopia: The Feminine as Allegory of the Modern." *The Making of the Modern Body: Sexuality and Society in the Nineteenth Century*. Ed. Catherine Gallagher and Thomas Laqueur. Berkeley: U California P, 1987. 220–29.

Bulgakov, Sergei. *Sophia: The Wisdom of God: An Outline of Sophiology*. West Stockbridge: Lindisfarne, 1993.

Butler, Judith. *Bodies That Matter: On the Discursive Limits of "Sex."* New York: Routledge, 1993.

Bynum, Caroline Walker. *The Resurrection of the Body in Western Christianity, 200–1336*. New York: Columbia UP, 1995.

Cameron, Sharon. *The Corporeal Self: Allegories of the Body in Melville and Hawthorne*. Baltimore: The Johns Hopkins UP, 1981.

Campbell, Joseph. *The Hero with a Thousand Faces*. Bollingen Series XVII. Princeton: Princeton UP, 1973.

———. *The Mythic Image*. New York: MJF Books, 1974.

Camporesi, Piero. *The Incorruptible Flesh: Bodily Mutation and Mortification in Religion and Folklore*. Trans. Tania Croft-Murray. Cambridge: Cambridge UP, 1988.

———. *Juice of Life: The Symbolic and Magic Significance of Blood*. Trans. Robert R. Barr. New York: Continuum, 1995.

Casey, Edward S. *Getting Back into Place: Toward a Renewed Understanding of the Place World*. Bloomington: Indiana UP, 1993.

———. "Getting Placed: Soul in Space." *Spring: An Annual of Archetypal Psychology*. Dallas: Spring, 1982. 1–26

Cavarnos, Constantine. *Orthodox Iconography*. Boston: Crestwood, 1977.

Ceronetti, Guido. *The Silence of the Body: Materials for the Study of Medicine*. Trans. Michael Moore. New York: HarperCollins, 1993.

Cobb, Noel. *Archetypal Imagination: Glimpses of the Gods in Life and Art*. Hudson: Lindisfarne, 1992.

Conger, John. "The Body as Shadow." *Meeting the Shadow: The Hidden Power of the Dark Side of Human Nature*. Eds. Connie Zweig and Jeremiah Abrams. Los Angeles: Tarcher, 1991. 84–87.

———. *Jung and Reich: The Body as Shadow*. Berkeley: North Atlantic, 1988.

Corbett, Lionel. *The Religious Function of the Psyche*. New York: Routledge, 1996.

Corbin, Alain. *The Foul and the Fragrant: Odor and the French Social Imagination*. Cambridge: Harvard UP, 1986.

Cowan, Bainard. "America Between Two Myths: *Moby-Dick* as Epic." *The Epic Cosmos*. Ed. Larry Allums. Dallas: Dallas Institute P, 1992. 217–46.

———. *Exiled Waters: Moby-Dick and the Crisis of Allegory*. Baton Rouge: Louisiana State UP, 1982.

Cowan, Donald. "The Self-Made Leader." *Classic Texts and the Nature of Authority*. Eds. Donald and Louise Cowan. Dallas: The Dallas Institute, 1993. 159–64

Cowan, Louise. "*Beloved* and the Transforming Power of the Word." *Classic Texts and the Nature of Authority*. Eds. Donald and Louise Cowan. Dallas: The Dallas Institute, 1993. 291–303.

———. "The Brothers Karamazov." University of Dallas, Irving, Texas. January 1985.

———. "Introduction: Epic as Cosmopoesis." *The Epic Cosmos*. Ed. Larry Allums. Dallas: The Dallas Institute P, 1992. 1–26.

———, ed. *The Terrain of Comedy*. Dallas: The Dallas Institute of Humanities and Culture, 1984.

Cox, Stephen D. *The Stranger Within Thee: Concepts of the Self in Late 18th. Century Literature*. Pittsburgh: Pittsburgh UP, 1980.

Curtis, Laura. "Raskolnikov's Sexuality." *Literature and Psychology*. 1991. 36, nos. 1–2. 88–105.

Davis, Clark. *After the Whale: Melville in the Wake of Moby-Dick*. Tuscaloosa: U Alabama P, 1995.

Dayananda, Y. J. "The Death of Ivan Ilych: A Psychological Study on Death and Dying." *Tolstoy's Short Fiction*. Trans. Michael Katz. New York: Norton, 1991. 423–35.

Desjarlais, Robert R. *Body and Emotion: The Aesthetics of Illness and Healing in the Nepal Himalayas*. Philadelphia: U Pennsylvania P, 1992.

Dimock, George. "The Name of Odysseus." *The Odyssey*. Trans. and ed. Albert Cook. New York: Norton, 1974. 406–24.

Dixon, Melvin. "The Black Writer's Use of Memory." *History and Memory in African-American Culture*. Ed. Genevieve Fabre and Robert O'Meally. New York: Oxford UP, 1994. 18–27.

Dodds. E.R. *The Greeks and the Irrational*. Berkeley: U California P, 1951.

———. "On Misunderstanding the *Oedipus Rex*." *Sophocles' Oedipus Rex*. Ed. Harold Bloom. New York: Chelsea House, 1988. 35–48.

Dostoevsky, Fyodor. *The Brothers Karamazov*. Trans. Constance Garnett, rev. Ralph E. Matlaw. New York: Norton, 1976.

———. *Crime and Punishment*. Trans. Jesse Coulson. Ed. George Gibian, Norton Critical Edition. 2nd. ed. New York: Norton, 1975.

———. *The Possessed*. Trans. Constance Garnett. New York: Heritage, 1959.

Doty, William G. "Hermes' Heteronymous Appellations." *Facing the Gods*. Ed. James Hillman. Dallas: Spring, 1994. 115–34.

———, ed. *Picturing Cultural Values in Postmodern America*. Tuscaloosa: U Alabama P, 1995.

Douglas, Mary. *Purity and Danger: An Analysis of the Concepts of Pollution and Taboo*. London: Ark, 1988.

Duff, Kat. "The Alchemy of Illness." *The Parabola Book of Healing*. Introd. Lawrence E. Sullivan. New York: Continuum, 1994. 45–53.

Edinger, Edward. *Melville's Moby-Dick: A Jungian Commentary*. New York: New Directions, 1978.

Egan, Jennifer. "The Thin Red Line." *The New York Times Magazine*, July 27, 1997, 21–25; 34, 40, 44, 49.

Eisler, Riane. *The Chalice and the Blade: Our History, Our Future.* New York: HarperCollins, 1988.

Elder, George. *The Body: An Encyclopedia of Archetypal Symbolism.* Vol. 2. The Archive for Research in Archetypal Symbolism. Boston: Shambhala, 1996.

———. "Crossroads." *Encyclopedia of Religion.* Vol. 4. Ed. Mircea Eliade. New York: Macmillan, 1987.

Emerson, Ralph Waldo. "The Over-Soul." *The American Tradition in Literature.* Rev. ed. Eds. Sculley Bradley, Richmond Beatty, et al. New York: Norton, 1957. 578–87.

Euripides. *The Bacchae and Other Plays.* Trans. Phillip Vellacott. New York: Penguin, 1973. 191–244.

Fagles, Robert. "Introduction." *Oedipus at Colonus. The Three Theban Plays.* Trans. Robert Fagles. New York: Penguin, 1984. 255–77.

———. "Introduction to *Antigone.*" *Sophocles: The Three Theban Plays.* Trans. Robert Fagles. Viking: New York, 1984. 33–54.

Feher, Michel, Ramona Naddaff, and Nadia Taze, eds. *Fragments for a History of the Human Body.* 3 vols. New York: Zone, 1989.

Felson-Rubin, Nancy. "Penelope's Perspective: Character from Plot." *Reading the Odyssey: Selected Interpretive Essays.* Ed. Seth L. Schein. Princeton: Princeton UP, 1996. 185–90.

Foucault, Michel. *The History of Sexuality:* Vol. 1, *An Introduction.* Trans. Robert Hurley. New York: Random House, 1980.

Gallagher, Catherine, and Thomas Laqueur, eds. *The Making of the Modern Body: Sexuality and Society in the Nineteenth Century.* Berkeley: U California P, 1987.

Gallop, Jane. *Thinking Through the Body.* New York: Columbia UP, 1988.

Gay, Peter. *The Bourgeois Experience: Victoria to Freud:* Vol. 1, *Education of the Senses.* New York: Oxford UP, 1984.

Gibson, A. Boyce. *The Religion of Dostoevsky.* Philadelphia: Westminster, 1973.

Giegerich, Wolfgang. "Killing and Consciousness." *Salt Journal* 1, no. 1 (1997): 39–43.

Gimbutas, Marija. *The Goddesses and Gods of Old Europe: Myths and Cult Images.* Berkeley: U California P, 1992.

———. *The Language of the Goddess.* San Francisco: HarperSanFrancisco, 1991.

Girard, Rene. *Deceit, Desire and the Novel: Self and Other in Literary Structure.* Trans. Yvonne Freccero. Baltimore: The Johns Hopkins UP, 1965.

———. *To Double Business Bound: Essays on Literature, Mimesis, and Anthropology.* Baltimore: The Johns Hopkins UP, 1978.

———. *Violence and the Sacred*. Trans. Patrick Gregory. Baltimore: The Johns Hopkins UP, 1977.

Glynn, Prudence. *Skin to Skin: Eroticism in Dress*. New York: Oxford UP, 1982.

Goldstein, Laurence, ed. *The Female Body*. Parts 1–2. *Michigan Quarterly Review* 29, no. 4 (1990); 30, no. 1 (1991).

Gordon, Sarah. "Flannery O'Connor, 'the Left-Wing Mystic' and the German Jew." SCMLA Convention, Houston, October 30, 1987.

Greenblatt, Stephen. "Mutilation and Meaning." *The Body in Parts: Fantasies of Corporeality in Early Modern Europe*. Eds. David Hillman and Carla Mazzio. New York: Routledge, 1997. 221–42.

Griffin, Susan. *Woman and Nature: The Roaring Inside Her*. New York: Harper, 1978.

Gustafson, Richard. "On *Ivan Ilych* and *Master and Man*—A Symbolic Structure." *Tolstoy's Short Fiction*. Ed. and trans. Michael Katz. New York: Norton, 1991. 461–70.

Hackel, Sergei. "The Religious Dimension: Vision of Evasion. Zosima's Discourse in *Brothers Karamazov*." *New Essays on Dostoevsky*. Ed. Malcolm Jones and Garth Terry. Cambridge: Cambridge UP, 1983.

Harris, Massimilla and Bud Harris. *Like Gold Through Fire: A Message in Suffering*. Alexander, North Carolina: Alexander Books, 1996.

Harris, Trudier. *Fiction and Folklore: The Novels of Toni Morrison*. Knoxville: U Tennessee P, 1994.

Hays, Peter L. *The Limping Hero: Grotesques in Literature*. New York: New York UP, 1971.

Heidegger, Martin. *Poetry, Language, Thought*. Trans. Albert Hofstadter. New York: Harper, 1975.

Hershman, Marcie. "The World and the Library." *Poets and Writers Magazine* 24, no. 6 (1996): 20–21.

Hillman, David, and Carla Mazzio, eds. *The Body in Parts: Fantasies of Corporeality in Early Modern Europe*. New York: Routledge, 1997.

Hillman, James. "Anima Mundi: The Return of the Soul to the World." *Spring: An Annual of Archetypal Psychology*. Dallas: Spring, 1982. 71–94.

———. "The Animal Kingdom in the Human Dream." *Eranos Jahrbuch* 51 (1982): 279–334.

———. *A Blue Fire: Selected Writings by James Hillman*. Ed. Thomas Moore. New York: HarperCollins, 1991.

———. *The Dream and the Underworld*. New York: Harper, 1979.

———. *Healing Fiction*. Barrytown: Station Hill, 1983.

———. "An Inquiry into Image." *Spring 1977*. Zurich: Spring, 1977. 62–88.

———. *Kinds of Power. A Guide to Its Intelligent Uses*. New York: Doubleday, 1995.

———. "Notes on Opportunism." *Puer Papers*. Irving: Spring, 1979. 152–68.

———. "Oedipus Revisited." *Oedipus Variations: Studies in Literature and Psychoanalysis*. Dallas: Spring, 1990. 87–169.

———. "Puer Wounds and Ulysses' Scar." *Puer Papers*. Dallas: Spring, 1979. 100–128.

———. *Revisioning Psychology*. New York: HarperCollins, 1992.

———. *The Soul's Code: In Search of Character and Calling*. New York: Random House, 1996.

Holquist, Michael. *Dostoevsky and the Novel*. Evanston: Northwestern UP, 1987.

The Holy Bible: The New Revised Standard Edition. Nashville: Holman, 1989.

Homer. *The Odyssey*. Trans. and ed. Albert Cook. New York: Norton, 1974.

Horder, John. "The Sick Image of My Father Fades." *The Rag and Boneshop of the Heart*. Eds. Robert Bly, James Hillman, and Michael Meade. New York: HarperCollins, 1992. 130.

Horvitz, Deborah. "Nameless Ghosts: Possession and Dispossession in *Beloved*." *Studies in American Fiction* 17, no. 2 (1989): 157–67.

Hubbs, Joanna. *Mother Russia: The Feminine Myth in Russian Culture*. Bloomington: Indiana UP, 1993.

Hunt, Lynn, ed. *Eroticism and the Body Politic*. Baltimore: The Johns Hopkins UP, 1991.

Hyde, Lewis. *The Gift: Imagination and the Erotic Life of Property*. New York: Random House, 1983.

Illich, Ivan. *H2O and the Waters of Forgetfulness*. Dallas: Dallas Institute, 1986.

———. "A Plea for Body History." March 1986. Unpublished.

Illich, Ivan, and Barry Sanders. *The Alphabetization of the Popular Mind*. San Francisco: North Point, 1988.

Irwin, John T. *American Hieroglyphics: The Symbol of the Egyptian Hieroglyphics in the American Renaissance*. Baltimore: The Johns Hopkins UP, 1983.

Jackson, Robert Louis. "The Triple Vision: Dostoevsky's 'The Peasant Marey.'" *Yale Review* (Winter 1978): 225–35.

Jager, Bernd. "Body, House and City." *Dwelling, Place and Environment*. Dordrecht/Boston/Lancaster: Martinus Nijhoff Publishers, 1985. 215–26.

Jones, Alexander, ed. *The Jerusalem Bible*. Garden City: Doubleday, 1966.

Jones, John. *Dostoevsky*. Oxford: Oxford UP, 1985.

Jones, Richard. *A Perfect Time*. Port Townsend: Copper Canyon Press, 1994.

Jung, Carl. *Aion: Researches into the Phenomenology of the Self*. 2nd ed. Vol. 9, 2 of *The Collected Works of C. G. Jung*. Bollingen Series XX. Princeton: Princeton UP, 1970.

————. *Alchemical Studies*. Trans. R. F. C. Hull. Vol. 13 of *The Collected Works of C. G. Jung*. Princeton: Princeton UP, 1983.

————. *Archetypes and the Collective Unconscious*. 2nd edition. Trans. R. F. C. Hull. Vol. 9, 1 of *The Collected Works of C. G. Jung*. Bollingen Series XX. Princeton: Princeton UP, 1969.

————. *Memories, Dreams, Reflections*. Trans. Richard and Clara Winston. New York: Random House, 1963.

————. *Nietzsche's Zarathustra: Notes of the Seminar Given in 1934–39*. Ed. James L. Jarrett. 2 vols. Bollingen Series XCIX. Princeton: Princeton UP, 1988.

————. "Psychology and Literature." *The Spirit in Man, Art, and Literature*. Trans. R. F. C. Hull. *The Collected Works of C. G. Jung*. Bollingen Series XX, Vol. 15. New York: Pantheon, 1966. 84–108.

————. "The Psychology of the Transference." *The Practice of Psychotherapy*. 2nd ed. Trans. R. F. C. Hull. *The Collected Works of C. G. Jung*. Vol. 20. 163–326. 1954.

————. *Vision Seminars*. Vol. II. Dallas: Spring, 1976.

Kanzer. Mark. "A Psychological View of Alyosha's Reaction to Father Zosima's Death." *The Brothers Karamazov and the Critics*. Ed. Edward Wasiolek. Belmont, Mass.: Wadsworth, 1967. 103–7.

Kearney, Richard. *The Wake of Imagination: Toward a Postmodern Culture*. Minneapolis: U Minnesota P, 1988.

Kenyon, Jane. *Otherwise: New and Selected Poems*. St. Paul: Graywolf P, 1996.

Kittelson, Mary Lynn. *Sounding the Soul: The Art of Listening*. Einsiedeln, Switzerland: Daimon, 1996.

Knox, Bernard. "Sophocles' Oedipus." *Sophocles' Oedipus Rex*. Ed. Harold Bloom. New York: Chelsea, 1988. 5–24.

Koerner, Joseph Leo. "The Mortification of the Image: Death as a Hermeneutic in Hans Baldung Grien." *Representations* 10 (Spring 1985): 52–101.

Kohut, Heinz. "Thoughts on Narcissism and Narcissistic Rage." *The Search for the Self: Selected Writings of Heinz Kohut: 1950–1978*. Vol. 2. Ed. Paul H. Ornstein. Madison: International UP, 1978. 615–58.

Komesaroff, Paul A., ed. *Troubled Bodies: Critical Perspectives on Post-modernism, Medical Ethics, and the Body*. Durham: Duke UP, 1995.

Kott, Jan. "The Memory of the Body." *The Memory of the Body: Essays on Theatre and Dance*. Evanston: Northwestern UP, 1992. 113–22.

Kristeva, Julia. *Strangers to Ourselves*. Trans. Leon S. Roudiez. New York: Columbia UP, 1991.

Kurosawa, Akira, dir. *Ikiru*. Takshi Shimura, Nobuo and Kyoko Seki. 1952. Videocassette. Media Home Entertainment. 134 min.

Lacan, Jacques. *Ecrits: A Selection*. Trans. Alan Sheridan. New York: Norton, 1977.

Lahr, John. "This Other England." *The New Yorker*, September 23, 1996, 50–57.

Laqueur, Thomas. *Making Sex: Body and Gender from the Greeks to Freud*. Cambridge: Harvard UP, 1990.

Lawlor, Anthony. *The Temple in the House: Finding the Sacred in Everyday Architecture*. New York: Putnam, 1994.

Lawlor, Robert. Interview with *Parabola. Parabola: The Magazine of Myth and Tradition* 18, no. 3 (1993): 11–18.

Lawrence, D. H. "The Grand Inquisitor." *The Brothers Karamazov*. Ed. Ralph Matlaw. New York: Norton, 1976. 829–36.

———. "Healing." *The Rag and Bone Shop of the Heart: Poems for Men*. Eds. Robert Bly, James Hillman, Michael Meade. New York: HarperCollins, 1992. 113.

———. *Studies in Classical American Literature*. New York: Viking, 1961.

Lear, Jonathan. *Open-Minded: Working Out the Logic of the Soul*. Cambridge: Harvard UP, 1998.

Ledbetter, Mark. "An Apocalypse of Race and Gender: Body Violence and Forming Identity in Toni Morrison's *Beloved*." *Picturing Cultural Values in Postmodern America*. Ed. William G. Doty. Tuscaloosa: U Alabama P, 1995. 158–72.

Leder, Drew. *The Absent Body*. Chicago: U Chicago P, 1990.

Levertov, Denise. "F." In *Fuel: Poems by Naomi Shihab Nye*. Rochester: Boa Editions, 1998. 5.

Levin, David Michael. *The Body's Recollection of Being: Phenomenological Psychology and the Deconstruction of Nihilism*. London: Routledge, 1985.

Lock, Margaret. "Cultivating the Body: Anthropology and Epistemologies of Bodily Practice and Knowledge." *Annual Review of Anthropology* 22 (1993): 133–55.

Lockhart, Russell A. "Cancer in Myth and Dream." *Spring: An Annual of Archetypal Psychology and Jungian Thought*. Dallas: Spring, 1977. 1–26.

———. *Words as Eggs: Psyche in Language and Clinic.* Dallas: Spring, 1983.

Lomperis, Linda, and Sarah Stanbury, eds. *Femininist Approaches to the Body in Medieval Literature.* Philadelphia: U Pennsylvania P, 1993.

Lopez-Pedraza. Rafael, *Hermes and His Children.* Zurich: Spring, 1977.

Lowe, Donald M. *The Body in Late-Capitalist USA.* Durham: Duke UP, 1995.

———. *History of Bourgeois Perception.* Chicago: U Chicago P, 1982.

Lowen, Alexander. *Narcissism: Denial of the True Self.* New York: Macmillan, 1985.

Lynch, James L. *The Language of the Heart: The Human Body in Dialogue.* New York: Basic, 1989.

Lynch, William. *Christ and Apollo: The Dimensions of the Literary Imagination.* Notre Dame: U. Notre Dame P, 1968.

———. *Images of Faith: The Dimensions of the Ironic Imagination.* Notre Dame: U Notre Dame P, 1975.

Martin, W. R. "A Note on Ruby and Revelation." *The Flannery O'Connor Bulletin,* 16 (1987): 23–25.

Mascia-Lees, Frances E., and Patricia Sharpe. "Introduction: Soft-Tissue Modification and the Horror Within." *Tattoo, Torture, Mutilation, and Adornment: The Denaturalization of the Body in Culture and Text.* Eds. Frances E. Mascia-Lees and Patricia Sharpe. Albany: SUNY P, 1992. 1–9.

Matlaw, Ralph. "Myth and Symbol in *The Brothers Karamazov.*" *The Brothers Karamazov and the Critics.* Belmont: Wadsworth, 1967. 109–19

Matthews, Caitlin. *Sophia: Goddess of Wisdom: The Divine Feminine from Black Goddess to World-Soul.* New York: HarperCollins 1992.

May, Rollo. *The Cry for Myth.* New York: Norton, 1991.

McMillan, Norman. "Dostoevskian Vision in Flannery O'Connor's 'Revelation.'" *The Flannery O'Connor Bulletin* 16 (1987): 16–22.

Meade, Michael. *Men and the Water of Life: Initiation and the Tempering of Men.* San Francisco: Harper, 1993.

Melville, Herman. *Moby-Dick.* Eds. Harrison Hayford and Hershel Parker. New York: Norton, 1967.

Merleau-Ponty, Maurice. *The Phenomenology of Perception.* Trans. Colin Smith. New York: Routledge, 1970.

———. *The Primacy of Perception.* Ed. James Edie. Chicago: Northwestern UP, 1971.

———. *The Prose of the World.* Trans. John O'Neil. Evanston: Northwestern UP, 1973.

Michel, Laurence. *The Thing Contained: Theory of the Tragic.* Bloomington: Indiana UP, 1970.

Miller, R. F., ed. *Critical Essays on Dostoevsky.* Boston: G. K. Hall, 1986. 234–42.

Milosz, Czeslaw. "Dostoevsky and Western Intellectuals." *Cross Currents: A Yearbook of Central European Culture* 5 (1986). 493–505.

Milton, John. *Paradise Lost.* Ed. Scott Elledge. New York: Norton, 1975. 2–286.

Moore, Thomas. *Care of the Soul: A Guide for Cultivating Depth and Sacredness in Everyday Life.* New York: HarperCollins, 1992.

———. *Soul Mates: Honoring the Mysteries of Love and Relationship.* New York: HarperCollins, 1994.

Morris, Marcia. *Saints and Revolutionaries: The Ascetic Hero in Russian Literature.* Albany: State U of New York P, 1993.

Morrisey, Robert J. "Preface." In Jean Starobinski's *Jean-Jacques Rousseau: Transparency and Obstruction.* Trans. Arthur Goldhammer. Chicago: U Chicago P, 1971.

Morrison, Toni. *Beloved.* New York: Knopf, 1992.

———. Interview with Toni Morrison. Home Vision Videocassette, Films Incorporated Co. 1989.

———. *Paradise.* New York: Knopf, 1998.

———. *Playing in the Dark: Whiteness and the Literary Imagination.* Cambridge: Harvard UP, 1990.

"Morrison, Toni." *Contemporary Authors: New Revision Series.* Vol. 42. 1994. 319–28.

Morson, Gary Saul. *The Boundaries of Genre: Dostoevsky's Diary of a Writer and the Traditions of Literary Utopia.* Austin: U Texas P, 1981.

———. "Verbal Pollution in *The Brothers Karamazov.*" *Critical Essays on Dostoevsky.* Ed. R. F. Miller. Boston: G. K. Hall, 1986. 234–42.

———. "Mythical Implications of Father Zosima's Religious Teaching." *Slavic Review* 38, no. 2 (1979).

———. "Prosaics: An Approach to the Humanities." *The American Scholar* 57, no. 4 (1988): 515–29.

Mulvey, Laura. *Fetishism and Curiosity.* Bloomington: Indiana UP, 1996.

Murav, Harriet. *Holy Foolishness: Dostoevsky's Novels and the Poetics of Cultural Critique.* Stanford: Stanford UP, 1992.

Nabokov, Vladimir. "Ivan Ilych's Life." *Tolstoy's Short Fiction.* Trans. Michael Katz. New York: Norton, 1991. 434–35.

Needleman, Jacob. *Time and the Soul.* New York: Doubleday, 1998.

Neumann, Erich. "The Fear of the Feminine." *The Fear of the Feminine: And Other Essays on Feminine Psychology.* Trans. Boris Matthews,

Esther Doughty, et al. Bollingen Series LXI.4. Princeton: Princeton UP, 1994. 227–82.

———. *The Great Mother: An Analysis of the Archetype.* Trans. Ralph Manheim. Bollingen Series XLVII. Princeton: Princeton UP, 1974.

New World Dictionary/Concordance to the New American Bible. New York: World, 1970.

Nietzsche, Friedrich. "The Birth of Tragedy." Trans. Clifton Fadiman. *The Philosophy of Nietzsche.* New York: Random House, 1954. 947–1088.

———. *The Will to Power.* Trans. Walter Kaufmann and R. J. Hollingdale. Ed. Walter Kaufmann. New York: Vintage, 1968.

Nye, Naomi Shihab. *Words Under the Words: Selected Poems (1995).* Portland: Far Corner Books, 1995.

O'Connor, Flannery. *The Habit of Being: Letters of Flannery O'Connor.* Ed. Sally Fitzgerald. New York: Vintage, 1980.

———. "On Her Own Work." *Mystery and Manners: Occasional Prose.* Eds. Sally and Robert Fitzgerald. New York: Farrar, Straus, 1969. 107–20.

———. "Parker's Back." *The Complete Stories of Flannery O'Connor.* New York: Farrar, Straus, Giroux, 1972. 510–30.

———. "Revelation." *Everything That Rises Must Converge.* New York: HarperCollins, 1993. 191–218.

———. "Writing Short Stories." *Mystery and Manners: Occasional Prose.* Eds. Sally and Robert Fitzgerald. New York: Farrar, Straus, 1969. 87–106.

Oliver, Mary. *Dream Work.* New York: Atlantic Monthly P., 1986.

Olson, Charles. *Call Me Ishmael.* New York: Reynall and Hitchcock, 1947.

Ong, Walter. *Orality and Literacy: The Technologizing of the Word.* London: Routledge, 1982.

———.*The Presence of the Word: Some Prolegomena for Cultural and Religious History.* New Haven: Yale UP, 1967.

Onians, Richard Broxton. *The Origins of European Thought: About the Body, the Mind, the Soul, the World, Time and Fate.* Cambridge: Cambridge UP, 1951.

Ouspensky, Leonid. *The Meaning and Language of Icons.* Trans. G. E. H. Palmer and E. Kadlvinsky. Boston: Beacon, 1952.

———. *Theology of the Icon.* Crestwood: St. Vladimir's Seminary P, 1978.

Ouspensky, Leonid, and Vladimir Lossky. *The Meaning of Icons.* Crestwood: St. Vladimir's Seminary P, 1952.

Outram, Dorinda. *The Body and the French Revolution: Sex, Class and Political Culture.* New Haven: Yale UP, 1989.

Palmer, Richard E. *Hermeneutics: Interpretation Theory in Schleiermacher, Dilthey, Heidegger, and Gadamer*. Evanston: Northwestern UP, 1969.

Paris, Ginette. *Pagan Grace: Dionysos, Hermes, and Goddess Memory in Daily Life*. Trans. Joanna Mott. Dallas: Spring, 1990.

———. *Pagan Meditations: Aphrodite, Hestia, Artemis*. Trans. Gwendolyn Moore. Dallas: Spring, 1986.

Parthe, Kathleen. "Tolstoy and the Geometry of Fear." *Tolstoy's Short Fiction*. Trans. Michael Katz. New York: Norton, 1991. 413–20.

Peck, M. Scott. *People of the Lie: The Hope for Healing Human Evil*. New York: Simon, 1983.

Peckham, Morse. *Beyond the Tragic Vision*. New York: George Braziller, 1962.

Phan, Peter C. *Culture and Eschatology: The Iconographical Vision of Paul Evdokimov*. New York: Peter Lang, 1985.

———. "Jesus Christ with an Asian Face." *Theological Studies* 57 (1996): 399–430.

Pinter, Harold. "Loving Shakespeare." *The Los Angeles Times Book Review*. February 14, 1999. 4.

Pocklington, Robb. "The Devil Made Them Do It: Hamlet and the Dionysian Paradigm." *CCTE Studies* 59 (1994): 18–26.

Porter, Roy. "Barely Touching: A Social Perspective on Mind and Body." *The Language of Psyche: Mind and Body in Enlightenment Thought*. Ed. G. S. Rousseau. Berkeley: U California P, 1990. 45–80.

Randall, William Lowell. *The Stories We Are: An Essay on Self-Creation*. Toronto: U Toronto P, 1995.

Rath, Sura. "Ruby Turpin's Redemption: Thomistic Resolution in Flannery O'Connor's 'Revelation.'" *The Flannery O'Connor Bulletin* 19 (1990): 1–10.

Rather, L. J. *Mind and Body in Eighteenth Century Medicine*. London: Wellcome Historical Medical Library, 1965.

Reeves, F. D. *The White Monk: An Essay on Dostoevsky and Melville*. Nashville: Vanderbilt UP, 1989.

Reid, Donald. *Paris Sewers and Sewermen: Realities and Representations*. Cambridge: Harvard UP, 1991.

Renker, Elizabeth. *Strike Through the Mask: Herman Melville and the Scene of Writing*. Baltimore: The Johns Hopkins UP, 1996.

Ricoeur, Paul. *The Symbolism of Evil*. Boston: Beacon, 1969.

Rilke, Ranier Maria. *Duino Elegies and The Sonnets to Orpheus*. Trans. A. Poulin Jr. Boston: Houghton, 1977.

Robinson, H. Wheeler. "Blood." *Encyclopedia of Religion and Ethics*. Ed. James Hastings. Vol. I. New York: Scribner's, 1928. 714–19.

Rohde, Erwin. "Appendix V." *Psyche: The Cult of Souls and Belief in Immortality Among the Greeks.* Vol. 2. New York: Harper, 1966. 588–90.

Romanyshyn, Robert. "The Abandoned Body, Homecoming, and the Fate of the Earth." University of the Incarnate Word, San Antonio, Texas, Fall 1993.

———. "The Despotic Eye and Its Shadow: Media Image in the Age of Literacy." *The Hegemony of Vision.* Ed. David Levin. U California P, 1994. 339–60.

———. *Psychological Life: From Science to Metaphor.* Austin: Texas UP, 1982.

———. *Technology as Symptom and Dream.* New York: Routledge, 1989.

Rosen, Nathan. "Style and Structure in *The Brothers Karamazov.*" *The Brothers Karamazov.* Trans. Constance Garnett; rev. Ralph E. Matlaw. New York: Norton, 1976. 841–51.

Rosenfeld, Herbert. "A Clinical Approach to the Psychoanalytic Theory of the Life and Death Instincts: An Investigation into the Aggressive Aspects of Narcissism." *Melanie Klein Today: Developments in Theory and Practice.* Vol. 1. Ed. Elizabeth Bott Spillius. New York: Routledge, 1996. 239–55.

Rothenberg, Rose Emily. "Psychic Wounds and Body Scars: An Exploration into the Psychology of Keloid Formation." *Spring, 1986.* Dallas: Spring, 1986. 141–53.

Rousseau, G. S., ed. *The Languages of Psyche: Mind and Body in Enlightenment Thought.* Berkeley: U California P, 1990.

Rousseau, Jean-Jacques. *The Confessions.* Trans. J. M. Cohen. New York: Penguin, 1953.

———. *Reveries of the Solitary Walker.* Trans. Peter France. New York: Penguin, 1989.

Roux, Jean-Paul. "Blood." *The Encyclopedia of Religion.* Ed. Mircea Eliade. Vol. 2. New York: Macmillan, 1987. 254–56.

Rushdy, Ashraf, H. A. "Daughters Signifyin(g) History: The Example of Toni Morrison's *Beloved.*" *American Literature* 64, no. 3 (1992): 567–97.

St. Theodore the Studite. *On the Holy Icons.* Trans. Catharine Roth. Crestwood: St. Vladimir's Seminary P, 1981.

Sanders, Clinton R. *Customizing the Body: The Art and Culture of Tattooing.* Philadelphia: Temple UP, 1989.

Sanders, Scott Russell. "Telling the Holy." *Parabola: The Magazine of Myth and Tradition* 18, no. 3 (1993): 4–9.

Sansonese, J. Nigro. *The Body of Myth: Mythology, Shamanic Trance, and the Sacred Geography of the Body.* Rochester: Inner Traditions International, 1994.

Sardello, Robert. "Angels and the Spiral of Creation." *The Angels.* Ed. Robert Sardello. Dallas: The Dallas Institute, 1994. 51–62.

——. "City as Metaphor, City as Mystery." *Spring: An Annual of Archetypal Psychology and Jungian Thought.* Dallas: Spring, 1982. 95–112.

——. *Facing the World with Soul: The Reimagination of Modern Life.* Hudson: Lindisfarne, 1992.

——. *Love and the Soul: Creating a Future for Earth.* New York: HarperCollins, 1995.

Scarry, Elaine. *The Body in Pain.* Baltimore: The Johns Hopkins UP, 1987.

——. "Introduction." *Literature and the Body: Essays on Populations and Persons.* Ed. Elaine Scarry. Baltimore: Johns Hopkins UP, 1988. vii–xxvii.

Schapiro, Barbara Ann. *Literature and the Relational Self.* New York: New York UP, 1994. 127–43.

Schilder, Paul. *The Image and Appearance of the Human Body: Studies in the Constructive Energies of the Psyche.* New York: International UP, 1950.

Schiller, Friedrich. *On The Aesthetic Education of Man.* Trans. Reginald Snell. New York: Continuum, 1989.

Schwartz, Joel. *The Sexual Politics of Jean-Jacques Rousseau.* Chicago: U Chicago P, 1984.

Segal, Carolyn Foster. "Morrison's *Beloved.*" *The Explicator* 51, no. 1 (1992): 59–61.

Segal, Charles. *Interpreting Greek Tragedy: Myth, Poetry, Text.* Ithaca: Cornell UP, 1986.

——. *Tragedy and Civilization: An Interpretation of Sophocles.* Cambridge: Harvard UP, 1981.

Seltzer, Mark. *Serial Killers: Death and Life in America's Wound Culture.* New York: Routledge, 1998.

Selzer, Richard. *Mortal Lessons: Notes on the Art of Surgery.* New York: Touchstone, 1976.

Sennett, Richard. *The Conscience of the Eye: The Design and Social Life of Cities.* New York: Knopf, 1990.

——. *Flesh and Stone: The Body and the City in Western Civilization.* New York: Norton, 1995.

Sexson, Lynda. *Ordinarily Sacred.* New York: Crossroad, 1982.

Shakespeare, William. *Hamlet.* 2nd ed. Ed. Cyrus Hoy. New York: Norton, 1992. 2–101.

Sheets-Johnstone, Maxine. *Giving the Body Its Due.* New York: State U of New York, 1992.

Shuman, Robert. *The Psychology of Chronic Illness: The Healing Work of Patients, Therapists, and Families.* New York: HarperCollins, 1996.

Skafte, Dianne. *Listening to the Oracle: The Ancient Art of Finding Guidance in the Signs and Symbols All Around Us.* New York: HarperCollins, 1997.

Slatkin, Laura M. "Composition by Theme and the *Metis* of the *Odyssey.*" *Reading the Odyssey: Selected Interpretive Essays.* Ed. Seth Schein. Princeton: Princeton UP, 1996. 223–38.

Slattery, Dennis. "*The Death of Ivan Ilych:* A Distinction Between Pain and Suffering." *New Directions in Death Education and Counseling: Enhancing the Quality of Life in a Nuclear Age.* Eds. Richard Pacholski and Charles Corr. Arlington: Forum for Death Education and Counseling, 1988. 185–94.

———. "Evil and the Negation of the Body in Flannery O'Connor's 'Parker's Back.'" *The Flannery O'Connor Bulletin* 17 (1988): 69–79.

———. "The Hysterical Body of Nature in Thebes and Salem Village." *New Orleans Review* 13, no. 2 (1986): 83–87.

———. "The Icon and the Spirit of Comedy in Dostoevsky's *The Possessed.*" *The Terrain of Comedy,* Ed. Louise Cowan. Dallas: The Dallas Institute P, 1984. 195–220.

———. *The Idiot: Dostoevsky's Fantastic Prince.* New York: Peter Lang, 1984.

———. "Imagining the Stuff of the World: Reflections on Gaston Bachelard and Ivan Illich." *New Orleans Review* 12, no. 3 (1989): 81–87.

———. "Is Memory Metaphorical or Is Metaphor Memorial? Dostoevsky's 'The Peasant Marei.'" *Ambiguities in Literature and Film.* Ed. Hans P. Braendlin. Tallahassee: Florida State UP, 1988. 23–32.

———. "Of Corpses and Kings: *Antigone* and the Body Politic." *Lit: Literature, Interpretation, Theory* 5, no. 2 (1994): 155–67.

———. "Pan, Myth, and Fantasy in Dostoevskii's *The Idiot.*" *Canadian-American Slavic Studies* 17, no. 3 (1983): 384–401.

———. "Speaking, Reflecting, Writing: The Myth of Narcissus and Echo." *South Central Bulletin* 4 (1983): 217–20.

———. "Watery Worlds/Watery Words: Ishmael's Write of Passage in *Moby-Dick.*" *New Orleans Review* 11, no. 2 (1984): 62–66.

———. "Whiteness." *Wild Turkey: A Literary Review.* Ed. Carol Cullar. Eagle Pass: The Maverick P, 1995.

Slochower, Harry. "The Quest for an American Myth: *Moby-Dick.*" *Mythopoesis: Mythic Patterns in the Literary Classics.* Detroit: Wayne State UP, 1970. 223–45.

———. "The Pan Slavic Image of the Earth Mother: *The Brothers Karamazov.*" *Mythopoesis: Mythic Patterns in the Literary Classics.* Detroit: Wayne State UP, 1970. 246–83.

Slotkin, Richard. *Regeneration Through Violence: The Mythology of the American Frontier, 1600–1800.* Middletown: Wesleyan UP, 1986.

Smith, Sidonie. *Subjectivity, Identity, and the Body: Women's Autobiographical Practices in the Twentieth Century.* Bloomington: Indiana UP, 1993.

Snell, Bruno. *The Discovery of the Mind: The Greek Origins of European Thought.* New York: Harper, 1960.

Sophocles. *Philoctetes.* Trans. David Grene. *Greek Tragedies.* Vol. 3. Chicago: U Chicago P, 1968. 43–106.

———. *The Three Theban Plays.* Trans. Robert Fagles. New York: Penguin, 1984.

Soyinka, Wole. *The Bacchae of Euripedes. Collected Plays.* Vol. 1. Oxford: Oxford UP, 1973. 235–307.

Spengler, Oswald. *The Decline of the West.* Abridged Edition. Trans. Charles Francis Atkinson. Ed. Arthur Helps. New York: Knopf, 1962.

Spicker. Stuart F., ed. *The Philosophy of the Body: Rejections of Cartesian Dualism.* Chicago: Quadrangle, 1970.

Stafford, Barbara Maria. *Body Criticism: Imaging the Unseen in Enlightenment Art and Medicine.* Cambridge, Mass. MIT, 1994.

Stallybrass, Peter, and Allon White. *The Politics and Poetics of Transgression.* Ithaca: Cornell UP, 1993.

Stanford, W. B. *The Ulysses Theme: A Study in the Adaptability of a Traditional Hero.* Dallas: Spring, 1992.

Starobinski, Jean. *Jean-Jacques Rousseau: Transparency and Obstruction.* Trans. Arthur Goldhammer. Chicago: U Chicago P, 1971.

———. *The Living Eye.* Trans. Arthur Goldhammer. Cambridge: Harvard UP, 1989.

Stein, Murray. *Practicing Wholeness: Analytical Psychology and Jungian Thought.* New York: Continuum, 1996.

Steiner, George. "Trotsky and the Tragic Imagination." *Language and Silence: Essays on Language, Literature and the Inhuman.* New York: Atheneum, 1976.

Strathern, Andrew J. *Body Thoughts.* Ann Arbor: U Michigan P, 1996.

Strong, Marilee. *A Bright Red Scream: Self-Mutilation and the Language of Pain.* New York: Viking, 1998.

Stroud, JoAnne, and Gail Thomas, eds. *Images of the Untouched: Virginity in Psyche, Myth and Community.* The Pegasus Foundation Series I. Dallas: Spring, 1982.

Sturrock, John. "Theory vs. Autobiography." *The Culture of Autobiography: Constructions of Self-Representation.* Ed. Robert Folkenflik. Stanford: Stanford UP, 1993. 21–37.

Synnott, Anthony. *The Body Social: Symbolism, Self and Society.* London: Routledge, 1993.

Tedlock, Dennis. Interview. "Where You Want to Be: An Investigation of the *Popul Vuh.*" Crossroads. *Parabola: The Magazine of Myth and Tradition* 18, no. 3 (1993): 43–53.

Terras, Victor. "The Art of Fiction as a Theme in *The Brothers Karamazov.*" *Dostoevsky: New Perspectives.* Ed. Robert Louis Jackson. Englewood Cliff: Prentice-Hall, 1984. 196–212.

Thevoz, Michel. *The Painted Body.* New York: Rizzoli, 1984.

Thompson, Diane Oenning. *The Brothers Karamazov and the Poetics of Memory.* Cambridge: Cambridge UP, 1991.

Thompson, William Irwin. *Evil and World Order.* New York: Harper, 1977.

Thomson, Rosemarie Garland. *Extraordinary Bodies: Figuring Physical Disability in American Culture and Literature.* New York: Columbia UP, 1997.

Tolstoy, Leo. *The Death of Ivan Ilych.* Trans. Aylmer Maude. *The Death of Ivan Ilych and Other Stories.* New York: Signet, 1960. 95–156.

Trace, Arthur. *Furnace of Doubt: Dostoevsky and The Brothers Karamazov.* Peru: Sugden, 1988.

Tracy, David. *The Analogical Imagination: Christian Theology and the Culture of Pluralism.* New York: Crossroads, 1985.

Turner, Bryan S. *The Body and Society: Explorations in Social Theory.* New York: Basil Blackwell, 1984.

Turner, Victor. "Bodily Marks." *The Encyclopedia of Religion.* Vol. 2. Ed. Mircea Eliade. New York: Random House, 1987. 269–75.

———. *Dramas, Fields, Metaphors: Symbolic Action in Human Society.* Ithaca: Cornell UP, 1974.

Unamuno, Miguel de. *Tragic Sense of Life.* Trans. J. E. Crawford Flitch. New York: Dover, 1954.

Vernant, Jean-Pierre. *Mortals and Immortals: Collected Essays.* Ed. Froma I. Zeitlin. Princeton: Princeton UP, 1991.

———. "The Spiritual Universe of the *Polis.*" *The Origins of Greek Thought.* Ithaca: Cornell UP, 1994. 49–68.

Voegelin, Eric. *The World of the Polis.* Baton Rouge: Louisiana State UP, 1956. Vol. 2 of *Order and History.* 4 vols. 1954–74.

Vogler, Christopher. *The Writer's Journey: Mythic Structure for Storytellers and Screenwriters.* Studio City: Michael Wiese Productions, 1992.

Wasiolek, Edward. "*The Brothers Karamazov:* Idea and Technique." *The Brothers Karamazov and the Critics.* Ed. Edward Wasiolek. Belmont, Mass.: Wadsworth, 1967. 118–44.

————. *Dostoevsky: The Notebooks for The Brothers Karamazov*. Chicago: U Chicago P, 1971.

Watkins, Mary. Interview with Dennis Patrick Slattery, Santa Barbara, California. June 18, 1998.

Watt, Ian. *Myths of Modern Individualism: Faust, Don Quixote, Don Juan, Robinson Crusoe*. Cambridge: Cambridge UP, 1996.

Whitman, Cedric. "Apocalypse: *Oedipus at Colonus*." *Sophocles: A Collection of Critical Essays*. Ed. Thomas Woodard. New York: Prentice-Hall, 1966. 146–74.

————. *Homer and the Heroic Tradition*. Cambridge: Harvard UP, 1958.

Whitmont, Edward C. *The Alchemy of Healing: Psyche and Soma*. Berkeley: North Atlantic Books, 1993.

————. "The Destiny Concept in Psychotherapy." *The Analytic Process: Aims, Analysis, Training*. Ed. Joseph B. Wheelwright. New York: Putnam, 1989. 185–98.

————. *Return of the Goddess*. New York: Crossroad, 1982.

Whitt, Margaret. "O'Connor's Secular Use of Religion." SCMLA Conference, Houston, October 30, 1987.

Willis, Susan. "Memory and Mass Culture." *History and Memory in African-American Culture*. Ed. Genevieve Fabre and Robert O'Meally. New York: Oxford UP, 1994. 175–87.

Wilson, Edmund. "Philoctetes: The Wound and the Bow." *The Edmund Wilson Reader*. Ed. Lewis M. Babney. New York: DaCapo P, 1997. 418–36.

Wyatt, Jean. "Giving Body to the Word: The Maternal Symbolic in Toni Morrison's *Beloved*." *PMLA*, 108, no. 3 (1993): 474–87.

Young, Dudley. *Origins of the Sacred: The Ecstasies of Love and War*. New York: Harper, 1992.

Zaner, Richard. *The Context of Self: A Phenomenological Inquiry Using Medicine as a Clue*. Athens: Ohio UP, 1981.

————. *The Problem of Embodiment: Some Contributions to a Phenomenology of the Body*. The Hague: Martinus Nijhoff, 1971.

Ziegler, Alfred. "Rousseauian Optimism, Natural Distress, and Dream Research." Zurich: *Spring*. 1976. 54–65.

Index